Privacy and Legal Issues in Cloud Computing

ELGAR LAW, TECHNOLOGY AND SOCIETY

Series Editor: Peter K. Yu, *Drake University Law School, USA*

The information revolution and the advent of digital technologies have ushered in new social practices, business models, legal solutions, regulatory policies, governance structures, consumer preferences and global concerns. This unique book series provides an interdisciplinary forum for studying the complex interactions that arise from this environment. It examines the broader and deeper theoretical questions concerning information law and policy, explores its latest developments and social implications, and provides new ways of thinking about changing technology.

Titles in the series include:

Copyright Law and the Progress of Science and the Useful Arts
Alina Ng

Transnational Culture in the Internet Age
Sean A. Pager and Adam Candeub

Environmental Technologies, Intellectual Property and Climate Change
Accessing, Obtaining and Protecting
Abbe E.L. Brown

Privacy and Legal Issues in Cloud Computing
Edited by Anne S.Y. Cheung and Rolf H. Weber

Privacy and Legal Issues in Cloud Computing

Edited by

Anne S.Y. Cheung
Professor of Law, University of Hong Kong, Hong Kong

Rolf H. Weber
Chair Professor of Law, University of Zurich, Switzerland

ELGAR LAW, TECHNOLOGY AND SOCIETY

Edward Elgar
PUBLISHING

Cheltenham, UK • Northampton, MA, USA

Published by
Edward Elgar Publishing Limited
The Lypiatts
15 Lansdown Road
Cheltenham
Glos GL50 2JA
UK

Edward Elgar Publishing, Inc.
William Pratt House
9 Dewey Court
Northampton
Massachusetts 01060
USA

Paperback edition 2016

A catalogue record for this book
is available from the British Library

Library of Congress Control Number: 2015930137

This book is available electronically in the Elgaronline
Law subject collection
DOI 10.4337/9781783477074

MIX
Paper from
responsible sources
FSC
www.fsc.org   FSC® C013056

ISBN 978 1 78347 706 7 (cased)
ISBN 978 1 78347 707 4 (eBook)
ISBN 978 1 78643 655 9 (paperback)

Typeset by Columns Design XML Ltd, Reading
Printed and bound in Great Britain by TJ International Ltd, Padstow

Contents

About the editors

Anne S.Y. Cheung

Anne S.Y. Cheung is Professor at the Faculty of Law, the University of Hong Kong. She received her legal education at the University of Hong Kong, the University of Toronto, the University of London and Stanford University. Her research interests are freedom of expression, privacy, and children's rights (including cyberbullying).

Anne is a committee member of the Hong Kong Press Council. She is one of the principal investigators of the CLIC Project (Community Legal Information Centre, www.hkclic.org), and a member of the Institute for Internet and Society, Berlin, Germany. She worked on the Open Net Initiative (Asia) Project to study online freedom of speech in the form of blogging in China. Currently, she is working with Privacy International (UK) to study privacy protection in Hong Kong and China.

Her works have been published in the *Harvard Journal of International Law Online* (selected as a Feature Article), *International Data Privacy Law* and the *Journal of Media Law*.

Rolf H. Weber

Rolf H. Weber is Ordinary Professor for Civil, Commercial and European Law at the University of Zurich, Switzerland. Since 2009, Rolf has been appointed as Visiting Research Professor at the University of Hong Kong (HKU). He has been working closely with the Law and Technology Centre and the Faculty of Law of HKU. His main fields of research are Internet and information technology law, international business law, media law, competition law and international financial law.

Rolf is Director of the European Law Institute and the Center for Information and Communication Law at the University of Zurich. Since 2008 Rolf has been a member of the Steering Committee of the Global Internet Governance Academic Network (GigaNet) and of the European Dialogue on Internet Governance (EuroDIG), and since 2009 he has been a member of the High-level Panel of Advisers of the Global Alliance for Information and Communication Technologies and Development

(GAID). In addition, he is engaged as an attorney-at-law. His research focus lies on the above-mentioned regulatory topics: his publication list is available at www.rwi.uzh.ch/lehreforschung/alphabetisch/weberr/person. html.

Contributors

Henry Chang

Henry Chang is the Information Technology Advisor at the Office of the Privacy Commissioner for Personal Data in Hong Kong. Henry advises the Privacy Commissioner and his office on privacy policies related to information and communications technologies, and monitors related ICT trends. He also advises on the investigation of complex cases that involve information systems. Henry's past experience includes being the head of spam regulation in Hong Kong's telecommunications authority and a regional information risk manager for a major investment bank.

Henry is a fellow of the British Computer Society. He holds degrees in Engineering Science, Informatics, Business Administration and Law. Dr Chang is an appointed technical expert in the IT Security Techniques subcommittee and Privacy Technologies working group of the International Organization for Standardization (ISO) and the Chair for the Technology Working Group of the Asia Pacific Privacy Authorities. He also holds certifications in privacy, IT security, ethical hacking and computer forensic investigation.

Alan Chiu

Alan Chiu is a partner in Hogan Lovells' IPMT. He has been qualified as a Hong Kong solicitor since 2004 and advises on a diversified range of contentious and commercial IP and IT matters in both Hong Kong and China, covering copyright, trademark, design, patent, trade secret, domain name, privacy, IP-related antitrust issues, manufacturing, sourcing and franchising, music and entertainment contracts as well as software and cloud agreements. Alan has substantive experience in IP litigation and has assisted a number of Fortune 500 companies, international multinational corporations and local blue chip companies to resolve their regional and cross-border IP and technology disputes. He also has a computer forensic background and advises on legal issues concerning computer security, IT compliance and Internet regulatory aspects. He is an accredited mediator of the Hong Kong International Arbitration Centre, the Law Society of Hong Kong and the Hong Kong

Mediation Accreditation Association and an affiliate member of the Information Security and Forensics Society. He currently serves as a member of the China Subcommittee of the International Trademark Association Anti-Counterfeiting Committee and the Technology Committee of the Law Society of Hong Kong. He has been appointed Adjunct Professor of Law by Hong Kong Shue Yan University.

K.P. Chow

K.P. Chow (University of California, Santa Barbara) is Associate Professor of the Department of Computer Science and Associate Director of the Center for Information Security and Cryptography (CISC) at the University of Hong Kong. Dr Chow's areas of research interest are computer forensics, cryptography, computer security, Internet surveillance and privacy. In the past few years, Dr Chow has been invited to be a computer forensic expert to assist the courts in Hong Kong.

Edward S. Dove

Edward Dove is a PhD student in the School of Law at the University of Edinburgh. Previously, he was Academic Associate at the Centre of Genomics and Policy at McGill University in Montreal, Quebec, Canada. He holds law degrees from McGill (BCL, LLB) and Columbia University (LLM). Edward's primary research interests are in the areas of privacy/data protection, data access and sharing, governance of international research collaboration, and socio-legal studies of genetic and genomics technologies. He is also a member of the International Cancer Genome Consortium's (ICGC) Working Group on Identifiability and Privacy.

Xiaoxi Fan

Xiaoxi Fan is a PhD research student in the Department of Computer Science at the University of Hong Kong. Her research interests include digital forensics, digital profiling and data mining. She is an affiliate member of the Information Security and Forensics Society, a local association that aims at advocating and enforcing professionalism, integrity and innovation in information security and computer forensics (www.isfs.org.hk).

Yann Joly

Yann Joly, PhD (DCL), Ad. E. is Lawyer Emeritus at the Bar of Quebec and the Research Director of the Centre of Genomics and Policy at

McGill University. He is also an Associate Professor in the Department of Human Genetics as well as the Biomedical Ethics Unit at McGill University. His research activities lie at the interface of intellectual property, medical law, biotechnology and bioethics. Professor Joly is the Data Access Officer of the International Cancer Genome Consortium (ICGC). In 2012, he received the Quebec Bar Award of Merit for Innovation for his work on the right to privacy in the biomedical field.

Terry Sheung-Hung Kaan

Terry Sheung-Hung Kaan is Co-Director of the University of Hong Kong's Centre for Medical Ethics and Law, a joint centre of the HKU Faculty of Law and the HKU Li Ka Shing Faculty of Medicine. He is also an associate professor in the Department of Law. His teaching and research interests centre primarily on biomedical law, biomedical ethics, and the regulation of biomedical research.

Bartha M. Knoppers

Bartha Maria Knoppers, PhD (Comparative Medical Law) Sorbonne (Paris I), currently holds the Canada Research Chair in Law and Medicine (Tier 1: 2001). She is Director of the Centre of Genomics and Policy at McGill University. She holds four Doctorates Honoris Causa, is a fellow of the American Association for the Advancement of Science, of the Hastings Center (Bioethics) and of the Canadian Academy of Health Sciences (CAHS), and is an Officer of both the Order of Canada and of Quebec. She was admitted to the Bar of Quebec in 1985.

Joe Kong

Joe Kong has been a computer forensic examiner since 1999 and is currently a part-time MPhil student at the University of Hong Kong. His major research area is digital forensics. Since 2002, he has been a certified forensic computer examiner of the International Association of Computer Investigative Specialists, an international non-profit corporation composed of computer forensic professionals dedicated to fostering and perpetuating educational excellence in this field (www.iacis.com). In addition, he is a full member of the Information Security and Forensics Society, a local association that aims at advocating and enforcing professionalism, integrity and innovation in information security and computer forensics (www.isfs.org.hk).

Geofrey Master

Geofrey Master is a partner in Mayer Brown's Business & Technology Sourcing (BTS) practice. He has broad experience in the full range of technology service transactions, including IT outsourcing and cloud computing. He also regularly works with data privacy and data security issues. Geof has represented clients in a wide range of industries, from start-up enterprises to national and global firms and including governmental entities. He has worked with clients in all geographies.

Prior to joining Mayer Brown in 2001, Geof worked for over ten years for Electronic Data Systems Corporation in various senior legal capacities, including five years as international general counsel with responsibility for all legal support requirements of EDS' non-US business. He was also previously an adjunct professor in business planning at the University of Texas School of Law. He is admitted to practice law in Hong Kong, the District of Columbia, New York and Texas.

Jean-Philippe Moiny

Jean-Philippe Moiny graduated in Law (University of Liège, Belgium) in 2008. He worked in the Privacy Department of CRIDS (Research Centre for Information, Law and Society) (University of Namur, Belgium) as a researcher from 2008 to 2013. He studied data protection, privacy, contract law and private international law in the context of social network sites and cloud computing. He also examined the legal rules related to the access to and reuse of public sector information. From 2009 to 2013, he was appointed to the Commission on Access to and Reuse of Administrative Documents, Reuse Section (Belgium Federal Appeal Committee). And from 2010 to 2013, he was also involved as an expert, for the Council of Europe, notably in the modernization of Convention no. 108 (data protection). Recently in 2013, he joined the Digital Economy Law Service of the Belgian Ministry of Economy (Directorate-General for Economic Regulation).

Chris Reed

Chris Reed is Professor of Electronic Commerce Law at Queen Mary University of London. He is a member of the Centre for Commercial Law Studies (CCLS). He joined the Centre in 1987 and is responsible for the University of London LLM courses in Information Technology Law, Internet Law, Electronic Banking Law and Telecommunications Law. Chris has published widely on many aspects of computer law, and research in which he was involved led to the EU directives on electronic signatures and on electronic commerce. From 1997–2000, Chris was Joint Chairman of the Society for Computers and Law, and in 1997–98 he acted as Specialist Adviser to the House of Lords Select Committee on Science and Technology. Chris participated as an expert at the European Commission/Danish Government Copenhagen Hearing on Digital Signatures, represented the UK Government at the Hague Conference on Private International Law and has been an invited speaker at OECD and G8 international conferences. He is a former director of CCLS, and from 2004–09 was Academic Dean of the Faculty of Law and Social Sciences.

Dominic N. Staiger

Dominic N. Staiger holds law degrees from Bond University, Australia (LLB with Honours) and the University of Zurich (MLaw). He is a licensed attorney-at-law (New York State Bar) and Visiting Scholar at Columbia University (New York). His research interests include privacy and data protection law with a focus on the legal implications of new technologies such as cloud computing, big data and the Internet of Things. Currently he is completing his PhD on 'Legal Compliance in the Cloud' and working as Researcher at the Chair of Prof. Rolf H. Weber. Prior to his legal career he founded an IT company, which he managed for six years.

George Yijun Tian

Dr George Tian is Senior Lecturer in Law at the University of Technology, Sydney and Uniform Domain Name Dispute Resolution Policy (UDRP) Neutral appointed by the World Intellectual Property Organization (WIPO). His research focuses on IP, antitrust law, privacy and digital media law. He is also a current research associate of the Cyberspace Law and Policy Centre at the University of New South Wales Law School. He previously served as a consultant of the International Labour Organization, a project coordinator of the Clayton Utz and a visiting fellow at the Harvard Law School and the Oxford Law School.

Peter K. Yu

Peter K. Yu holds the Kern Family Chair in Intellectual Property Law and is the founding director of the Intellectual Property Law Center at Drake University Law School. Born and raised in Hong Kong, he has served as Wenlan Scholar Chair Professor at Zhongnan University of Economics and Law in Wuhan, China and a visiting professor of law at the

University of Haifa, the University of Hong Kong, the University of Strasbourg and Washington and Lee University. He is the author or editor of six books and more than 100 law review articles and book chapters.

Preface

This edited volume began life in an academic conference entitled 'Up in the Cloud: Legal and Privacy Challenges in Cloud Computing' held by the Faculty of Law of the University of Hong Kong (HKU) in July 2013. Over several hot summer days, the conference brought together local and international experts from academe, industry, the legal professions and regulatory authorities to explore the complex legal and privacy challenges brought about by rapidly evolving cloud computing technology. Most of the conference presenters agreed to contribute a chapter to this volume, and this book has also been further strengthened by the inclusion of several commissioned chapters. Because cloud computing, and the legal issues surrounding it, is a relatively new area of study, it is hoped that this book will be welcomed by all who have an interest in law and technology, whether from an academic or a practical perspective.

In the course of writing and editing this book, we have incurred many debts. In particular, we are greatly indebted to Professor Peter Yu of Drake University, whose ready willingness to assist us with his specialist knowledge in law and technology and encouragement at all stages of publication were invaluable to the project's success. We are also exceedingly grateful to Dr Clement Chen, Anne's senior research assistant at the time of writing and now a postdoctoral research fellow at the Faculty of Law, HKU. Clement took great care in checking references and spent countless hours searching for answers to our seemingly never-ending queries. His intelligent and devoted labour, meticulous and unremitting care in editing and footnote compilation, and unfailingly pleasant, good-humoured and informative responses were an indispensable aid throughout this project.

This book project has been made possible by the kind support of the Research Grants Council of the Hong Kong Special Administrative Region Government (GRF743010).

Introduction: a walk in the clouds

Anne S.Y. Cheung and Rolf H. Weber

Cloud computing is fast becoming an integral part of daily life, with people's activities in the physical world or on personal computers increasingly moving to web-based services 'up in the cloud'. The cloud allows us to access our documents, photos, and video files from anywhere in the world. Many of us are customers of Dropbox and Google, amongst other cloud service providers.[1] Be it online searching, media streaming or WhatsApping, we are all in the cloud. In addition, many businesses have purchased computing resources through cloud service providers rather than acquiring their own physical IT assets. The ubiquity of the cloud is also attracting considerable research attention, with researchers from academic and research institutions carrying out investigations into various aspects of cloud computing, from ensuring the efficient and effective use of such computing to infrastructure issues, cloud service models and cloud security. Leading IT analyst firm Gartner claims that by 2016,[2] cloud computing will account for the bulk of all new IT spending, whereas consulting firm McKinsey estimates that the total annual economic impact of cloud technology could reach US$6.2 trillion by 2025.[3] Furthermore, according to McKinsey, most of that impact ($1.2–5.5 trillion) could take the form of the additional surplus

---

[1] Dropbox reports that its number of users reached 300 million in May 2014. See Kaylene Hong, 'Dropbox Reaches 300m Users, Adding on 100m Users in Just Six Months' (*Thenextweb*, 29 May 2014), http://thenextweb.com/insider/2014/05/29/dropbox-reaches-300m-users-adding-100m-users-just-six-months, accessed 9 August 2014. Google claimed in June 2014 that its cloud-based storage service, Google Drive, has more than 190 million active users. See 'Meet the New Google Drive' (*Google Drive Blog*, 25 June 2014), http://googledrive.blogspot.hk/2014/06/meet-new-google-drive_25.html, accessed 9 August 2014.
[2] 'Gartner Says Cloud Computing Will Become the Bulk of New IT Spend by 2016' (*Gartner*, 24 October 2013), www.gartner.com/newsroom/id/2613015, accessed 9 August 2014.
[3] James Manyika, Michael Chui, Jacques Bughin, Richard Dobbs, Peter Bisson and Alex Marrs, 'Disruptive Technologies: Advances that Will Transform

generated by the cloud delivery of services and applications to Internet users, with the remainder resulting from the use of cloud technology to improve enterprise IT productivity.[4] In other words, 'cloud' is no longer a mere buzzword for cool technology, but rather represents a significant paradigm shift in technological advancement and our daily lives.

Whilst cloud computing is providing us with unprecedented convenience, and thus unleashing commercial and social innovation, it has also led to great uncertainty concerning a multitude of individual rights, such as the right to privacy, security and intellectual property, particularly because of its reliance on cross-border data hosting and outsourcing. This book discusses and analyses various approaches to addressing these problems, in particular issues pertaining to security, personal data protection, contracting and licensing, jurisdiction, regulatory framework reform and content regulation. It also looks at the specific implications for cloud computing, information ownership, geographic management and bio-medical practice. The major jurisdictions studied are the United States and the European Union.

Most cloud companies are techno giants based in the US (including Google and Amazon), whilst the European Union takes pride in its privacy protection regime.[5] Given the rise of global data flows, this situation has triggered intriguing dynamics, not only for the companies and cloud users in those two jurisdictions but also for those in other areas. Individual chapters discuss the implications of cloud computing in Belgium, Australia, the UK, China and Hong Kong.

Containing the forces of technology within the existing legal landscape has long constituted an uphill battle. Computer scientists are always one step ahead of the barely imaginable and thinking ahead to the next generation of tools and gadgets that will change the world as soon as technology catches up with innovation. Whilst the law does not wish to act so quickly that it stifles innovation, it also does not want to lag so far behind as to be useless. In joining the battle over how law and policy can appropriately tackle the challenges of cloud computing, this book brings together international experts from academe (legal and computer science) and industry, as well as legal professionals and representatives of the

---

Life, Business, and the Global Economy' (May 2013) 61, www.mckinsey.com/insights/business_technology/disruptive_technologies, accessed 9 August 2014.

  [4] Ibid.
  [5] Mark Scott, 'European Firms Turn Privacy into Sales Pitch' (*NYTimes Bits Blog*, 11 June 2014), http://bits.blogs.nytimes.com/2014/06/11/european-firms-turn-privacy-into-sales-pitch/?_php=true&_type=blogs&_php=true&_type=blogs&_php=true&_type=blogs&_r=2, accessed 9 August 2014.

regulatory authorities, to explore the complex legal and privacy challenges brought about by rapidly evolving cloud computing technology.

The opening chapter (by Joe Kong, Xiaoxi Fan and K.P. Chow) takes up the subject of cloud computing by providing a basic introduction to the latest agreed definition of cloud computing, its corresponding models and its various deployment methods. Moreover, it gives an overview of the information security and privacy issues related to cloud computing, and offers a hybrid legal-technological solution. Contrary to common belief, encryption is not a silver bullet to resolving personal data privacy and security problems. Accordingly, the authors discuss the advantages and disadvantages of various encryption technologies. Regardless of how much companies invest in information security enhancement, incidents of malicious system attacks, accidental data loss and deletion are still worryingly common. Kong and his team argue that personal data privacy and data security are the responsibility of both cloud service providers and users.

Chapters 2 and 3 turn their attention to the regulatory challenges posed by cloud computing. In Chapter 2, Henry Chang examines these challenges primarily from the perspective of data protection authorities (DPAs). The diverse nature of cloud markets and the complex offerings of cloud service providers in each, create considerable challenges for DPAs when it comes to the protection of personal data stored in the cloud. As a cloud service can be considered a special form of outsourced service, this chapter begins with a general description of the data protection challenges that arise when outsourcers are used to store and/or process personal data. It then goes on to analyze the three cloud-related issues that raise the greatest concerns amongst organizational users, including issues of cross-border data transfer between jurisdictions, the loose subcontracting arrangements entered into by cloud service providers, and the standard terms and conditions they offer. Chang also assesses the advice given by DPAs to both organizational users and consumers around the world on the use of cloud computing.

Sticking to the theme of regulatory challenges, Rolf H. Weber in Chapter 3 concentrates on examining the available regulatory instruments for cloud computing, namely the *ex ante* concept of sector-specific regulation and the dimensions of *ex post* competition law. In doing so, he places emphasis on the problems associated with imprecise EU legislation affecting cloud computing growth and the concept of 'net neutrality'. Furthermore, the chapter addresses the risks of vertical integration, that is, contractual relations between an Internet service provider and a cloud provider leading to subsequent discrimination against other providers. To further foster the growth of cloud computing, Weber argues that introducing sector-specific regulation constitutes the most sensible choice, as it would allow a more determinative assessment of a party's rights and obligations.

In the midst of our examination of cloud-related privacy, security and regulatory concerns, Anne Cheung in Chapter 4 asks the fundamental question of what personal data is and what it should be. The current definition of personal data in most jurisdictions often hinges on whether the data can be linked to an identifiable or identified person. However, with the ongoing advancement and growing use of re-identification technology, coupled with the huge amount of data being processed and stored in the cloud across the globe, data can be easily 're-personalized'. This situation leads to the next logical question, which is whether anonymous, anonymized, pseudonymous or fragmented data can or should be considered personal data. The implications for the process and storage of such data in the cloud and the sale of consumer and health data cannot be underestimated. Thus, Cheung argues that a more nuanced definition and understanding of personal information/data is needed. In analyzing the current US approach and the proposed EU Data Protection Regulation, she further argues that a harmonized definition that factors in harm and risk, predictability, and flexibility in the shifting technological landscape should be formulated.

Chapters 5 and 6 confront the thorny issues of cross-border data flows and jurisdiction that crop up in any discussion of the Internet and the cloud. In Chapter 5, Dominic Staiger addresses the challenges created through cross-border data transfers on the cloud from the EU to the US, and reviews the legal response to these challenges under the current EU Data Protection Directive and the proposed EU Data Protection Regulation. In particular, he highlights issues related to the inadequacies of the Safe Harbor framework and the definitional ambiguities in the proposed EU regulation. The chapter further analyses the effects of such ambiguities and inadequacies on the actors involved in different cloud service types and scenarios, and discusses the key points that these actors should keep in mind.

Jean-Philippe Moiny in Chapter 6 defines the concept of jurisdiction, and illustrates the many jurisdictional conflicts that occur in attempting to regulate the cloud, whether we are talking about regulating relations between private parties (civil liability) or between individuals and states (for example, criminal investigation), or larger regional bodies such as the EU, or concerned with federated entities or special administrative regions such as Hong Kong. The chapter shows that zoning of the cloud and Internet is emerging, if not already in operation, and that it is likely to speed up if cloud computing ever reaches its full potential.

Chapters 7 to 10 can be seen as forming the second part of this book, as each of their authors has chosen to elaborate upon various substantive areas of law in relation to cloud computing. In Chapter 7, Chris Reed points out that cloud users, and those whose information is processed by cloud providers, are naturally concerned that they may somehow lose their legal rights to that information once it enters the cloud. They are also concerned, or at least ought to be concerned, about who has the rights to the metadata and other information that cloud service providers generate in using that information. Reed argues that rights analysis is not the appropriate way to address this issue. Copyright law and the law of confidential information establish quite clearly who possesses these rights, and use of the cloud does not generally overturn them. What the cloud does instead is radically change the degree of control a rights owner has over the use and disclosure of information. To a certain extent, this is a matter that can be addressed in contracts, but building a contractual framework that incorporates all necessary cloud players is cumbersome and difficult. Most of the related issues can be more appropriately resolved through the establishment of cloud community norms, incorporated in appropriate governance mechanisms, and through greater accountability on the part of cloud actors concerning how information has and will be used.

Directly on the subject of copyright, Chapter 8 delves into questions about how the collection, handling and distribution of content and personal information can be appropriately undertaken in the new cloud environment. George Tian examines the recent development of cloud-related content regulations in various jurisdictions (the US, the UK, the EU, Japan, China and Australia) from a macro policy development perspective. A number of recent cases highlighting the potential for new and emerging cloud computing services to infringe copyrights or enable their customers to do so are discussed. Drawing lessons from the US and Australia, Tian provides practical suggestions for future content regulation and policy reform in Asia.

Revolving around the theme of copyright, Peter Yu in Chapter 9 explores how cloud platforms can be used to facilitate the worldwide distribution of copyrighted entertainment content. He examines the problems posed by existing markets, which are segmented based on legal and territorial boundaries and distribution and licensing arrangements. Yu then discusses how cloud platforms can better meet consumer demand for entertainment content in a highly globalized world. The chapter outlines the potential challenges and complications that arise from the

use of cloud platforms and distributors, and offers preliminary suggestions for the changes that are needed in the legal, business and technological environments.

Moving on from copyright concerns, Terry Kaan in Chapter 10
explores the challenges and concerns specific to the storage and use of
healthcare information in the cloud. He sounds a note of caution in
arguing that, in the rush to embrace cloud technology, insufficient
attention has been paid to the much more fundamental issues and
challenges raised by the transformation of data from analogue to digital
form. In economically and technologically advanced countries, healthcare
information is rapidly being moved from the analogue to the digital
domain. Whilst it is widely assumed that the basic nature of the
information remains essentially unchanged in this transformation, this
chapter makes the argument that it in fact inevitably entails fundamental
changes to the very nature of the stored information. By analyzing the
experience of several jurisdictions, Kaan makes a general inquiry into the
challenges and pitfalls that institutional data owners, policy planners and
IT database system designers need to keep in mind when preparing to
store healthcare information in the digital and cloud domains.

The remaining two chapters more pointedly underscore the practical
concerns of cloud technology for researchers and for those parties
involved in licence agreements. In Chapter 11, Edward Dove, Yann Joly
and Bartha Knoppers remind us that the biggest challenge in 21st century
data-intensive genomic science is developing the vast computer infrastructure and advanced software tools necessary to perform comprehensive analyses of genomic datasets for biomedical research and clinical
practice. Researchers are increasingly turning to cloud computing both as
a solution to integrate data from genomics, systems biology, and biomedical data mining and as an approach to analyzing data to solve
biomedical problems. Whilst cloud computing provides several benefits,
such as lower costs and greater efficiency, it also raises a number of legal
issues. In this chapter, the authors discuss several key legal issues (data
control, security, confidentiality, transfer and accountability) from an
international legal perspective and based on a review of several publicly
available cloud service providers' terms of service. These issues should
be borne in mind by genomic research organizations when they negotiate
legal arrangements for storing genomic data on the servers of large
commercial cloud service providers. Diligent genomic cloud computing
means leveraging security standards and evaluation processes as a means
to protect data, and entails many of the same good privacy practices that
researchers should always consider in safeguarding local infrastructure.

In Chapter 12, Alan Chiu and Geofrey Master revisit the issue of data ownership but from the perspective of content licensing. They ask this question: when a user uploads data to the cloud, whether in the form of a photo, text, soundtrack or logo, has he or she surrendered any ownership rights of that data? The answer depends very much on the nature and scope of the content licence agreed between the parties concerned. Content licences generally apply in any cloud computing context. The scope of that licence, defined in the terms of service agreement, often varies in accordance with the nature and features of the cloud services being used. There are typically significant differences between the licensing terms of public and private clouds. In this final chapter, the authors provide an overview of intellectual property (IP) licensing on the Internet, particularly in the context of cloud services, and discuss in detail some of the challenges to licensing in the cloud computing arena. They also discuss other intellectual property considerations that arise when engaging cloud services for private or business use. The chapter concludes with some thoughts about the future for IP licensing in cloud services.

Careful readers are likely to spot an inconsistency in this collection, that is, the use of 'data' as both a singular and a plural by different authors. As international consensus has yet to be reached over which usage is correct, the editors have decided to let the inconsistency remain. Our task is to provide useful navigational tools for crossing and recrossing the frontier between theory and practice, between regulation and innovation, and to clear away some of the clouds along the meandering path of law and technology.

1. Introduction to cloud computing and security issues

Joe Kong, Xiaoxi Fan and K.P. Chow

I. INTRODUCTION[1]

The evolution of the Internet and the widespread adoption of virtualization[2] technology have brought cloud computing to the forefront of innovation in the early 21st century, a circumstance in which computation has become per-use service-based. Cloud users can now process data and utilize storage platforms through high bandwidth networks at low cost and high efficiency. At its most basic and general level, cloud computing technology refers to the delivery of information technology resources as a service to multiple customers through the Internet: a process whereby software, shared resources and information are held on remote servers designed and established by the respective network or infrastructure operator. Consequently, the handling of this data is under the control of service providers, and this is known as 'the cloud'.[3] In other words, cloud computing enables information to be accessible anywhere to anyone with an Internet connection.

The centralization of computing infrastructure and the change in the global computing landscape have allowed individual users and business enterprises to perform their activities round-the-clock with the advantage

---

[1] Part of the Introduction and Section II of this chapter are taken from Anne S.Y. Cheung, Ricci Ieong, K.P. Chow and Rolf H. Weber, 'Challenges to Personal Data Protection in Cloud Computing' (2013) 6 Journal of Law and Economic Regulation 105.

[2] Virtualization is a technology that combines computing resources to present one or many operating environments using methodologies like hardware and software partitioning, partial or complete machine simulation, and others. Susanta Nanda Tzi-cker Chiueh and Stony Brook, 'A Survey on Virtualization Technologies' (*RPE Report*, 2005) 1–42.

[3] European Commission, 'A Comprehensive Approach on Personal Data Protection in the European Union', COM (2010) 609 final 2.

of device and location independence. Many of us who are using webmail, social networking services, web conferencing and online music services may already be in the cloud. At the same time, the use of cloud computing in the business community has begun to expand because cloud computing supports scalable and virtualized computer-related resources using the Internet. Such a model does not require its users to have the necessary expertise in or control over the cloud infrastructure, and this technology can be implemented using different deployment approaches or architectures. Businesses utilizing cloud services can save huge costs such as being able to use central processing unit cycles without having to buy their own mainframe computers, storing data and documents without having their own storage networks, and using expensive software and being able to provide it to their clients without having to buy the software themselves. Functioning through a 3G/4G network, the portability of computation has come to a stage where cloud users can share their data resources freely at any time, at any location, from any device or with any person. The prominent cloud service providers (CSPs) offering a variety of services include VMware, Sun Microsystems, Rackspace US, IBM, Amazon, Google, BMC, Microsoft, Ubuntu and Yahoo.[4] Most of them rely on the use of virtual machines (VMs), which are software implementations of computers used to execute programmes.

As we can imagine, the benefits of cloud computing are enormous.[5] Through this model, individuals, businesses and governments can rent services and store data at a much cheaper price than buying new equipment and software themselves. Cloud computing can also reduce the waste of information systems resources, increase the efficiency of data centres, save significant energy and lower operating costs.[6] It is also a further developed technical model of the previously applied point-to-point business outsourcing processes.

---

[4] John J. Barbara, 'Cloud Computing: Another Digital Forensic Challenge' (*DFI News*, 30 October 2009), www.dfinews.com/articles/2009/10/cloud-computing-another-digital-forensic-challenge, accessed 28 July 2014.
[5] Mark Taylor and Matteo Matteucci, 'Cloud Computing' (2010) 16 *Computer and Telecommunications Law Review* 57, 58–9; Laurel Delaney, '10 Benefits of Cloud Computing' (*Verio*), www.verio.com/resource-center/articles/cloud-computing-benefits/, accessed 28 July 2014.
[6] A survey in 2011 showed that 80 percent of organizations which had adopted cloud computing had reduced costs by 10–20 percent. Other benefits of cloud computing are mentioned in the European Commission, 'Unleashing the Potential of Cloud Computing in Europe', COM (2012) 529 final; and Dan Svantesson and Roger Clarke, 'Privacy and Consumer Risks in Cloud Computing' (2010) 26 *Computer Law and Security Review* 391.

On account of its significance, cloud technology was recognized as one of the top ten information technologies in 2012 and the personal cloud as one of the top ten strategic technologies in 2013.[7] It was predicted by Gartner that by 2016, more than 50 percent of Fortune/Global 1000 companies will have stored customer-sensitive data in a public cloud,[8] which means that the cloud revolution will have significant implications not only for technology development but also for new business model design and the economy at large. It is estimated that by 2014, the public cloud services market in the European Union (EU) alone will reach €11 billion in revenue, amounting for 3.6 percent of the total IT market.[9] Globally, the total revenue from public IT cloud services exceeded €17 billion (US$21.5 billion) in 2010 and the forecast is that it will reach €58 billion (US$72.9 billion) in 2015.[10] In 2011, Neelie Kroes, Vice-President of the European Commission for Digital Agenda, urged Europe to move from being 'cloud-friendly' to 'cloud-active'.[11] In 2012, the European Commission announced the adoption of the Cloud Computing Strategy for the European Union and the establishment of a European Cloud Partnership that has included private industry and public sector users.[12]

---

[7]   Tom Donoghue, 'Gartner Lists Top 10 IT Technologies for 2012' (*Integration Developer News*, 19 October 2011), www.idevnews.com/stories/4888/ Gartner-Lists-Top-10-IT-Technologies-for-2012, accessed 28 July 2014; 'Gartner Identifies the Top 10 Strategic Technology Trends for 2013' (*Gartner*, 23 October 2012), www.gartner.com/newsroom/id/2209615, accessed 14 July 2014.

[8]   'Gartner Reveals Top Predictions for IT Organizations and Users for 2012 and Beyond' (*Gartner*, 1 December 2011), www.gartner.com/it/page.jsp?id= 1862714, accessed 28 July 2014.

[9]   European Commission, 'Commission Adopts Its Cloud Computing Strategy' (*European Union*, 19 September 2012), http://europa.eu/rapid/press-release_ AGENDA-12-30_en.htm, accessed 3 August 2014.

[10]   Benjamin Fox, 'Prepare to Invest Billions in the Cloud, EU Warns Businesses' (*EU Observer*, 20 September 2012), http://euobserver.com/economic/ 117610, accessed 28 July 2014.

[11]   Neelie Kroes, 'Towards a European Cloud Computing Strategy', speech delivered at World Economic Forum Davos (*European Union*, 27 January 2011), http://europa.eu/rapid/pressReleasesAction.do?reference=SPEECH/11/50, accessed 28 July 2014.

[12]   European Commission, 'Digital Agenda: New Strategy to Drive European Business and Government Productivity via Cloud Computing' (*European Union*, 27 September 2012), http://europa.eu/rapid/pressReleasesAction.do?reference= IP/12/1025&format=HTML&aged=0&language=EN&guiLanguage=en, accessed 28 July 2014.

Yet, the vast potential of cloud computing also brings with it unprecedented challenges. Among various concerns,[13] the most pressing ones are personal data protection and information security.[14] OWASP (Open Web Application Security Project), a commonly referenced worldwide organization focused on improving the security of application software, named personal data protection as one of the top ten issues for the cloud computing environment.[15] The majority of the survey results have confirmed that the information security issue is the critical hurdle for users when considering switching to the cloud computing environment.[16] It is also known that the US government does not store classified data in the public cloud for national security reasons.[17] The above concern is certainly understandable since, by putting our personal data and information on remote servers, we may easily lose control over our data. Moreover, in most cases, we do not know how, where, by whom our personal data is being processed.

To understand and tackle security concerns in the cloud, we will start off in Section II by explaining the meaning of cloud computing and its various deployment models which entail different personal data concerns. Then in Section III we will explore how new security issues arise in the cloud computing environment. Although some may argue that the nature of cloud computing does not differ much from current Internet and web technology, a closer look at the nature of the non-standardization of different models, resource sharing and outsourcing will reveal different

---

[13]   For a discussion of the new challenges that cloud computing poses to competition law, e-commerce and network regulation, see Jasper P. Sluijs, Pierre Larouche and Wolf Sauter, 'Cloud Computing in the EU Policy Sphere: Interoperability, Vertical Integration and the Internal Market' (2012) 3 *Journal of Intellectual Property, Information Technology and E-Commerce Law* 12.

[14]   The Info Sec Guidelines 2002 of the OECD (Organisation for Economic Co-operation and Development) is now in revision. In 2012, the OECD launched a broad consultation to review its 2002 Security Guidelines for Information Systems and Networks and delivered its November 2012 Report. See OECD, 'The Role of the 2002 Security Guidelines: Towards Cybersecurity for an Open and Interconnected Economy' (2012) OECD Digital Economy Papers No. 209, http://dx.doi.org/10.1787/5k8zq930xr5j-e, accessed 28 July 2014.

[15]   Kroes (n 11).

[16]   Ponemon Institute, 'Ponemon Releases Cloud Service Provider Study' (*Ponemon*, 2 May 2011), www.ponemon.org/blog/ponemon-releases-cloud-service-provider-study, accessed 28 July 2014.

[17]   Nancy J. King and V.T. Raja, 'Protecting the Privacy and Security of Sensitive Consumer Data in the Cloud' (2012) 28 *Computer Law and Security Review* 308, 310.

sets of challenges to security. Critical and unique issues highlighted in this chapter with respect to the cloud environment are the sharing of roles and responsibilities between cloud service providers and data users, with illustrations of the problems of security. Finally, in Section IV, we offer solutions that can enhance security in the cloud environment. Although the industry model is still in its infancy, it may be an answer in view of the gap between legal regulation and innovation.

In this chapter, users of cloud services in a non-private capacity (whether corporate or public administration, business enterprises, or individuals) are referred to as 'users' or 'customers', whereas individuals using such services in a private capacity are referred to as 'consumers'.[18]

II. WHAT IS CLOUD COMPUTING?

A. Definition and Features

As mentioned briefly at the start of this chapter, cloud computing is a service whereby information, software, and shared resources are provided as a utility to electronic devices such as computers over the Internet. Although there is no single definition of cloud computing, the formulation by the United States National Institute of Standards and Technology (NIST) has gained wide recognition and has provided an authoritative guideline.[19] It defines cloud computing as 'a model for enabling convenient, on-demand network access to a shared pool of configurable computing resources (for example, networks, servers, storage, applications, and services) that can be rapidly provisioned and released with minimal management effort or service provider interaction'.[20] Embedded in this definition are five essential characteristics of cloud computing: (1) on-demand self-service; (2) broad network access; (3) resource pooling and location independence; (4) rapid elasticity; and (5) measured services.[21]

---

[18]   This use of terminology follows that of W. Kuan Hon, Christopher Millard and Ian Walden, 'Who Is Responsible for "Personal Data" in Cloud Computing? The Cloud of Unknowing, Part 2' (2012) 2 *International Data Privacy Law* 3.

[19]   European Commission (n 6).

[20]   Peter Mell and Timothy Grance, 'The NIST Definition of Cloud Computing' SP 800-145 (*National Institute of Standards and Technology Information Technology Laboratory*, September 2011), http://csrc.nist.gov/publications/nist pubs/800-145/SP800-145.pdf, accessed 28 July 2014.

[21]   Ibid 2.

First, through *on-demand self-service* features, end-users are empowered to directly control and manage IT resource provisioning, meaning that they have unilateral access to different cloud services whenever required. Second, for most cloud environments, IT resources can be managed and controlled through *broad network access* or a web browser, regardless of the physical location of one's devices (for example, laptops, smartphones or personal computers). Hence, the service is location independent and enables us to work 'through the cloud'. Third, due to the software running on the servers that provide cloud resources, it enables *resource pooling and location independence*, which is one of the most important aspects of the nature of cloud computing, by enabling the effective use of resource sharing between various users and consumers around the world in different data centres. Resource pooling is also known as multi-tenancy in the cloud as a large number of users and consumers can share costs and resources on single systems, which makes cloud systems more efficient and cost-effective.[22] Fourth, as IT resources are expected to be shared and provisioned when needed in real time, availability of resources appears to be virtually 'unlimited'. In fact, the system has been made to be more elastic, scalable, and customized to meet needs and demands. In the cloud environment, choices and options for users and consumers can be built into the software platform, whereas the cloud service providers (suppliers) can profit from the *economies* of scale.[23] Finally, any piece of IT equipment, storage, or computation power can be converted into a *measurable* charging scheme. Cloud service providers then have controls over both the storage and infrastructure, or either one, depending on the delivery model and the service level agreement between the users and the consumers. The latter two groups will have to pay for the services based on the agreed service charge.

B. Service Models

Cloud computing is not entirely new to the market and can be viewed as a collective repackaging of IT services. An analogy can be drawn between cloud computing and serviced apartments in real estate. When one owns a house, one can modify and configure anything within that house, but the house owner also has to replace or to fix any malfunctioning facilities within the house. Whereas for serviced apartments, one can just focus on managing one's living space and enjoying the services

---

[22] Sluijs and others (n 13) 14.
[23] Ibid.

while all other activities such as maintaining the building and the services, such as electricity and plumbing, within the house will be handled by the service provider. The tenant's requirements are stated in their service level agreement with the landlord.

Likewise, in the cloud environment, the services to be provided by the cloud service providers should be defined (in a service catalogue) and available for users to choose from. In other words, a cloud service is like a tenancy arrangement for computing facilities. A landlord with a large house can establish a flexible multi-tenancy arrangement with more than one tenant for an undetermined timeframe. Anyone can join as a tenant to use the computing facilities, or leave the cloud architecture when they need to, but the choice of service is pre-defined in the contract. In other words, no matter which type of service model (infrastructure, platform or software) is used, the clients (users or customers) rely on the cloud service provider to manage and maintain the shared servers, data storage and systems.

In the first model, that of Infrastructure-as-a-Service (IaaS), the cloud service providers offer basic computing infrastructure such as processing power and/or storage (for example, virtual remote servers, CPU power, network bandwidth and storage capacity) to customers and consumers who are responsible for installing their own operating systems and applications. These providers are often specialized market players that can rely on a physical, complex infrastructure that spans several geographic areas.[24] However, security and privacy provisions beyond the basic infrastructure have to be managed by the users. Examples are Rackspace and Amazon EC2 and S3.

In the second model, that of a Platform-as-a-Service (PaaS), the cloud service providers provide a platform and tools (for example, operating system, database management, security and workflow management, and web servers) to customers and consumers so that they can construct, install and develop their own applications. These services are targeted mainly at market players that use a PaaS to develop and host proprietary application-based solutions to meet in-house requirements or to provide services to third parties.[25] Security and privacy provisions are split between the cloud providers and the cloud users. Examples are Google's App Engine and Microsoft's Windows Azure.

---

[24] Article 29 Data Protection Working Party, 'Opinion 05/2012 on Cloud Computing' (WP 196, 1 July 2012), http://idpc.gov.mt/dbfile.aspx/WP196.pdf, accessed 4 February 2015.

[25] Ibid.

In contrast to the above models, there is a third model, that of Software-as-a-Service (SaaS). In this model, in addition to providing basic computing infrastructure and platforms, the cloud service providers will also provide application software. In other words, various application services are delivered and made available to end-users. Well-known examples are Facebook, Google Maps and YouTube. In the cases of web hosting and email management, a company can set up its own web server and email server by purchasing, installing and configuring the servers. With the SaaS model, the company management team can also decide not to own the server but to simply pay for the already installed and configured server together with software. The IT team just needs to load the web server content or email addresses. Consequently, these services often replace conventional applications being installed on the local systems of the users, resulting inevitably in the outsourcing of the storage and processing of data to cloud service providers.[26] Security and privacy provisions are carried out mainly by the cloud service provider. Users do not have control over the cloud infrastructure or applications, except for some administrative or preferential settings.

The above three service models are not mutually exclusive. Instead, they often run as an integrated or multi-layered service. For instance, a cloud service may involve layers of different providers. In the case of Dropbox, data users consider it to be a SaaS, while Dropbox itself uses Amazon's IaaS infrastructure.[27]

C. Deployment Models

Besides service models, there are also four major deployment models for cloud computing environments – public, private, community and hybrid clouds – in which a deployment model refers to the scheme of resource sharing. With respect to security and privacy for different cloud service deployment models, the level of protection would depend on the effectiveness of the relevant policies, the robustness of the security and privacy controls, and the extent of the transparency of the performance and management details of the cloud environment. Besides the above, the choice of service model is also an important indicator of the scope of the control that a cloud user has over the cloud environment.

---

[26] Ibid.

[27] W. Kuan Hon, Christopher Millard and Ian Walden, 'The Problem of "Personal Data" in Cloud Computing: What Information Is Regulated? – The Cloud of Unknowing' (2011) 1 *International Data Privacy Law* 211, 212.

In public clouds, resources are provisioned dynamically for public users and accessed through the Internet from a third-party provider in a self-service manner. In contrast, private clouds are used exclusively by a single organization. They can be managed by a third party or used as an internal resource, and can be hosted off-site or on the company's premises. Likewise, in a community cloud, organizations or companies within a specific community share infrastructure that can be managed by either a third party or the community itself, and can be hosted off-site or within the community's premises. Lastly, a hybrid cloud is a combination of two or more clouds where the individual cloud entities have maintained their uniqueness even though they are bound into one cloud.

Among the four deployment models, the private cloud gives the consumers the highest degree of control while the public cloud gives the lowest. In between is the hybrid cloud, constituting a combination of different deployment models. Coupled with the various service models, the provision of cloud services can involve complicated legal issues depending on the flow of personal data through the chain of cloud services, the roles and responsibilities of the cloud service providers and their sub-providers, and the location of the cloud service providers. For instance, public clouds are commonly located in different jurisdictions, entailing issues of trans-border data transfer which will be discussed further in Chapter 5 and Chapter 6.

III. SECURITY CHALLENGES IN THE CLOUD ENVIRONMENT

Regardless of which service model or deployment model of cloud computing is involved, security remains a core concern.

A. General Security Concerns

In the old days, if the computer of one's neighbour was being hacked, one might dismiss it by saying 'It's not my business', but in the present era of shared infrastructure in the cloud, everyone is at risk. Even though cloud computing has been deployed and used in production environments since the 1990s,[28] security has continued to be a pressing concern. In 2010, a survey conducted by Harris Interactive for Novell revealed that

---

[28]   John Viega, 'Cloud Computing and the Common Man' (2009) 42(8) *Computer* 106; Kevin McPartland, 'Moving Beyond Buy-Side Cloud Computing Myths' (*Wall Street and Technology*, 10 July 2014), www.wallstreetandtech.com/

90 percent of more than 200 IT leaders at large enterprise organizations were concerned about cloud security and 50 percent of them viewed security concerns as the primary barrier to adopting the cloud.[29] In 2011, a survey conducted by International Data Corporation (IDC) showed that 47 percent of 500 IT executives were concerned about the threat to security posed by cloud computing.[30] Cisco's CloudWatch 2011 report for the UK revealed that 76 percent of 250 IT decision makers in large UK companies cited security and privacy as top barriers to adopting the cloud.[31]

This general fear and concern is not without grounds. The Cloud Security Alliance in 2013 identified nine major threats to cloud computing.[32] The first threat is related to data breaches, which refers to the intentional or unintentional release of secure information to an untrusted environment, involving financial information, personally identifiable information, personal health information, and so on. It is a security incident in which sensitive, protected or confidential data is copied, transmitted, viewed, stolen or used by an individual unauthorized to do so. For instance, a malicious hacker behind a virtual machine (VM) could use side-channel timing information to extract private cryptographic keys being used by other VMs on the same server. The second threat involves data loss, including not only the deletion of data by malicious hackers but also by careless CSPs or natural or human-induced disasters. The third threat to cloud computing is account or service traffic hijacking. For instance, if attackers gain access to another's credentials, they can eavesdrop on another's activities and transactions, and then manipulate data, return falsified information and redirect another's clients to illegal

---

infrastructure/moving-beyond-buy-side-cloud-computing-myths/a/d-id/1297183, accessed 11 July 2014.

[29] 'Novell Survey Reveals Widespread and Accelerating Enterprise Adoption of Private Clouds' (*Novell*, 5 October 2010), www.novell.com/news/press/2010/10/novell-survey-reveals-widespread-and-accelerating-enterprise-adoption-of-private-clouds.html, accessed 16 July 2014.

[30] Aaron Ricadela, 'Cloud Security Is Looking Overcast' (*BusinessWeek*, 1 September 2011), www.businessweek.com/magazine/cloud-security-is-looking-overcast-09012011.html, accessed 16 July 2014.

[31] Anh Nguyen, 'Only Seven Percent of UK IT Services in the Cloud, Says Survey' (*IT World*, 7 September 2011), www.itworld.com/cloud-computing/200657/only-seven-percent-uk-it-services-cloud-says-survey, accessed 16 July 2014.

[32] Ted Samson, '9 Top Threats to Cloud Computing Security' (*InfoWorld*, 25 February 2013), www.infoworld.com/t/cloud-security/9-top-threats-cloud-computing-security-213428?page=0,0&source=footer, accessed 28 July 2014.

sites. The fourth threat is the problem of insecure APIs[33] which will impact the security of the implementation of system management, provisioning, orchestration and monitoring of cloud services. The fifth threat is the denial of service (DoS) when an attacker fails to knock out the cloud service entirely but manages to use up the VM's processing time, rendering the applications unable to provide their service. The sixth threat involves malicious insiders gaining direct access or making modifications to the systems and application data. The seventh threat concerns abuse of the cloud by outsiders. For example, a hacker can make use of cloud servers to launch a DDoS attack[34] or share pirated software. The eighth threat is concerned with inadequate due diligence checks carried out when an organization moves its IT operations to the cloud without having adequate resources, or is not sufficiently familiar with cloud technology, and therefore does not have adequate or proper security measures for protecting its data. Finally, there is the problem of technology vulnerabilities when cloud service providers use software that is not designed to offer strong isolation properties in a multi-tenant architecture.

1. Challenges inherent in the cloud infrastructure

One needs to bear in mind that transitioning to cloud computing involves a transfer to the cloud provider of the responsibility and control of data and systems that were previously under the organization's direct control. The major tradeoff is that one shifts risk and loses control to gain flexibility, availability and to save costs in shared, remote resources. Yet, this increases the potential threat from hackers, cybercriminals and their malware.

As mentioned earlier in Section II.B, depending on the service model used, cloud infrastructure security is a responsibility shared between the cloud service providers (CSPs) and the users. The users are generally responsible for host based security while the CSPs are responsible for

---

[33] Application Programming Interface (API) is a language and message format used by an application programme to communicate with the operating system or some other control programme such as a database management system or communications protocol. See 'Definition of: API' (*PC Magazine Encyclopedia*), www.pcmag.com/encyclopedia/term/37856/api, accessed 4 August 2014.
[34] Distributed Denial of Service (DDoS) attack is the most advanced form of DoS attack which uses many computers to launch a coordinated DoS attack against one or more targets. See Christos Douligeris and Aikaterini Mitrokotsa, 'DDoS Attacks and Defense Mechanisms: Classification and State-of-the-Art' (2004) 44(5) *Computer Networks* 643, 645.

network based security. This split of responsibilities has another significant impact on IaaS because the CSPs supply basic resources such as machines, disks and networks, while the users are responsible for the operating system, the software environment necessary to run *their* applications, and the data placed into the cloud computing environment. In contrast, for a SaaS or a PaaS arrangement, the infrastructure, software and data are the primary responsibility of the CSP as the user has little control over any of these features.

The cloud is composed of four deployment models (public, private, community and hybrid) and three delivery models (IaaS, SaaS and PaaS). For a system with multiple components, security depends not only on the correct implementation of components, but also on the interactions among different components. Complex interactions among components would increase vulnerability. In the cloud environment, logical separation managed by software is used rather than a physical separation of resources. An attacker could disguise itself as a legitimate user to obtain access to the cloud service, exploit vulnerabilities from within the cloud environment and then compromise the separation mechanisms to gain unauthorized access to other tenants of the cloud server. Exposing the remote administrative interfaces of cloud computing to a user on the Internet would increase the risks of intrusion compared to the relatively secure direct connections needed for system administration in a traditional data center. In the cloud environment, some system administration functions may be supported by the CSP. The latter may perform the functions with remote administrative access. Both these activities introduce additional security risks. Hence, great damage may be caused by a malicious insider in the cloud computing environment. In particular, public cloud computing environments, most of which run on either SaaS or PaaS systems, are extremely complex because of the potential risks of trust or data breaches being involved. Sharing an infrastructure with unknown outside parties can be a major drawback for some applications, and strong security mechanisms should be used for logical separation.

In other words, the cloud environment promotes the integration of many networked computers while at the same time concealing the structure behind it. Users' access to security audit trails in the cloud can be difficult or even impossible. This shortcoming has provided camouflage for perpetrators of malicious activity to pose as legitimate customers, making it more difficult for security practitioners to track down the perpetrator's activities through permissible means. If data content cannot be monitored, such online storage and the anonymity of users' identities could impose an arduous task on security practitioners when they try to uncover or detect any unlawful activities that are associated with virtual computers in the cloud.

2. New relations between providers and users

In the cloud environment, where security issues are concerned, the emphasis is typically placed on cloud service providers while the role of users and consumers is often overlooked. For instance, web browsers are mostly used by the client-side to access cloud computing services. There may be other lightweight applications running simultaneously on the client's desktop or mobile devices used to access the cloud services. It is not surprising that the various plug-ins and extensions for web browsers are ill-famed for their security problems since those add-ons do not provide automatic updates and thus increase the persistence of vulnerabilities. Ensuring secure access from mobile devices such as smartphones or tablets is made even more difficult by the preloaded operating systems which might become outweighed by malware over time and collapse. Besides that, their small size and portability can result in the loss of physical control while the limited built-in processing power plus the weak security mechanisms are usually inadequate and can be easily circumvented by attackers. The growing availability of mobile networks and the use of social media, personal webmail and other public cloud storage systems on mobile devices are a concern, since these software and services have been increasingly used to serve as paths for social engineering attacks and have a negative impact on the security of the underlying cloud service platform. Moreover, cloud applications are often delivered to users through custom-built native apps instead of a web browser. There is always a chance of having a backdoor Trojan keystroke logger, or other type of malware, embedded in the apps running on a mobile device.

B. Implications for IT Management

From the above perspective, cloud computing represents a significant paradigm shift away from the conventional IT security management of an organizational data centre to a de-perimeterized infrastructure that is open to use by a potential adversary. The decisions about transitioning organizational data, applications and other resources to a cloud computing environment require an organization to take a risk-based approach to analysing available security and privacy options. The information technology governance practices of the organization that pertain to the security policies, procedures, implementation, testing, use and monitoring of deployed or engaged services should be extended to include the use of the cloud computing environment. When shifting risk from locally managed servers and services to the cloud, one should not forget the key areas of security concern, that is, confidentiality (the data should not be exposed, exploited or leaked), integrity (the data should be correct, attestable and not corrupted) and availability (access to the data is not disabled and service is not denied).

Based on the above-mentioned threats, the Cloud Security Alliance recommends a defensive, in-depth strategy that includes computer, storage, network, application and user security enforcement and monitoring.[35]

IV. SOLUTIONS TO SECURITY AND PRIVACY THREATS

A. General Solutions

Indisputably, as we have explained earlier, cost reduction and efficiency enhancement are the primary motivation for computer users needing major computer processing power to move towards a cloud environment. At the same time, security and privacy have become the primary interest and concern of CSPs.

To provide a 'solution' to the challenge to privacy inherent in cloud computing, configuration control, vulnerability testing, security audits and patching of platform components, greater consistency and system platform hardening should be offered by the CSP.[36] In addition, better resilience and disaster recovery strategies need to be built into the cloud computing environment to cope with sudden bursts of service demands and distributed denial of service attacks. Furthermore, the provision of better backup and restore procedures will enable cloud services to provide a more reliable off-site repository for an organization's data.[37]

It is essential for cloud users to oversee and manage how the CSPs maintain the security of the computing environment and ensure data

---

[35] Ted Samson (n 32).

[36] Hewlett-Packard Development Company, '5 Cloud Security Concerns You Must Address' (May 2012), www.snt.hr/about_us/company/WhitePapSecurity. pdf, accessed 17 July 2014.

[37] Healthcare Information and Management Systems Society, 'Cloud Security Toolkit' (CS03 – Cloud Security 101, February 2012), www.himss.org/files/HIMSSorg/content/files/PrivacySecurity/CS03_Cloud_Security_101.pdf, accessed 17 July 2014.

confidentiality. The default offering of CSPs generally does not reflect a specific security and privacy need. To determine a suitable service from a risk perspective requires a full understanding of the operation of the users' business or organization, and the users' concerns about potential threats to it. The selected cloud computing solution should be configured, deployed and managed to meet the identified security and privacy requirements.

B.   Service Level Agreements

Other than simply implementing the default offering of a CSP, a negotiated service agreement can document the assurance of the CSP that it will accomplish the customer's and consumer's requirements to protect critical data and applications on the cloud.

Service Level Agreements (SLAs) refer to binding agreements between a service provider and its customer or consumer that have now become an important part of the cloud service delivery model.[38] These agreements specify the conditions under which a service is to be delivered. Traditional SLAs did not cover security aspects. In 2011, Bernsmed outlined how to have a cloud SLA cover security aspects. It allows the easier selection of cloud services from different CSPs with defined security levels.[39] In their suggested SLA lifecycle, the CSP should first publish its security services. When a potential user plans to use a cloud service, they will then negotiate a specific SLA with the CSP about the security requirements and the security services offered by the CSP. If both parties agree on the SLA, the CSP and the user will commit to the SLA and the services will be provisioned by the CSP. Following this, the user can monitor the service to ensure that the negotiated SLA is being implemented by the CSP. If the user wants to change the requirements or detects any violations of the SLA, it may result in renegotiation of the SLA. After the services are provided, the SLA will be terminated and all resources will be freed.

---

[38]   Karin Bernsmed, Martin Gilje Jaatun, Per Hakon Meland and Astrid Undheim, 'Security SLAs for Federated Cloud Services', paper presented at the Sixth International Conference on Availability, Reliability and Security (ARES), Vienna, 22–6 August 2011, 202.

[39]   Karin Bernsmed, Martin Gilje Jaatun, Per Hakon Meland and Astrid Undheim (n 38).

C. Data Encryption

Cloud computing has additional privacy issues as it is operating as a co-tenant platform. It is important that new security design principles for privacy should be considered. For instance, a group of cloud servers might run different types of applications simultaneously for 1,000 users, and one of those applications might have no purpose other than spying on the other 999, which the CSP may be unaware of. To protect the user, data should be encrypted, and that data would only be decrypted when it is actually being processed, and the results after computations would be re-encrypted again. In addition, a new design for inside-out security should be deployed where all network-connected data must be able to defend itself from attacks at any endpoint. The system must have an awareness of timeline, identity, location and content, with well-defined user access policies. For example, when millions of users need access to cloud resources, user provisioning and de-provisioning should be simple, scalable and efficient.

In other words, if we apply ordinary encryption to cloud storage, it will prevent the cloud provider from processing the data, and will confine the cloud's role to being just simple storage. There are two kinds of encryption which can be applied to achieve trusted data sharing over untrusted CSPs, namely incremental encryption and homomorphic encryption.

1. Incremental encryption

In cryptography, the term 'plaintext' refers to data in its original plain form while 'ciphertext' refers to data in its encrypted form. In incremental encryption, plaintext is encrypted incrementally several times using different encryption keys. Incremental encryption allows the computation of the final ciphertext based on the initial ciphertext and the change in the plaintext.[40] It can encrypt data multiple times with different keys, and produce a final ciphertext which can be decrypted in a single decryption by a single key. The scheme allows changing the encryption key without decrypting the data first, thus it enables the re-encryption of data in an untrusted environment. During the sharing, the data is always in its encrypted form, though at different stages it may be encrypted with different keys. There is no single stage in which the data is decrypted into its plain form before it is delivered to the authorized users. For example,

---

[40] Chunming Rong, Son T. Nguyen and Martin Gilje Jaatun, 'Beyond Lightning: A Survey on Security Challenges in Cloud Computing' (2013) 39(1) *Computers & Electrical Engineering* 47.

the cloud user *U1* encrypts all his documents using his key *K1*. When *U1* wants to share one of the documents *D1* with another user *U2*, *U1* can incrementally encrypt the document *D1* with another key *K2*. The user *U2* can then decrypt the incrementally encrypted document *D1* with another key *K3*. In the sharing process, the document *D1* never appears in plain form until it is delivered to and decrypted by the authorized user *U2*.

2. Homomorphic encryption

Homomorphic encryption allows the CSP storing the ciphertext to perform certain operations without decrypting the ciphertext. With homomorphic encryption, the CSP can perform operations on the data without decrypting the data, that is, the encrypted data never appears in plain form during the data processing. Unfortunately, at the moment there is no practical homomorphic encryption scheme that can be implemented in the cloud computing environment.

D. Hardware-Anchored Security

In 2013, Ryan proposed hardware-anchored security.[41] Under this scheme, the CSP can decrypt the data when the CSP needs to perform processing on it. The main idea is that the decryption key is bound to the programme. The CSP can use the key to process the data using the designated programme, while no other programme is allowed to use the key. The CSP uses special hardware to store the keys which makes them accessible only to designated programmes. Hardware-anchored security in the style of Excalibur is a more versatile and applicable approach.[42]

E. Remove Sensitive Data

Data encryption provides a good way for protecting data confidentiality but it often requires the sacrifice of a certain degree of efficiency and flexibility in data processing. Instead of encrypting all the data, another way to ensure data confidentiality is to remove the sensitive data and just store non-sensitive data in the cloud.[43] For example, when handling data containing personally identifiable information, the client can remove the

---

[41] Mark D. Ryan, 'Cloud Computing Security: The Scientific Challenge, and a Survey of Solutions' (2013) 86(9) *Journal of Systems and Software* 2263.

[42] Mark D. Ryan (n 41).

[43] Shucheng Yu, Wenjing Lou and Kui Ren, 'Data Security in Cloud Computing' in Sajal K. Das, Krishna Kant and Nan Zhang (eds), *Handbook on*

unique identifying information to protect user privacy. This method preserves efficiency and flexibility in data processing as the distribution and management of keys are not required.

V. CONCLUSION

Given that cloud computing has become part of our lives, data security and privacy have become an increasing area of concern for both service providers and users. No matter what line of business, branch of government or online engagement one is dealing with, once we decide to use the cloud, preventing unauthorized access to information resources will become a major consideration. This chapter has highlighted the security issues unique to the architecture of cloud computing. The solutions lie in strengthening in-built technological security capabilities and management, reaching new types of contractual arrangements between service providers and users and in adopting encryption technology.

Data must be secured while at rest, in transit and in use, and access to the data must be controlled. Standards for communications protocols and public key certificates allow data transfers to be protected using cryptography and can usually be implemented with similar effort in SaaS, PaaS and IaaS environments. Any cloud computing solution should be properly configured, deployed and managed to meet the security and privacy requirements of customers and consumers using the solution. Organizational or business data must be protected in a manner consistent with the organization's or business's policies, whether in the organization's or business's computing centre or in the cloud. In addition, security and privacy controls should be implemented correctly and operate as intended throughout the system lifecycle. Accountability for security and privacy in cloud deployments cannot be delegated entirely to cloud providers. To a certain degree, it also remains an obligation for users to fulfill.

As cloud service providers endeavour to come to grips with having to tackle security challenges in the constantly morphing clouds, users should also grapple with newly arising concerns and not be too easily dazzled by digital cloud wizardry. We all want to live in a smarter cloud at a fast rate and at low cost, but we also need to factor data security into the total equation.

Securing Cyber-Physical Critical Infrastructure (Waltham, Massachusetts, United States: Elsevier 2012) 389.

2. Data protection regulation and cloud computing

Henry Chang

I. INTRODUCTION

The benefits of cloud computing make it appealing to a wide range of organizational customers: from small and medium enterprises to non-government organizations, which lack the expertise or resources to manage a complex and costly internal information technology (IT) infrastructure, to large multinational corporations that are attracted by the potential cost savings. However, despite the management and cost advantages of cloud computing, there are a number of information security and privacy protection concerns in particular, when the cloud is used to process or handle personal data. These concerns result from organizational customers' apparent lack of control over and oversight of the way in which personal data are protected and managed therein.

This chapter covers the issues that organizational customers need to consider if they decide to engage the services of cloud providers. It first outlines the basic data protection principles underpinning the obligations of data users/controllers,[1] and then describes the common data protection concerns that organizations have when engaging outsourcers, of which cloud providers are considered as a special type. Finally, the chapter outlines several characteristics of the business model that many cloud providers adopt and how those characteristics affect the protection of personal data privacy. Throughout the discussion, recommendations from data protection authorities (DPAs) are provided, where applicable.

---

[1] Many data protection laws define data users/controllers as the entities that collect, use and/or store personal data belonging to individuals, that is, data subjects. Any reference to a data user in this chapter also refers to a data controller.

II. CLOUD SERVICE AND DEPLOYMENT MODELS

There are many classifications and features of cloud computing. For the purposes of this chapter, however, only the following service models and deployment models are considered relevant to personal data privacy protection: private and public cloud service models, as well as software as a service (SaaS) and platform/infrastructure as a service (PaaS/IaaS) deployment models (for definitions and a discussion of private, public, community and hybrid clouds, please see Chapter 1).[2]

The two relevant service models are private and public clouds. Given private clouds are meant for the exclusive use of individual organizations, organizational customers should be in a position to mandate all the necessary controls to safeguard personal data that they have entrusted to their cloud providers. In contrast, public clouds are meant to be shared by multiple customers with varying needs. By definition, public cloud providers tend to make their clouds as generic as possible in order to appeal to as many customers as possible. As such, the level of controls exercised by organizational customers of public clouds is inevitably lower when compared with those using private clouds.

As far as personal data protection is concerned, the main distinction between various deployment models is that, under the SaaS model, the cloud provider also supplies and very often operates the relevant software for data users. In this model, the software that the cloud provider offers may not be fully customizable to data users' compliance and security requirements because of the former's need to serve a large number of customers with the same software. It should also be noted that some SaaS providers interact directly with data users' customers, which renders the roles and responsibility of each party, in terms of who is collecting what personal data for what purposes, even fuzzier. The PaaS and IaaS models, in contrast, allow data users to install their own software, which can safely be assumed to be more readily compliant with specific business, security and regulatory requirements of the data users.

---

[2] Peter Mell and Timothy Grance, 'The NIST Definition of Cloud Computing' SP 800-145 (*National Institute of Standards and Technology Information Technology Laboratory*, September 2011), http://csrc.nist.gov/publications/Pubs SPs.html#800-145, accessed 9 June 2014.

III. WHY CLOUD COMPUTING IS A CONCERN TO DATA PROTECTION AUTHORITIES

Cloud computing is without question a very attractive business enabler, offering such benefits as a short lead time, minimal investment and ease of use for any business initiative or operation that requires IT support. Gartner, a leading IT research and advisory firm, estimated that the cloud market would grow from US$111 billion in 2012 to US$244 billion in 2017.[3] Amidst the attractiveness of cloud technology, however, it is important to keep in mind the inherent risks that many of its character-istics pose to personal data privacy protection, risks that relate primarily to the apparent lack of control and oversight a data user retains when it entrusts personal data to a third party such as a cloud provider for processing or storage. The Article 29 Working Party, set up under Article 29 of the Data Protection Directive 95/46/EC,[4] is made up of representa-tives of the DPAs of each European Union (EU) Member State, the European Data Protection Supervisor and the European Commission. Amongst its aims are to advise the European Commission and make recommendations to the EU on all matters related to the protection of personal data. It considers the lack of control over and lack of infor-mation about cloud operations to be the two major risks associated with cloud use.[5]

---

[3] Ed Anderson, Lai-ling Lam, Yanna Dharmasthira, Chad Eschinger, Susan Cournoyer, Cathy Tornbohm, Jeffrey Roster, Bianca Francesca Granetto, Gian-luca Tramacere, Dean Blackmore, Joanne M. Correia, Laurie F. Wurster, Tom Eid, Ruggero Contu, Venecia K. Liu, Fabrizio Biscotti, Chris Pang, Dan Sommer, T.J. Singh, Andrew Frank, Hai Hong Swinehart, Alan Dayley, Jie Zhang, Morgan Yeates, Rajesh Kandaswamy, Douglas Toombs and Gregor Petri, 'Forecast: Public Cloud Services, Worldwide, 2011–2017, 4Q13 Update (2013)' (*Gartner*, 26 December 2013), www.gartner.com/doc/2642020/forecast-public-cloud-services-worldwide, accessed 9 June 2014.

[4] EU Data Protection Directive 95/46/EC of the European Parliament and of the Council of 24 October 1995 on the protection of individuals with regard to the processing of personal data and on the free movement of such data [1995] OJ L 281, 31–50.

[5] Article 29 Working Party, 'Opinion 5/2012 on Cloud Computing' (WP 196, 1 July 2012), http://ec.europa.eu/justice/data-protection/article-29/documentation/opinion-recommendation/files/2012/wp196_en.pdf, accessed 9 June 2014.

Under many data protection laws, including those of Canada,[6] the EU,[7] Hong Kong[8] and New Zealand,[9] data users take ultimate responsibility for and are held accountable for the security and use of the personal data in their possession even when they outsource the processing thereof to other parties. Amongst the measures they should therefore take are ensuring that the personal data is not used for any purpose other than that originally specified, is kept no longer than necessary and is protected against unauthorized or accidental access, processing, erasure, loss or use no matter whether they are processing the personal data themselves or have entrusted a third party to do so. Accordingly, to fulfil their obligations under the law, data users must ensure that adequate controls are specified in both their requirements and any contract they negotiate with outsourced data processors.

Although the engagement of cloud services may be considered a form of outsourcing,[10] data users may find the model of engagement somewhat different from the usual outsourcing model. With the exception of private clouds, where the cloud service is fully dedicated to one customer and its requirements,[11] data users may be unable to exert the level of control they typically can in a one-to-one relationship with a traditional outsourcer. Data users may also be unaware of some cloud characteristics that have a potentially negative impact on personal data privacy.

IV. GENERAL DATA PROTECTION PRINCIPLES

It is not the case, however, that cloud computing is beyond the reach of current data protection laws. More than 100 jurisdictions have enacted

---

[6] 'Cloud Computing for Small and Medium-Sized Enterprises: Privacy Responsibilities and Considerations' (*Office of the Privacy Commissioner of Canada*, June 2012), www.priv.gc.ca/information/pub/gd_cc_201206_e.asp, accessed 9 June 2014.

[7] Article 29 Working Party (n 5).

[8] 'Information Leaflet on Cloud Computing' (*Office of the Privacy Commissioner for Personal Data, Hong Kong*, November 2012), www.pcpd.org.hk/english/publications/files/cloud_computing_e.pdf, accessed 9 June 2014.

[9] 'Cloud Computing: A Guide to Making the Right Choices' (*Office of the Privacy Commissioner of New Zealand*, February 2013), www.privacy.org.nz/assets/Files/Brochures-and-pamphlets-and-pubs/OPC-Cloud-Computing-guidance-February-2013.pdf, accessed 9 June 2014.

[10] 'Cloud Computing for Small and Medium-Sized Enterprises' (n 6); 'Information Leaflet on Cloud Computing' (n 8).

[11] Mell and Grance (n 2).

data protection laws since 1973.[12] Broadly speaking, the majority of them follow the core principles of the original Organisation for Economic Co-operation and Development (OECD) Privacy Guidelines on the Protection of Privacy and Transborder Flows of Personal Data (OECD Guidelines hereafter) published in 1980.[13] The OECD Guidelines were updated in 2013,[14] and the nine core principles are summarized below.[15] Where applicable, the specific principles relevant to clouds are further elaborated upon.

1. Collection Limitation Principle

The collection of personal data should be purpose-driven. The means of collection should also be lawful and fair, and, where appropriate, the data users should notify the data subjects the purpose of data collection and obtain their consent.

This principle of collection limitation generally applies to personal data collected for business purposes and to the manner in which personal data collection takes place. However, if data users are engaging SaaS cloud services such as a calendar service being used directly by customers of the data user, the cloud providers concerned are in fact interacting directly with data subjects, and may be able to collect more information about those data subjects than the data users intended. For example, they may collect information on data subjects' usage patterns

---

[12]   Graham Greenleaf, 'Global Data Privacy Laws 2013: 99 Countries and Counting' (2013) 123 *Privacy Laws & Business International Report* 10.

[13]   OECD, 'Recommendation of the Council Concerning Guidelines Governing the Protection of Privacy and Transborder Flows of Personal Data' C(80)58/FINAL; H.P. Gassmann, 'OECD Guidelines Governing the Protection of Privacy and Transborder Flows of Personal Data' (1976) 5(2) *Computer Networks* 127. According to Greenleaf, by 2013, 32 out of the 34 OECD member countries had enacted data protection laws implementing the OECD Guidelines. He further implies that the majority of the data protection laws in various jurisdictions (101 at the time of writing) follow at least 11 of the 15 separate principles from the OECD and Council of Europe requirements. Graham Greenleaf, 'Scheherazade and the 101 Data Privacy Laws: Origins, Significance and Global Trajectories', http://papers.ssrn.com/sol3/papers.cfm?abstract_id=2280877, accessed 7 August 2014.

[14]   OECD, 'Recommendation of the Council Concerning Guidelines Governing the Protection of Privacy and Transborder Flows of Personal Data', as amended on 11 July 2013 by C(2013)79, www.oecd.org/sti/ieconomy/oecd_privacy_framework.pdf, accessed 7 August 2014.

[15]   The core principles are taken from Parts II and III of the OECD Guidelines (n 14).

and the locations from which they use the software. In such cases, whether data subjects are aware of the collection of their personal data and the entity collecting them (that is, who the data user is) needs to be carefully analysed.

2. Purpose Specification Principle

The purposes for which personal data is collected should be specified no later than at the time of collection. In addition, when the collected data no longer serves a given purpose, it should be erased or anonymized if practicable.

This principle requires data users to ensure that the personal data they entrust to cloud providers is not kept longer than necessary if it no longer serves a purpose or is intended/scheduled for erasure.

3. Use Limitation Principle

Personal data should not be disclosed, made available or otherwise used for purposes other than those originally specified except with the consent of the data subject.

This principle requires data users to ensure that the personal data they entrust to cloud providers is not being used for purposes beyond those originally collected for and/or agreed upon.

4. Data Quality Principle

Any personal data collected should be relevant to the purposes for which it is to be used. To the extent necessary for those purposes, personal data should be accurate, complete and kept up to date.

5. Security Safeguards Principle

Personal data should be protected by reasonable security safeguards against such risks as loss, unauthorized access or use, destruction, modification or disclosure.

This principle requires data users to ensure that the personal data they entrust to cloud providers is being protected in the same way it would be if handled by the data users themselves.

6. Openness Principle

There should be a general policy of openness concerning developments, practices and policies with respect to the handling of personal data.

7. Individual Participation Principle

An individual should have the right to confirm whether a data user has held his or her personal data. He or she should also be entitled to obtain a copy of such data within a reasonable period of time and in a reasonable manner, and to have the data erased, rectified, completed or amended as appropriate.

When engaging cloud services, data users must ensure that cloud providers are able to support data users' obligations concerning the fulfilment of data access and data correction requests. This principle may be particularly challenging when a data user is using a SaaS provider, as the entire software system is designed and operated by the cloud provider. If the aforementioned requirements were not taken into consideration at the design stage or the cloud providers are unaware of the data users' obligations, it is the data users that would eventually shoulder the legal responsibility for any failure to honour data access and correction requests.

8. Accountability Principle

Data users should be accountable for compliance with measures that give effect to the foregoing principles, as well as with measures to address incident response and breach handling.

If data users are to engage cloud services that involve personal data, they should formally assess all privacy impacts through a privacy impact assessment. Furthermore, data users should ensure that the cloud providers they choose have appropriate incident response and breach handling procedures in place.

9. Principle of Free Flow and Legitimate Restrictions

A jurisdiction may restrict the transfer of personal data to another jurisdiction that does not substantially observe the foregoing data protection principles.

This final principle requires data users to establish the legal basis for entrusting personal data to cloud providers that may then transfer it to other jurisdictions.

V. CHALLENGES ARISING FROM CLOUD BUSINESS MODELS

Data users engaging cloud services should observe all of the data protection principles listed above. Owing to the nature of cloud services, they should pay particular attention to the purpose specification, use limitation and security safeguards principles. This section discusses how these principles relate to data protection in the cloud, with specific reference to various cloud business models.

A. Outsourcing

As previously noted, the use of the cloud constitutes a specific form of outsourcing. As such, all of the challenges related to outsourcing involving the processing of personal data apply. These challenges typically include the following areas.

1. Technical safeguards for identity management and authentication

One of the appealing features of the cloud, particularly the public cloud, is its ability to be accessed in the Internet from anywhere. Whilst this feature meets the mobility needs of the data users, it also allows easier access for hackers. The security safeguards principle stipulates that a secure identity management system for authenticating and authorizing legitimate users be in place to protect the personal data stored in the cloud.

2. Proper exit plan, data erasure and data portability

The handling of data after a cloud contract has ended, or after fulfilment of the original purpose of their collection, should be well thought through. A formal 'exit plan' defining how personal data should be handled and protected in the event of contract completion or mid-term termination is advised. Furthermore, the contract should contain a provision ensuring that when personal data is no longer needed or is erased, it is indeed permanently erased and no longer in the cloud provider's possession.[16] These steps will ensure that the purpose specifications and use limitation principles are observed.

---

[16] Article 29 Working Party (n 5); 'Cloud Computing for Small and Medium-Sized Enterprises' (n 6); 'Information Leaflet on Cloud Computing' (n 8); 'Cloud Computing' (n 9).

3. Limitation on data use in the cloud

Cloud providers are often in a position to receive, handle and/or access personal data provided by multiple customers. In line with the use limitation principle, cloud providers should be formally reminded that they cannot retain or use the personal data entrusted to them beyond the terms outlined by individual customers.[17] They should also be reminded that they must not aggregate the personal data of multiple customers for new or previously undisclosed purposes.

In other cases, data users may be engaging a SaaS that their customers directly use and/or access (such as a cloud-based payment gateway). When customers interact directly with the SaaS application (the payment gateway), the SaaS cloud providers may be in a position to collect additional information about these customers, such as their patterns and locations of access and the types of device used. Data users must think carefully about who owns such information and what limitations should be imposed on its use in accordance with the purpose specifications principle.

4. Obligations under individual participation principle

Again, if data users are using a SaaS with which their customers interact directly, they need to ensure that the provider of that SaaS is capable of helping the former to meet their obligations by respecting an individual's right to personal data access and correction. In other words, the SaaS provider may need to provide an end-to-end mechanism for fulfilling access and correction requests from data subjects, or at least support data users in doing so, within a reasonable time frame.

5. Formal data breach management and notification arrangements

The accountability principle stipulates that data users should be prepared for all eventualities and, among other things, pre-develop a data breach handling and notification plan. When a data user engages outside parties such as cloud providers to handle personal data on its behalf, this plan should involve the active participation of the cloud providers if it is to be meaningful and effective.[18]

---

[17]   Article 29 Working Party (n 5).
[18]   'Cloud Computing for Small and Medium-Sized Enterprises' (n 6); 'Information Leaflet on Cloud Computing' (n 8).

B. Trans-Border Data Flows

Many jurisdictions with data protection legislation have trans-border data flow restrictions in place that prohibit the transfer of personal data outside their jurisdictions by data users unless specific conditions are met. Examples include the National Privacy Principle 9 of the Australian Privacy Act 1988,[19] Article 25 of the EU Data Protection Directive 95/46/EC[20] and Section 114B of the New Zealand Privacy Act 1993.[21] Typically, such conditions include the consent of the data subjects and/or assurance that the jurisdictions to which the personal data will be transferred have implemented the same standards of data protection.

Even in cases in which jurisdictions do not have explicit trans-border data flow restriction in their data protection laws, such as Hong Kong's Personal Data (Privacy) Ordinance[22] and the Canadian Personal Information Protection and Electronic Documents Act,[23] data users cannot simply move collected personal data across borders without considering regulatory limitations because data users are always responsible for the protection and use of the personal data in their custody. If they choose to transfer the data they collect outside their own jurisdictions and any misuse or data breach occurs as a result, they will be held responsible by the DPAs in the jurisdictions in which they operate. Furthermore, they may also have to find a way to assure their customers that their personal data being transferred to other jurisdictions will be afforded the same level of protection as if it resides locally.

To allow a computing resource to be fully utilized in a time-efficient manner, cloud providers often locate their data centres in multiple jurisdictions to allow the same resource to be shared by customers operating in different time zones, with peak hours – and hence heavy demand – occurring at different times of the day. Another feature of cloud computing is that cloud providers can dynamically allocate their

---

[19] Privacy Act 1988 (Cth) sch 3 item 9, before amendment in 2012. This principle regulates the private sector. It has been replaced by 'Australia Privacy Principle 8' under the Privacy Amendment (Enhancing Privacy Protection) Act 2012 (Cth) sch 1 item 8.

[20] EU Data Protection Directive 95/46/EC (n 4).

[21] The New Zealand Privacy Act 1993. The section concerns the transfer of information received from another state to a third state. It has been amended by the Privacy (Cross-Border Information) Amendment Act 2010.

[22] Personal Data (Privacy) Ordinance, Cap 486, s 33. This section is currently not in effect.

[23] The Canadian Personal Information Protection and Electronic Documents Act [2000] SC, c 5.

resources to customers in a flexible and optimized way to ensure that spare resources are efficiently utilized. The result is that customer data may be located in and/or moved to data centres in different jurisdictions rather rapidly. After all, cloud providers with data centres in more than one location often stress their superior ability to ensure data availability. If one data centre is affected by a natural disaster or infrastructure failure, customers' data can be shifted seamlessly to distant data centres that remain unaffected. There is always a danger, however, that cloud providers will be unable to easily identify the location of their customers' data in a timely fashion.[24]

When engaging the services of cloud providers, data users need to seriously consider the following implications of trans-border data flows.

1. Risks of storing data in jurisdictions without adequate data protection laws

The risks for data users of storing personal data in jurisdictions without data protection laws are obvious. First, such locations impose no minimum legal standard on the staff of cloud providers. Accordingly, staff may be unaware of any data protection principles requiring them to respect the original purpose of the personal data entrusted to them and to protect the personal data physically and electronically in accordance with its sensitivity. Second, there is no incentive or reason, apart from possible contractual obligations, for the staff in such jurisdictions to follow any such data protection principles. The absence of any legal sanctions if anything goes wrong discourages them from spending any additional time or energy on data protection compliance.

2. Risks of storing data in other jurisdictions

Regardless of whether other jurisdictions have data protection laws in place, the personal data stored there become automatically subject to the laws of those jurisdictions. Data users need to familiarize themselves with those laws to understand the implications they have for their customers. For example, data stored in other jurisdictions may be subject to monitoring and/or access by law enforcement agencies without court warrants. In such circumstances, the transferral of customers' personal data to other jurisdictions exposes such data to unexpected disclosure and regulation by foreign authorities, data users may have a duty to inform their customers that their personal data will be stored in a foreign jurisdiction, as well as the implications of such storage.

---

[24]   Article 29 Working Party (n 5).

3. International efforts to facilitate cross-border data flows

The issues of cross-border data flows have been known for some time. Numerous international efforts have been made to facilitate easier trans-border data flows, and these efforts have progressed with varying degrees of maturity and relevance.

The Safe Harbour Agreement was negotiated between the European Commission and US Department of Commerce to allow personal data from the EU to be transferred to US companies that have signed the agreement and are committed to certain Safe Harbour principles. The agreement ensures that the data protection standard is adequate for a transfer under EU Data Protection Directive 95/46/EC.[25]

Binding corporate rules (BCR) are another vehicle according to which trans-border data flows may be permitted within a corporation operating across multiple jurisdictions. BCR allow a company to be approved by a lead EU regulator by undertaking to comply with EU Data Protection Directive 95/46/EC when processing personal data outside the EU. A detailed discussion of the EU-US data transfer framework can be found in Chapter 5. Data users should note, however, that cloud providers approved under the Safe Harbour Agreement or BCR have no obligation to offer or adhere to the requirements of those schemes when dealing with non-EU customers. The potential customers of such approved cloud providers must therefore determine exactly what services or contracts they are being offered.

The Asia-Pacific Economic Cooperation (APEC) Cross-Border Privacy Rules[26] (CBPR) constitute an intergovernmental agreement available to APEC economies that have enacted their own data protection laws. A set of rules has been developed, and companies operating across the APEC economies may apply to become verified third-party accountability agents appointed by regulators in the economies in question.[27] Similar to the case with the Safe Harbour Agreement and CBPR, it is likely that only large companies will have the necessary resources to complete the verification process. If cloud providers operating in APEC economies are

---

[25]   Rolf H. Weber and Dominic N. Staiger, 'Legal Challenges of Trans-Border Data Flow in the Cloud' (2013) 3 Weblaw IT-Jusletter.

[26]   'The Cross Border Privacy Rules System: Promoting Consumer Privacy and Economic Growth across the APEC Region' (*Asia-Pacific Economic Cooperation*, 5 Sep 2013), www.apec.org/Press/Features/2013/0903_cbpr.aspx, accessed 9 June 20104.

[27]   Asia-Pacific Economic Cooperation, 'APEC Cross-Border Privacy Rules System Program Requirements' (March 2012), www.apec.org/~/media/Files/Groups/ECSG/CBPR/CBPR-ProgramRequirements.pdf, accessed 7 August 2014.

verified to comply with the CBPR, they should be in a position to demonstrate to APEC data users their commitment to personal data privacy, as their entire cloud operations are subject to the jurisdictions and regulatory oversight within APEC. The CBPR regime is still relatively new, however, with only a few economies and companies having joined to date.

4. Compensation controls

One compensating control that data users may consider when engaging the services of cloud providers is to determine the exact locations in which their personal data will reside. They should then discern whether those locations have data protection laws comparable to those of their own jurisdictions and, if necessary, specify the locations in which the cloud providers are allowed to store their personal data.[28] In addition, it would also be useful to ensure that the cloud provider staff who have access to that data are equally aware of the relevant data protection laws.[29] Data users also need to consider whether a cloud provider's claim to be compliant with international efforts to facilitate trans-border data flows is relevant to their decision to use that provider. These seemingly obvious and straightforward compensating controls are not without their challenges, as not all cloud providers are willing to disclose the locations of their storage facilities, let alone allowing customers to specify a 'white list' of locations in which their data can be stored. However, potential customers should continue to make such demands in an effort to force cloud providers to realize the importance of transparency over storage locations and eventually provide customers with location choices.

C. Subcontracting Arrangements

Amongst the many attractive features of cloud computing are scalability and elasticity. Scalability means that cloud resources can be expanded or contracted as needed by data users. Elasticity means that such expansion and contraction can be met very quickly and often at the touch of a button.[30] The implication is that cloud providers have sufficiently large resources to cater for unpredictable demands. In reality, however, it is more likely that they will instead shift to or share the economic risk with others by establishing a series of outsourcing arrangements.[31] In such

---

28   Article 29 Working Party (n 5).
29   'Information Leaflet on Cloud Computing' (n 8).
30   Mell and Grance (n 2).
31   'Information Leaflet on Cloud Computing' (n 8).

arrangements, cloud providers build and own a core capacity themselves. When that capacity is depleted to a certain level, they will enter into an outsourcing arrangement to obtain extra capacity (be it hardware or manpower) temporarily to meet demand. As demand from data users can go down as well as up, these additional resources are obtained temporarily until such time as the cloud provider is certain they will be required on a permanent basis.

The potential concern with such outsourcing arrangements, however, is that the cloud providers may or may not need the spare capacity in practice. Hence, how much effort they will exert to build in and/or negotiate the necessary controls in their contracts with outsourcers remains uncertain. The main risk of subcontracting lies in the potential loss of control. In the case of the cloud, the contractual relationships are between the cloud providers and the subcontractors, but the latter also serve all of the former's customers. Therefore, the contract between cloud provider and subcontractor is unlikely to be tailor-made to meet the regulatory requirements of each and every data user.

What further complicates the matter is that very few cloud providers are transparent about their subcontracting arrangements. Hence, potential customers are not in a position to gauge the severity of the risks involved. If cloud providers engage in subcontracting arrangements, data users need to take the following issues into consideration.

1. Lack of formal contractual relationship

When it engages in subcontracting, a cloud provider's operations are potentially supported by a range of outside parties. In addition to data users' inability to specify the necessary controls to subcontractors, subcontractors enjoy no direct contractual relationship with data users. In the event of any breach or misuse of personal data caused by subcontractors, data users will be unable to hold them contractually liable. This lack of a direct contractual relationship with data users substantially weakens the sense of responsibility and loyalty that subcontractors feel. Accordingly, they may not feel obliged to alert all users, with whom they may not have a strong contractual relationship, about any data breaches they suffer. In extreme cases, subcontractors can walk away from catastrophic data breaches, leaving data users to face the full legal consequences. In any event, data users need to remember that the resulting legal and reputational damage to them cannot be realistically compensated for by suing either the cloud provider or its subcontractors for breach of contract.

2. Lack of privacy awareness and/or legal sanctions

As previously noted, if subcontractors entrusted with the processing of personal data are located in jurisdictions without data protection laws, they could suffer from a lack of knowledge and/or respect for personal data protection, which poses risks to data users. As in the aforementioned case, they may be able to walk away from a catastrophic data breach or incident of misuse without being subject to any legal sanctions.

3. Judgement call

It is thus of the utmost importance that data users determine the outsourcing policy and practice of any cloud provider whose services they intend to engage, and then exercise judgement concerning whether adequate controls over outsourcing arrangements and subcontractors are in place.

D. Standard Offerings

Many cloud providers, particularly those offering public cloud solutions, offer only a limited number of predefined cloud solutions/packages to their customers. Data users looking to work with such providers should look very carefully at the details of their offerings to ensure that all of their requirements under the principles of purpose specification, use limitation and security safeguards will be met.

1. Security/compliance gap

Data users who discover that the offerings of potential cloud providers do not meet their security/compliance requirements should not consider those providers. Should they choose to ignore the gap and accept using inadequate cloud solutions, they will be putting both the personal data they have collected and their business reputation at risk. A better way of dealing with inadequate cloud offerings would be to discuss the relevant issues with the cloud providers concerned, giving them an opportunity to customize or otherwise improve the problematic offerings until the data users are comfortable with them and are confident that they are in compliance with the principles of purpose specifications, use limitation and security safeguards.

2. Verification

Even if cloud providers are willing to customize or otherwise improve their offerings to ensure they meet all data user imposed requirements, the next challenge for data users is on how to ensure that additional controls are indeed in place and executed properly. In traditional outsourcing arrangements, auditing rights are generally included in the contract but the situation is more challenging for cloud providers, whose operations and boundaries are somewhat fluid. The development of new and innovative means by which cloud service providers can demonstrate their level of compliance with the requirements or expectations of data users is a matter of urgency.

Certification involving independent assessment may be one way for them to demonstrate conformity with predetermined standards. However, data users who are unfamiliar with the workings of these standards and the certification process could be misled by the creative use of a certification reference in cloud providers' marketing materials. To better protect themselves, data users should thus familiarize themselves with the scope of the security and auditing standards commonly used or claimed by cloud providers, and assess their relevance and adequacy on a case-by-case basis.

CONCLUSION: THE CHALLENGES TO DATA USERS

Data users are ultimately held responsible for the proper handling of all personal data in their possession. Such responsibility is not a transferable legal obligation, and thus the outsourcing of personal data processing to a cloud provider does not shift the legal liability to that provider. The main challenge for data users utilizing cloud systems is therefore to figure out a way to maintain control and oversight akin to managing the personal data themselves.

Once they have understood the main data protection principles outlined in this chapter, particularly the principles of purpose specifications, use limitation and security safeguards, data users looking to engage the services of cloud providers should carry out proper risk assessments of all potential offerings to identify any gaps that may exist between those offerings and their own requirements. Any gaps identified must then be addressed by implementing appropriate controls to avoid or at least reduce the risk.

Data users should always be mindful of the need to avoid accepting too much risk. Instead, they should find a cloud solution with sufficient protection to meet their requirements or find a cloud provider that is prepared to customize its solutions and demonstrate compliance with those requirements. It is clear that public clouds targeting consumers or low-cost markets are less likely to satisfy control and compliance requirements if used to process personal data. In addition to risk avoidance and/or reduction measures, which are essentially designed to prevent risks from materializing, data users may also consider more sophisticated measures such as encryption. If data users apply such measures as 'strong' cryptographic algorithms, robust implementation (software products), complex passwords and proper key management to encrypt personal data stored in the cloud, then they should be able to maintain a high level of data confidentiality as they will be the only party capable of decrypting the data. Concerns over access and/or misuse by unauthorized parties will thus be greatly alleviated.

In sum, cloud use is appealing but fraught with challenges in terms of personal data privacy protection. A top-down approach that begins with an understanding of basic data protection principles and followed by a risk assessment of the gaps between cloud offerings and required controls and requirements would constitute a good start to tackling these challenges.

3. Legal safeguards for cloud computing

Rolf H. Weber

I. INTRODUCTION

Cloud computing technology is subject to a manifold number of legally prescribed and voluntary safeguards and boundaries. These include legislation which ensures the protection of an individual's personal data, a competition law framework maintaining an open and accessible cloud market and the concept of 'net neutrality'. Although aimed at improving the rights of customers, such legislation is in practice ill-tailored to the needs of cloud computing providers and, thus, poses significant challenges in its daily application. The following chapter addresses the applicable legal safeguards for cloud computing and highlights potential measures that cloud providers can implement to ensure compliance.

In practice, access and portability of data are of central importance. Three possible scenarios can be envisaged in regard to an individual's access to data stored in the cloud and the available technical framework for a transfer into another cloud system. Under the first scenario, the cloud market is broken down into various actors with their own individual systems based on self-developed proprietary technologies. In a second scenario, a few cloud providers dominate the market, but allow for data to be transferred between the varying systems. Ideally, the third approach with a universal data standard, open interfaces and open source software should be sought, as it provides the highest efficiency gains by making use of a global cloud.[1] Thus, ensuring open systems through enhanced data portability will be one of the main future challenges facing

---

[1] Michael Donohue and Dimitri Ypsilanti, 'Briefing Paper for the ICCP Technology Foresight Forum', Organisation for Economic Co-operation and Development, N 22–4, www.oecd.org/internet/ieconomy/43933771.pdf, accessed 27 May 2014.

regulators worldwide. It is, therefore, important that government procurement takes these issues into account and requires its cloud suppliers to fulfil a uniform data standard. Such action will put pressure on cloud providers to ensure data portability and access.[2]

The hereinafter-discussed legal safeguards can stem from sector-specific regulation or from general competition law. After a short introduction to the two different regulatory systems the chapter analyses the possible design of specific normative provisions by discussing the main pillars of sector-specific regulation, namely interoperability and data portability, network neutrality, vertical integration control as well as electronic commerce requirements. The analysis shows that sector-specific regulation is only partially in a position to meet the requirements of an appropriate legal framework for cloud computing.

As a consequence, general competition law must be invoked in order to overcome regulatory weaknesses. Major issues to be dealt with are interoperability and data portability on the one hand and the limitations of vertical integration on the other hand.

The chapter concludes with a short discussion of other legal safeguards such as information security, data protection and data flows, intellectual property and related issues as well as the regulatory boundaries of cloud contracts.

II. AVAILABLE REGULATORY INSTRUMENTS

The available regulatory instruments for cloud-based systems can be grouped into economic regulation, to which sector-specific regulation and competition law belong, and into general legal safeguards, such as data security, data protection or business-related regulations which due to their scope touch and concern cloud computing.

Economic regulation embraces two main forms of state intervention being based on two different regulatory regimes, namely competition law and sector-specific regulation:

(i)   Competition law, usually referred to as *ex post* regulation, is characterized by the fact that competition authorities intervene if market participants jeopardize free competition by way of restrictive agreements or abusive behaviour in the market. Exceptionally,

---

[2]   Donohue and Ypsilanti (n 1) para. 48.

in the case of a merger, competition authorities are allowed to pre-emptively block a structural change in the market.

(ii) In contrast, sector-specific regulation is a form of (at least partial) *ex ante* regulation, which tries to lay the ground for competition: it is only admissible in those markets (for example, natural monopolies) in which forces and actors fail to ensure workable competition.[3]

Competition rules are considered to be generally applicable norms without regard to the particularities of a certain market, they are usually backward looking, that is, they rely on historical evidence. Sector-related regulations are specifically designed to meet the requirements of a certain market: they are forward looking (*ex ante*). Sector-specific regulation is adopted in market segments in which competition pressure is weak or even non-existent and, therefore, the systematic abuse of market power is likely.[4]

Both approaches have their strengths and weaknesses: competition law is quite general and does not normally provide specific solutions, but is very flexible. Sector-specific regulation contains precise terms which provide certainty for regulatory bodies and concerned undertakings: it normally provides faster and more effective solutions.[5]

Competition law is applicable across the whole economy, notwithstanding the existence of any sector-specific regulation, which, in contrast, is usually formulated against the backdrop of competition law. Consequently, whilst competition rules try to protect open markets in general, sector-specific regulation often focuses on promoting entry into markets deemed to lack sufficient competition. As a principle it may be stated that the existence of even extensive regulation does not free an undertaking from the obligation to comply with general competition

---

[3] Peter Alexiadis, 'Balancing the Application of Ex Post and Ex Ante Disciplines, Rights and Remedies in a Liberalised and Competitive Internal Market: Square Pegs in Round Holes?' (*Gibson Dunn*, March 2012) 139, www.gibsondunn.com/publications/Documents/Alexiadis-BalancingtheApplication ofExPostandExAnteDisciplines.pdf, accessed 27 May 2014.

[4] Alexiadis (n 3) 139.

[5] Rolf H. Weber, *Regulatory Models for the Online World* (Zurich, Schulthess Verlag 2002) 116.

rules. Sector-specific regulation is designed to avoid undesirable developments and ensures market access for interested undertakings.[6]

At the institutional level, sector-specific supervisory bodies and competition authorities are meant to coordinate their actions. From a procedural perspective, sector-specific regulation has the objective of establishing an adequate market structure: therefore, the concrete norms are to be applied at first sequence, followed by the general competition law rules.

Since cloud computing has close relations to technical (fixed or mobile) infrastructures, an interaction between sector-specific regulation and competition law is unavoidable. Even if overarching regulation for cloud computing, as an IT service, is not available on an international or regional level, specific rules are in place, for example, on network regulation as well as on content regulation which play an integral role in the cloud computing markets.[7]

III. SECTOR-SPECIFIC REGULATION

Several problems can be dealt with by sector-specific regulation, namely: (i) interoperability and data portability; (ii) network neutrality; (iii) vertical integration; and (iv) electronic commerce issues. Hereafter, the EU electronic communications framework will be addressed in more detail. This regulatory framework, having been revised in 2009, is based on four Directives: the Framework Directive,[8] the Access Directive,[9] the Authorisation Directive,[10] and the Universal Service Directive.[11] Corresponding to

---

[6]   Jasper P. Sluijs, Pierre Larouch and Wolf Sauter, 'Cloud Computing in the EU Policy Sphere' (2012) 1 JIPITEC 12, 17, www.jipitec.eu/issues/jipitec-3-1-2012/3320/sluijs.pdf, accessed 27 May 2014.

[7]   Rolf H. Weber in cooperation with Mirina Grosz and Romana Weber, *Shaping Internet Governance: Regulatory Challenges* (Zurich, Schulthess Verlag 2009) 203–5.

[8]   Directive 2002/21 on a common regulatory framework for electronic communications networks and services (Framework Directive) [2002] OJ L 108/33.

[9]   Directive 2002/19 on access to, and interconnection of, electronic communications networks and associated facilities (Access Directive) [2002] OJ L 108/7.

[10]   Directive 2002/20 on the authorization of electronic communications networks and services (Authorisation Directive) [2002] OJ L 108/21.

[11]   Directive 2002/22 on universal service and users' rights relating to electronic communications networks and services (Universal Service Directive) [2002] OJ L 108/51.

the legal nature of Directives,[12] the respective rules are to be implemented at the national level.

A. Interoperability and Data Portability

The EU regulatory framework defines an 'electronic communications' service' as a service wholly or mainly consisting of the conveyance of signals on electronic networks, including telecommunications' services, but excluding service providing or exercising editorial control or content transmitted using electronic communications' networks and services.[13] Theoretically, cloud computing could be summarized under the term electronic services if the activity is concerned with services in the form of sending signals on electronic communications networks.[14] However, such a kind of business restriction to sending signals does not apply in the daily practice of cloud computing.

Cloud computing providers offer an IT-related service enabling the storing and processing of data. Usually they are dependent on an Internet service provider (ISP) to facilitate the sending and receiving of signals on the networks, that is, cloud computer providers are not establishing the communications infrastructure nor are they associated with the respective services, meaning that regulations on electronic communications do not hit the core of cloud computing services.[15] Nevertheless, this technical assessment does not mean that a cloud service provider would exercise editorial control over content transmitted.

The Access Directive of the EU contains interconnection requirements with corresponding powers for the national regulatory agencies: however, these requirements only concern electronic communications' service providers. Therefore, the regulatory framework seems of little support for enhancing data portability and interoperability of cloud services.[16]

B. Network Neutrality

The relationship between cloud computing providers and ISPs is exposed to the network neutrality discussion focusing on the question whether an

---

[12] The four separate Directives were amended in the 2007 review by Directive 2009/136 amending Directives 2002/22, 2002/58 and 2009/140 [2009] OJ L 337, 11.

[13] Framework Directive (n 8) Art. 2(c).

[14] Sluijs, Larouche and Sauter (n 6) 23.

[15] Ibid.

[16] Ibid.

ISP may intervene in the communications process. For example, an ISP may introduce different speeds of delivery or pricing structures for bandwidth.[17] From a substantive angle, the problem of introducing a model of differentiated quality of service (QoS) for different services is at stake.[18] Obviously, network neutrality is significant for cloud computing since the delivery of the services is usually time sensitive (not allowing for slow processes) and price structuring could jeopardize the price schemes of the cloud services' providers.

Nevertheless, it should not be overlooked that priority services and differentiated pricing schemes could also enable cloud computing providers to offer different kinds of services and make the reliability of these services dependent on the chosen service option.[19] A particular problem occurs in the case of scarce resources, for example, when the bandwidth is limited in mobile broadband. In this context, the questions on network operators' compliance with the neutrality principle must be examined.

The EU regulatory framework does not contain specific network neutrality provisions, but addresses the transparency element according to the policy that regulatory interventions in the market would not be legitimate providing the network customers are sufficiently informed of the network operator practices and network management principles. Transparency policy should overcome the potentially negative effects of non-compliance with the network neutrality principle.[20] Nevertheless, national legislators are entitled to introduce specific rules which could have an impact on bandwidth management. For example, the Netherlands has introduced, the second country in the world to do so, a net neutrality provision into its Telecommunications Act of 2012.[21] Ultimately, a certain fragmentation of national markets cannot be avoided. However, from the EU perspective this consequence is acceptable since it would be

---

[17]   On the network neutrality principle in general, see Simon Schlauri, 'Network Neutrality as a New Regulatory Principle of Telecommunications Law' in Indra Spiecker genannt Döhmann and Jan Krämer (eds), *Network Neutrality and Open Access* (Baden-Baden, Nomos 2011) 43–51.

[18]   Sluijs, Larouche and Sauter (n 6) 24.

[19]   Ibid.

[20]   Schlauri (n 17) 51.

[21]   Emőke Maembe, 'Net Neutrality in Europe' (*European Commission*, 7 February 2013) 12, http://ec.europa.eu/consumers/empowerment/minutes/minutes_0708022013_p04_en.pdf, accessed 27 May 2014; Iljitsch van Beijnum, 'Netherlands Becomes World's Second "Net Neutrality" Country' (*Ars Technica*, 10 May 2012), http://arstechnica.com/tech-policy/2012/05/netherlands-becomes-worlds-second-net-neutrality-country/, accessed 27 May 2014.

in the national interest to introduce a competitive environment in favour of their own national market participants.

Looking from this angle, the main problem for cloud computing providers consists in the fact that different regulations might have to be considered for different national markets, notwithstanding the trans-national character of cloud computing services. This fragmentation could cause additional transaction costs even if the regulations are transparent and the network management can be forecast.[22] Apart from the costs, it might also become more difficult to guarantee a certain processing quality and speed to customers of cloud computing services: 'Clouds are especially vulnerable to this situation as their main service comprises outsourced, computationally intensive – and thus bandwidth-hungry – processes, often for corporate clients with a strong demand for reliability as they depend on cloud services to operate their business'.[23]

A possible 'countermeasure' could consist of improved standardization of procedural and service-related rendering of cloud computing. As a negative impact of standardization a certain weakening of competition between the cloud computing providers can hardly be avoided.

C. Vertical Integration

As mentioned,[24] a cloud computing provider does not offer 'electronic communications' services' over 'electronic communications' networks'; therefore, such a service provider does not usually fall under the EU regulatory framework on electronic communications, but it is subject to competition law in respect of vertical integration.[25] Consequently, the electronic communications' framework of the EU does not play a direct role in this context.

However, as discussed hereafter, cloud computing services are likely to fall within the term of 'information society services'. Whether this assessment leads to certain access requirements under the EU regulatory framework has not yet been clarified. At first instance, the fact that certain services have a specific purpose does not qualify them for access

---

[22] 'Guidelines for Quality of Service in the Scope of Net Neutrality' (*Body of European Regulators for Electronic Commerce*, 26 November 2012) 13, http://berec.europa.eu/eng/document_register/subject_matter/berec/regulatory_best_practices/guidelines/1101-berec-guidelines-for-quality-of-service-in-the-scope-of-net-neutrality, accessed 27 May 2014.

[23] Sluijs, Larouche and Sauter (n 6) 25.

[24] See heading III.A in this chapter.

[25] Ibid heading IV.C.

rights to infrastructure even if content providers face similar access problems. In principle, the corresponding challenges are not significantly different from those of electronic communications' networks and services, meaning that an application by analogy does not seem to be excluded, particularly since the recent amendments to the Access Directive have included information society services and broadcast content services.[26]

D. Electronic Commerce

(i)   Electronic commerce regulations often rely on different notions than electronic communications regulations, namely on the term of 'information society services'. For example, EU Directive 1998/34 uses the definition of a 'service normally provided for remuneration, at a distance, by electronic means and at the individual request of a recipient of services'.[27]

Cloud computing services can be considered as a type of information society service. Therefore, in EU countries, the E-Commerce Directive 2000/31 is applicable,[28] mainly containing rules being relevant in the cloud computing context in respect of jurisdictional issues and of secondary liability for cloud computing services. Thereby, the specific functions of the different Internet service providers are to be taken into account.

The main function of an access provider consists of making Internet access available: therefore, the access provider can become liable to the users for lack of Internet access, which constitutes a contractual non-performance. An often common issue is the assessment of whether certain malfunctions of the Internet are attributable to the access provider. The access provider is only exercising a 'transport' function since normally the material is carried through an automatic technical process. The fact that the access provider makes it technically possible for the user to get access to illegal

---

[26]   Sluijs, Larouche and Sauter (n 6) 23–4.

[27]   Council Directive 98/34, last amended by Council Directive 2006/96 [2006] OJ L 363/81 Art. 1 para. 2.

[28]   Council Directive 2000/31/EC of the European Parliament and of the Council of 8 June 2000 on certain legal aspects of information society services, in particular electronic commerce, in the internal market (E-Commerce Directive).

content is not considered a non-diligent behaviour per se (Art. 12 of the EU E-Commerce Directive).[29]

The notion of secondary liability as regulated in the E-Commerce Directive encompasses the question whether service providers could become liable for actions of their users. According to the E-Commerce Directive, a distinction must be drawn between a 'mere' access provider, a 'caching' provider and a 'hosting' provider.[30] Since a cloud computing provider is actually designing and rendering individual services, the provision on secondary liability of access providers would not be applicable.

(ii) Cloud computing providers offering contents and services can be qualified as hosting providers. Therefore, when a cloud computing provider has knowledge of illegal activities or illegal materials, the respective data must be removed. If the cloud computing provider, however, does not have any control over the recipient of the service, the secondary liability is limited to injunctive relief.[31] Nevertheless, it should not be overlooked that the secondary liability provisions of the E-Commerce Directive are debated in the European Courts,[32] and that the introduction of appropriate safe harbour provisions is being discussed.[33]

It seems that a new, redefined approach to the hosting provisions stated in Article 14 of the E-Commerce Directive[34] is necessary in light of the evolving new technologies such as cloud computing. However, it would not seem justifiable to impose a burden on a cloud provider to control a customer's data if a hosting provider is not required to do so. The main technological difference lies in the decentralized provisioning of a scalable service, thus making supervision of data much harder to achieve than on a single hosting server. As technology is evolving so are the forms of cloud

---

[29] Rolf H. Weber, 'Internet Service Provider Liability: The Swiss Perspective' (2010) 1 JIPITEC 145.

[30] E-Commerce Directive (n 28) Arts 12–14.

[31] Sluijs, Larouche and Sauter (n 6) 26.

[32] Patrick Van Eecke and Maarten Truyens, 'EU Study on the Legal Analysis of a Single Market for an Information Society: Liability of Online Intermediaries' (November 2009) 3, http://ec.europa.eu/information_society/newsroom/cf/document.cfm?doc_id=842, accessed 29 January 2015; Joanna Kulesza, 'Delfi v Estonia before the ECHR: Editorial Liability for Internet Service Providers?' (*Jusletter IT*, 11 December 2013), http://jusletter-it.weblaw.ch/issues/2013/11-Dezember-2013.html, accessed 27 May 2014.

[33] Van Eecke and Truyens (n 32) 28.

[34] E-Commerce Directive (n 28).

computing. Meanwhile, cloud computing and hosting services have merged into a new product called cloud hosting.

In contrast to the old dedicated hosting where web data was processed and stored on one server in a specific location, cloud hosting allows storage and processing to take place in various locations. The data is shifted to a server centre where the costs are lowest and which is available to perform the required operations. This again highlights the incompatibility of cloud technology with the current law, created through inflexible definitions in legislation such as the E-Commerce Directive.

(iii) The E-Commerce Directive is not very clear as far as jurisdictional rules are concerned since, according to its purpose, the new framework does not intend to establish additional rules on private international law. However, the preamble provides for the reservation that the traditional rules should not restrict the freedom to provide information society services.[35] As a principle, EU countries are not allowed to interfere with the cross-border provision of information society services. The applicable legal framework should be based on the rules of the country of domicile of the services' provider.[36] Therefore, if a cloud computing provider complies with the rules at its domicile, services could be delivered to customers in other countries.[37] Nevertheless, a specific problem consists in the fact that the E-Commerce Directive addresses EU states, not private enterprises such as the network operators and the ISP. Since the Directive does not enjoy horizontal effects, the regulatory tools to streamline cloud computing operations seem weak.[38]

IV. COMPETITION LAW

As mentioned, competition law provisions are not sector related, but generally apply across all markets.[39] As seen on many occasions, competition law plays an increasingly important role in IT markets.

---

[35] E-Commerce Directive (n 28) Preamble.
[36] E-Commerce Directive (n 28) Art. 3.
[37] Michael Hellner, 'The Country of Origin Principle in the E-Commerce Directive: A Conflict with Conflict of Laws?' (2004) 12 *Eur Rev Priv L* 193, 194.
[38] Sluijs, Larouche and Sauter (n 6) 25.
[39] See above heading I.

A. Market Definition

The application of competition law in respect of restrictive agreements or the abusive behaviour of a market dominant enterprise requires the definition of the relevant product/service as well as geographic and temporal markets. Usually the definition of the relevant market is based on the concept of demand-side substitutability, to be accessed and determined by a qualitative analysis of product/service characteristics and intended product/service use.[40]

In the case of cloud computing, an upstream market (cloud computing provider) and a downstream market (ISP) are to be taken into account:

(i)   On the upstream level, the notion of the relevant market could be limited to individual types of cloud computing services (in other words, IaaS, SaaS, PaaS (infrastructure/software/platform as a service)). The justification for such a 'narrow' differentiation lies in the fact that the three types of services differ in characteristics and use.[41] However, this approach does not properly take into account the supply-side substitutability since cloud computing services rely on mass customization. Only if the providers can exploit economies of scope by ensuring a vast amount of services at limited cost the large investments into the facilities can be justified.[42]

(ii)   As far as the downstream level is concerned, a distinction between broadband access and narrowband access is possible, as well as a distinction between fixed and mobile access to communications' networks. Nevertheless, in view of the most recent technological developments, such a kind of differentiation of sub-markets is becoming less convincing over time.[43]

A special problem concerns the market definition of wholesale call termination: according to common practice, each respective network is establishing its own relevant market as no choice to deal with another operator exists other than the operator to which the

---

[40]   Jared Kagan, 'Bricks, Mortar and Google: Defining the Relevant Antitrust Market for Internet-Based Companies' (2010) 55 *New York Law School Law Review* 285.
[41]   Sluijs, Larouche and Sauter (n 6) 18.
[42]   Ibid.
[43]   Ibid.

calling party subscribes (the terminating operator).[44] A similar reasoning could be applied to cloud computing services since usually a customer can communicate with the cloud computing provider only through a specific ISP.[45]

The geographical market definition has to take into account the fact that clouds are built on the premise of ubiquity, mobility and pervasiveness, making purely national markets too narrow; moreover, the geographic market scope must encompass the inherent cross-border business.[46] Therefore, in principle, the cloud computing market is global, but subject to linguistic and/or cultural market delimitations for specific services.[47] On the downstream level, an ISP can be subject to national regulation (for example, on interconnection and roaming practices): consequently, geographic markets are more fragmented and national issues can play a role.[48]

B. Interoperability and Data Portability

Interoperability and data portability are important for cloud computing services' recipients since otherwise existing contractual relations can hardly be changed (excluding the choice of another provider) and the customer becomes completely dependent on the services of the once chosen provider. Competition law refers to the so-called customer lock-in situation which is regarded as abusive conduct of a market dominant enterprise.[49] Such kind of customer lock-in leads to aggravated dependence on a specific cloud computing provider (CCP).[50] The first problem in the analysis of potentially illegal behaviour concerns the question of whether the cloud computing provider has a dominant position in the market. This assessment depends on the above-discussed market definition. Usually, court practice applies a competition law approach that facilitates the assumption of market dominance[51] and the assessment of

---

44   Recommendation 2003/311 of 11 February 2003 on relevant product and service markets within the electronic communications sector susceptible to ex ante regulation in accordance with Directive 2002/21 [2003] OJ L 114/45.
45   Sluijs, Larouche and Sauter (n 6) 19.
46   Weber (n 5) 48.
47   Kagan (n 40) 283.
48   Sluijs, Larouche and Sauter (n 6) 19.
49   Ibid.
50   Ibid.
51   Case 27/76, *United Brands v Commission* [1978] ECR, 207.

market entry barriers.[52] At first instance, fierce competition seems to exist between various enterprises active in the cloud computing market. Nevertheless, changing a provider is in practice often difficult and causes substantive costs; thus, the customer cannot easily get detached from its existing cloud computing provider.[53]

The conduct of a market dominant enterprise can lead to anti-competitive foreclosure, particularly in the case of a high market share. In such a situation, the customer might have difficulties to port data from one cloud provider to another provider or work together with two or more cloud providers simultaneously. Even if this scenario does not easily fit into the broad types of abusive conduct identified in the Guidance Paper of the EU Commission,[54] the customer is tied in to certain investments in relation to the customization of services and the relocation of private/proprietary information on the cloud provider's facilities.[55]

Competition laws, therefore, have to encourage non-proprietary cloud systems by closely monitoring the actions of dominant cloud service providers such as Google, Amazon and Microsoft. If these decide to shield their cloud offerings against other systems, such action might violate competition law due to their dominant market position.

C. Vertical Integration

Apart from the vertical integration of two enterprises by way of a merger between a cloud provider and an ISP, vertical restraints can also be based on restrictive agreements or abusive market behaviour.

Restrictive agreements

EU competition law is concretizing the general provision of Article 101 of the Treaty on the Functioning of the European Union (TFEU) on restrictive vertical agreements through Regulation 330/2010 on Vertical

---

[52] Case 85/76, *Hoffmann-La Roche v Commission* [1979] ECR, 461.

[53] More optimistic in the assessment, however, Sluijs, Larouche and Sauter (n 6) 19.

[54] Communication from the Commission: Guidance on the Commission's Enforcement Priorities in Applying Article 82 of the EC Treaty to Abusive Exclusionary Conduct by Dominant Undertakings [2009] OJ C 45/7, paras 32–90.

[55] Sluijs, Larouche and Sauter (n 6) 20.

Restraints,[56] the so-called block exemption regulation, together with the Guidelines on Vertical Restraints released by the Commission.[57] The key factor in the assessment of vertical agreements is the existence of market power. Regulation 330/2010 exempts contractual arrangements, if both parties hold less than 30 per cent market share in their respective markets. Again, the market definition plays a major role: the more the market is fragmented (for example, in IaaS, SaaS, PaaS), the more likely the mentioned market ratio will be exceeded.[58]

(i) Threshold exceeded: If either party would exceed the 30 per cent threshold, the block exemption of Regulation 330/2010 would not be applicable and the vertical arrangement must be assessed under Article 101 TFEU. Therefore, the decisive fact consists in the question whether suitable alternatives in the form of other cloud providers are available. Since cloud computing services are offered on a global scale, the substitutability criterion should be fulfilled; however, an alternative to the given ISP is usually not present.[59]

(ii) Below threshold: If the market share threshold of 30 per cent is not exceeded, the vertical arrangement can be justified if it does not contain a so-called black list restriction which defeats the application of Regulation 330/2010.[60] Such kinds of black list issues are resale price, maintenance provisions and long-lasting non-compete obligations.[61]

Abusive market behaviour

(i) Market dominance: Another competition law restriction is abusive behaviour in the case of market dominance according to Article 102 TFEU. Market dominance is assessed along the lines of the described market definitions:[62] the narrower the market is designed, the more likely market dominance exists. Vertical integration of a cloud provider by an

---

[56] Commission Regulation 330/2010 of 20 April 2010 on the application of Art. 101 para. 3 TFEU to Categories of Vertical Agreements and Concerted Practices [2010] OJ L 102/1, http://eur-lex.europa.eu/LexUriServ/LexUriServ. do?uri=OJ:L:2010:102:0001:0007:EN:PDF, accessed 27 May 2014.

[57] Commission Guidelines on Vertical Restraints [2010] OJ C 130/1.

[58] Sluijs, Larouche and Sauter (n 6) 22.

[59] Ibid.

[60] Regulation No 330/2010 (n 56).

[61] Regulation 330/2010 (n 56) Art. 5.

[62] See heading III.A in this chapter.

ISP which does not fulfil the requirements of a dominant market position is not governed by competition law.[63]

In practice, abusive behaviour often consists of margin squeezes or predatory pricing.[64] Currently, the cloud computing market is dominated by only a handful of big providers: these are Microsoft, Google and Amazon. Smaller companies are emerging; however, they focus mostly on a limited market segment targeting mainly the more profitable commercial usage as private cloud users are accustomed to receiving basic cloud services free of charge (in other words, cloud email, limited cloud storage).

Because the above-mentioned big corporations have already set up the required infrastructure, they might be inclined to deter further competition. Amazon could consider a predatory pricing strategy as its servers are also used for its main business, the sale of goods. Offering its unused hardware capacity is only a further add-on and does not necessarily need to be sustainably priced. Over the last year, a sharp fall in cloud service prices has occurred. Amazon was the first to reduce its prices, quickly followed by Microsoft and other market participants.[65] On the face of it, this development seems to be an advantage for the cloud user, but on closer view the dominant market position of the big providers is cemented. Furthermore, the market entry barrier is increased for new competitors due to the smaller profit margins which results in an extended duration to recoup the initial outlay for new hardware and software. Thus, big corporations with established hardware and software systems as well as the financial resources, which are already active in the market, are put at an advantage.

In addition, classifying any action as predatory pricing is difficult as generally procompetitive pricing is allowed. An exact assessment of the circumstances and timing of the parties is therefore essential in determining whether a party is selling under its costs in order to drive competition out of the market.

---

[63] Jasper Sluijs, 'Network Neutrality and Internal Market Fragmentation', TILEC Discussion Paper No 2012-015, 17.

[64] Bruce H. Kobayashi, 'The Law and Economics of Predatory Pricing', George Mason University Law and Economics Research Paper Series 08-41, 1, http://papers.ssrn.com/sol3/papers.cfm?abstract_id=1154052, accessed 27 May 2014.

[65] Larry Dignan, 'Cloud's Price Race to Zero: Microsoft Cuts Azure Pricing, Eyes Amazon' (*ZDNet*, 9 March 2012), www.zdnet.com/blog/btl/clouds-price-race-to-zero-microsoft-cuts-azure-pricing-eyes-amazon/71246, accessed 27 May 2014.

The most critical issue in the context of abusive market behaviour is access. An example is the refusal of an ISP to deal with a non-affiliated cloud computing provider given the fact that the ISP is tied into a vertically integrated scheme with another cloud computing provider.[66]

The detailed competition law assessment of such a situation depends on the interpretation of the Commission's Guidance Paper on Article 102 TFEU providing its opinion on the interpretation of the relevant term 'discrimination'.[67] Furthermore, the European Courts often deal with the abusive behaviour of IT and telecommunications' enterprises.[68] An example is Wanadoo,[69] a France Telecom subsidiary engaged in the sale of Internet access which was provided with Asymmetric Digital Subscriber Line (ADSL) services by its parent whilst competing on the market with other providers. The other market participants were required to buy the ADSL service from France Telecom, which had a monopoly on the service. However, Wanadoo sold its services to customers below the actual 'production' costs and thus utilized a deliberate strategy of predation aimed at pre-empting the strategic market for high-speed Internet access at the expense of its competitors.[70] Whilst the customers were better off in the short term because of this predatory pricing, they would have ultimately had to bear higher costs once the competitors disappeared from the market. Therefore, the European Court of Justice (ECJ) sanctioned France Telecom for its anti-competitive conduct.[71]

This case vividly shows that the potential for market abuse and anti-competitive conduct is real. Recently, German Telekom announced that it will cap all its customers' broadband connections to a maximum

---

[66]   Sluijs, Larouche and Sauter (n 6) 20.

[67]   Guidance Paper (n 54).

[68]   Gönenc Gürkaynak, Derya Durlu and Margaret Hagan, 'Antitrust on the Internet: A Comparative Assessment of Competition Law Enforcement in the Internet Realm' (2013) 14 *Business Law International* 51.

[69]   Case 202/07 P, *France Télécom SA v Commission of the European Communities* [2009] ECJ I-02369, http://curia.europa.eu/juris/document/document.jsf;jsessionid=9ea7d2dc30dbf104c0c0db854cfbb7a2b47ce4657504.e3 4KaxiLc3qMb40Rch0SaxuNb310?text=&docid=73807&pageIndex=0&doclang=EN&mode=lst&dir=&occ=first&part=1&cid=85937, accessed 27 May 2014.

[70]   Alberto Alemanno and Marco Ramondino, 'The ECJ France Télécom/Wanadoo Judgment: To Recoup or Not to Recoup? That "Was" the Question for a Predatory Price Finding under Article 82 EC' (2009) 6 ELR 1.

[71]   Case 202/07 P (n 69).

gigabyte amount.[72] This cap would, however, not apply to data received from services provided by its partner (a movie and sound streaming portal). It remains to be seen whether other ISPs will follow this example. If so, the potential usage of cloud computing would be seriously impaired as it relies heavily on bandwidth due to its decentralized nature.

(ii) Refusal to supply: Another critical behaviour could consist of the refusal to supply a service, either actual or constructive. An illegal vertical integration is to be assumed in the case of cloud computing provider/ISP integration with subsequent foreclosure of rival cloud computing providers upstream (or rival ISPs downstream).[73] Generally, however, duties to supply a service are considered to have the potential of exerting an adverse effect on innovation. Ensuring steady market access by forcing a certain supply from ISPs will likely outweigh the potentially detrimental effect a decision not to supply services to a party would have. Essentially competition would break down as it can only take place in a market in which the ISPs currently regulate access. A 'must-carry'[74] rule could mitigate the potential limitations ISPs try to place on cloud providers' broadband communication.

The European Courts have analysed the respective problems mainly in the *Bronner* and *Microsoft* cases. In *Bronner*, a three-pronged test was introduced, looking at the questions of whether the essential facility (the infrastructure of an ISP) is indispensable for a service (of a cloud

---

[72] Kai Biermann, 'Telekom drosselt fast alle Kunden' (*Zeit Online*, 3 May 2013), www.zeit.de/digital/internet/2013-05/telekom-drossel-2016, accessed 27 May 2014.

[73] Sluijs, Larouche and Sauter (n 6) 21.

[74] Directive 2009/140/EC of the European Parliament and of the Council of 25 November 2009 amending Directives 2002/21/EC on a common regulatory framework for electronic communications networks and services, 2002/19/EC on access to, and interconnection of, electronic communications networks and services, and 2002/20/EC on the authorization of electronic communications networks and services [2009] OJ L 337/37; Directive 2009/136/EC of the European Parliament and of the Council of 25 November 2009 amending Directive 2002/22/EC on universal service and users' rights relating to electronic communications networks; Directive 2002/58/EC concerning the processing of personal data and the protection of privacy in the electronic communications sector and Regulation (EC) No 2006/2004 on consumer protection cooperation [2010] OJ L 337/11, Art. 31(1).

computing provider) to reach its customers, regardless of whether alternative methods of carriage fall within the same market.[75] The test addressed the question of whether the dominant party's refusal was 'likely to eliminate all competition on the part of the undertaking seeking access'.[76] Additionally, in the *Microsoft* case it was held that it had to be proven that access to the interoperability information held by Microsoft was indispensable to compete in the workgroup server market.[77] Applying this reasoning to a potential market abuse situation in which an ISP refuses access to a competing cloud provider, the determinative factor would be whether such action is likely to eliminate all competition by other cloud providers. As an ISP fulfils a central function in the free flow of data, such a decision not to service a cloud provider or user will seriously impair the functioning of the Internet. Thus, the ISP must give the cloud provider access; otherwise, competition on the market would not be possible, or only operate in a negligible fashion.

The case surrounding Article 9a of the German Telecommunications law of 2004 (Telekommunikationsgesetz) highlighted that the implementation of regulatory measures aimed at ensuring competition on the market has to be taken by the National Regulatory Authorities (NRA) and not by the national legislator.[78] In this case, the German parliament essentially passed a blanket exemption applicable to parts of the German Telekom network, thus limiting the abilities of the NRA to regulate these networks. In essence, the independency required from a market regulator was undermined by allowing the legislator to interfere in its decision-making process. The ECJ correctly concluded that Germany had violated EU law.[79] The NRAs are better equipped to assess a market

---

75   Case C-7/97, *Bronner v Mediaprint* [1998] ECR I-07791.
76   Ibid 38.
77   Case T-201/04, *Microsoft v Commission* [2007] ECR II-03601, 33.
78   Case C-424/07, *European Commission v Federal Republic of Germany* [2009] EC I-11431, 97.
79   Art. 8(4) of Directive 2002/19/EC of the European Parliament and of the Council of 7 March 2002 on access to, and interconnection of, electronic communications networks and associated facilities (Access Directive); Arts 6 to 8(1) and (2), 15(3) and 16 of Directive 2002/21/EC of the European Parliament and of the Council of 7 March 2002 on a common regulatory framework for electronic communications networks and services (Framework Directive); and Art. 17(2) of Directive 2002/22/EC of the European Parliament and of the Council of 7 March 2002 on universal service and users' rights relating to electronic communications networks and services (Universal Service Directive).

situation on a case by case basis and act accordingly by imposing *ex ante* measures.[80]

Article 114 TFEU allows EU institutions to harmonize laws across the EU when they diverge to such an extent that it jeopardizes the internal market. The boundaries of the EU's competence in taking measures to achieve its goal are not fully clear. On the one hand, the ECJ has expressed its view that mere disparities between regulatory approaches are insufficient to justify harmonization action and that an actual and real obstacle is required.[81] On the other hand, subsequent cases have indicated that the court has understood that rapid technological development will invariably lead to a differing approach across the member states and thus a degree of flexibility is necessary to allow the EU institutions to achieve their objective of harmonizing diverging national legislations.[82] Nevertheless, any harmonization regulation must be closely linked to the objective of the regulatory framework.[83] It has been argued that consumer protection under Article 95(3) EC would justify an increase in harmonization of the telecommunications market even if negative consequences of such action can be envisaged for market operators.[84] Thus, it seems that the ECJ would not overturn efforts by the Commission to regulate network management.[85]

In order to realize the efficiency gains brought about by the use of cloud computing, vertical integrations must be closely scrutinized as they could potentially have a significant effect on the growth of cloud technology in the future.[86] Cloud computing providers are able to utilize a variety of ISPs which in turn also makes an ISP seem more attractive to a customer because of the cloud systems that can potentially be used

---

[80] Case C-424/07, *European Commission v Federal Republic of Germany* (Advocate General Opinion) [2009] EC I-11431, 66.

[81] Case C-376/98, *Germany v Parliament and Council* (Tobacco Advertising I) [2000] ECR I-8419, 84.

[82] Case C-217/04, *UK v European Parliament and Council* [2006] ECR I-3789, 61.

[83] Ibid 47.

[84] Case C-58/08, *The Queen, on the Application of Vodafone Ltd and Others v Secretary of State for Business, Enterprise and Regulatory Reform* (International Roaming) [2010] NYR, 69.

[85] Sluijs (n 63) 27.

[86] Andrew Odlyzko, 'Network Neutrality, Search Neutrality, and the Never-Ending Conflict between Efficiency and Fairness in Markets' (2009) 8 *Rev of Network Econ* 40, 57.

through its network.[87] In the US, a cloud provider agreement with all ISPs is easy to achieve as there are only a few big providers. However, in Europe every country has a few providers; thus, reaching an agreement with all of them is nearly impossible.[88] Furthermore, the network management policies in most EU countries differ, which creates issues as to a uniform transfer between EU members.

Europe has recently seen an increase in cases relating to broadband access. The *Telecom Italia* case in 2013 highlights how network infrastructure owners abuse their dominant position and try to deter competition by treating orders from their internal divisions favourably to those of others.[89] Imposing heavy fines, such as the 103.794 million euro fine on Telecom Italia seems warranted due to the huge impact service access has on every single Internet user and service provider.[90]

The EU has left the market open by allowing the ISPs to manage traffic within the boundaries of competition law as long as they communicate their actions clearly to customers. As a countermeasure to any imbalance created, the national regulators can set minimum standards that have to be maintained in regard to all network transmissions.[91] Ultimately, a differing level of service provided in various member states will affect the customers through different pricing and access. This result is not in line with the goal of one internal European market without boundaries.

Nevertheless, suggestions have been made to distinguish the necessary harmonization process by focusing 'on the areas where its benefits are the highest, in particular given the possibilities of economies of scale provided by the technology or cross-country externalities, and where its costs are the

---

[87]   Rochet Tirole and Jean Tirole, 'Platform Competition in Two-Sided Markets' (2003) 1 *J EEA* 990.

[88]   Sluijs, Larouche and Sauter (n 6) 12.

[89]   'TLC: Antitrust, Telecom Italia Abused its Dominant Position in the Network Infrastructure, Total Fine of €103.794 Million' (*Autorità Garante della Concorrenza e del Mercato*, 10 May 2013), www.agcm.it/en/newsroom/press-releases/2052-a428-tlc-antitrust-telecom-italia-abused-its-dominant-position-in-the-network-infrastructure-total-fine-of–103794-million.html, accessed 27 May 2014.

[90]   Ibid.

[91]   Filomena Chirico, Ilse Van der Haar and Pierre Larouche, 'Network Neutrality in the EU' [2007] TILEC Discussion Paper DP 2007–030.

lowest, in particular given the heterogeneity of national preferences and choices or the need to allow for regulatory experimentation'.[92]

Ensuring a uniform approach to regulation has many benefits. Mainly it will enable ISPs to offer the same service across all EU countries (economies of scale) and supply cloud users with a reliable and uniform service throughout the EU.[93] Cloud providers are especially interested in a uniform framework as they otherwise would have to deal with situations in which data transmitted through a country with low regulatory standards, and thus low base service levels, affects their customers in another EU member state where the service level is high. Interestingly, it seems as if the EU members are creating incentives to implement stricter legislation than that at EU level.

V. GENERAL LEGAL SAFEGUARDS

A. National Information Security Directive and Cloud Access by Foreign and National Governments

1. National Information Security Directive

The EU is debating a proposal for a directive on information security which aims at raising the level of preparedness across all member states in regard to information security issues affecting more than one member state. In doing so, the members shall set their own legal framework and infrastructure allowing for cross-border information sharing and risk identification. Also, the internal structures in terms of a national authority and a computer emergency response team need to be set up. The authority is required to collect data and identify incidents which pose risks to national information security. As these systems are linked across all member states, a uniform approach is necessary in order to identify and prevent the spreading of an incident across the member states. The standardization process of cloud services could potentially create 'systemic' risks based on the uniform use of protocols and other technologies. Once these are breached or otherwise affected, all cloud providers would be facing the same challenges; thus, a European coordination framework seems warranted.

---

[92] Philippe Defraigne and Alexandre De Streel, 'Where Should the European Union Intervene to Foster the Internal Market for eComms?' [2011] 63 *Communications & Strategies* 81.

[93] Sluijs (n 63) 10.

2. Cloud access by foreign and national governments

Data access by governments and their intelligence organs has become a prevalent topic in the media as it touches and concerns every IT user. In particular, the US approach has been criticized as being not transparent and by far too intrusive into the liberties of its own as well as foreign citizens. In general, one can say that data access by an intelligence agency targeting foreign subjects is hardly regulated and nearly any form of measures to obtain foreign information is allowed. However, when the agency wants to gain information about citizens of its own country, specific formal procedures must be followed, which vary heavily especially between the US and the EU member states. Most noteworthy in the context of cloud computing is the fact that a transfer under the safe harbour framework of the EU[94] is still considered as compliant with EU law despite the extensive access rights of the US intelligence agencies.[95]

Often cloud services create a false sense of security as the users are not aware where the data is actually processed and stored. Nevertheless, access to this data is easily available once it is stored in a fixed location such as a US cloud server. No contractual undertaking, be this the safe harbour framework or any other undertaking, will stop public authorities from accessing the user's data. In these cases, public law such as the Patriot Act of 2001 or the Foreign Intelligence Surveillance Act of 1978 trump any such agreement. However, voluntary disclosure can generally be prevented through contractual undertakings. In order to succeed in a breach of contract suit based on prohibited voluntary disclosure, the claimant would have to find a way around the mentioned statutory indemnity (in other words, filing the claim against a foreign subsidiary based on foreign law). Another often neglected fact is that the US cloud companies and their international subsidiaries (in particular EU subsidiaries) are subject to the US disclosure laws and can be required to hand over data which is stored anywhere in the world. If they do not follow such a request, they may face severe penalties.

Entrusting information to the cloud must only be done when the users are certain that the information contained is not confidential or important in any form. Thus, journalists especially, should consider using alternative technologies or encrypting all data sent into the cloud in order to ensure that no other party gains access to it. At this level, some situations might even raise human rights issues where minority groups/refugees

---

[94] See Chapter 8 in this book.

[95] Rolf H. Weber and Dominic N. Staiger, 'Datenüberwachung in der Schweiz und den USA' (*Jusletter*, 12 September 2013), http://jusletter.weblaw.ch/article/de/_11802?lang=de, accessed 27 May 2014.

communicate through the cloud and could subsequently be harmed or killed if their information falls into the wrong hands.

B.   Data Protection and Data Flows

Data protection laws are an integral part of the cloud computing framework.[96] In the EU, they are currently governed by the Data Protection Directive[97] and, after a successful legislative process, by the new Data Protection Regulation.[98] They ensure that personal data, being data from which a person can be identified, is subject to extra protection and is not disclosed to parties which do not require and are not entitled to receive this information.

C.   Intellectual Property and Related Issues

A manifold number of questions on intellectual property rights arise in the context of cloud computing. These can be related to software supplied by the cloud provider or software used on a cloud provider's servers originating from the customer. Other aspects such as data stored and accessed by cloud customers also raise intellectual property (IP) issues.[99]

In order to file an action, the infringer needs to be identified first, which in most instances will be hard to achieve due to the international nature of cloud services and the use of IP addresses. Thus, in most cases, an action is brought against the cloud provider as the facilitator of the infringement. Such actions are a major concern for the users and suppliers of cloud computing services. Currently, no legal framework exists for intellectual property laws tailored to cloud computing. Thus, general intellectual property rights apply. Determining the national laws which will govern an individual case is complex.

---

[96]   See Chapter 4 and Chapter 5.

[97]   Directive 95/46/EC of the European Parliament and of the Council of 24 October 1995 on the protection of individuals with regard to the processing of personal data and on the free movement of such data [1995] OJ L 281.

[98]   Proposal for a Regulation of the European Parliament and of the Council on the protection of individuals with regard to the processing of personal data and on the free movement of such data (General Data Protection Regulation) COM (2012) 11 final.

[99]   For a short summary of provider liability for uploaded data, see Neville Cordell, 'Intellectual Property in the Cloud' (*Allen and Overy*, May 2013), www.allenovery.com/SiteCollectionDocuments/Intellectual_property_in_the_cloud_May_2013.PDF, accessed 27 May 2014.

However, as a first step, any cloud customer should ensure that it is granted a contractual indemnity for potential IP violations caused by the cloud provider's software. In addition to this fairly regular scenario, where the cloud provider grants access to a standard software environment, customers often use open source software to meet their specific needs. This software is further refined (either by the customer or the provider) and adjusted precisely to the customer's specifications. A cloud provider could later use this 'new' software and distribute it to its other customers whilst infringing the developing customer's IP rights.[100] On the one hand, a customer should therefore carefully review its contracts to ascertain whether a right to use and further distribute the software is being granted to the cloud provider. On the other hand, a cloud customer might only want to gain short term access to specific individualized open source cloud software in order to acquire a certain know-how.[101]

D.   Regulatory Boundaries of Cloud Contracts

Cloud computing contracts are subject to the general contract laws of the jurisdiction where they are formed. When dealing with private end users of a service the main regulatory provisions affecting such contracts are based in consumer protection law. In order to maintain a balance in bargaining power between the rights of an inexperienced individual and a big cloud computing provider, safeguards are put into place by various legislators. Often cloud providers will limit or even exclude any duty to keep the service available as well as require an indemnification for any data loss, destruction, disclosure and so forth.[102] For example, the UK has implemented the Unfair Terms in Consumer Contracts Regulations 1999 in which Section 5(1) provides that when a significant imbalance exists in the parties' rights and obligations to the detriment of the consumer, such a term will be considered as unfair.

However, this protection only applies to consumers and not to the 'main subject matter' of the contract. Ultimately, it remains up to the courts to show their willingness to expand the application of the law to cloud contracts and thus bar certain one-sided provisions of cloud contracts which are common today. If the suggestions of the published

---

[100]   Hon W. Kuan, Christopher Millard and Jan Walden, 'Negotiating Cloud Contracts' [2012] 16 *Stan Tech L Rev* 1, 126.

[101]   IP-related issues are discussed in detail in Chapters 7–10.

[102]   'Google Cloud Platform Terms of Service' (*Google Developers*), https://developers.google.com/cloud/terms, accessed 27 May 2014.

guidance note are followed, one can expect that a consumer-favourable interpretation will be applied.

Once a cloud contract is breached by a provider, the user will face the challenge of receiving back the data transferred into the cloud. Potentially, a cloud provider could take its user's data 'hostage', requiring the payment of an additional fee or a disclaimer of any rights under the contract. These risks are one of the biggest challenges cloud computing technologies face as in essence the user loses control of the data sent into the cloud. The data then can be stored and processed anywhere in the world, making any kind of enforcement action impossible. It seems advisable that the cloud provider is at least located in the EU and that only a European cloud is used. This gives the user recourse to European laws and enables enforcement within the EU. However, the legislation in the member states as to contractual duties and rights varies; thus, enforcing a cloud contract or claiming damages in another member state still poses a challenge. The EU should consider implementing a sector-specific cloud computing law dealing exactly with such contractual issues in order to overcome discrepancies within the EU and thus foster the development of a European cloud.

VI. OUTLOOK

Sector-specific regulation catering for the need of cloud providers, especially in regard to rights associated with the flow of data from and to an ISP, seems to be a solution in addressing the seemingly growing restrictions on competition. Any lack in innovation caused by such regulation on the side of the ISP would likely be compensated by the cloud service providers as these are interested in innovative technologies facilitating a faster flow of data. Without such measures, cloud service providers will increasingly be faced with the challenge of actually being able to deliver their services to customers. This is not only inconvenient for the customers but will add huge costs to the economy because of the lost competitive advantage which is generally to be gained by using more efficient technology such as cloud computing. The risks associated with a vertical integration, that is, an ISP and cloud provider merging, could also be reduced through regulation enforcing supply of the ISP's service. The ISP must then ensure that it treats its cloud provider in the same manner as other providers.

Also, new approaches to the protection of intellectual property rights in the digital world need to be developed and the respective obligations of cloud providers must be more precisely defined. In particular, the

E-Commerce Directive requires further clarification in regard to its liability protection under Article 14 in order to set a clear and reliable framework for cloud providers.

Even well-known cloud providers such as Apple with its iCloud do not have their own servers but use those of their competitors, such as Amazon's or Microsoft's cloud servers.[103] Guidance through professional industry standards can educate cloud users of these risks and thus put additional pressure on cloud providers to provide transparent accounts of how they perform the services they offer.

---

[103] Gavin Clarke, 'Apple's iCloud Runs on Microsoft and Amazon Services: Who Says Azure Isn't Cool and Trendy Now' (*The Register*, 2 September 2011), www.theregister.co.uk/2011/09/02/icloud_runs_on_microsoft_azure_and_amazon, accessed 27 May 2014.

4. Re-personalizing personal data in the cloud

Anne S.Y. Cheung

I. INTRODUCTION

Any personal data legal regime hinges upon whether personal data are utilized. As fundamental and obvious as that statement may seem, identification of the common constitutive elements of personal data has proved to be a difficult task.[1] A study covering the 36 data protection laws of 30 countries, for example, found a lack of consensus on what personal data even are.[2] Despite the absence of harmonization, however, the study also found the definitions of personal data in most countries revolve largely around the notion of 'identified' and/or 'identifiable'

---

[1] For instance, under section 6(1) of the Privacy Act in Australia, as amended in 2013, personal information is defined as information or an opinion about an identified individual, or an individual who is reasonably identifiable: (a) whether the information or opinion is true or not; and (b) whether the information or opinion is recorded in a material form or not. It was formerly defined as information or an opinion (including information or an opinion forming part of a database), whether true or not, and whether recorded in a material form or not, about an individual whose identity is apparent, or can reasonably be ascertained, from the information or opinion. The Privacy Act 1988 (Cth), as amended by Act No. 13, 2013, www.comlaw.gov.au/Details/ C2014C00076, accessed 13 March 2014. For the background to the debate surrounding the Act, see Australian Government, 'Australian Government: First Stage Response to the Australian Law Reform Commission Report 108, *For Your Information: Australian Privacy Law and Practice*' (October 2009). For details of the debate in the European Union, see the discussion in Section II of this chapter.
[2] William B. Baker and Anthony Matyjaszewski, 'The Changing Meaning of "Personal Data"' (IAPP Privacy Academy, Baltimore, 30 September 2010), www.privacyassociation.org/resource_center/the_changing_meaning_of_personal_ data, accessed 12 March 2014.

individuals.[3] The current definition in the European Union, for instance, encompasses both types of individuals, whilst the US legal regime protects only the former.[4]

Although the debate surrounding the concept and definition of personal data has broad repercussions for the governance of personal data in general, it is particularly pertinent to the cloud environment in which data are exposed on a global scale. Regardless of which service or deployment model of cloud computing is involved, the rights of data subjects (whether businesses or individuals), the responsibilities of data controllers and a host of other legal regulations are issues of concern when personal data are collected, used, stored or processed.[5] Unsurprisingly, data subjects tend to view their data as personal data, whereas cloud service providers are inclined to think otherwise in their efforts to save costs and facilitate further technological and business advances through data use.[6]

A plausible solution that may balance the interests of data subjects and cloud operators is to bring personal data protection into line with

---

[3]   Ibid.

[4]   Council Directive 95/46/EC on the Protection of Individuals with Regard to the Processing of Personal Data and on the Free Movement of such Data (EU Data Protection Directive) [1995] OJ L281/31, art. 2. In contrast to the EU model, there is no comprehensive federal law in the US governing personal data. Personal data protection has been described as 'fragmented' because it often depends on the type of data and the entities in control, although the Federal Trade Commission has played a key role in influencing the development of personal data regulations, policies and company practices. Daniel J. Solove and Woodrow Hartzog, 'The FTC and the New Common Law of Privacy' (2014) 114 *Columbia Law Review* 583. For further discussion, see Section II of this chapter.

[5]   For instance, article 12 of the EU Data Protection Directive governs the accessibility and correction of personal data, whilst article 17 covers data security and article 25 data transfer. Personal data must be processed by the data controller, which is defined as 'the natural or legal person, public authority, agency or any other body that alone or jointly with others determines the purposes and means of the processing of personal data', in compliance with the data principles listed under article 6 of the EU Data Protection Directive (n 4).

[6]   A 2013 survey showed that 66 per cent of 1300 organizations that had adopted cloud computing had reduced costs by 23 per cent. Luis Columbus, 'Making Cloud Computing Pay' (*Forbes*, 10 April 2013), www.forbes.com/sites/louiscolumbus/2013/04/10/making-cloud-computing-pay-2/, (accessed 15 July 2014).

technological innovation. Encryption technology has contributed significantly to the confidentiality of personal data,[7] but strongly encrypted data take much longer to process and render applications difficult to run.[8] A more viable option is to anonymize data in such a way that individuals are de-identified. Although data anonymization is widely used in medical research,[9] the findings of various studies suggest that data can rarely be truly anonymized using current technology.[10] Further, the explosion of data in the big data era has further shown perfect anonymization to be an illusion.[11] The situation requires us to question our existing understanding of the character of personal data and the possible risks their use (or misuse) entails. Thus, one of the burning legal issues in the personal data protection arena is whether anonymous, anonymized and pseudonymous data should be viewed as personal data (the distinctions amongst these concepts will be dealt with in Section II of this chapter). Whilst some law reformers in Europe argue that none of these three categories of data should be classified as personal data,[12] American scholars have proposed

---

[7] W. Kuan Hon, Christopher Millard and Ian Walden, 'The Problem of "Personal Data" in Cloud Computing: What Information Is Regulated? – The Cloud of Unknowing' (2011) 1(4) *International Data Privacy Law* 211, 217.

[8] Strong encryption refers to one-way encryption that prohibits re-identification. Ibid 220. It is, however, necessary for data to remain unencrypted to be useful for data processing purposes. W. Kuan Hon, Eleni Kosta, Christopher Millard and Dimitra Stefanatou, 'Cloud Accountability: The Likely Impact of the Proposed EU Data Protection Regulation' (2014) Queen Mary School of Law Legal Studies Research Paper 172/2014, 11, http://papers.ssrn.com/sol3/papers.cfm?abstract_id=2405971, accessed 1 April 2014.

[9] For example, the Clinical Practice Research Datalink, which is managed by the UK Department of Health, contains over 5 million active patient records (and over 13 million overall). It boasts of having the world's largest database of anonymized, longitudinal primary care medical records and links to secondary care datasets for national and international research. 'The Clinical Practice Research Datalink' (*National Cancer Institute*, 10 December 2013), http://epi.grants.cancer.gov/pharm/pharmacoepi_db/cprd.html, accessed 13 March 2014.

[10] Paul Ohm, 'Broken Promises of Privacy: Responding to the Surprising Failure of Anonymization' (2010) 57 *UCLA Law Review* 1701.

[11] Viktor Mayer-Schonberger and Kenneth Cukier, *Big Data: A Revolution That Will Transform How We Live, Work, and Think* (New York: Houghton Mifflin Harcourt 2013) 155.

[12] The Committee on Civil Liberties, Justice and Home Affairs, 'Report on the Proposal for a Regulation of the European Parliament and of the Council on the Protection of Individuals with Regard to the Processing of Personal Data and on the Free Movement of Such Data (General Data Protection Regulation)' (PE 501.927v05-00, 21 November 2013) 26, 63, 64, 200, www.europarl.europa.eu/

a number of largely risk-based regimes.[13] In addition to examining the issues involved in this ongoing debate, this chapter advocates a more nuanced legal definition and understanding of privacy that takes into account the different levels of data personalization and argues that a truly contextual approach to personal data protection should factor in continuous technological assessment of the nature of data.

Section II of this chapter begins by outlining the shifting legal landscape of the definition of personal data, focusing on the two key elements of identified and identifiable data. Although examples from a variety of jurisdictions are presented, the main focus is on the EU and the US. EU law is an obvious choice for any study concerned with the topic of personal data protection, as it is impossible to ignore the EU's comprehensive and elaborate legal scheme governing such protection, particularly its extraterritorial effect in requiring an adequate level of protection in countries to which its citizens' data are transferred.[14] At the same time, given the globalized nature of technology companies, it is also necessary to understand the US legal landscape. Section III then illustrates the increasingly blurred line between personal data and supposedly fully anonymous data by analysing the debate over the re-identification of individuals from seemingly anonymous data. The conceptual distinction between anonymous, anonymized and pseudonymous data is explained in this part of the chapter, which also delves into judicial decisions that reflect the growing body of jurisprudence recognizing new categories of data as personal data. Technological advances increasingly mean that every item of data has the potential to constitute personal data, which has wide implications for cloud service providers, particularly for those storing medical data in the cloud. Another pressing concern is the use of Internet users' information for marketing purposes. Finally, Section IV brings the chapter to a close by explaining why the current suggested approaches to personal data reform are inadequate and why a continuous risk assessment regime governing cloud service

---

sides/getDoc.do?pubRef=-//EP//NONSGML+REPORT+A7-2013-0402+0+ DOC +PDF+V0//EN, accessed 14 March 2014; Commission, 'Proposal for a Regulation of the European Parliament and of the Council on the Protection of Individuals with Regard to the Processing of Personal Data and on the Free Movement of Such Data (General Data Protection Regulation)' COM (2012) 11 final (the proposed General Regulation).

[13]   Ohm (n 10) 1704, 1774; Paul M. Schwartz, 'Information Privacy in the Cloud' (2013) 161 *University of Pennsylvania Law Review* 1623, 1655.

[14]   EU Data Protection Directive (n 4) art. 25; Rolf H. Weber, *Regulatory Models for the Online World* (The Hague: Kluwer Law International 2002) 156.

providers is necessary. The terms 'personal data' and 'personal information' are used interchangeably throughout this chapter, primarily because 'personal data' is a legal term used in the EU, whereas 'personal information' is more commonly used in the US.[15]

II. THE SHIFTING LEGAL LANDSCAPE OF PERSONAL DATA: IDENTIFIED VERSUS IDENTIFIABLE

Central to the legal regime governing personal data is the definition of such data. Cloud storage providers are reported to have delivered more than one exabyte of data under contract in 2012 alone.[16] However, it remains unclear exactly how much of this vast amount of data is personal data, and how much should be viewed as such. Further, whether information becomes personal data is dependent upon the decisions made throughout the data processing process in the cloud environment.[17] Hence, the definition of personal data is pivotal to the debate.

Under article 2 of the EU Data Protection Directive of 1995, personal data constitute 'any information relating to an identified or identifiable natural person (data subject)'.[18] Although the exact meaning of an 'identified person' is not delineated in the Directive, the Article 29 Data Protection Working Party defines it as a natural person distinguishable from all other members within a group.[19] The Directive defines an identifiable person, in contrast, as 'one who can be identified directly or

---

[15] For a discussion of the nuances between 'personally identifiable information' and 'personal data', see William B. Baker and Anthony Matyjaszewski, 'The Changing Meaning of "Personal Data"' (*International Association of Privacy Professionals Resource Center*, 30 September 2010), www.privacy association.org/resource_center/the_changing_meaning_of_personal_data, accessed 21 April 2013.

[16] One exabyte is 1 billion gigabytes. 'The State of Cloud Storage: 2013 Industry Report – A Benchmark Comparison of Performance, Availability and Scalability' (*Nasuni*, 2013) 1, www.nasuni.com/rs/nasuni/images/Nasuni-White-Paper-State-of-Cloud-Storage-2013.pdf, accessed 18 March 2014.

[17] Paul M. Schwartz, 'Information Privacy in the Cloud' (2013) 161 *University of Pennsylvania Law Review* 1623, 1646.

[18] EU Data Protection Directive (n 4).

[19] Article 29 Data Protection Working Party, 'Opinion 4/2007 on the Concept of Personal Data' (WP 136, 20 June 2007) 12. The Article 29 Working Party is an independent European advisory body set up under Article 29 of the EU Data Protection Directive.

indirectly, in particular by reference to an identification number or to one or more factors specific to his physical, physiological, mental, economic, cultural or social identity'.[20] In other words, whilst 'identified' in this context generally refers to data being used to determine the specific identity of an individual or to distinguish said individual from the other members of a group, 'identifiable' points only to the possibility of being identified.[21]

The personal data legislation in various jurisdictions has a similar framework for distinguishing between identified and identifiable persons. For instance, the Hong Kong Personal Data (Privacy) Ordinance defines personal data as any data that relate directly or indirectly to a living individual from which it is reasonably practicable for the identity of that individual to be ascertained.[22] The notions of both identified and identifiable are implied by the Hong Kong legal regime. The Australia Privacy Act defines personal information as 'information or an opinion about an identified individual, or an individual who is reasonably identifiable'.[23] Different from the Hong Kong and Australian legislation, most related legislation in the US adopts the term 'personally identifiable information' (PII), or a close variation thereof, referring to information that identifies a person or to a list of specific types of data that constitute PII.[24] Take the Video Privacy Protection Act as an example. It defines PII as 'information which identifies a person',[25] whilst the Children's Online Privacy Protection Act stipulates that 'personal information' is 'individually identifiable information about an individual collected online', comprising first and last name, physical address, social security number, telephone number and email address.[26] The Health Insurance Portability and Accountability Act (HIPAA), in contrast, embraces the concepts of both identified and identifiable, considering individually identifiable health information to be any information that identifies the individual or 'with

---

[20]   Directive 95/46/EC of the European Parliament and of the Council of 24 October 1995 on the Protection of Individuals with regard to the Processing of Personal Data and on the Free Movement of Such Data [1995] OJ EC 23/6.

[21]   Ibid 12.

[22]   Personal Data (Privacy) Ordinance, Cap 486, Laws of Hong Kong, 25 April 2013.

[23]   Privacy Act 1988 (Cth) (n 1).

[24]   Paul M. Schwartz and Daniel J. Solove, 'The PII Problem: Privacy and a New Concept of Personally Identifiable Information' (2011) 86 *New York University Law Review* 1814, 1831–2.

[25]   Video Privacy Protection Act of 1988, 18 USC para. 2710(a)(3).

[26]   Children's Online Privacy Protection Act of 1998, 15 USC paras 6501–6.

respect to which there is a reasonable basis to believe that the information can be used to identify the individual'.[27]

Clearly, data that do not constitute personal data are subject to far less, if any, legal regulation. If 'identified' refers to specific individuals being distinguished, whereas 'identifiable' points to the possibility thereof, the former term is inevitably narrow, whilst the latter is broad and inclusive, and arguably even ever-expanding given the forever advancing nature of technology.[28] In 1995, the EU Data Protection Directive confined the scope of 'identifiable' under recital 26 to all 'means likely reasonably to be used either by the controller or by any other person to identify the said person'.[29] The primary considerations are what means are available to identify an individual and the extent to which such means are readily available to the data controller. The hint provided by article 2 of the Directive is that one should look for such nominative identifiers as identification number, address or health data.[30] Under recital 26, the Directive also envisages the need to allow room for flexibility and technological innovation by exempting from the need for protection any 'data rendered anonymous in such a way that the data subject is no longer identifiable'.[31]

However, such approaches based on established categories of identifiers and on existing anonymization technology may no longer be helpful. As explained in greater detail in the following section, technological advances have rendered it common practice to aggregate and combine

---

[27] HIPAA of 1996, Pub L No 104-191, 110 Stat 1936 (1996) s.1171(6)(i)(ii).

[28] Paul M. Schwartz and Daniel J. Solove, 'Reconciling Personal Information in the United States and European Union' (2014) 102 *California Law Review* 877.

[29] EU Data Protection Directive (n 4).

[30] Luiz Costa and Yves Poullet, 'Privacy and the Regulation of 2012' (2012) 28 *Computer Law & Security Review* 254, 255.

[31] Recital 26 of the EU Data Protection Directive (n 4) states:

Whereas the principles of protection must apply to any information concerning an identified or identifiable person; whereas, to determine whether a person is identifiable, account should be taken of all the means likely reasonably to be used either by the controller or by any other person to identify the said person; whereas the principles of protection shall not apply to data rendered anonymous in such a way that the data subject is no longer identifiable; whereas codes of conduct within the meaning of Article 27 may be a useful instrument for providing guidance as to the ways in which data may be rendered anonymous and retained in a form in which identification of the data subject is no longer possible.

bits of seemingly non-personal information to identify individuals and even to contact or profile them. Arguably, any data constitute a form of potential identifier, and anonymization techniques have become so powerful in the 21st century that complete anonymization may no longer be feasible.[32]

The General Data Protection Regulation (the proposed General Regulation) proposed by the European Commission in 2012 in large part constitutes an endeavour to address the various concerns raised and challenges posed by the rapid advancement of technology, including the need to formulate a new definition of personal data.[33] Article 4(2) of the proposed General Regulation defines personal data as 'any information relating to a data subject'. A data subject, in turn, is defined under article 4(1) as:

> an identified natural person or a natural person who can be identified, directly or indirectly, by means reasonably likely to be used by the controller or by any other natural or legal person, in particular by reference to an identification number, location data, online identifier or to one or more factors specific to the physical, physiological, genetic, mental, economic, cultural or social identity of that person.

In brief, under the proposed definitions, the concept of personal data has been expanded to include 'any information' relating to a data subject, whereas the standard of 'identifiable' has been replaced by any direct or indirect means that are reasonably likely to be used. The list of nominative identifiers has also been expanded to include new categories such as location data and online identifiers. Nevertheless, to a large extent, recital 23 of the proposed General Regulation merely reiterates recital 26 of the Directive by continuing to rely on the concept of 'identifiable' and excluding the category of anonymous data (defined as data that can no longer be identifiable from the proposed regulatory regime).[34] In addition, recital 24 of the proposed General Regulation

---

[32]   Ohm (n 10).

[33]   The proposed General Regulation (n 12).

[34]   Recital 23 of the proposed General Regulation (n 12) states that:

The principles of protection should apply to any information concerning an identified or identifiable person. To determine whether a person is identifiable, account should be taken of all the means likely reasonably to be used either by the controller or by any other person to identify the individual. The principles of data protection should not apply to data rendered anonymous in such a way that the data subject is no longer identifiable.

For the text of recital 26 of the EU Data Protection Directive, see n 31.

stipulates that 'identification numbers, location data, online identifiers or other specific factors as such need not necessarily be considered as personal data in all circumstances'.[35]

It can thus be seen that the proposed General Regulation offers more protection to personal data by broadening the very concept of personal data to include all information whilst allowing room for flexibility by taking into account the 'indirect means' likely to be used to identify individuals. Still, the critical issue remains whether an individual is capable of being identified based on all means likely to be used and by reference to available information. There is still a broad continuum of identifiable information, including anonymous or pseudonymous information, that requires different levels of identification effort.[36] Furthermore, the explicit exclusion by both the Directive and proposed General Regulation of the regulation of anonymous data without clarifying the detailed requirements of what constitutes such data indirectly provides industry with a powerful incentive to develop and apply more effective anonymization techniques.[37] At the same time, as the following discussion demonstrates, whether data can be sufficiently anonymized to render them a genuine form of non-personal data remains highly debatable.

III. THE MYTH OF DATA ANONYMIZATION: WHEN ALL DATA ARE PERSONAL DATA

The apparent assumption in excluding anonymous data from legal regulation is that data records can be made irreversibly anonymous and

---

[35] Recital 24 of the proposed General Regulation (n 14) states that:

When using online services, individuals may be associated with online identifiers provided by their devices, applications, tools and protocols, such as Internet Protocol addresses or cookie identifiers. This may leave traces which, combined with unique identifiers and other information received by the servers, may be used to create profiles of the individuals and identify them. It follows that identification numbers, location data, online identifiers or other specific factors as such need not necessarily be considered as personal data in all circumstances.

[36] Schwartz and Solove (n 28) 11.

[37] Recital 26 of the EU Data Protection Directive (n 31) and recital 23 of the proposed General Regulation (n 34). See also Christopher Kuner, 'The European Commission's Proposed Data Protection Regulation: A Copernican Revolution in European Data Protection Law' (2012) *Bloomberg BNA Privacy and Security Law Report* 1, http://ssrn.com/abstract=2162781, accessed 18 March 2014.

that data subjects can be rendered non-identifiable.[38] When the Article 29 Working Party gave its opinion on cloud computing, it placed the anonymization of data on a par with their erasure.[39] Similarly, in speaking on security and control in the cloud environment, Neelie Kroes, Vice-President of the European Commission and European Commissioner for the Digital Agenda, urged that data records be made irreversibly anonymous before further use is made of them.[40] Anonymization is thought to be the perfect 'silver bullet' solution for the reuse of data, for privacy and security, and for innovation and business purposes.[41] With the continued advancement of re-identification technology, however, data are not what they used to be. What exactly are anonymous data, then?

A.   Anonymous versus Anonymized Data

As mentioned earlier in the chapter, both recital 26 of the Data Protection Directive and recital 23 of the proposed General Regulation define anonymous data as 'data rendered anonymous in such a way that the data subject is no longer identifiable' by all means reasonably likely to be used either by the controller or by any other person able to identify the individual in question. In response to the proposed General Regulation, the European Parliament has formulated another definition, taking anonymous data to be 'personal data that has been collected, altered or otherwise processed in such a way that it can no longer be attributed to a data subject',[42] specifically stipulating that 'anonymous data shall not be considered personal data'. The European Parliament has also proposed

---

[38]   Another example is article 6(e) of the EU Data Protection Directive, which allows the keeping and further processing of personal data if they are kept in a form that does not permit identification of the data subjects. The Article 29 Working Party interpreted this as either the erasure of data or true data anonymization. Article 29 Data Protection Working Party 01037/12/EN, 'Opinion 05/2012 on Cloud Computing', WP 196 (1 July 2012) 11, http://ec.europa.eu/justice/data-protection/article-29/documentation/opinion-recommendation/files/2012/wp196_en.pdf, accessed 22 March 2014.

[39]   Ibid.

[40]   Neelie Kroes, 'Cloud Computing and Data Protection' (Speech/10/686, 25 November 2010), http://europa.eu/rapid/press-release_SPEECH-10-686_en.htm?locale=en, accessed 22 March 2014.

[41]   Ohm (n 10) 1736.

[42]   The Committee on Civil Liberties, Justice and Home Affairs (n 12) Amendment 34.

that there could be 'alleviations' concerning the use of pseudonymous data,[43] the proposed definition for which is:

> any personal data that has been collected, altered or otherwise processed so that it of itself cannot be attributed to a data subject without the use of additional data which is subject to separate and distinct technical and organizational controls to ensure such non-attribution, or that such attribution would require a disproportionate amount of time, expense and effort.[44]

In other words, the use of pseudonymous data involves explicit identifiers being replaced with codes, thus rendering the linking of those data to the specific individuals concerned possible.[45]

The foregoing legal definitions are premised on the notions that: (1) data can be made non-identifiable; (2) that certain means are more likely than others to be used; and (3) that the relevant perspective is that of the data controllers or similar persons/entities. However, actual data analysis and research call these presumptions into question. For example, Harvard University Professor Latanya Sweeney, who specializes in data re-identification research, reminds us that the term 'anonymous' implies that the data can no longer be manipulated or linked in such a way as to identify an individual.[46] An obvious example is when data are collected with no identifiers and never linked to an individual, such as in the case of questionnaires returned by mail without a name or return address.[47] However, for data analysis to have practical use, one cannot get rid of all identifiers. In addition, Sweeney points out that in most cases there are major difficulties in ensuring that data are completely anonymous because of the unusual or even unique information appearing within the data themselves. In addition, different datasets can often be easily matched to re-identify the individuals therein owing to the presence of certain personal characteristics.[48] Although there are various ways of maintaining data confidentiality to differing degrees, Sweeney contends that this process should be described as the 'de-identification' of data and

---

[43] Ibid. Amendments 36 and 61.
[44] Ibid.
[45] Ibid.
[46] Latanya Sweeney, 'Weaving Technology and Policy Together to Maintain Confidentiality' (1997) 25 *Journal of Law, Medicine & Ethics* 98, 100.
[47] The Boston Consulting Group, 'The Value of Digital Identity' (*Liberty Global*, November 2012), www.lgi.com/PDF/public-policy/The-Value-of-Our-Digital-Identity.pdf, accessed 27 March 2014.
[48] Sweeney (n 46) 100–101.

the final product as 'de-identified' data.[49] The use of such terminology is reflected in some US legislation. For example, the HIPAA Administrative Simplification Rules require the 'de-identification of protected health information' before its use and/or disclosure.[50] However, the more commonly used term when personal identifiers such as names, identity card numbers or credit card numbers are removed is 'anonymized data'.[51]

B.   The Debate over Anonymized Data

The current and suggested definitions for personal data, data subjects, anonymous data and pseudonymous data in the European Union regime in essence refer to anonymized data. Still, the critical issue remains the regulation of the 'identifiability' of data, which is dependent on the means that are likely and reasonably available and the parties with the ability to use them. It is thus rather unsurprising that the European Parliament's proposals to exempt anonymous data from the regulatory regime and to introduce a lesser standard for pseudonymous data have been met with caution by more than 100 leading European academics.[52] Such a position has been described as 'dangerous' by these scholars, as it would allow seemingly protected data to be used to re-identify individuals.[53] Viviane Reding, the European Commissioner for Justice, Fundamental Rights and Citizenship, has warned against the simple use of pseudonymous data to bypass legal regulation for the same reason, that is, individuals may be easily identified.[54]

---

[49]   Ibid.
[50]   Section 164.514(a) of the HIPAA Administrative Simplification Rules defines the standard for the de-identification of protected health information as follows: 'Health information that does not identify an individual and with respect to which there is no reasonable basis to believe that the information can be used to identify an individual is not individually identifiable health information'. 45 CFR s. 164.514(a).
[51]   Hon et al. (n 7) 214.
[52]   'More than 100 Leading European Academics Are Taking a Position' (*Data Protection in Europe*, 14 February 2013), www.dataprotectioneu.eu/, accessed 13 March 2014.
[53]   Ibid.
[54]   Simon Taylor, 'Reding Warns against Identity Changes to Bypass Data Privacy' (*European Voice*, 4 April 2013), www.europeanvoice.com/article/imported/reding-warns-against-identity-changes-to-bypass-data-privacy/76859.aspx, accessed 24 March 2014.

1. Nature of identifiers

Inherent within the legal definition of personal data is reliance on explicit identifiers to distinguish individuals. Both the current and proposed EU laws in this arena mention the 'means reasonably likely to be used' with reference to specific identifiers, including identification numbers and location data. Similarly, much US legislation shares this approach in singling out identifiers. The HIPAA lists 18 categories of information to be removed to avoid identification. They include social security numbers, vehicle identifiers and health plan beneficiary numbers.[55] The belief that underpins such legislation is that, once these identifiers are removed (and these categories of identifiers are considered to be particularly telling in identification terms), data can be anonymized or de-identified and are thus no longer personal. As noted earlier, however, aside from the fact that data can rarely, if ever, be fully anonymized, another fundamental issue is that this list of identifiers is far from exhaustive. Rather, as the following discussion shows, it is ever-expanding, and data that we have yet to contemplate can in fact contain revealing identifiers.

(a) Browser-generated information　One controversial example related to both cloud computing and Internet usage in general is browsing habits. In *Vidal-Hall v Google Inc.*, the High Court of Justice in England and Wales was asked to consider whether the tracking and collating of information relating to Internet users' usage on a particular Internet browser by Google constituted the misuse of personal data under the UK Data Protection Act 1998.[56] To determine the answer, the Court had to decide whether the claimants could establish a good case that personal data were involved. The case arose out of a complaint that Google had been collecting information from the claimants' computers or other devices used to access the Internet, including their personal characteristics, interests, wishes or ambitions, and then later sold this to various companies that subsequently sent targeted advertisements to the claimants. This form of information is known as browser-generated information: 'information which is automatically submitted to websites and services by a browser on connecting to the Internet'.[57]

---

[55]　45 CFR (n 50) s. 164.514(2)(i).
[56]　[2014] EWHC 13 (QB); appeal confirmed in *Google Inc v Vidal-Hall & Ors* [2015] EWCA Civ 311.
[57]　Ibid [27].

Google's defence was that browser-generated information is not private, but rather anonymous, as the information is collected and aggregated before being sent to separate websites and advertising services.[58] The Court was far from convinced by this argument for the simple reason that if there were no personal value in the information, then Google would not have collected and collated it to earn 'spectacular revenues' by selling it for targeted advertising.[59] The Court further pointed out that the fact that Google itself did not identify any of the individuals from whom it collected browser-generated information was irrelevant because those individuals were identifiable to third parties such as advertising companies.[60]

Indeed, the use of browsing habits to identify individual customers has become common practice in the marketing arena, which invites us to question the entire notion of anonymous or anonymized data. *The Wall Street Journal* reported that 75 per cent of the top 1000 websites include code from social networks such as Facebook and Twitter to match individuals' identities with their Internet browsing activities.[61] There are in fact specialist companies that track particular categories of shoppers to mine their data for third parties. For example, Dataium LLC tracks car shoppers to provide car dealers with information on potential customers, including how serious those customers are about buying a car. Like Google, Dataium's defence is that it does not provide dealers with detailed customer information but only analysis of customers' interests.[62] However, when customers forward their email address to dealers, they can be identified right away.

(b) Data fingerprints   The aforementioned examples demonstrate that previously neglected categories of information can easily become 'linkable data fields'.[63] In addition to the above-cited cases litigated before the

---

[58]   Ibid [115].

[59]   Ibid.

[60]   Ibid [117].

[61]   Jennifer Valentino-Devries and Jeremy Singer-Vine, 'They Know What You're Shopping For' (*The Wall Street Journal*, 7 December 2012), http://on line.wsj.com/news/articles/SB10001424127887324784404578143144132736214, accessed 13 March 2014.

[62]   Ibid.

[63]   Ohm (n 10) 1735. A data field refers to a single category of data (typically displayed as a column), with a field heading in a database, such as 'surname' or 'age'. Such fields apply to all records listed, meaning that, for each individual, the surname and age fields contain his or her corresponding data. Daniel Chandler and Rod Munday, 'Field' in *A Dictionary of Media and*

courts, a Japanese researcher discovered that each individual's seating posture (counting the contours of the body, posture and weight distribution) is unique and can thus be used with 98 per cent accuracy for identification purposes.[64] Japanese scientists are using this discovery to develop an anti-theft system for cars.[65] In another study, Cambridge scholars proved that the 'Likes' feature of Facebook can reveal an individual's personality and identity with 85 per cent accuracy, and this information is currently publicly available by default.[66] Contrary to the prevailing belief that the digital record gathered by Facebook is merely a form of generic data, the Cambridge study demonstrated that surprisingly accurate estimates of Facebook users' race, age, IQ, sexuality, personality, substance use and political views can be inferred from automated analysis of their Facebook Likes alone.[67] Similar to web search queries and browsing histories, researchers have found that sensitive information can be extracted from the Likes feature of Facebook using relatively unsophisticated techniques, a finding with profound ethical implications when that information is used for targeted advertising and consumer profiling.

Together these examples constitute strong evidence that reliance on identifiers as a reference to benchmark personal data is likely to be under-inclusive and no longer helpful.

2. Re-identification through data aggregation and combination

Beyond the ever-advancing technologies that enable one to unlock the personal side of previously hidden or seemingly meaningless data,

---

Communication (2011), www.oxfordreference.com.eproxy2.lib.hku.hk/view/ 10.1093/acref/9780199568758.001.0001/acref-9780199568758-e-0973, accessed 15 July 2014.

[64] This study was conducted by Professor Shigeomi Koshimizu at the Advanced Institute of Industrial Technology in Tokyo. Mayer-Schonberger and Cukier (n 11) 77.

[65] Ibid.

[66] 'Digital Records Could Expose Intimate Details and Personality Traits of Millions' (*Research, University of Cambridge*, 11 March 2013), www.cam.ac.uk/ research/news/digital-records-could-expose-intimate-details-and-personality-traits-of-millions#sthash.CFln1BYz.dpuf, accessed 26 March 2014; Michal Kosinskia, David Stillwella and Thore Graepelb, 'Private Traits and Attributes are Predictable from Digital Records of Human Behavior' (2013) *Proceedings of National Academy of Sciences of the United States of America*, www.pnas.org/content/ early/2013/03/06/1218772110.full.pdf+html, accessed 26 March 2014.

[67] Ibid.

re-identification techniques have also been widely used to identify individuals through the aggregation and combination of data or datasets.

(a) The power of data combination   Data mining technologies allow the combination of data from different sources, which then easily permits the identification of individuals.[68] Two notorious examples are the America Online (AOL) study of search queries and Netflix movie ratings.

In 2006, AOL launched the AOL Research Project, the stated aim of which was to support an open research community, by posting on its website 20 million search queries made by 650,000 users of AOL's search engine, thereby documenting their activities during a three-month period.[69] All of the data were pseudonymized in the sense that obviously identifying information such as usernames and IP addresses had been replaced by unique identification numbers. However, this veil of pseudo-anonymity was quickly lifted by two *New York Times* reporters who used pieces of seemingly non-revealing information, such as '60 single men', 'tea for good health' and 'landscapers in Lilburn, GA' to trace a 60-year-old widow in Georgia.[70] This discovery eventually resulted in the dismissal of the AOL researchers responsible for the project and the resignation of AOL's then chief technology officer.[71]

Paralleling the AOL story, in the same year, Netflix, the 'world's largest online movie rental service', publicly released 100 million records disclosing nearly half a million users' film ratings for the previous five years. It offered a US$1 million prize to anyone who could improve its film recommendation system by at least 10 per cent. Like AOL, Netflix had ostensibly pseudonymized all of the rating information. Whilst it took three years for the winner to claim the $1 million prize, it took just two weeks for researchers to announce that they could identify individual

---

[68]   Data mining refers to 'the process of extracting useful information from a disparate collection of databases, files, and other sources such as web pages. A typical data mining operation might be carried out by a bank to discover the financial profile of customers who opt for a particular type of credit card. Data mining software often uses some artificial intelligence technology and quite a lot of statistical theory'. Darrel Ince, 'Data Mining' in *A Dictionary of the Internet* (2013), www.oxfordreference.com.eproxy1.lib.hku.hk/view/10.1093/acref/97801 91744150.001.0001/acref-9780191744150-e-824, accessed 4 April 2014.

[69]   Ohm (n 10) 1717–18.

[70]   Michael Barbaro and Tom Zeller Jr., 'A Face Is Exposed for AOL Searcher No. 4417749' *The New York Times* (9 August 2006), www.nytimes.com/ 2006/08/09/technology/09aol.html, accessed 29 March 2014.

[71]   Ibid.

subscribers from the records Netflix had released.[72] Two researchers from the University of Texas compared the Netflix records with those of the Internet Movie Database (IMDb), on which users also have an opportunity to rate films, and identified individuals with 84 per cent accuracy.[73] If an additional piece of information was available, specifically the date a rating was posted, their accuracy rate skyrocketed to 99 per cent.[74]

The AOL story illustrates that an individual can be identified given sufficient data, whereas the Netflix story shows that cross-matching databases can achieve the same result. To further demonstrate how easy it is to identify an individual, Sweeney has set up a database on which one can key in an individual's sex, birth date and ZIP code (if a US resident), and the site will generate that individual's identity[75] with a claimed 87 per cent accuracy rate.[76]

These examples show how combination technology is being used to unlock the dormant value of data to trace specific individuals.[77]

(b) Legal response Realizing the potential and risks of combining and cross-matching data, a number of judges and lawmakers have attempted to tackle the issue. In *Northwestern Memorial Hospital v. Ashcroft*,[78] for example, US Appeals Court Judge Richard Posner ruled that even redacted medical records (those from which protected information identifying individual patients has been removed)[79] are a form of personally identifiable information because of the potential for the information therein to be easily combined with information available on the Internet to identify particular individuals. The case arose from a challenge by the applicant hospital against a Department of Justice subpoena seeking the

---

[72] Ohm (n 10) 1721.

[73] Arvind Narayanan and Vitaly Shmatikov, 'How to Break Anonymity of the Netflix Prize Dataset' (*arXiv*, 2006), http://arxiv.org/abs/cs/0610105, accessed 29 March 2014; Steve Lohr, 'Netflix Cancels Contest Plans and Settles Suit' (*New York Times Bits Blog*, 12 March 2010), http://bits.blogs.nytimes.com/2010/03/12/netflix-cancels-contest-plans-and-settles-suit/, accessed 29 March 2014.

[74] Ibid.

[75] 'How Unique Are You?' (*Data Privacy Lab*, 2013), http://aboutmyinfo.org/, accessed 28 March 2014.

[76] Interview with Sweeney. Caroline Perry, 'You Are Not So Anonymous' (*Harvard Gazette*, 18 October 2011), http://news.harvard.edu/gazette/story/2011/10/you%E2%80%99re-not-so-anonymous/, accessed 28 March 2014.

[77] Mayer-Schonberger and Cukier (n 11) 107.

[78] [2004] 362 F 3d 923.

[79] See discussion in Section II.B(2)(a) of this chapter.

medical records of certain patients upon whom late-term abortion procedures had been performed. Although all of the medical records sought had
been redacted, the Court held that most medical records are sensitive by
nature, with that sensitivity lying beyond the HIPAA's remit, particularly
in the case of a controversial issue such as abortion.[80] In endorsing the
decision of a previous authority, the court specifically stated that
'whether the patients' identities would remain confidential by the exclusion of their names and identifying numbers is questionable ... information that in the cumulative can make the possibility of recognition
very high'.[81] Judge Posner sympathized with the patients concerned,
noting that it was completely understandable that these women would be
frightened to have their redacted records entered into the trial record,
given that persons of their acquaintance or even any skilful Googlers
could sift through them and combine them with other information to
expose the women to threats, humiliation and obloquy.[82] He made clear
that certain kinds of medical information should be seen as highly
sensitive and, even if anonymized or de-identified, should not be disclosed to the public because of the potential for combination with other
information to identify, and potentially cause harm to, the individuals
concerned. The logic of this reasoning is likely to have wider implications for research using medical data and for the processing of personal
data in cloud-based bio-banks (please see the discussion in Chapter 11).

More recently, the US state of California in 2013 amended its law on
personal information to include regulation of the practice of data combination by imposing new requirements on the operators of commercial
websites or online services that collect the personal information of
Californian consumers.[83] Under section 1798.29 of the California Civil
Code, as amended, the definition of personal information has been
expanded to include an individual's first name or first initial and last
name in combination with any one or more of five stated categories of
data fields if any is unencrypted: (1) social security number; (2) driver's
licence number or California identification card number; (3) bank
account number or credit or debit card number in combination with any
required security code, access code or password that would permit access

---

[80]   Ibid 929.

[81]   Ibid; the Court relied on *Parkson v Central DuPage Hospital*, 435 NE 2d
144.

[82]   Ibid.

[83]   Personal Information: Privacy SB-46 (2013–2014) reg sess, ch 396, Cal
Stat (enacted), http://leginfo.legislature.ca.gov/faces/billNavClient.xhtml?bill_id=
201320140SB46, accessed 28 March 2014.

to an individual's financial records; (4) medical information; and (5) health insurance information.[84] The definition also now includes a username or email address in combination with a password or security question and answer that would permit access to an online account.[85] All of this information is subject to a specific duty of notice of breach and security requirement.[86] Whilst such specific identifiers suffer the same under-inclusiveness as those discussed in Section II.B(2)(a) of this chapter, California's new approach to regulating the combination of certain categories of unencrypted information constitutes a move in the right direction.

The need to regulate data combinations should not be underestimated, particularly in the cloud era. Google was fined 900,000 euros by the Spanish authorities in 2013 after the company was found to have violated Spanish privacy laws by combining the data of its users across nearly 100 services without their consent.[87] The practice was also condemned by the Dutch personal data authority, which criticized Google for 'spinning an invisible web of personal data' to trap individual users.[88] Svantesson and Clarke had sounded the alarm bell back in 2010 when the Internet giant declared in its privacy statement that the company might combine the information that users had supplied within their accounts not only with information from other Google services but also with that of third parties.[89] Google had defended the practice in 2009, claiming that information available on the Internet or in the public record should not be regarded as private or confidential.[90] Google could thus easily construct user profiles for any of its users with extraordinary precision and detail, and could also share those profiles and the information therein with other companies and cloud users. Perhaps owing to its legal confrontation with the authorities in Spain and the Netherlands, Google eventually amended

---

[84] Cal Civ Code s.1798.29(g)(1).

[85] Ibid s.1798.29(g)(2).

[86] Ibid ss1798.29 and 1798.82.

[87] 'Spain Levies Maximum Fine over Google Privacy Policy' (*BBC News*, 20 December 2013), www.bbc.com/news/technology-25461353, accessed 28 March 2014.

[88] 'Google Violated Dutch Data Protection Laws, Says Watchdog' (*BBC News*, 29 November 2013), www.bbc.com/news/technology-25154252, accessed 28 March 2014.

[89] Dan Svantesson and Roger Clarke, 'Privacy and Consumer Risks in Cloud Computing' (2010) 26 *Computer Law & Security Review* 391, 394.

[90] Ibid.

its privacy policy, confining the combination of information to Google services alone.[91]

IV. NAVIGATING THROUGH THE CLOUD

The power of re-identification technology urges reconsideration of the definition of personal data. The prevailing understanding of such data as any information relating to an identified or identifiable natural person by means reasonably likely to be used by the data controller or any other person/entity is inevitably overly broad in the cloud era for several reasons. First, technology has rendered any form of information potentially identifiable. Most information can now be readily re-personalized, either through deep analysis of the information itself (as seen in the cases of browser-generated information and individuals' seating posture) or through its combination with other data or datasets. With enough information, the data in question can be linked back to the individual concerned. Second, the means reasonably likely to be used are evolving so rapidly that they are often not even contemplated at the time of data collection. Third, data controllers may not be the party that will reuse the anonymized or pseudonymous data for secondary use. The Netflix example demonstrates that bloggers, reporters and computer science researchers can easily re-identify individuals from a pool of statistical data within a short period of time. In light of these factors, the European Parliament's proposed amendment to redefine a data subject as 'an identified natural person or a natural person who can be identified, directly or indirectly, by means reasonably likely to be used by the controller or by any other natural or legal person, *working together with the controller*'[92] is likely to give inadequate protection to the individuals concerned. On the one hand, if the definition is too sweeping, it will impose an undue burden on the many data controllers or processors in the cloud. On the other, confining the definition to identified persons and

---

[91]   Google Privacy Policy (20 December 2013 version): 'We may combine personal information from one service with information, including personal information, from other Google services – for example to make it easier to share things with people you know. We will not combine DoubleClick cookie information with personally identifiable information unless we have your opt-in consent'. See 'Privacy Policy' (*Google*, 20 December 2013), www.google.com/policies/privacy/, accessed 28 March 2014.

[92]   The Committee on Civil Liberties, Justice and Home Affairs (n 12) Amendment 76.

known categories of identifiers or imposing restrictions only on controllers and those working with them is too narrow. The test of whether any data constitute personal data needs to be dynamic, as even information that is not originally personal in nature may become so if the holders of that information process it for other purposes to identify individuals.

Many scholars have pointed to the urgent need to ask hard questions about the nature of data and the realistic risks of individuals being identified on the basis of any given data. For instance, Hon, Millard and Walden suggest that when a person's identity may not realistically be traced from anonymized, pseudonymized, encrypted or fragmented data, that set of data should not be seen as personal data.[93] In such cases, they say, cloud processors are often in a 'cloud of unknowing' and should not be asked to shoulder all of the legal duties under the EU Data Protection Directive.[94] In contrast, when technologies allow the combination of data from different sources so as to identify individuals, different sets of duties should be imposed.[95] Thus, rather than applying the simple test of identification, these scholars argue that the definition of personal data should be based on the realistic risk of identification after taking into account all means reasonably likely to be used to identify an individual.[96] On the other side of the Atlantic, American scholars have proposed entirely different regimes that are largely risk-based in nature. For example, Paul Ohm argues that the power of re-identification technology and the 'fragility of anonymisation' have rendered the classification of personal data meaningless and that we should move to a cost and harm paradigm in regulating data flows instead.[97] Paul Schwartz and Daniel Solove offer the alternative model of personal identifiable information 2.0 (PII 2.0), with a different set of legal rules to apply along the continuum of identified and identifiable data.[98] Schwartz further advocates that, in the cloud context, the focus of legal regulation be on the risks of decision-making with personal data rather than on the mere automation of processing choices.[99]

Building on the work of these and other scholars, this chapter contends that we need a regime that adopts a nuanced definition of personal data

---

[93] Hon et al. (n 7).
[94] Ibid 219.
[95] Ibid 215.
[96] Ibid 217.
[97] Ohm (n 10) 1704, 1774.
[98] Schwartz and Solove (n 24) 1814.
[99] Paul M. Schwartz, 'Information Privacy in the Cloud' (2013) 161 *University of Pennsylvania Law Review* 1623, 1655.

that takes into account different levels of data personalization, incorporates regular assessments of the risks associated with identification, including the reuse of data, and factors in a policy of accountability based on the harm and benefit to society at large rather than on data subjects' consent.

A.   New Measures for Personal Data

1.   New rules for de-identified data

Despite the current paradigm and definition of personal data being problematic, it would be impractical to get rid of the concept of personal data entirely, as we need a yardstick for legal regulation. As previously noted, because most data are potentially personal data, the EU's proposed General Regulation has rightly defined personal data as any information relating to an individual. However, to prevent the adoption of an over-encompassing approach, the focus must then be on regulation of the potential to re-identify individuals. At one end of the spectrum should be identified data (data that clearly identify or single out individuals) subject to clear regulations, and at the other end should be anonymous data (the very few exceptional cases in which data cannot be linked to any individuals) excluded from regulation. Most cases are likely to fall into the category of pseudonymous data (anonymized or de-identified data), which require careful consideration. In the proposals of both the European Parliament and the European Council,[100] pseudonymous data fall into a kind of halfway house category intended for less stringent regulation.[101] The emphasis in both proposals is rightly on non-attribution to a specific data subject without the use of additional information, 'as long as such additional information is kept separately and subject to technical and organisational measure[s] to ensure non-attribution'.[102] It has been suggested that pseudonymous data can be stored in the cloud, whilst the key used to de-reference the values of the

---

[100]   Council of the European Union, 'Proposal for a Regulation of the European Parliament and of the Council on the Protection of Individuals with regard to the Processing of Personal Data and on the Free Movement of Such Data (General Data Protection Regulation)' [2013] ST 17831/13 INIT, http://register.consilium.europa.eu/doc/srv?l=EN&t=PDF&gc=true&sc=false&f=ST%2 017831%202013%20INIT, accessed 31 March 2014.

[101]   Hon et al. (n 8) 9. Under recital 68(a) of the proposal by the European Council, data breach notification does not apply to pseudonymous data. Ibid.

[102]   European Council (n 100) Article 4; the Committee on Civil Liberties, Justice and Home Affairs (n 12) Amendment 77.

data or to re-identify individuals needs to be stored and applied only on physical premises.[103] Further, the subsequently re-identified data can be used only in secure transactional systems.[104] However, the afore-mentioned duty of non-attribution and overall duty of confidentiality within the proposals seem to apply only to organizations internally. In contrast, the US Federal Trade Commission (FTC) has recommended a more robust system of de-identification and accountability.[105] Rather than toiling with the concepts of anonymous (or anonymized) and pseudony-mous data, the FTC acknowledges that the de-identification of data is not foolproof, and thus there is always a possibility that individuals will be re-identified. Accordingly, it recommends that companies robustly de-identify, and publicly commit to making no attempts to re-identify, data, and contractually require the same public commitment from any downstream users with which they share information. Such requirements should extend to the sharing of data with third parties owing to the possibility of subsequent attribution by later parties.

2. Data quality and size

When considering threats external to organizations, data quality and size also need to be taken into account. Data quality refers to the nature, sensitivity and linkability of data to individuals,[106] with the latter referring to the different degrees of data identifiability or levels of effort required to identify an individual. An example of good-quality data is the information presented in Google Flu Trends. Regardless of whether its predictions are accurate,[107] the information that Google gathers from the online web search queries submitted by millions of individuals are abstracted at a high level and safely aggregated.[108] Data quality is affected by data size. As mentioned earlier in our discussion, the size of

---

[103] Alan Murphy, 'Storing Data in the Cloud Raises Compliance Challenges' (*Forbes*, 19 January 2012), www.forbes.com/sites/ciocentral/2012/01/19/storing-data-in-the-cloud-raises-compliance-challenges/, accessed 16 July 2014.

[104] Ibid.

[105] Federal Trade Commission, *Protecting Consumer Privacy in an Era of Rapid Change* (FTC Report March 2012) 21–2, www.ftc.gov/sites/default/files/documents/reports/federal-trade-commission-report-protecting-consumer-privacy-era-rapid-change-recommendations/120326privacyreport.pdf, accessed 17 July 2014.

[106] Ohm (n 10) 1766.

[107] Charles Arthur, 'Google Flu Trends is No Longer Good at Predicting Flu, Scientists Find' (*The Guardian*, 27 March 2014), www.theguardian.com/technology/2014/mar/27/google-flu-trends-predicting-flu, accessed 2 April 2014.

[108] Schwartz and Solove (n 24) 1882.

a database is determinative of how easy it is to link the information therein to an individual. The larger in size it is, the easier that link is to make. However, the law seems to be silent on the amount of data that data controllers may collect, how long they may retain them, what data may or may not be combined and whether stricter security measures are needed for large databases. Ohm argues that new quantitative limits and guidelines should be enacted to address these issues.[109] Such limits and guidelines would undoubtedly have an impact on cloud services given the vast quantity of data stored in the cloud, but are certainly deserving of further consideration.

In sum, in determining what constitutes personal data, we must also consider the quality and quantity of the data in question. Ultimately, the core issue in personal data protection is identity protection.

B.   Risk Assessment of the Disclosure and Reuse of Data

Equally important is regulation of the disclosure and reuse of personal data, including pseudonymous data, because third parties may identify the individuals concerned through data combination. The risks and adverse effects of profiling through data mining and data combination are well recognized. Data brokers have been collecting, analysing, selling and linking consumer identities without our knowledge for some time.[110] For example, Acxiom, the largest data broker in the US and a marketing giant, holds an average of 1500 pieces of information on each of more than 200 million Americans.[111] It is estimated that each piece of information that users post on Facebook is worth five US cents and that each Facebook user is worth US$100 as a source of information.[112] When a cloud service is provided, the Internet becomes both a rich source and

---

[109]   Ohm (n 10) 1767.

[110]   The FTC uses the term 'data broker' to refer to those that 'collect and aggregate consumers' personal information from a wide range of sources and resell it for an array of purposes, such as marketing, verifying an individual's identity, and preventing financial fraud'. Prepared Statement of the FTC, 'What Information Do Data Brokers Have on Consumers, and How Do They Use It?' 113th Sen (18 December 2013), www.ftc.gov/sites/default/files/documents/public_statements/prepared-statement-federal-trade-commission-entitled-what-information-do-data-brokers-have-consumers/131218databrokerstestimony.pdf, accessed 2 April 2014.

[111]   Steve Kroft, 'The Data Brokers: Selling Your Personal Information' (*CBS News*, 9 March 2014), www.cbsnews.com/news/the-data-brokers-selling-your-personal-information/, accessed 2 April 2014.

[112]   Mayer-Schonberger and Cukier (n 11) 119.

pool of data. At present, there is limited regulation of the secondary use of data in most jurisdictions, particularly when they take the ostensible form of non-personal data (anonymized or pseudonymized data). Ultimately, this is an issue of data security, relating to the obligations of data controllers to protect against unauthorized data access, use and disclosure by third parties.

However, it can be argued that there are legitimate reasons to reuse pseudonymous data, such as in pharmaceutical trials and medical data research or for other legitimate purposes that serve the public interest. In such cases, scholars have recommended that clear guidelines be set, with minimum standards established for the de-identification of datasets and independent reviews of the risk of re-identification before data disclosure.[113] Many have advocated that a specific model be used to measure the continuum of risk involved. For example, Hon et al. and others use the 'realistic risk of identification'[114] as a benchmark, whereas Schwartz and Solove suggest the 'substantial risk of being identified'.[115] More concretely, Ohm recommends that any risk assessment takes account of: (1) the data-handling techniques used by database owners; (2) the nature of information release, with the public disclosure of data being subject to stricter scrutiny; (3) the quantity of data involved; (4) the likely motives and economic incentives for anyone to re-identify the data; and (5) the trust culture in a particular industry or sector, that is, the existing standard of fiduciary duty or duty of confidentiality in that sector.[116] Furthermore, as data identification and combination technologies are advancing at a rapid pace, I contend that any risk assessment concerned should be carried out on a regular basis rather than only at the stages of data collection, de-identification and disclosure.

C. Accountability

Many of the foregoing measures are dependent on the compliance framework of the data controllers and the organizations or companies concerned because individuals often have no idea that their data are being collected, used and processed or that they have been re-identified, let alone being asked to give their informed consent for the unknown, future and secondary use of those data. It is therefore important to formulate an alternative privacy framework that is based less on consent and more on

---

113   Hon et al. (n 7) 215.
114   Ibid 224.
115   Schwartz and Solove (n 24) 1882.
116   Ohm (n 10).

holding data controllers accountable for a particular reuse of data based on risk and the likely adverse impact (harm) on data subjects when the unauthorized disclosure and use of data takes place. The EU currently affords sensitive personal data special protection. Recital 33 of the EU Data Protection Directive specifies that data 'which are capable by their nature of infringing fundamental freedoms or privacy should not be processed unless the data subject gives his explicit consent'. Although the categories of sensitive data are likely to be controversial in different contexts and cultures,[117] the 'sensitive' nature of certain data reveals the underlying values and harm concerned. For example, data related to an individual's religious beliefs, race and health (particularly sensitive health information such as HIV status) may lead to discrimination against that individual.[118] Google's online advertisement Google AdSense has been accused of racial bias against African Americans,[119] thus arguably violating the rights to equality and autonomy. Similarly, data that point to age may lead to targeted advertisements against children, the elderly or other vulnerable groups in society, reflecting an imbalance of power. Bearing in mind the threat of harm arising from the re-identification of certain data, organizations need to ensure that sensitive data, which may perhaps be better described as critical data, are stored separately from the general network. They also need to ensure that access to such data is carefully monitored, that their combination with other data cannot easily take place and that their public disclosure is impossible.

---

[117]   Article 8 of the EU Data Protection Directive prohibits the processing of personal data revealing 'racial or ethnic origin, political opinions, religious or philosophical beliefs, trade-union membership, and the processing of data concerning health or sex life', unless data subjects provide their explicit consent or other conditions under article 8(2) are satisfied.

[118]   It was recently reported that the US Federal Bureau of Investigation (FBI) has been collecting racial and ethnic information to map communities around the country based on crude stereotypes about which groups commit various types of crime. Seeta Gangadharan, 'Knowing Is Half the Battle: Combating Big Data's Dark Side through Data Literacy' (*Slate*, 2 April 2014), www.slate.com/blogs/future_tense/2014/04/02/white_house_big_data_and_privacy_review_we_need_federal_policy_about_digital.html?wpisrc=burger_bara, accessed 4 April 2014.

[119]   Latanya Sweeney, 'Discrimination in Online Ad Delivery' (2013) 56(5) *Communications of the ACM* 45.

V. CONCLUSION

We leave 'data fingerprints' everywhere, including in the cloud, without fully realizing it.[120] The personal data privacy that we have long enjoyed, or at least thought we enjoyed, has turned out to be an illusion. Personal data have a distinct lifecycle – what was once de-personalized can be re-personalized. Further, re-identification technology has become increasingly advanced and common in the age of big data and computing in which data are processed globally.

Understandably, data subjects would like all of the data they store in the cloud to be treated as personal data so as to be entitled to personal data protection, including retaining control over those data in the form of consent, accessibility, security and notification of any data breach. Data controllers (businesses, organizations and researchers alike) feel otherwise. To encourage innovation and the responsible use of data, we need a new concept of personal data that takes into account the distinct lifecycle of such data: their evolving nature and capacity to be re-identified. The analysis in this chapter makes clear that proper personal data management and technological tools need to address the rising concerns over data quality and quantity and potential risk and harm in the shifting landscape of personal data protection. We need continuous assessments of the privacy implications of given data and their linkability to real individuals. Finally, it is high time that we move from a consent-based to an accountability-based legal regime governing personal data.

---

[120]   Ohm (n 10) 1723.

5. Cross-border data flow in the cloud between the EU and the US

Dominic N. Staiger

I. INTRODUCTION

The flow of data across borders, in particular that of personal data, from the European Union (EU) to the US poses significant challenges for cloud providers as well as their European business clients. Critical but unresolved issues include agreeing on standards for the required data protection which must be observed in relation to the identifiability of personal data, as well as the contractual rights granted to the cloud provider and its customers under various Terms of Service (ToS).[1] Furthermore the necessary level of control and the accompanying degree of responsibility under European data protection laws also warrant a closer analysis in the context of cloud computing.[2]

Due to the vast technological changes over the last two decades, laws relating to data protection have had to be constantly adapted to technological advancements in order for their regulatory purpose to be achieved. Unfortunately any enactment or amendment of law requires a significant period of time. For instance, the Data Protection Directive[3] (DPD) was enacted in the mid-1990s to address concerns raised by personal data transfers to countries outside the EU. At the time the DPD was passed, cloud computing did not exist and the main application of the legislation focused on simple point to point transfers from a European

---

[1]   Rolf H. Weber and Dominic N. Staiger, 'Cloud Computing: A Cluster of Complex Liability Issues' (2014) 20 Web JCLI, http://webjcli.org/article/view/303/418, accessed 11 February 2015.

[2]   Rolf H. Weber and Dominic N. Staiger, 'Legal Challenges of Trans-Border Data Flow in the Cloud' (13 May 2013) Jusletter IT, http://jusletter-it.weblaw.ch/issues/2014/15-Mai-2014.html, accessed 11 February 2015.

[3]   Directive 95/46/EC of the European Parliament and of the Council of 24 October 1995 on the protection of individuals with regard to the processing of personal data and on the free movement of such data [1995] OJ EC 23/6.

sender to a foreign recipient.[4] By the early 21st century, the situation had changed completely. Now, not only has the potential of cloud computing been recognized, the challenges it poses have urged a new legal response (please see the discussion in Chapter 4). Recognizing this, the European Parliament initiated a reform process which resulted in the first draft of a European Data Protection Regulation (DPR)[5] in 2012. In regard to personal data transfers to locations outside of the EU, some issues that had been identified in the DPD were addressed, others remain unresolved. This chapter will focus on the data protection implications that arise from a personal data transfer from the EU to the US, taking into account the draft DPR as last revised in October 2013 as well as the DPD which is still in force at the time of writing.

As a starting point, the definitions under the DPD will be introduced, highlighting the controller/processor distinction and its importance to cloud computing. Subsequently, the application of the DPD to a personal data transfer will be addressed before an in-depth analysis of such transfers to the US is carried out.

II. DATA PROTECTION FRAMEWORK IN THE EU

A. Definition of Personal Data

At the core of the European data protection framework lies the definition of personal data created in the mid-1990s. It includes any data from which an individual person is identifiable.[6] Despite such a seemingly simple definition, technological progress continues to create challenges for its interpretation today. For example, anonymous data does not generally lead to the identification of an individual. However, by merging an anonymous data set together with another anonymous data set, an

---

[4] Neil Robinson, Hans Graux, Maarten Botterman and Lorenzo Valeri, 'Review of the European Data Protection Directive' (2009) 6, www.hideproject. org/downloads/references/review_of_eu_dp_directive.pdf, accessed 2 July 2014.

[5] European Commission, Proposal for a regulation of the European Parliament and of the Council on the protection of individuals with regard to the processing of personal data and on the free movement of such data (General Data Protection Regulation) COM [2012] 11/4 draft 2012 and draft as of 7 October 2013, www.europarl.europa.eu/meetdocs/2009_2014/documents/libe/dv/comp_am_art_01-29/comp_am_art_01-29en.pdf, accessed 2 July 2014 (Data Protection Regulation hereinafter).

[6] Data Protection Regulation (n 5) art. 4(2).

individual person can potentially be identified via a computerized calculating process such as is commonly used in Big Data[7] technologies. Thus a person can become identifiable when three independent variables are known,[8] for example, hair colour, age and favourite restaurant.[9] (For a further discussion of this matter, please see Chapter 4.) Additionally, personal data can be altered to prevent or hinder identification. The three most common approaches employed in this regard are encryption, pseudonymization or anonymization. When data is encrypted it is generally no longer classed as personal data because 'if you cannot view data, you cannot identify data subjects'.[10]

Nevertheless, such an assessment will strongly depend on the type of encryption used and the security level it provides.[11] Anonymized and pseudonymized data is altered through a one-way measure which cannot easily be reversed. The question in these instances is: whether or not a person can be identified through available direct or indirect identifiers. Commonly the use of the same variable will enable identification through outside data sets by comparing the variables and deriving a pattern from which the process can be reversed.[12] Deleting such direct identifiers was previously considered an adequate measure by European courts, nevertheless, this view might change in the future due to technologies such as cloud systems which allow for a much easier identification based on the availability of vast amounts of data.[13] The volume of data being

---

[7]   'Big Data' refers to the processing of vast amounts of data *in order* to determine correlations between data sets that provide valuable information for various commercial purposes.

[8]   Iain Hrynaszkiewicz, 'Preparing Raw Clinical Data for Publication: Guidance for Journal Editors, Authors, and Peer Reviewers' (2010) 340 *British Medical Journal* 181, 2.

[9]   W. Kuan Hon, Christopher Millard and Ian Walden, 'The Problem of "Personal Data" in Cloud Computing' (2011) 1 *IDPL* 211, 215.

[10]   Ibid 211.

[11]   W. Kuan Hon, Eleni Kosta, Christopher Millard and Dimitra Stefanatou, 'Cloud Accountability: The Likely Impact of the Proposed EU Data Protection Regulation' (2014) Queen Mary School of Law Legal Studies Research Paper 172/2014, 10–13.

[12]   Article 29 Working Party, 'Opinion 4/2007 on the Concept of Personal Data' (WP 136, 20 June 2007) 12–15.

[13]   Joined cases C-92/09 *Volker und Markus Schecke GbR* and C-93/09 *Hartmut Eifert v Land Hessen* [2009] OJ C 13/6 15.1.2011 assume that deleting names adequately anonymizes the recipients of certain funds.

processed in the cloud is growing exponentially. Invariably the accumulation of data will slowly but steadily lower the efforts required to identify and attribute specific characteristics to an individual.

The DPR defines personal data as data from which a natural person 'can' be identified.[14] In light of the above-mentioned forms of data, further clarification would be warranted in order to ensure legal certainty for cloud providers. For cloud service providers, it is essential to know when the data they store or process is personal and, thus, whether they must observe the requirements laid down by the DPR in order to transfer the data to the US in compliance with EU data protection laws. Compared to the DPD, including a special definition of pseudonymous data[15] appears to be a positive first step towards the realization that IT is constantly changing and legislative action is necessary to address the needs of the market. The proposed definition requires that additional data which in combination with other data could identify a person must be stored separately and subjected to special protective measures.[16] Also a definition of encrypted data was included, requiring the data to be unintelligible to an unauthorized person.[17]

However, maintaining a definition of personal data which depends on the encryption or anonymization technique used by a customer is unsatisfactory as it also affects the cloud provider's classification as controller or processor.[18]

In addition to the general classification of personal data regarding a person's identifiability, the DPR also addressed the problems associated with genetic and biometric data by including a definition in the DPR and imposing special requirements on processing this type of data. It is well known that Facebook, running also on a cloud infrastructure, is able to run biometric identification (in other words, facial recognition) over their user profiles allowing for the identification of an individual person. The physical characteristics of a person can also be analysed through this method. To what extent this data can be used for commercial purposes is

---

[14] Data Protection Regulation (n 5) art. 4(2).

[15] Ibid art. 4(2a).

[16] Ibid art. 83(1b).

[17] Ibid art. 4(2b); see W. Kuan Hon, Christopher Millard and Ian Walden, 'What Is Regulated as Personal Data in Clouds?' in Christopher Millard (ed.), *Cloud Computing Law* (Oxford: OUP 2013) 167–78, for a discussion on encryption, anonymization and pseudonymization.

[18] W. Kuan Hon, Christopher Millard and Ian Walden, 'Who Is Responsible for Personal Data in Clouds?' in Christopher Millard (ed.), *Cloud Computing Law* (Oxford: OUP 2013) 211.

subject to the contract governing the relations between the parties. Access to this data by governmental agencies is also possible under certain circumstances.[19]

Furthermore, the mentioned definition in the DPR draws a further distinction as to special categories of personal data.[20] These categories include data which relates to race origin, political opinions, religion, philosophical beliefs, sexual orientation, trade union activities, genetic or biometric data, data concerning health or sex life, administrative sanctions, judgments, criminal convictions or suspected offences. This data cannot be processed unless certain specific requirements are fulfilled.[21] Such a provision is of particular importance for cloud service providers which offer a social media service including the processing of such data. In this context an exception applies where the data subject has 'manifestly made data public'.[22] The cloud provider is then no longer under a general prohibition regarding the processing of this information.

B.   Definition of Processing

The term 'processing' under the DPR is of central importance to cloud providers as it triggers the application of the DPR once their actions fall under this definition. Processing is described as any operation or set of operations which is performed upon personal data.[23] The DPR includes a list of examples of such operations. For cloud computing purposes the terms such as *collection, storage, adaptation or alteration, use, disclosure by transmission, dissemination or otherwise making available, alignment or combination, erasure or destruction*[24] are invariably applicable in some form. In practice this means that every type of cloud service provider, including IaaS, PaaS, SaaS, XaaS[25] will carry out a processing

---

[19]   The Uniting and Strengthening America by Providing Appropriate Tools Required to Intercept and Obstruct Terrorism Act of 2001 (USA PATRIOT Act), Pub. L. No. 107–56, 115 Stat 272 (2001); and Foreign Intelligence Surveillance Act of 1978, 50 U.S.C. ch. 36.

[20]   It has been suggested that the definition of personal data should place a greater focus on the risk of harm and its expected severity; Christopher Millard, 'Opinion: The Future of Privacy (part 2) – What Might Privacy 2.0 Look Like?' (2008) 5 *Data Protection Law and Policy* 8–11.

[21]   Data Protection Regulation (n 5) art. 9(1).

[22]   Ibid art. 9(2)(e).

[23]   Ibid art. 4(3).

[24]   Ibid.

[25]   'Infrastructure as a service' (IaaS) is the provision of hardware (calculating capacity and storage). 'Platform as a service' (PaaS) provides the hardware and

operation at some point during the course of supplying its cloud service. It is therefore important for a cloud provider to be aware that when any form of European personal data is involved in the cloud process this will generally trigger the enforcement of the DPR. Once the application of the DPR to the conduct of a cloud provider is established one must then turn to the control exerted over the processing which determines the amount of responsibility that must be shouldered by a cloud provider under the DPR.

C. Controller and Processor Distinction

The level of responsibility for the processing determines the amount of obligation that is imposed under the DPD or the DPR. Two types of actors are distinguished in this regard. A controller determines the purposes, conditions and means of the processing of personal data whereas a processor processes personal data on behalf of the controller.[26] As practice has shown, this seemingly simple definition poses some major challenges for cloud providers as well as data protection experts. By expanding the scope of the DPR to such an extent, any cloud computing provider will ultimately be classed as a processor, if not a controller.

The Article 29 Working Party, an advisory body set up by the DPD, addressed this issue in its Working Paper 169 (WP169).[27] Primarily cloud providers were considered to be processors as long as they do not act in a manner which is inconsistent with their instructions. Generally the instructions do not contain a right to cater advertising specifically to the controller, which is common practice in cloud services targeted at private consumers. Thus in a social media context when a user uploads data to a social media site running on a cloud and the provider then alters its advertising based on the personal data received it will be deemed to be a controller for the purposes of the DPD and the DPR.

However, it has been argued that such an approach fails to distinguish the qualitative level of the actual functions carried out by the provider.[28] So, for example, an IaaS provider supplies the hardware resources

---

basic software platform for further software implementation. 'Software as a service' (SaaS) offers remote access to software through a browser. 'XaaS' stands for providing of any form of capability through a communication link.

[26] Data Protection Regulation (n 5) art. 4(5) and (6).

[27] Article 29 Working Party, 'Opinion 1/2010 on the Concepts of "Controller" and "Processor"' (WP 169, 16 February 2010).

[28] Hon, Millard and Walden (n 17) 208.

required by the customer despite having little or no control over the data that is processed as access to the system is granted through an automated structure and billed accordingly. In such a case, the cloud user determines the 'means' of processing thus informing the IaaS provider of the type of resources it requires. The Article 29 Working Party has expressed its view in its Working Paper 169 that there must be a certain leeway for these providers in deciding on the exact means by which the resource is supplied. Focusing on the 'effective means' of processing, the Article 29 Working Party introduced a possible further element in defining an actor in a cloud setting as a controller, as the power to determine the 'effective means' is traditionally and inherently reserved for the controller and is essential to the core processing.

In practice, this means that the controller must inform the processor of the required essential means of processing, leaving non-essential means such as organizational and technical questions to the processor (in other words, IaaS provider).[29] To what extent the processor is allowed to determine these factors on its own remains open to debate.[30] However, the WP169 has expressed its view that 'the cloud client may task the cloud provider with choosing the methods and the technical or organisational measures to be used to achieve the purpose of the controller'.[31] It seems that the clearer and more precise the instructions given by the controller are, the more likely the processor will remain a mere processor rather than a controller.[32] This concept is more akin to an agency concept where the processor carries out the mandate given to it by the controller.[33] However, both the DPD and the DPR do not contain a concept of 'effective means' thus leaving it open to authorities to determine in an individual case what conduct amounts to that of a controller.[34] In daily cloud practice such an environment does not encourage cloud providers to expand their business as they lack the legal certainty required to carry out their activities in conformity with EU laws.

---

[29]   Article 29 Working Party (n 12) 14–15.
[30]   For example, security decisions might be so critical that they must be defined as essential means.
[31]   Article 29 Working Party, 'Opinion 5/2012 on Cloud Computing' (WP196, 1 July 2012) 8.
[32]   Article 29 Working Party (n 12) 13, 28, 29.
[33]   Article 29 Working Party (n 12) 26: 'The contract should include a sufficiently detailed description of the processor's mandate'.
[34]   See Data Protection Regulation (n 5) art. 4(5), which defines the controller as the party that determines purpose and means of processing.

The European data protection authorities should therefore clearly and uniformly define how they will interpret the controller/processor distinction.[35] Giving practical examples of common situations in a cloud environment would provide the necessary guidance required by the industry.

In light of the underlying service that is provided by various cloud providers, a new category must be created for providers who are neither controllers nor processors under the current definition of the DPD as well as the DPR. These include providers that offer a standard service such as the supply of hardware which a user can then access and use to process personal data. If the provider does at no time have access to or control over the data, nor is taking any other measures to impact the processing of the data, the provider should not be classed as a controller.[36] It is rather the self-service fashion and use by the customer that should be determinative in this regard. Thus before a cloud provider becomes a processor for the purposes of the DPD or the DPR, the provider should be required to have knowledge of the processing of personal data on its systems as well as control over it in the form of access to the data.[37]

D. Applicability of the Data Protection Regulation and Directive

The material scope of the DPR extends to partly or fully automated processing, whereas the method of processing is irrelevant.[38] Thus a natural person posting or utilizing personal data in the cloud (in other words, on a cloud-based social network) would be subject to the legislation. In order to avoid such a situation, the DPR incorporates in article 2(2)(d) an exception for exclusively household or domestic use in circumstances where it can reasonably be expected that only a limited number of persons will gain access to such data. This also includes activities such as private sales or family related activities without any connection to a professional or commercial purpose. Importantly, even if the data is used by a private individual based on these grounds, a cloud provider which processes the data on request of the person subject to the

---

[35] Commentators tend to assume that all providers are processors; Daniele Catteddu and Giles Hogben, *Cloud Computing: Benefits, Risks and Recommendations for Information Security* (Heraklion: European Network and Information Security Agency, 2009) 66.

[36] Hon, Millard and Walden (n 18) 211.

[37] Ibid.

[38] Data Protection Regulation (n 5) art. 4(3).

exception must still conduct the processing in accordance with the data protection principles laid down by the DPR in article 5.

The DPD and the DPR do not apply to public authorities in relation to actions carried out in connection with criminal investigations.[39] Under the DPD there is a real risk that non-EU cloud customers using a cloud service provider, which maintains data centres in the EU for the processing of personal data (EU or non EU), will be subjected to the DPD. Also the law seems to favour discounting a potential establishment in order to impose the DPD through the low threshold of 'using EU equipment' under article 4(1)(c) DPD. Applying the DPD to non-EU controllers which essentially only want to use an EU provider's infrastructure to process their non-EU personal data seems to be a big hindrance for the further expansion of a European cloud computing market. Foreign non-EU controllers have no incentive at all to use EU cloud providers, which will subject them to uncertain EU data protection laws.

As processing includes the transfer of personal data, the DPR as well as the DPD apply to the party transferring data outside the EU, be this a controller or a processor.[40] A processor in a foreign country is generally not subject to the DPR or the DPD. However, under the DPR the scope has been extended to situations in which the foreign party 'targets' EU customers.[41] Yet this does not require the customers to prove that the cloud providers have the intention of developing an activity of a certain scale with other member states in order to meet the 'manifest intention' requirement established by the European Court of Justice (ECJ).[42] Practical enforceability issues also arise in these situations as addressed in section III below.

Before a data transfer is legally allowed, justification for the collection and processing must be provided under the DPR. In contrast to the DPR, the DPD does not include such a provision, thus for an analysis of the grounds for justification under the DPD one must turn to the applicable member state's implementation of the DPD.

---

[39]   Data Protection Directive (n 3) art. 2(2)(e).

[40]   See Data Protection Regulation (n 5) art. 4(3) for a definition of processing that includes transmission and dissemination.

[41]   For a non-exhaustive list of the factors involved in ascertaining whether or not a targeting has taken place, see C-585/08 *Peter Pammer v Redderei Karl Schlüter GmbH & Co KG* and C-144/09 *Hotel Alpenhof GesmbH v Oliver Heller* [2010] ECR I-12527, 93.

[42]   Ibid 82.

The DPR requirements for lawful processing found in article 6, are based on article 7 of the DPD. The most controversial justification is the one on consent by the data subject through entering into a contractual arrangement with the service provider processing the data.[43] Specific conditions of consent which previously were not included in the DPD are now laid down in article 7 of the DPR. In any event the burden of proof in establishing the data subject's consent to the processing of their data is on the controller.[44] Such consent will no longer be classed as freely given where the cloud provider uses default options under which the data subject must object to the processing or when pre-ticked boxes are used in online forms.[45] Once a specific processing cannot be justified based on directly given consent, the justification that the processing is required for the performance of the contract can potentially be employed.[46] However, the central difference in the current approach under the DPD is a 'legitimate interest' exception under which a controller or the third party to whom the data is disclosed can process it under certain circumstances.[47] In any case it must meet the reasonable expectations of the data subject. Furthermore, this provision might not be available in situations where the fundamental rights and freedoms of the data subject are affected. One can expect that the court will closely follow the rights enshrined in the Charter of Fundamental Rights of the European Union in interpreting this limitation.

The extent to which fundamental rights must be concerned in order to trigger the application of the exception remains open to interpretation by the data protection authorities, thus clarification through a guidance document seems necessary.

E. Personal Data Transfers within the EU

Once personal data is identified as being on European territory or the DPR applies due to the targeting exception, certain limitations apply to the data. Within the EU the data can be transferred freely as the data protection level will be equalized once the DPR comes into force and is

---

[43] Data Protection Regulation (n 5) art. 6(1)(a).

[44] Data Protection Regulation (n 5) art. 7(1); see Article 29 Working Party, 'Opinion 15/2011 on the Definition of Consent' (WP 187, 2011).

[45] Data Protection Regulation (n 5) art. 7 recital 32.

[46] Ibid art. 6(1)(b).

[47] W. Kuan Hon and Christopher Millard, 'How Do Restrictions on International Data Transfers Work in Clouds?' in Christopher Millard (ed.), *Cloud Computing Law* (Oxford: OUP 2013) 262.

applicable throughout the EU. Article 1(3) of the DPR expressly points out that no processing or transfer of personal data within the EU shall be restricted by the DPR. Any processing in the cloud or storage in the cloud is therefore possible without restrictions as long as the data does not leave the EU and is processed in a server centre within the EU. The level of protection afforded by Swiss data protection standards is currently seen as being equivalent to the European level.[48] Therefore a transfer of such data to and from the EU is allowed without restrictions.

III. PERSONAL DATA TRANSFERS FROM THE EU TO THE US

As one of the core attributes of cloud computing is its scalability and processing based on the location where provisioning costs are lowest, personal data will invariably need to be transferred abroad in order to maximize the efficiency gains provided by technology. For example, personal data could be processed more cheaply in a country where it is night-time and thus server calculating capacity is not required by local businesses as their employees are not at work.

In order to benefit from this situation, a European company must be able to transfer the data to another more cost-efficient country. However, the data protection standards in these countries are often lower than the EU's and are very hard to enforce. The issue of enforceability has been addressed under the proposed DPR. Article 25 requires a controller which is not established in the EU to designate a representative in the EU. This is akin to article 4(2) of the DPD. Exceptions to this rule apply if the third country provides an adequate standard of data protection or if the controller processes data relating to less than 5000 data subjects within any 12 month period.[49]

The territorial scope of the DPR extends to all processing of personal data in the context of an establishment of a controller or processor in the EU, regardless of where the processing takes place. Additionally, when the personal data of a data subject in the EU is being processed by a controller or processor not established in the EU, it will be subject to the DPR if the processing is related to the offering of goods or services to

---

[48] Data Protection Directive (n 3) art. 24; European Commission, 'Commission Decision of 26 July 2000 pursuant to Directive 95/46/EC of the European Parliament and of the Council on the Adequate Protection of Personal Data Provided in Switzerland' [2000] OJ L 215, 25/08/2000, 1–3.
[49] Data Protection Regulation (n 5) art. 25(2)(a) and (b).

data subjects in the EU or the monitoring of such persons.[50] This leads to the DPR having a very wide territorial scope as even a US cloud provider offering its services to European customers must adhere to the data protection requirements imposed by the EU laws. The provisions of the DPR clarify this rule by requiring it to be apparent that the controller is envisaging the offering of services to data subjects residing in one or more EU member states.[51] However, if there are no European subsidiaries of the company or any other physical presence in the EU, the enforcement of any claim will remain challenging.[52]

The extension of the scope to monitoring activities will in future pose some challenges for providers as well data protection authorities. It includes the tracking as well as the collection of data related to a data subject in the EU with the intention of using or potentially using this data to create a profile of that person or making a decision in relation to that person. Importantly this also extends to predicting personal preference, behaviours and attitudes. Today most social service providers already collect data about their customers to cater their service more specifically to the needs of each individual and thus may fall under the DPR's definition.[53]

In contrast to the DPR, the DPD describes a two-stage process in determining the applicable law:[54]

(i)   does the data controller have an 'establishment' on the territory of an EU Member State, and (ii) does the controller process personal data in the context of activities of that establishment? If the answer to both questions is yes, then that Member State's implementation of the DPD will apply to such personal data processing, wherever in the world it takes place – whether outside or inside the European Economic Area (EEA).[55]

---

[50]   Data Protection Regulation (n 5).

[51]   Ibid art. 3 recital 20.

[52]   Julia Black, 'Constructing and Contesting Legitimacy and Accountability in Polycentric Regulatory Regimes', (2008) 2 *Regulation and Governance* 137, 143.

[53]   'Facebook Data Collection and Use Policy' (*Facebook*), www.facebook.com/about/privacy/, accessed 2 July 2014.

[54]   Data Protection Directive (n 3) art. 4(1)(a).

[55]   W. Kuan Hon, Julia Hörnle and Christopher Millard, 'Data Protection Jurisdiction and Cloud Computing: When Are Cloud Users and Providers Subject to EU Data Protection Law? The Cloud of Unknowing, Part 3' (2011) Queen Mary School of Law Legal Studies Research Paper No. 84/2011, 9, http://papers.ssrn.com/sol3/papers.cfm?abstract_id=1924240, accessed 2 July 2014.

For both the DPD and the DPR, the classification of an establishment is a key factor.[56] It appears that the European Court of Justice provides some guidance requiring 'both human and technical resources necessary for the provision of particular services'[57] to be permanently available. In regard to data centres in the EU being used by a foreign cloud customer (controller) this interpretation needs to be closely examined. As a data centre requires buildings and employees, it will probably amount to an establishment if owned by the customer. However, if the customer only rents a rack, cage or server from a third party cloud provider in the EU, it becomes increasingly difficult to classify this as the customer's establishment.[58] Furthermore, the activities of that establishment are important. The wording in 'the context of the activities of an establishment' *was given a wide interpretation by the courts.*[59] However, it has been suggested that this has mainly been done for policy reasons and should be more closely linked to the 'processing activities of the establishment as a controller who determines the purposes and means of that processing'.[60] In contrast to this interpretation one could argue that a data centre has no 'own activities' as it carries out only a passive technical activity as a processor, thus it has never processed in the 'context of its activity as controller'.[61] One must therefore closely examine the establishment of a customer in the EU (such as a sales office) in order to determine the context of the activities, but if the customer does not have an office in the EU and the data centre cannot be classified as an establishment the establishment grounds do not apply.[62]

If a data centre owner has a one-man office in the EU, the Article 29 Working Party has expressed its view that in order to be an establishment the office must be 'actively involved in the activities in the context of

---

[56]   Weber and Staiger (n 2) N 90.

[57]   Case C-390/96 *Lease Plan Luxembourg SA v Belgian State* [1998] ECR I-2553.

[58]   Hon, Hörnle and Millard (n 55) 19.

[59]   *Republica Italiana v David Carl Drummond, George de los Reyes, Peter Andrew Fleischer, Desikan Arvind*, Ordinary Tribunal of Milan (24 February 2010) Sentenza n 1972/2010 (penal decision against individual officers of Google for violations of Italian data protection laws).

[60]   Hon, Hörnle and Millard (n 55) 11.

[61]   Serge Gutwirth, Yves Poullet, Paul de Hert and Ronald Leenes (eds), *Computers, Privacy and Data Protection: An Element of Choice* (Dordrecht: Springer 2011) 48.

[62]   Ibid.

which the processing of personal data takes place'.[63] This supports the view that the active involvement of the data centre owner in the processing is necessary to classify it as an establishment. Mostly, this will not apply as the processing is under the control of the cloud customer, who pays the data centre for the use of its facilities for its processing activities.

As a first step, a cloud user should therefore determine where the equipment of the cloud provider is located in order to ascertain whether or not a cross-border transfer of data outside the EU has occurred. A party transferring personal data from the EU into a cloud which is not based on EU servers must closely scrutinize how the service is provided. Subsequently, at a second stage, the different server locations must be ascertained to determine which transfer method under European law is available and most appropriate to the circumstances.

A.   Personal Data Transfer Requirements under EU Law

Any transfer outside the EU must fall under one of the exceptions provided by the DPR. These include:

Transfers under an adequacy decision by the EU
Transfers by way of appropriate safeguards
Transfers by way of binding corporate rules (BCR)[64]
Transfers under an article 44 exception.[65]

The concept of determining adequacy by the European Commission as well as the BCR and the appropriate safeguards (contractual clauses) have already been employed in the DPD.[66] Essentially the European Commission will decide based on the list of factors mentioned in article 41 of the DPR whether or not a non-EU country fulfills an adequate standard of data protection which would allow the transfer of personal

---

[63]   Article 29 Working Party, 'Opinion 8/2010 on Applicable Law' (WP 179, December 2010) 12.

[64]   Article 29 Working Party, 'Working Document: Transfers of Personal Data to Third Countries – Applying Article 26(2) of the EU Data Protection Directive to Binding Corporate Rules for International Data Transfers' (WP 74, 3 June 2003) 6.

[65]   Rolf H. Weber, *Regulatory Models for the Online World* (Zurich: Kluwer Law International 2002) 156.

[66]   Data Protection Directive (n 3) arts 25 and 26.

data to that country. In doing so, the Commission must define the territorial and sectorial application of its decision.

One of the most commonly used data transfer mechanisms is the so-called Safe Harbor agreement[67] which allows personal data transfers from the EU to the US. In essence it requires the US counterpart receiving the information to have conducted a self-assessment of its data protection systems and be registered with the Department of Commerce. In doing so, they state that they adhere to the minimum standard set by the EU DPD. Once this procedure is completed, the company is seen as a safe harbour for personal data outside the EU, thus the European Commission has approved transfers to the US in these situations. Nevertheless, one should not forget that the data protection standards in the US are much lower than they are in the EU, being sectorial in nature and varying between different states. Additional concerns have been raised regarding compatibility with EU law where the data is being accessed by US intelligence agencies and used for their own purposes. This debate has increasingly received attention in light of the revelations of Edward Snowden.[68] Accordingly the first challenge has been the case brought against Facebook, based on the argument that the transfer of personal data to the US is no longer legally possible due to the extensive surveillance rights of the US authorities.[69] In considering these arguments, the Irish Data Protection Commissioner concluded that at the time of entering into the Safe Harbor agreement, the European Commission was aware of the US surveillance framework, thus their decision to allow transfers under the agreement is still valid.[70] Therefore in practice, the Safe Harbor agreement remains the best and easiest solution for US cloud providers with server locations in the US.

If there has been no adequacy decision by the Commission or a determination that a third country's data protection is inadequate, two possibilities are open to the cloud providers. The first is a transfer under

---

[67] For more information on the Safe Harbor agreement, see www.export.gov/safeharbor/.

[68] Rolf H. Weber and Dominic N. Staiger, 'Datenüberwachung in der Schweiz und den USA' (25 November 2013) Jusletter IT,http://jusletter. weblaw.ch/juslissues/2013/735.html, accessed 11 February 2015.

[69] Rolf H. Weber and Dominic N. Staiger, 'Spannungsfelder von Datenschutz und Datenüberwachung in der Schweiz und in den USA' (15 May 2014) Jusletter IT, N 9, http://richterzeitung.weblaw.ch/jusletter-it/issues/2014/15-Mai-2014. html, accessed 11 February 2015.

[70] Response from the Irish Data Protection Commissioner (*Europe versus Facebook*, 23 July 2013), www.europe-v-facebook.org/Response_23_7_2013.pdf, accessed 2 July 2014.

the appropriate safeguards exception. It requires the cloud provider to adduce appropriate safeguards to data protection through a legally binding instrument. This can take the form of article 43 BCR or be accomplished through a so-called European Data Protection Seal.[71] Secondly, standard clauses and individual contractual clauses are possible; however, the latter require prior approval by the authorities whereas standard clauses and the BCR do not need specific authorization.[72] These measures apply equally to cloud providers in their capacity as controllers or processors.

In contrast to the Safe Harbor agreement, which is limited to US–EU transfers and only applies to certain transfers or categories thereof, BCR are applicable within the institution or corporate structure which ensures the enforcement of the DPD in transferring data to any party governed by them.[73] They can be indicative of compliance with the Safe Harbor principles, but are not determinative as the above-mentioned approval process through the US Department of Commerce must be followed. At a bare minimum, they must grant enforceable rights to the data subject and must be legally binding on the entire corporate structure governed by them.[74] The BCR must therefore apply to and be enforceable on the controller's group of undertakings and also cover the external subcontractors who are bound by these rules. In contrast to the DPD, the DPR sets out the minimum requirements of such BCR, ensuring further legal certainty for cloud businesses.

Today, many cloud providers include in their Terms of Service (ToS) a provision stating either that they fulfill the Safe Harbor principles in regard to transfers to the US or that they will not transfer the data to another country unless it has a data protection standard that is equivalent to or higher than the originating country.[75] It is therefore central for the cloud customer to understand what service is being offered at what stage of processing and by whom. For example, Dropbox uses Amazon S3 as its storage service provider and states on its website that the data will only be transferred in an encrypted fashion.[76] However, such transparent

---

[71] Data Protection Regulation (n 5) art. 42(2)(aa).
[72] Data Protection Regulation (n 5) art. 42(3).
[73] Article 29 Working Party (n 64).
[74] Weber and Staiger (n 2) N 93–4.
[75] See clauses 5.1 and 12 of 'Complete Privacy Statement' (*Symantec*), www.symantec.com/en/uk/about/profile/policies/privacy.jsp, accessed 2 July 2014.
[76] 'Security Overview' (*Dropbox*), www.dropbox.com/privacy#security, accessed 2 July 2014.

communication is not a common practice. Thus, a cloud customer who is thinking of utilizing a cloud service provider should make the necessary enquiries.

In light of the potential enforcement of a data subject's rights, the new DPR offers significant improvements. In particular article 19(2b) is of importance in regard to a technical solution. It states that: 'In the context of the use of information society services, and notwithstanding Directive 2002/58/EC, the right to object may be exercised by *automated means* using a *technical standard* which allows the data subject to clearly express his or her wishes' (emphasis by author).[77] Thus the data subject could enforce his or her data protection requirements by way of a standard certificate used in his or her browser. This automated data certificate would store the user's data protection settings and could automatically object to a use by a provider who has not complied with the set standard.

B. Personal Data Transfers to a Sub-Processor

The cloud environment is often multilayered, including a number of different service providers, such as an IaaS provider supplying the necessary hardware to run the software of an SaaS provider. In such instances one must consider the subsequent processing that takes place once the personal data has left the EU under one of the mentioned exceptions.

New requirements will be introduced in the DPR, including an obligation to seek approval before using a sub-processor.[78] As the use of sub-processors is general practice in the cloud industry, especially in multilayered cloud services (in other words, an SaaS running on an IaaS in the EEA), imposing such a restriction will likely deprive the users of cloud computing technologies of some of the cloud's main advantages unless a right to do so can be included in the standard contract terms.[79] Article 30 of the DPR imposes additional security obligations on

---

[77]   Data Protection Regulation (n 5) art. 19(2b).
[78]   Data Protection Regulation (n 5) art. 26(d).
[79]   Christopher Millard, Ian Walden, W. Kuan Hon and Alan Cunningham, 'Response to the UK Ministry of Justice's Call for Evidence on the European Commission's Data Protection Proposals' (5 March 2012) Queen Mary, University of London, 6, www.cloudlegal.ccls.qmul.ac.uk/docs/65220.pdf, accessed 2 July 2014.

processors.[80] These requirements apply to cloud providers being processors despite the fact that they may not know that the controlling customer is processing personal data as they are only supplying the capabilities for various possible processing activities.[81]

However, the processor must ensure that it has retained the right to transfer the data to a sub-processor under its contract with the controller. In any case, the sub-processor must adhere to the minimum data protection requirements set by the controller in its contract with the processor. No further extension of powers is allowed as the processor cannot transfer more power to the sub-processor than what the processor has been given by the controller. Thus once personal data is transferred to the US from an EU controller under the Safe Harbor agreement the US processor must then ensure that its subsequent processor in the US is also registered with the Department of Commerce under the Safe Harbor agreement. If the subsequent processor intends to transfer the data abroad to a third country, one of the exceptions under the DPR must also apply to the transfer as if the data were transferred from an EU location directly. Such an approach is necessary to ensure that the data protection level advocated by the EU is maintained. In practice there is no possibility of legally imposing these obligations directly through the DPR on such a third party.[82] However, the processor could be liable as party to the Safe Harbor agreement or for a breach of the contractual arrangement or the BCR entered into with the controller. The proposed DPR would allow for fines of up to 5 per cent of the worldwide turnover of the corporation in breach, which should act as a strong deterrent.[83]

C. Information Policies

In order for a cloud customer to effectively exercise his or her rights, knowledge of the actions undertaken by the cloud provider are necessary. In this regard, the DPR requires that the data subject be informed about the purpose, type and duration of the data collected as well as any disclosure to third parties or the sale of the data.[84] This information is

---

[80]   Such as implementing appropriate technical and organizational measures according to the findings of a data protection impact assessment under Article 33.

[81]   Weber and Staiger (n 2) N 97.

[82]   Although a contractual agreement is possible, a third-party independent certification is often agreed upon.

[83]   Data Protection Regulation (n 5) art. 79(2a)(c).

[84]   Ibid art. 13a.

essential for the data subject to determine whether or not the agreed use of his or her data has been violated and in order for him or her to enforce and protect his or her rights. Once the data subject is aware of third party disclosures or transfers to another country with which he does not agree, the previously given consent can be withdrawn.[85] The right to withdraw such consent is a pillar of the data subject's rights. Unless one of the standard scenarios of data transfers to third countries under an adequacy decision is present the data subject might find that the safeguards taken in an individual case are inadequate and thus object to the transfer on these grounds.[86] Additionally the controller must provide information where it has identified through an impact assessment that the data subject's personal data may be at high risk.[87]

Any withdrawal of consent must be made to be as easy as was giving consent to the processing of the personal data in the first place. In order to comply with this requirement cloud providers must establish procedures for the withdrawal of consent and offer an effective way for withdrawing consent, for example through completing an online form. Nevertheless, once consent is withdrawn, in most cases the cloud provider will no longer be able to offer its services to the customer. Thus a right to terminate the relationship must be included in the cloud contract with the customer.[88]

In addition to the basic requirement of consent, the DPR requires the consent to be narrowly tailored. It must be limited to the purpose for which the data is processed and not include a general right to process the data under the contractual relationship. It shall lose its validity once the purpose for which the consent was given ceases to exist. However, the cloud provider is also prevented from making its service conditional on the consent to the processing of data that is not necessary for the execution of the contract or the provision of service.[89]

Once the above-mentioned particulars[90] have been supplied, the controller must provide specific information as to whether or not a transfer to a third country is intended. This includes information as to whether or not an adequacy decision exists in regard to the country in question, or whether a transfer is intended under articles 42–3 or 44(1)(h) of the DPR,

---

[85]   Ibid art. 7(3).

[86]   Ibid art. 14(1)(g).

[87]   Ibid art. 14(1)(h).

[88]   Generally, this would include a deletion requirement for the data upon termination. Article 29 Working Party (n 31) 3.1.4.3.

[89]   Data Protection Regulation (n 5) art. 7(4).

[90]   Ibid art. 13a.

in which case reference to the appropriate safeguards has to be made together with the means to obtain a copy of them.[91]

D.   Disclosure to Third Parties

In light of the current international developments in the area of surveillance, cloud customers must inform themselves about third party access when storing or processing data in the cloud. Under current US law (the Foreign Intelligence Surveillance Act[92] (FISA) and the Patriot Act[93]), government agencies have extensive rights in accessing data on US servers as well as data stored internationally by a US company. The access rights to the data of US citizens are limited. However, there are no boundaries to the right to access the data of foreign nationals or companies once it is determined that no infringement of a US citizen's constitutional rights is likely to be involved.[94]

As current developments have shown, personal data will need further protection going beyond the Safe Harbor agreement as the current legal boundaries are not sufficient to protect a party from government and third party access. A cloud contract should address this issue and in particular the extent and support of the cloud provider in resisting a request for information from a third party. Under no circumstances should the cloud provider contractually be allowed to voluntarily disclose information. The US has allowed such disclosure and excluded any liability by the cloud provider under the FISA's disclosure provision.[95] This stands in strong contrast to the European requirements under which the controller must inform the data subject of any disclosure to public authorities within a period of 12 months after giving the notice required under article 13a DPR.[96]

Besides the clear-cut distinction between a cloud provider requiring access to data during cloud hosting and simple data storage, another dimension that needs to be considered is social media in the cloud. In this context, the disclosure of personal data is essential for the cloud service to work as the received data forms an integral part of the business

---

[91]   Data Protection Regulation (n 5) art. 14(g).
[92]   Foreign Intelligence Surveillance Act (n 19).
[93]   USA PATRIOT Act (n 19).
[94]   Weber and Staiger (n 2) N 46.
[95]   Ibid N 37. It remains to be seen if this is enforceable in its current form.
[96]   Data Protection Regulation (n 5) art. 14(1) (ha).

concept of the cloud provider.[97] This situation is further complicated through an increased blurring of social media and hosting services (in other words, Flickr: offering blogging and different interest group interactions).

Where the data is sensitive for business, it becomes more of a contractual issue and other technical methods need to be employed to ensure the protection of the data.

Not only third parties but also the cloud service provider has an interest in accessing and monitoring the data of its customers. On the one hand, it has to ensure that the data complies with its terms (contains no copyright infringement or criminal data), and on the other hand, the information can also be useful for marketing and business analytics.

The DPR would require the cloud provider (controller) to ensure that only personal data necessary for a specific purpose is being processed and that no data is retained, disseminated or collected beyond the minimum required for that purpose.[98] This provision aims at ensuring that personal data is not distributed to an indefinite number of parties and that the data subject is able to retain a certain degree of control. In a cloud environment the effects of such a limitation strongly depend on the type of cloud service offered. If personal data is processed within a company structure such as for marketing statistics, the processing goals and mechanisms are much clearer as compared to a situation in which a cloud service provider offers a cloud social media service directly to a vast number of individuals. In the individual customer context, the cloud provider will be processing the data for a number of different purposes such as marketing, supply of service and security reasons. The more complex and multilayered a service offering becomes, the harder it will be for the provider to ensure that the data is only processed for the specific purpose of providing the service. Especially as the service might be linked to the provider's right to supply tailored advertisements, this provision requires some further clarification.

IV. CONCLUSION

In light of the above analysis it has become clear that personal data transfers in the cloud from the EU to the US are far more complex than

---

[97] Lilian Edwards and Ian Brown, 'Data Control and Social Networking: Irreconcilable Ideas?' in A. Matwyshyn (ed.), *Harboring Data: Information Security, Law, and the Corporation* (Palo Alto: SUP 2009).

[98] Data Protection Regulation (n 5) art. 23(2).

the Safe Harbor agreement would suggest. Cloud providers must keep up to date on any changes to the Safe Harbor agreement and in particular to its implementation by the American authorities. Self-assessing one's own data protection compliance carries an inherent incentive to only fulfill the most basic level of protection in order to keep costs down. As there are no regular independent tests of company data protection standards the risk of detection remains low. European regulators are faced with the difficulty of enforcing personal data protection abroad in a country where such protection generally does not exist. Commercial realities, however, put a limit on the extent to which data flow can be controlled as all major cloud providers are US based. Thus, without allowing transfers to the US, EU companies would not be able to participate in the benefits of cloud computing. A European cloud is possible but would substantially increase costs, and cost is one of the main reasons for using cloud computing in the first place. New approaches will have to bridge this gap between the legitimate interests of individuals and the commercial realities of the cloud. In particular, social media as one of the main drivers of personal data dissemination will need to be better addressed by regulation. Individuals are often not aware of the disclosure involved when they use a cloud social media service. Thus appropriate safeguards in the form of providing information to the customers and establishing regulatory boundaries are necessary.

6. Cloud and jurisdiction: mind the borders

Jean-Philippe Moiny*

I. INTRODUCTION

Broadly speaking, the cloud is 'everything as a service' (XaaS),[1] provided through a communications link, including software as a service
(SaaS), the platform as a service (PaaS) and infrastructure as a service
(IaaS). It causes 'a change in perspective from seeing the computer as a
box to seeing the computer as a door'[2] that opens onto a transnational
environment of people and devices interconnected by the Internet. Some
authors consider that 'Cloud Computing is a natural evolution of the
Internet'.[3] Others judge that cloud computing equates to 'Internet Computing', and they conclude that '[i]t is also the beginning of a new

---

    *   The author is a jurist in the Digital Economy Law Service of the Belgian
Federal Public Service Economy. This chapter reflects the author's personal
views.
    [1]   Terms are borrowed from Daryl C. Plummer, Thomas J. Bittman, Tom
Austin, David W. Cearley and David Mitchell Smith, 'Cloud Computing:
Defining and Describing an Emerging Phenomenon' (*Gartner*, 17 June 2008) 5,
www.emory.edu/BUSINESS/readings/CloudComputing/Gartner_cloud_computing_
defining.pdf, accessed 18 January 2014.
    [2]   Clay Shirky, quoted by Jeffrey F. Rayport and Andrew Heyward, 'Envi-
sioning the Cloud: The Next Computing Paradigm' (*Marketspace*, 2009) 11,
http://marketspacenext.files.wordpress.com/2011/01/envisioning-the-cloud.pdf,
accessed 8 July 2011.
    [3]   Russell Craig, Jeff Frazier, Norm Jacknis, Sealan Murphy, Carolyn
Purcell, Patrick Spencer and JD Stanley, 'Cloud Computing in the Public Sector:
Public Manager's Guide to Evaluating and Adopting Cloud Computing' (*Cisco
IBSG White Paper*, 2009) 2, www.cisco.com/web/about/ac79/docs/wp/ps/Cloud_
Computing_112309_FINAL.pdf, accessed 18 January 2011.

Internet based service economy: the Internet centric, Web based, on demand, Cloud applications and computing economy'.[4]

The Internet enables the cloud's internationality: this internationality causes a need for jurisdictional issues to be discussed. These issues already existed at the advent of the mainstream use of the Internet, and are now exacerbated in the cloud. The latter seems beyond territories and beyond the jurisdiction of authorities' territories and authorities (the United States, the European Union (EU) and regions such as Hong Kong, and so on).

Section II of this chapter recalls the notion of jurisdiction and underlines the ability of various authorities to easily assert jurisdiction over the cloud. Section III focuses on how the EU and Belgian private international law (private IL) solves conflicts of jurisdiction. It defines the competence of European judges to decide international cloud-related cases, the limits to the applicability of the laws of Member States to these cases, and the freedom of cloud providers and users to choose a competent court and the applicable law. Section IV of this chapter illustrates how the targeting or accessibility of an online service is decisive in determining the competent court and applicable law. It then focuses on the related 'geo-determined' intents of cloud providers and users. As a consequence of how authorities assert their jurisdiction and how cloud providers may want to avoid some assertions of jurisdiction, access to services is limited and borders are erected in the cloud.

II. JURISDICTION

'Jurisdiction concerns the power of the state under international law to regulate or otherwise impact upon people, property and circumstances'.[5] Jurisdiction in public international law (IL) should not be confused with the competence *of a court* to try a case or the competence *of law* to regulate a situation in private IL (section III),[6] but to some extent such competencies are interrelated.

---

[4] V. Srinivasa Rao, N.K. Nageswara Rao and E. Kusuma Kumari, 'Cloud Computing: An Overview' (2009) 9(1) JATIT 71, 76, www.jatit.org/volumes/research-papers/Vol9No1/10Vol9No1.pdf, accessed 18 January 2014.

[5] Malcolm N. Shaw, *International Law* (Cambridge: Cambridge University Press, 2008) 645.

[6] See Pierre Mayer, 'Droit international privé et droit international public sous l'angle de la notion de compétence' (1979) RCDIP 10–21.

Formally, on the one hand, prescriptive jurisdiction (in French, *'compétence normative'*) is the power to enact rules of general (acts, governmental decrees, and so on) or individual (court decisions[7] (*adjudicative jurisdiction*), decisions of an administrative body, and so on) application.[8] On the other hand, enforcement jurisdiction (in French, *'compétence d'exécution'*) is the power to take concrete actions, such as measures of constraint, to ensure the effective application of the rules by their subjects[9] (for example, evidence-seeking, execution measures). These jurisdictions are treated differently in public IL, as will be shown below.

Public IL forms the basis of an authority's jurisdiction,[10] conferring upon it grounds for international jurisdiction:[11] mainly territory and nationality. Its purpose, therefore, is to set the limits of an authority's competence.[12] Since the cloud crosses territories, many authorities may claim jurisdiction over the same international situation, relying on one or another principle, which affects people abroad. It is therefore essential to determine how jurisdiction is territorially limited by public IL.

It is clear from the *Lotus* case[13] that an authority may not exercise its *enforcement* jurisdiction within the territory of another authority without the assent of that latter authority or permission obtained by a rule of international law.[14] It is, however, debatable whether or not an authority may enforce within the limits of its own territory any rule with an extraterritorial reach: does the *Lotus* jurisprudence authorize a limitless

---

7   See Jean Combacau, 'Les sujets internes en droit international' in Jean Combacau and Serge Sur (eds), *Droit international public* (Paris: Montchrestien 2006) 357; Francis A. Mann, 'The Doctrine of International Jurisdiction Revisited after Twenty Years' (1984) 3 RCADI 67; Brigitte Stern, 'L'extraterritorialité "revisitée": où il est question des affaires Alvarez-Machain, Pâte de Bois et de quelques autres ...' (1992) 38 AFDI 252–3.

8   See Pierre-Marie Dupuis, *Droit international public* (Paris: Dalloz 1998) 74; Patrick Dailler, Mathias Forteau and Alain Pellet with the collaboration of Daniel Müller and Nguyen Quoc Dinh, *Droit international public* (Paris: Dalloz 2009) 565.

9   Dupuis (n 8) 75.

10   Dominique Carreau, *Droit international* (Paris: Pedone 2001) 332.

11   Nguyen Quoc Dinh, *Droit international public* (Paris: LGDJ 1975) 356.

12   Stern (n 7) 250–51.

13   SS Lotus, *France v Turkey*, [1927] PCIJ (ser A) No 10 (Sept 7).

14   Ibid [18–19].

exercise of *prescriptive* jurisdiction?[15] The possibility of a positive answer has been minimized and criticized:[16] prescriptive jurisdiction would also be territorially limited. In this sense, it is assumed that: 'States are generally considered to be authorised to exercise jurisdiction if they could advance a legitimate interest based on personal or territorial connections of the matter to be regulated'.[17]

But the nature of that link is not clearly established in public IL:

> Although it is precisely public international law that is theoretically supposed to restrain private international law, *the indeterminacy of the public international law rules of jurisdiction*, the territorial principle in particular, *makes these rules so malleable that they may justify nearly every jurisdictional assertion.*[18]

As a consequence, authorities have broad discretion to freely define the territorial reach of their jurisdictions, alone (national/local law) or jointly with other authorities (international conventions, EU Regulations, and so on). Therefore, the practice of each individual state becomes of utmost importance.

The cloud is moreover territorially anchored, which makes it easy to link it to authorities territorially and contributes to the risk of potential concurrent assertions of jurisdiction. On the one side, the cloud concerns service providers and users having a nationality, a domicile and residence somewhere else. On the other side, '[t]he cloud itself is a network of data centres',[19] that is, located in buildings on the ground: the Internet backbone (switches, routers, fibres, and so on) is also territorially rooted.

Before long, many authorities may legally and legitimately claim jurisdiction to ensure compliance of their own public policy over the Internet and the cloud. As the European Court of Justice (ECJ) puts it:

---

[15] Regarding the States' competence and the rules of private IL, see Mayer (n 6) 537–83.

[16] See Shaw (n 5) 654; Ian Brownlie, *Principles of Public International Law* (Oxford: Clarendon Press, Oxford University Press 1990) 302; Robert Jennings and Arthur Watts, *Oppenheim's International Law*, vol 1 (Burnt Mill: Longman 1993) 478–9; Mann (n 7) 19–33.

[17] Cedric Ryngaert, *Jurisdiction in International Law* (Oxford: Oxford University Press 2008) 22.

[18] Ibid [17] (emphasis added).

[19] Rayport and Heyward (n 2) 3.

First, ... a Member State cannot be denied the right to extend to the Internet the application of the unilateral restrictive rules which it adopts for legitimate purposes in the public interest simply because that technological medium has a character that is in essence transnational. Secondly, it is undisputed that Member States are not deprived of legal means enabling them to ensure, as effectively as possible, compliance with the rule which they lay down in relation to actors operating on the Internet and falling, for one reason or another, within their jurisdiction.[20]

There, technology helps authorities enable website blocking (whose efficacy is relative) to enforce local law online and to erect borders. The ECJ recognized the importance of such an enforcement measure:

A measure which implements the national legislation at issue in the main proceedings, such as the injunction which the judge ... imposed on the Ladbrokes companies in order to block access to their Internet site for persons residing in the Netherlands ... is an indispensable element of the protection in respect of games of chance that is intended to be provided by the Netherlands within its own territory ... That implementing measure merely ensures the effectiveness of Netherlands legislation concerning games of chance. Without such a measure, the prohibition laid down by [that legislation] would be ineffective ...[21]

The tone is set. How jurisdictional assertions are arbitrated by private IL will now be illustrated.

III. PRIVATE INTERNATIONAL LAW

This section focuses only on civil law in the EU and in Belgium, in particular on the two basic questions arising from international situations: which judge is competent and which law applies? Thereby, it is assumed that the user is domiciled and has his or her habitual residence in an EU Member State in which the cloud provider has (and had) no presence.

---

[20]   Joined cases C-316/07, C-358/07 to C-360/07, C-409/07 and C-410/07 *Markus Stoß and Others* [2010] ECR I-08069, paras 86–7.

[21]   Case C-258/08 *Ladbrokes Betting & Gaming Ltd and Ladbrokes International Ltd v Stichting de Nationale Sporttotalisator* [2010] ECR I-04757, paras 43–4.

A. Competent Judge

In EU law, 'Brussels I' Regulation (Brussels I),[22] which will be replaced by Regulation 'Brussels I*bis*' (Brussels I*bis*),[23] defines which courts are competent to decide cases in civil and commercial matters in the EU (for example, privacy, intellectual property, contract and tort law in general). If Brussels I does not apply, for instance, if the defendant party is not domiciled in the EU,[24] then national law applies for identifying the competent judge (the private IL Code (PILC) in Belgium).[25]

1. Forum selection clause

The complicated question of the validity of a choice-of-court agreement can only be addressed briefly. Article 23 of Brussels I offers the possibility to choose a (or the) court(s) *of a Member State* if one or more of the parties at stake is domiciled in a Member State.[26] It also sets the formal conditions of such a choice. However, in consumer contracts the consumer is notably protected if the cloud provider, being domiciled or established in another Member State, 'directs' its activities to the Member State in which the consumer is domiciled:[27] he or she may submit their claim to the courts of the Member State in which they are

---

[22] Council Regulation (EC) 44/2001 of 22 December 2000 on jurisdiction and the recognition and enforcement of judgments in civil and commercial matters [2001] OJ L12.

[23] Regulation (EU) 1215/2012 of the European Parliament and of the Council of 12 December 2012 on jurisdiction and the recognition and enforcement of judgments in civil and commercial matters [2012] OJ L351, will apply from 10 January 2015 (art. 81).

[24] Council Regulation (EC) No 44/2001 of 22 December 2000 on jurisdiction and the recognition and enforcement of judgments in civil and commercial matters (Brussels I), however, sometimes applies when the defendant is not domiciled in the EU (see arts 15.2, 22 and 23). The spatial scope of the Brussels I*bis* Regulation Proposal for a Regulation of the European Parliament and of the Council on jurisdiction and the recognition and enforcement of judgments in civil and commercial matters [2010] COM 748/3 is slightly different, see arts 4 and 6 and, for example, see (n 26) and (n 30) and related text.

[25] 'Loi du 16 juillet 2004 portant le Code de droit international privé' [2004] MB; Brussels I (n 24) art. 2.1; Regulation 1215/2012 (n 22) art. 4.1.

[26] See Brussels I (n 24) art. 23.3 if no party is domiciled in a Member State. Brussels I*bis* (n 24) art. 25 applies regardless of the party's domicile, see also (n 32) and (n 33) and related text.

[27] The criterion is discussed in section IV of this chapter. If the provider is only established in the EU, the contract must fall within the activities of this establishment, Brussels I (n 24) art. 15.2.

domiciled.[28] As agreed, a choice of forum depriving this consumer of his or her right may only be concluded *after the dispute has arisen*.[29] The effect of a forum selection within general terms and conditions is therefore limited. Brussels I*bis* will protect the consumer even if the other party has no establishment within the EU.[30]

If the courts of a *third state* (for example, US courts) are chosen, in principle Brussels I does not apply: the involved court of a Member State (for example, Belgium) would apply the *lex fori* including conflict of laws rules (PILC).[31] However, this position is being debated,[32] and Brussels I*bis* does not lead to the end of the discussions.[33] Under the PILC, a forum selection is effective against a consumer only if it has been agreed to after the dispute has arisen.[34] If another Member State's law applies (Belgian courts are not involved) which does contain such prohibition, the forum selection in a consumer contract could nevertheless be unfair according to Directive 93/13.[35] According to the PILC, a professional user will be bound by a jurisdiction clause unless it is foreseeable that the foreign decision will not be recognized or enforced in Belgium.[36]

---

[28]   Brussels I (n 24) arts 16.1 and 16.2. Proceedings may be brought against him or her only before the courts of that Member State.

[29]   Brussels I (n 24) art. 17.1–17.3.

[30]   Brussels I*bis* (n 24) arts 17–19.

[31]   Case C-387/98 *Coreck Maritime GmbH v Handelsveem BV and Others* [2000] ECR I-09337, para. 19.

[32]   According to an opposite opinion, Brussels I would apply and a court could not decline its jurisdiction in favour of the non-EU court chosen. For this debate, see Francesca C. Villata, 'Choice-of-Court Agreements in Favour of Third States' Jurisdiction in Light of the Suggestions by Members of the European Parliament' in Fausto Pocar, Ilaria Viarengo and Francesca C. Villata (eds), *Recasting Brussels I* (Padova: CEDAM 2012) 219.

[33]   Brussels I*bis* (n 24) art. 25 still concerns the choice of a/the court(s) of a Member State.

[34]   PILC art. 97, para. 3.

[35]   See art. 3 and Annex 1(q) of Directive 93/13/EEC of the Council of 5 April 1993 on unfair terms in consumer contracts [1993] OJ L95. Regarding this question and the case law of the ECJ, see Jean-Philippe Moiny, 'Cloud computing: validité du recours à l'arbitrage? Droits de l'Homme et clauses abusives (partie I)' (2011) 77 RLDI 102–3. This Directive applies notwithstanding the choice of the law of a non-EU country, if the contract has a close connection to the territory of the Member States (art. 6).

[36]   PILC art. 7.

2. Default rules

If the parties did not agree on a forum, apart from the general rule *actor sequitur forum rei*,[37] Article 5.3 of Brussels I will apply in tort, *delict* or *quasi-delict matters* if the defendant is domiciled in a Member State.[38] This disposition is discussed in section IV of the chapter. If the defendant is not so domiciled, the national law of the court involved will determine the competent judge (for example, the PILC encompasses similar provisions[39]).

In non-consumer contracts, if the defendant is domiciled in a Member State, the courts of the place of performance of the obligation in question are competent. That is, unless otherwise agreed, the courts where the cloud services were provided or should have been provided under the contract are competent.[40] Otherwise, national law again determines the competent court. The PILC provides that Belgium courts will be competent if the contractual obligation was entered into in Belgium or if it is (or should be) performed there.[41]

Where is a cloud service performed/provided? Can this question be answered for all cloud services (SaaS, PaaS and IaaS) at once? Technically, cloud services are performed in data centres. Taking into consideration the locations of the IaaS or the locations of the hardware where the PaaS or SaaS are run would be simple, but these locations can be irrelevant. In such a case, should the place where a service is accessed by its user be relevant? The ubiquitous access of cloud services removes the viability of such a criterion. Pleading the contrary would certainly lead to unwanted forum shopping. It could rather be argued that the service is performed where the user normally uses the service, where the service provider supervises and manages the service, or even partially at each place. This shows the importance of including an appropriate provision in the contract, keeping in mind that such a clause may not circumvent the legal regime of forum selection clauses.

B. Applicable Law

1. Conflict of laws rules

Two kinds of rules/methods exist to determine the applicable law and both are used at the EU and Belgian levels: the bilateral (or multilateral)

---

[37] Brussels I (n 24) art. 2.
[38] Brussels I*bis* (n 24) art. 7.2.
[39] PILC arts 5 para. 1 and 96.2.
[40] Brussels I (n 24) art. 5.1 (b).
[41] PILC art. 96 (1°).

rules (or methods), and the unilateral rules (or methods).[42] The 'Rome II'
Regulation (Rome II)[43] and the 'Rome I' Regulation (Rome I),[44] defining
the law applicable to non-contractual and contractual obligations, respectively reflect the multilateral method: they define, in the EU, which law
applies in which situations. Member States, however, nevertheless retain
some margin to apply their own 'provisions that cannot be derogated
from by agreement' or their own 'overriding mandatory provisions', and
to safeguard the 'public policy of the forum'.[45] Such provisions (for
example, data protection,[46] consumer protection, online gambling regulation[47]), relating to public policy aspects, in principle depend on a
unilateral rule of applicability. In French, these *'lois de police'* or *'lois
d'application immédiate'*[48] have their own scope of application and do
not define which other law would apply if they do not.

In contractual matters, Rome I enshrines the principle of the freedom
to choose the applicable law;[49] exceptionally, another law will supplant
the law chosen in the contract, for instance if mandatory provisions, as
just evoked, apply. For example, if a cloud service provider directs its
service to the country of habitual residence of a consumer, a choice of
law cannot deprive this consumer of the 'protection afforded to him by
provisions that cannot be derogated from by agreement' according to the

---

[42]   Henri Batiffol and Paul Lagarde, *Traité de droit international privé*, vol 1
(Paris: LGDJ 1993) 423–5; Dominique Bureau and Horatia Muir Watt, *Droit
International Privé, Tome 1* (Paris: PUF 2007) 332–9.

[43]   Regulation (EC) 864/2007 of the European Parliament and of the Council
of 11 July 2007 on the law applicable to non-contractual obligations (Rome II)
[2007] OJ L199.

[44]   Regulation (EC) 593/2008 of the European Parliament and of the Council
of 17 June 2008 on the law applicable to contractual obligations (Rome I) [2008]
OJ L177.

[45]   Rome II (n 43) arts 16 and 26 and Rome I (n 44) arts 6.2, 9 and 21.

[46]   See Directive 95/46/EC of the European Parliament and of the Council of
24 October 1995 on the protection of individuals with regard to the processing of
personal data and on the free movement of such data [1995] OJ L281, art. 4, and
Belgian privacy law, 'Loi du 8 décembre 1992 relative à la protection de la vie
privée à l'égard des traitements de données à caractère personnel' [1993] MB,
art. 3*bis*; Jean-Philippe Moiny, 'Facebook au regard des règles européennes
concernant la protection des données' (2010) 2 *European Journal of Consumer
Law* 256–9.

[47]   'Loi du 7 mai 1999 sur les jeux de hasard, les paris, les établissements de
jeux de hasard et la protection des joueurs' [1999] MB.

[48]   François Rigaux and Marc Fallon, *Droit international privé* (Brussels: De
Boeck & Larcier 2005) 129–34 and 138–40.

[49]   Rome I (n 44) art. 3.1.

law of this country (for example, the prohibition of unfair terms in consumer contracts),[50] unless it is considered that the service is to be supplied exclusively in a country other than that in which the consumer has his or her habitual residence.[51]

Outside the material scope of Rome I (for example, regarding agreements on the choice of a court[52]), Member States' private IL will apply. The PILC, however, makes Rome I rules applicable in matters excluded from Rome I, unless it says otherwise.[53]

In non-contractual matters, the general rule of Rome II provides that 'the law applicable to a non-contractual obligation arising out of a tort/delict shall be the law of the country in which the damage occurs'.[54] Cloud providers and users are less free. They may agree on an applicable law *before* the event giving rise to damage only if they pursue a commercial activity.[55] Otherwise, for example, if the user is a consumer, parties may only choose the applicable law *after* this event has occurred.[56] Furthermore, in both cases, depending on the location of the elements of the situation, the choice of law shall not prejudice the application of certain legal provisions.[57]

Copyright and privacy are especially at stake in the cloud. Regarding the former, Rome II contains a special mandatory rule: the 'law applicable to a non-contractual obligation arising from an infringement of an intellectual property right shall be the law of the country for which protection is claimed'.[58] This rule is a consequence of the territorial scope of intellectual property. The location of the establishment of the cloud providers and the users therefore does not matter.

Concerning privacy and rights relating to personality, Rome II does not apply,[59] but Member States' private IL does. The PILC specifies that the law applicable to a breach of privacy or of a personality right is the law of the country in which the causal event or the damage occurred (or may occur), at the choice of the victim, unless the tortfeasor can show that he or she could not foresee that the damage would occur in the country at

---

50   Ibid art. 6.2.
51   Ibid art. 6.4(a).
52   Ibid art. 1.2(e).
53   PILC art. 98, para. 1, alinéa 2.
54   Rome II art. 4.1.
55   Ibid art. 14.1(b).
56   Ibid art. 14.1(a).
57   Ibid art. 14.2–3.
58   Ibid art. 8.1.
59   Ibid art. 1.2(g).

stake.[60] For instance, a cloud provider established in the US who makes information relating to a Belgian user public could face a claim based on the horizontal effect of Article 8 of the European Convention of Human Rights (ECHR)[61] combined with civil liability rules.[62] But if the user falsely represented him- or herself as a US resident (notably by using a proxy server) when they joined the service, the cloud provider may argue that he or she was not able to foresee the occurrence of damage in the country of the user's residence (for example, in Belgium). Neither will the law of the place in which the damage occurs apply if the parties chose another applicable law *after* the dispute has arisen.[63]

Regarding data protection, a unilateral mandatory rule[64] has been set in EU and Member States laws.[65] Briefly, a cloud provider who processes personal data (and is therefore a data controller) has to fully apply the national implementation of Directive 95/46 (for example, the Belgian Privacy Act) in two situations:[66] firstly, if the data processing is part of the activities of a Belgian establishment of this provider, and secondly, if the latter is established outside the EU, in case it uses equipment (for example, a data centre, cars with cameras such as Google Street View cars, users' mobile phones, a data processor, and so on) located in Belgium for the purpose of that processing. This latter criterion was abandoned in the draft EU Data Protection Regulation in favour of a targeting approach.[67]

---

[60] PILC art. 99 para. 2 and art. 100.

[61] Convention for the Protection of Human Rights and Fundamental Freedoms, Rome, 4 November 1950.

[62] See art. 1382 of the Belgian Civil Code.

[63] PILC art. 101.

[64] See Directive 95/46 (n 46) art. 4 and Belgian privacy law (n 46) art. 3*bis*.

[65] More exactly, European Economic Area (EEA) states are concerned.

[66] Article 29 Working Party, 'Opinion 8/2010 on Applicable Law' 0836-02/10/EN (WP 179, 16 December 2010), http://ec.europa.eu/justice/policies/privacy/docs/wpdocs/2010/wp179_en.pdf, accessed 18 January 2014.

[67] See Commission proposal for a Regulation of the European Parliament and of the Council on the protection of individuals with regard to the processing of personal data and on the free movement of such data (General Data Protection Regulation) COM [2012] 11 final, art. 3.2(a), and European Parliament legislative resolution of 12 March 2014 on the proposal for a regulation of the European Parliament and of the Council on the protection of individuals with regard to the processing of personal data and the free movement of such data (first reading), art. 3.2(a), www.europarl.europa.eu/sides/getDoc.do?type=TA&language=EN&reference=P7-TA-2014-0212, accessed 29 April 2014. This point is discussed later.

2. Substantive international obligations

Besides conflict of laws rules, international obligations of a material/ substantive nature could *require* an exercise of jurisdiction or *limit/forbid* it. Such obligations influence conflicts of law resolution.

For instance, it can be argued that parties to the ECHR have a positive obligation to apply the Convention to international situations involving private persons such as cloud providers and users (the horizontal effect[68]). In a certain way, privacy applies between individuals in the information society through the prism of data protection.[69] European data protection provisions (Convention 108 of the Council of Europe[70] and EU Directive 95/46) can be seen as fulfilling such a positive obligation through the transborder data flows (TBDF) regime,[71] or through the full application of EU data protection law to data controllers established abroad.[72] The TBDF regime aims at enabling the international flow of information without jeopardizing European data protection rules. To this end, the European Commission (and the Council of Europe) accepts that personal data leaving Europe is subject to 'adequate' but not equivalent data protection rules: the jurisdictional assertion exists but is smoothed.[73] Such a reserve in international situations also appears in the case law of

---

[68] Regarding this effect, see Jean-Philippe Moiny, 'Cloud Based Social Networks Sites: Under Whose Control?' in Alfreda Dudley-Sponaugle, James Braman and Giovanni Vincenti (eds), *Investigating Cyber Law and Cyber Ethics: Issues, Impacts and Practices* (Hershey: IGI Global 2011) 156–7, and the references cited by the author.

[69] Nevertheless, ECHR (n 61) art. 8 also applies.

[70] Convention for the Protection of Individuals with regard to Automatic Processing of Personal Data, Strasbourg, 28 January 1981.

[71] Yves Poullet, 'Pour une justification des articles 25 et 26 de la directive européenne no 95/46/CE en matière de flux transfrontières et de protection des données' (2003) Comm com électr 17–21; Directive 95/46 (n 46) arts 25 and 26; Additional Protocol to the Convention for the Protection of Individuals with regard to Automatic Processing of Personal Data regarding Supervisory Authorities and Transborder Data Flows, Strasbourg, 8 November 2001, art. 2.

[72] Directive 95/46 (n 46) art. 4.1(c); see Commission proposal (n 67) art. 3.2(a) and Parliament's position at first reading (n 67) art. 3.2(a).

[73] To some extent, the modernization of Convention 108 threatens this attenuation, see art. 12.1 of the Proposed Modernized Text adopted by the Consultative Committee of the Convention for the Protection of Individuals with regard to Automatic Processing of Personal Data (T-PD Bureau) in its 29th plenary meeting (27–30 November 2011), www.coe.int/t/dghl/standardsetting/ dataprotection/TPD_documents/T-PD(2012)04Rev4_E_Convention%20108%20 modernised%20version.pdf, accessed 20 January 2014.

the European Court of Human Rights *only* when *flagrant* breaches of the ECHR are condemned, to permit international cooperation.[74]

Summarily, the ECHR is neither absolute[75] nor universal.[76] Nevertheless, internationality certainly does not provide a general and automatic excuse to ignore it.[77] Furthermore, the positive obligations to apply the ECHR to international private situations remain to be delimited.

Authorities may otherwise be required to refrain from applying national law. The creation of an EU internal market and the integration of the markets pursued by the World Trade Organization (WTO) are good illustrations. For instance, the internal market clause of the E-commerce Directive limits the applicability of national law between EU Member States.[78] In the legal domain coordinated by the Directive, the law applicable to the provision of an information society service may not be 'stricter' than the law of the Member State in which the provider is established.[79] Finally, Data Protection Directive 95/46 also contains an internal market clause: Member States may not restrict or prohibit the free flow of personal data between them for data protection reasons.[80] A Regulation should replace that rule.[81]

---

[74] European Court of Human Rights, *Bosphorus Hava Yollari Turizm Ve Tikaret Anonim Sirketi v Ireland* [2005] ECHR 2005-VI, para. 15; *Soering v The United Kingdom* [1989] Series A, para. 112; *Drozd and Janousek v France and Spain* [1992] 14 EHRR 745, para. 110; *Pellegrini v Italy* [2001] ECHR 2001-VIII, as interpreted in *Lindberg v Sweden* [2004] ECtHR App no 48198/99; *Iribarne Pérez v France* [1995] 22 EHRR 153; *Maumousseau and Washington v France* [2007] ECtHR App no 39388/05.

[75] Jean-Philippe Moiny, 'Cloud computing: validité du recours à l'arbitrage? Droits de l'Homme et clauses abusives (partie II)' (2012) 78 RLDI 100–103. However, some dispositions suffer no derogation (for example, art. 3).

[76] *Bankovic and Others v Belgium and Others* [2001] ECHR 2001-XII, para. 80.

[77] For example, the responsibility of the parties remains even when they transfer competences to an international organization, see *Matthews v The United Kingdom* ECHR 1999-I, para. 32; *Bosphorus v Irlande* (n 74) para. 154.

[78] See Directive 2000/31/EC of the European Parliament and of the Council of 8 June 2000 on certain legal aspects of information society services, in particular electronic commerce, in the Internal Market (Directive on Electronic Commerce) [2000] OJ L178, art. 3.

[79] Joined cases C-509/09 *eDate Advertising GmbH v X and Olivier Martinez* and C-161/10 *Robert Martinez v MGN Limited* [2011] ECR I-10269, para. 68.

[80] Directive 95/46 (n 46) art. 1.

[81] Commission proposal for a Regulation of the European Parliament and of the Council on the protection of individuals with regard to the processing of personal data and on the free movement of such data (General Data Protection

IV. BORDERED CLOUD

Private IL rules take into consideration the mere accessibility of a cloud service in the EU and its targeting an EU Member State. As a consequence, if a cloud provider wishes to avoid EU jurisdiction, it has to geographically limit its offer. The cloud is then bordered. Targeting expresses the geo-determined intent of the cloud provider, as the mere accessibility of a service could too. In addition, it will be shown below that the geo-determined intent of the user could also be relevant.

A. The Geo-Determined Intent of Cloud Providers

1. Competent court

The necessity for a provider to 'direct his activities to a State' (the targeting) is required by the rules protecting consumers in Brussels I.[82] According to the *Pammer* and *Hotel Alpenhof* cases,[83] these rules apply if there is an explicit or implicit *intention* of the professional to reach the consumers *of the Member State(s)* at stake and to contract with them.[84] This can be seen as a 'geo-determined' intent, a kind of subjective territoriality that can be identified in the facts of a case by national courts through the combination of objective elements instantiated by the ECJ.[85]

The ECJ had to judge if Article 5.3 of Brussels I[86] needed such a geo-determined intent in order to justify competence at the location where the damage occurred. According to this Article as interpreted by the *Mines de potasse* judgment,[87] in matters relating to tort, *delict* or *quasi-delict*, a tortfeasor domiciled in the EU may be sued, at the option of the victim, in the courts of the Member State where the damage occurred or may occur, or in those Member States in which a causal

---

Regulation) (n 67) and the European Parliament legislative resolution of 12 March 2014 on the proposal for a regulation of the European Parliament and of the Council on the protection of individuals with regard to the processing of personal data and the free movement of such data (n 67).

[82] Brussels I (n 24) part 2.1.

[83] Joined cases C-585/08 *Peter Pammer v Reederei Karl Schlüter GmbH & Co KG* and C-144/09 *Hotel Alpenhof GesmbH v Oliver Heller* [2010] ECR I-12527.

[84] *Pammer* and *Hotel Alpenhof* (n 83) paras 65–8 and 75–94.

[85] See section IV.A.3.

[86] Regulation 1215/2012 (n 23) art. 7.2.

[87] Case C-21/76 *Handelskwekerij GJ Bier BV v Mines de potasse d'Alsace SA* [1976] ECR 01735.

event took place or may take place. In *eDate Advertising*,[88] involving the breach of personality rights by means of content placed on an Internet website, the ECJ decided that the accessibility of the website and content in the territory of the Member State at stake could lead to damage there.

More precisely, the ECJ has maintained its *Shevill* jurisprudence[89] and has adapted it to the Internet. A person who claims a breach of his or her rights of personality can submit a liability claim to the court of each Member State in which the litigious content is accessible, but only in respect of the damage directly caused in that specific Member State. The victim can also submit the claim in respect of all the damage caused to the court of the Member State in which the publisher of the content is established.[90] The ECJ then added a new forum: the alleged victim has the right to submit his or her claim *in respect of all the damages caused* to the court of the place of their 'centre of interests'. 'Centre of interests' is defined as the place of his or her habitual residence, or even a place where other factors (such as a professional activity) may establish the existence of a particularly close link with that place.[91]

The absence of a specific 'geo-determination' of a website is not decisive with regard to the application of Article 5.3 of Brussels I in intellectual property matters, as shown by two ECJ cases: *Wintersteiger v Products4U*,[92] a trademark case, and *Pinckney*,[93] a copyright case.

In the first case, involving the use of Google AdWords, the Court, concerning the competence based on the place where the damage occurred, deemed that:

> an action relating to infringement of a trade mark registered in a Member State through the use, by an advertiser, of a keyword identical to that trade mark on a search engine website operating under a country-specific top-level domain of another Member State may be brought before the courts of the Member State in which the trade mark is registered.[94]

---

[88]   *eDate Advertising* and *Martinez* (n 79).

[89]   Case C-68/93 *Fiona Shevill and Others v Presse Alliance SA* [1995] ECR I-00415.

[90]   *eDate Advertising* and *Martinez* (n 79) paras 42 and 52.

[91]   Ibid paras 48–9.

[92]   Case C-523/10 *Wintersteiger AG v Products 4U Sondermaschinenbau GmbH* [2012] ECR.

[93]   Case C-170/12 *Peter Pinckney v KDG Mediatech AG* [2013] ECR.

[94]   *Wintersteiger v Products 4U* (n 92) para. 29. Thanks to the place of the causal event, the courts of the Member State of the place of establishment of the advertiser are competent, para. 38.

In *Pinckney*, the ECJ considered that Article 5.3 of Brussels I 'cannot depend on criteria which are specific to the examination of the substance and which do not appear in that provision',[95] such as the geo-determined intent of its provider. It only matters that a harmful event *may occur* in the territory at stake. In *Pinckney*, that likelihood may arise 'from the possibility of obtaining a reproduction of the work to which the rights relied on by the defendant pertain from an Internet site accessible within the jurisdiction of the court seized'.[96] Then if the protection granted by the State of the court seized 'is applicable only in that Member State, [this court] only has jurisdiction to determine the damage caused within [that] Member State'.[97] Consequently, a cloud provider runs the risk of being obliged to appear before a Member State's court to answer a claim under the copyright law of that State, if the cloud service is accessible there.

As already explained, the Member States' private IL applies if the defendant is not domiciled within the EU. In Belgium, the legislator had the intention that Article 96.2 of the PILC is interpreted as Article 5.3 of Brussels I. Nevertheless, Belgian courts might consider that the case law of the ECJ would not be the proper way to address cases involving non-EU domiciled defendants, and that the mere accessibility of a cloud service is not enough, no matter what kind of legal claim is at stake.

2. Applicable law

As opposed to international competence, a geo-determined intent could be required more often regarding applicable law. Rome I relating to consumer contracts may require the geo-determined intent of the cloud service provider to apply. In that regard, the case law of the ECJ under Brussels I rules protecting consumers can be transposed *mutatis mutandis*.

The geo-determined intent of the website provider has especially been required in intellectual property matters. In its judgment in *L'Oréal v eBay*,[98] the Court underlined that the mere accessibility of a website within the EU is not enough to find a breach of a trademark law due to an online offer for sale or advertisement of a product protected by a trademark. Such an offer or advertisement has to target consumers in the

---

[95] *Pinckney* (n 93) para. 41.
[96] Ibid para. 44.
[97] Ibid para. 45. More precisely, see para. 47.
[98] Case C-324/09 *L'Oréal SA and Others v eBay International AG and Others* [2011] ECR I-06011.

territory of the national trademark, or in one or more territories covered by the community trademark, depending on the right at stake.[99]

In a copyright case, the *Donner* judgment,[100] the Court considered that:

> a trader who directs his advertising at members of the public residing in a given Member State and creates or makes available to them a specific delivery system and payment method, or allows a third party to do so, thereby enabling those members of the public to receive delivery of copies of works protected by copyright in that same Member State, makes, in the Member State in which the delivery takes place, a 'distribution to the public' under Article 4(1) of Directive 2001/29.[101]

Considering the *sui generis* right on databases, the ECJ again referred to the geo-determined intent to localize an act of re-utilization within the meaning of Article 7 of Directive 96/69[102] in the *Football Dataco* case:

> [T]he mere fact that the website containing the data in question is accessible in a particular national territory is not a sufficient basis for concluding that the operator of the website is performing an act of re-utilisation caught by the national law applicable in that territory concerning protection by the *sui generis* right ... The localization of an act of re-utilisation in the territory of the Member State to which the data in question is sent depends on there being evidence from which it may be concluded that the act discloses an intention on the part of its performer to target persons in that territory.[103]

The geo-determined intent of the cloud service provider could generally be decisive with regard to national public policy law rules applicable to the national territory. This has been the case in Belgium concerning the applicability of market practices and consumer protection legislation.[104]

---

[99]   Ibid paras 62–7.

[100]   Case C-5/11 *Criminal proceedings against Titus Alexander Jochen Donner* [2012] ECR.

[101]   Ibid para. 30.

[102]   Directive (EC) 96/69 of the European Parliament and of the Council of 8 October 1996 amending Directive 70/220/EEC on the approximation of the laws of the Member States relating to measures to be taken against air pollution by emissions from motor vehicles [1996] OJ L282.

[103]   Case C-173/11 *Football Dataco Ltd and Others v Sportradar GmbH et Sportradar AG* [2012] ECR, paras 36 and 39.

[104]   'Loi du 6 avril 2010 relative aux pratiques du marché et à la protection du consommateur' [2010] MB (this law is codified in book VI of the Belgian Economy Law Code); Jean-Philippe Moiny, 'Droit international et droit européen – L'intention "géodéterminée": un facteur de rattachement confirmé?' (2012) 48–49 RDTI 237.

De lege ferenda, the future EU Data Protection Regulation could also bind a data controller not established in the European Economic Area but nevertheless offering services to data subjects in the Union.[105] The geo-determined intent might become relevant to define the offer of a service to these data subjects, as could already be the case with the E-privacy Directive applying 'to the processing of personal data in connection with *the provision of* publicly available electronic communications services *in public communications networks in the Community*'.[106]

3. Evidence of the intent

The international nature of the activity of cloud providers and the use of a language or a currency other than the language or currency generally used in the state in which the cloud provider is established are relevant in view of geo-determined intents.[107] The use of a country code top level domain (ccTLD) appears, 'in the absence of any evidence to the contrary' (for example, a ccTLD used for a pun), 'to be targeted at consumers in the territory' of the country code.[108] '[T]he establishment of contact at distance … and the reservation of goods or services at a distance, or *a fortiori* the conclusion of a consumer contract at a distance are also relevant'.[109] Interpreting Article 15.1(c) of Brussels I, the ECJ considered that the existence of a causal link between the means used by the professional to direct his or her activities and the conclusion of a

---

[105] See Article 3.2(a) of the Commission proposal (n 67) and of the Parliament's position at first reading (n 67). The first leaked draft EU data protection regulation explicitly mentioned the direction of the data controller's activities (art. 2, 2 (scope), of unofficial document [...] (2011) XXX draft v56, 29 November 2011, www.statewatch.org/news/2011/dec/eu-com-draft-dp-reg-inter-service-consultation.pdf, accessed 18 January 2014); EU Working Party 29 (n 66) 24.

[106] Directive 2002/58/EC of the European Parliament and of the Council of 12 July 2002 concerning the processing of personal data and the protection of privacy in the electronic communications sector (Directive on privacy and electronic communications) [2002] OJ L 201, art. 3.1 (emphasis added).

[107] *Pammer* and *Hotel Alpenhof* (n 83) para. 93.

[108] *L'Oréal v eBay* (n 98) para. 66.

[109] Case C-190/11 *Daniela Mühlleitner v Ahmad Yusufi and Wadat Yusufi* [2012] ECR, para. 44. In the case at stake, concerning consumer protection in private IL, the conclusion of such contract could be seen as a condition of the applicability of these rules. See Jean-Philippe Moiny and Bertel De Groote, '"Cyberconsommation" et droit international privé' (2009) 37 RDTI 29–31.

contract with the consumer constitutes evidence of a geo-determined intent.[110] These elements are of course not exhaustive.[111]

It can be asked whether or not a cloud provider would be considered to have a geo-determined intent as soon as it effectively knows, or has serious reasons to know, that it offers its service to residents of a certain territory and nevertheless carries on providing the service. On the one hand, there is a presumption that it does not have such knowledge if users circumvented the 'geolocation barriers' it set.[112] On the other hand, measures faking the geo-determination (as a mere unapplied disclaimer) will never prevent the finding of a geo-determined intent.

Convincingly Dan Jerker Svantesson argues that website providers have many technical means at their disposal to define the audience of their website.[113] In that regard one could consider that the mere access-ibility of a service does amount to geo-determination more often than expected.[114] Most probably, cloud providers will block access to their services to users in certain locations if the cloud providers do not want to be subjected to the respective jurisdictional assertions of those locations.

The question of the geo-determined intent of service providers is certainly not settled, and in any case it needs to be addressed on a case-by-case basis.

B. Geo-Determined Intent of Users

There could be an interest in having cloud services not geo-determined to EU users, but nevertheless accessible to them. This would offer them the possibility to knowingly and wilfully subject themselves to the (different) rules of another authority, to take advantage of an opportunity they value

---

[110] Case C-218/12 *Lokman Emrek v Vlado Sabranovic* [2013] ECR, para. 32.

[111] The ECJ also evoked other elements in the case of the online re-utilization of the content of a database, see *Football Dataco* (n 103) paras 40–42.

[112] Users should pay attention to the interpretation courts could give to the prohibition of unauthorized access to information systems, see Moiny (n 68) 177–81 and the references cited by the author.

[113] Dan Jerker B. Svantesson, 'Time for the Law to Take Internet Geoloca-tion Technologies Seriously' (2012) 8(3) *Journal of Private International Law* 473.

[114] Svantesson concludes that 'focus should not be on whether a content-provider has "targeted" a particular forum as commonly is the case at present. Rather, we should focus on whether that content-provider has "dis-targeted" the forum, in other words, has taken steps to avoid contact with the forum in question', ibid 486.

(a service for instance) but not available on their national market. In this context, could not the geo-determined intent of the user be relevant in jurisdictional issues?

Firstly, consumer protection is not absolute.[115] If a consumer travels to another country to buy something, his or her national consumer protection law is not supposed to protect them there.[116] Metaphorically, should he or she not be able to 'travel' on the Internet also? If yes, it would be critical that he or she knowingly and purposefully crosses the borders (geo-determined intent). He or she would know if the service at stake is not targeted at them (no geo-determined intent of the service provider), in contrast to the goods and services on the market in their home nation (geo-determined intent of the provider). A consumer could be interested in accessing a cutting-edge cloud service not (yet) designed for his or her residential market, and knowingly accept different consumer protection laws.

Secondly, neither are human rights absolute: individuals may in some circumstances renounce some rights.[117] In that regard, consent plays a crucial role.[118] The data protection TBDF regime constitutes another illustration. Exceptionally, personal data may be transferred to a foreign country with no adequate level of protection if the data subject has given his or her unambiguous consent.[119] In other words, a user may knowingly and freely consent to the application of less favourable rules of data protection abroad. The draft regulation maintains that exception.[120] Some geo-determined intent of the user (the *consent* to the processing of personal data *abroad*) is therefore taken into consideration.

V. CONCLUSION

It has been shown that authorities may exercise their jurisdiction over the cloud and the Internet according to public IL. The conflicts arising from

---

[115] *Pammer* and *Hotel Alpenhof* (n 83) para. 70.

[116] See however *Mühlleitner* (n 109), where the professional directed his activities to the Member State of the consumer.

[117] There are limits to rights and freedoms, for example, privacy (ECHR art. 8, para. 2) and freedom of expression (ECHR art. 10, para. 2), and a renunciation of some guarantees enshrined in the ECHR is possible, see (n 75).

[118] Moiny (n 75).

[119] Directive 95/46 (n 46) art. 26.1(a); proposed modernized Convention 108 (n 73) art. 12(a).

[120] Commission proposal (n 67) art. 44.1(a) and Parliament's position at first reading (n 67) art. 44.1(a).

concurrent assertions of jurisdictions are solved through private IL in civil matters. These rules permit, but also limit, the cloud providers' and users' ability to choose the competent court and applicable law. In private IL, the accessibility of a cloud service or the geo-determined intent of its provider may be decisive. Thereby, it is suggested that the geo-determined intent of users could matter if a cloud service is merely accessible to these users.

In conclusion, as a consequence of the way jurisdiction is asserted and the way cloud or Internet service providers may not want to avoid the jurisdiction of some authorities, the cloud and the Internet are already purposefully and legally bordered. Users have experienced this. This is not new and will continue, since a global harmonization of law, and of the values and interests the law serves, is an imperialist pipe dream.

7. Information in the cloud: ownership, control and accountability

Chris Reed

Cloud users, and those whose information is processed by cloud users, are naturally concerned that they might somehow lose their legal rights to information once it enters the cloud. They are also concerned, or at least ought to be concerned, about who has the rights in the metadata and other information which cloud service providers generate about, and by using, that information. But a focus on rights may not be the best way to address this issue. Copyright and the law of confidential information establish quite clearly who possesses the rights, and use of the cloud does not usually upset rights ownership.

What the cloud does do, is to change radically the *control* which a rights owner has over the use and disclosure of information. To some extent this is a matter which can be addressed in contracts, but building a contractual framework which incorporates all the necessary cloud players is cumbersome and difficult. This chapter will suggest that most of these control problems are more appropriately resolved through cloud community norms, incorporated in appropriate governance mechanisms, and through accountability on the part of cloud actors about how information will be and has been used.

I. OWNERSHIP

The concept of ownership is deeply embedded in human psychology. So important is it that individuals tend to place a higher value on things that they already own than on identical objects which they do not, the so-called 'endowment effect'.[1] The effect is even stronger if the

---

[1]   Daniel Kahneman, Jack L. Knetsch and Richard H. Thaler, 'Experimental Tests of the Endowment Effect and the Coase Theorem' (1990) 98 *Journal of Political Economy* 1325.

individual considers that he or she has earned, or deserves, the owned thing.[2] It is also observed in relation to intangibles such as intellectual property (IP), and authors of IP value their creations even higher than those who have purchased IP created by another.[3]

This creates problems when forming cloud computing relationships. Customers will be using cloud platforms to store information which they have created or acquired, and to generate new information. But these platforms are owned and operated by the cloud service provider, not the customer. Thus customers tend to fear that they might somehow lose ownership of this highly valued information.

The overvaluing of ownership leads to an excessive focus on maintaining IP rights, even though there is no appreciable likelihood of any loss of ownership here. It also means that insufficient attention is paid to the question of control over that information, which *is* an area where cloud use presents real risks which need to be guarded against. Achieving a solution is challenging, and the chapter makes some suggestions as to how this might be managed.

Cloud customers tend to think of information ownership as being like their ownership of other kinds of property. Of course, this is not strictly accurate. Information in digital form is generally not any kind of personal property, but instead is protected by a combination of the laws of intellectual property, confidence and contract, among others. The composite effect of these laws gives customers a set of rights in respect of their information which is very similar in effect to owning physical property. For convenience, this composite will be referred to here as 'ownership' of the information, even though the term is not strictly accurate. Privacy rights can supplement this 'ownership' by providing additional control over its use, but as these rights are personal rather than proprietary, even in the weakest sense, they are not considered further here.

A.   Information Placed in the Cloud

Where information has originated outside the cloud, that information will already have an established ownership status. This information will most likely take the form of data, which the customer intends to process using

---

   2   George Loewenstein and Samuel Issacharoff, 'Source Dependence in the Valuation of Objects' (1994) 7 *J Behavioral Decision Making* 157, 165.
   3   Christopher Buccafusco and Christopher Sprigman, 'Valuing Intellectual Property: An Experiment' (2010) 96 *Cornell LR* 1.

the cloud service, or software which will run on the cloud platform. Placing this information in the cloud will not per se change its ownership.

The primary form of ownership of information is via intellectual property. The IP rights most likely to be relevant are copyright and, in the EU, database right, but we need to recognize that information may also receive trade mark or patent protection.

National copyright laws across the world recognize that copyright subsists in works in digital form, but these laws differ in their conceptions of what constitutes a work. English law, and the law of those countries whose law originated from England, protects all works[4] where sufficient labour, skill or judgement has been used in their creation.[5] There is no requirement for creativity per se, but information will not be protected if its creation required minimal effort[6] or if what is created is too minimal to be recognized as a work.[7] Civil law countries, which protect authors' rights rather than copyright, tend to demand a minimum level of creativity to qualify for protection. Germany is perhaps the clearest example, requiring there to be a creative step (*Gestaltungshöhe*) to distinguish a work from mere information.[8] Prior to the EU Software Directive[9] the German courts had held that some types of software (such as operating systems) were functional, rather than creative, and were thus not protected by author's right.[10] This is still likely to be the position for purely functional information such as data tables. Although the US is a common law jurisdiction, its Supreme Court has rejected the 'sweat of

---

[4] With the exception of databases in England – Copyright, Designs and Patents Act 1988, s. 3(1)(a) as amended by Copyright and Rights in Databases Regulations 1997, SI 1997/3032, reg. 5.

[5] *Ladbroke (Football) Ltd v William Hill (Football) Ltd* [1964] 1 WLR 273. A similar view is taken in many other common law jurisdictions – *Desktop Marketing Systems Pty Ltd v Telstra Corporation Limited* [2002] FCAFC 112 (Federal Court of Australia).

[6] *GA Cramp & Sons Ltd v Frank Smythson Ltd* [1944] AC 329.

[7] *Exxon Corporation v Exxon Insurance Consultants International Ltd* [1982] ch. 119 (no copyright on the word 'Exxon'), *Hitachi Ltd v Zafar Auto and Filter House* [1997] FSR 50, 58 (Copyright Board, Karachi, Pakistan; no copyright on the word 'Hitachi').

[8] *Brombeer Muster*, BGH decision of 27 January 1983, 1983 GRUR 377.

[9] Directive 91/250/EEC on the legal protection of computer programs [1991] OJ L 122/42, which requires a computer program to be the author's 'own intellectual creation' to qualify for protection by copyright (art. 1(3)).

[10] *Inkasso-Programm*, BGH decision of 9 May 1985, 1986 IIC 681; *Betriebs-system*, BGH decision of 4 October 1990, 1991 IIC 723.

the brow' test found in English law, and now requires a minimal level of creativity for copyright protection.[11] However, the level of creativity required is lower than, for example, Germany.[12]

If the law applicable to creation is that of an EU Member State then information in the form of a database receives *sui generis* protection under the Database Directive. For a database[13] to qualify for this protection there must have been 'qualitatively and/or quantitatively a substantial investment in either the obtaining, verification or presentation of the contents'.[14] If so, the maker of the database has the right 'to prevent extraction and/or re-utilization of the whole or of a substantial part, evaluated qualitatively and/or quantitatively, of the contents of that database'.[15] Protection lasts for 10 years from first making the database available to the public or 15 years from its creation, whichever is the shorter.[16]

From this we can conclude that the majority of the information which customers place in the cloud will be protected by copyright or database right, though the scope of those rights will vary from country to country. The initial owners of these IP rights will be the authors, or more likely the employers or assignees of those authors. These principles will also apply to information placed in the cloud by service providers, third party software houses and database proprietors. The only way ownership of IP can be lost is via a formal assignment of ownership or, in some countries, a dedication of the work to the public domain. The mere uploading of information to a cloud platform or service does none of these.

It is, though, always possible that the contract between the customer and provider might contain terms affecting information ownership. But if a sample of these terms is examined it becomes clear that service providers make no attempt to assert ownership rights in the customer's

---

[11]   *Feist Publications Inc v Rural Telephone Service Company Inc* 499 US 340 (1990).

[12]   *BellSouth Advertising and Publishing Corp v Donnelly Information Publishing Inc* 933 F 2d 952 (11th Cir 1991) (holding that copyright subsists in Yellow Pages telephone directories due to the minimal creativity in devising the business categories under which listings are set out).

[13]   '"Database" shall mean a collection of independent works, data or other materials arranged in a systematic or methodical way and capable of being individually accessed by electronic or other means', Directive 96/9 on the legal protection of databases [1996] OJ L77, 20, art. 1(2).

[14]   Art. 7(1).

[15]   Art. 7(1), subject to the Lawful User's Rights (Art. 8(1)).

[16]   Art. 10.

IP.[17] Indeed, they are more likely to state expressly that ownership remains with the customer. Typical examples of such terms include (emphasis added):

> By using our Services you provide us with information, files, and folders that you submit to Dropbox (together, 'your stuff'). *You retain full ownership to your stuff. We don't claim any ownership to any of it.*[18]
>
> Some of our Services allow you to submit content. You retain ownership of any intellectual property rights that you hold in that content. *In short, what belongs to you stays yours.*[19]   •
>
> *You own all of the content and information you post on Facebook ...* [20]

However, all service providers use their terms to obtain permission to make certain uses of the customer's IP. This is discussed in section II below, and in more detail in Chapter 8.

The second field of law which is relevant to information ownership is that relating to the protection of confidential information or trade secrets. The international consensus on a minimum level of protection is set out in Article 39(2) of the Agreement on Trade-Related Aspects of Intellectual Property Rights (TRIPS Agreement), which provides that protection must be given to information which:

(a) is secret in the sense that it is not, as a body or in the precise configuration and assembly of its components, generally known among or readily accessible to persons within the circles that normally deal with the kind of information in question;

(b) has commercial value because it is secret; and

(c) has been subject to reasonable steps under the circumstances, by the person lawfully in control of the information, to keep it secret.

---

[17] Simon Bradshaw, Christopher Millard and Ian Walden, 'Standard Contracts for Cloud Services' in Christopher Millard (ed.), *Cloud Computing Law* (Oxford: Oxford University Press 2012) ch. 3, 57–8.

[18] 'Dropbox Terms of Service' (*Dropbox*), www.dropbox.com/privacy#terms, accessed 1 February 2014.

[19] 'Google Terms of Service' (*Google*), www.google.com/intl/en/policies/terms/, accessed 1 February 2014.

[20] 'Facebook Statement of Rights and Responsibilities' (*Facebook*), www.facebook.com/legal/terms, accessed 1 February 2014.

Many jurisdictions, including England, also protect non-commercial information which is confidential in nature and has been received subject to an obligation of confidence, express or implied.[21]

Much of the information uploaded to the cloud, whether protected by IP rights or not, will be of a confidential nature, and the owner of that information therefore needs protection against actual or anticipated unauthorized disclosure. The continued maintenance of confidence in the information is important because once the information becomes known outside the confidential relationship it loses its protection[22] except, to some extent, as against a wrongful discloser in breach of confidence.[23]

An obligation of confidence can arise because the information is imparted in circumstances where the recipient would expect to be obliged to maintain confidence,[24] but cloud service providers will have no way of deciding which parts of the customer's information are confidential, nor will customers necessarily understand how far the information made available by the provider is confidential. Thus a confidentiality obligation is most conveniently created by means of contractual terms.[25]

As with IP rights, an owner's rights of confidentiality will not be affected by placing the information in the cloud so long as all those who thereby have access to the information are under an obligation to maintain its confidence. The nature of commercial cloud computing relationships would seem to suggest that the service provider impliedly undertakes to maintain confidence in the customer's information, and this may be stated expressly in the terms of service.[26] The issue is more complex in relation to services such as Facebook or LinkedIn, which are used to maintain a one-to-many relationship with 'friends', network

---

[21]   *Coco v AN Clark (Engineers) Ltd* [1969] RPC 41.

[22]   *Attorney-General v Guardian Newspapers Ltd (No 2)* [1990] 1 AC 109; *Public Systems Inc v Towry and Adams* (Ala 1991) 587 So 2d 969 (Alabama, US).

[23]   *Seager v Copydex* [1967] RPC 349.

[24]   *Saltman Engineering v Campbell* [1948] 65 RPC 203.

[25]   If there are no express terms for information ownership, a court is likely to find implied terms. The difficulty with implied terms is that although the court's analysis of their content is derived from the nature of the relationship between the parties, this analysis occurs after the event. By definition, the court would not be asked to determine the terms if the parties had a common understanding of the permitted uses of information within that relationship, and so one of them is certain to be disappointed – see the Australian decision in *Trumpet Software Pty Ltd v OzEmail Pty Ltd* [1996] 34 IPR 481 (Federal Court of Australia).

[26]   'Salesforce Master Subscription Agreement', cl. 8.1 (*Saleforce*), www.saleforce.com/assets/pdf/misc/salesforce_MSA.pdf, accessed 29 May 2014.

members and others. Here the nature of the provider's confidentiality obligations is less obvious, because of the more open nature of the relations between users, and drafting contractual terms which reflect the complexity of the normative expectations of users is probably inappropriate. I will return to this point in section IV below.

Finally, contract law plays a role in determining ownership rights through the terms of service for the cloud computing relationship. This contract is likely to clarify the copyright and confidentiality relationships in two ways. First, it is commonplace for the agreement to acknowledge the IP rights that the various players own, thus preventing any question of equitable assignments of IP rights arising. Second, the agreement might define obligations of confidentiality which each player owes to the others, including any limitations on those obligations,[27] and agree the confidentiality position once the relationship terminates, though terms about the confidentiality of customer information are only common in commercial cloud contracts.

B.   Information Generated in the Cloud

Application of IP laws to information generated in the cloud, whether by the customer or the service provider, produces exactly the same ownership results as we saw in section I.A above so far as copyright is concerned. The author of the information will be the customer or provider (or more likely, an employee acting in the course of employment), which means that copyright in the information will belong to the author or his or her employer.[28] So long as the applicable law is that of a Berne Convention[29] country then copyright comes into existence immediately the work is created, which under English law is when it is recorded,[30] and that copyright subsists in all other Berne countries without the requirement for further formalities.

---

[27]   For example, a provider may receive demands for access to information under law enforcement or anti-terrorist legislation. Whether the provider intends to co-operate voluntarily or require a court order, and how far the provider will inform the customer of the demand, are matters to explain in the service terms.

[28]   Copyright, Designs and Patents Act 1988, s. 11(2) for England. Employers seem to universally own the economic rights in works created in the course of employment, although the position for moral rights may vary.

[29]   Berne Convention for the Protection of Literary and Artistic Works, www.wipo.int/treaties/en/ip/berne/, accessed 29 May 2014.

[30]   Copyright, Designs and Patents Act 1988, s. 3(2).

The lack of a fixed geography for the cloud means, however, that it may be hard to discover precisely *where* the information was first recorded. This is unlikely to be a problem so far as subsistence of copyright is concerned, because the national treatment provisions of the Berne Convention depend only on a work having a 'country of origin' in a Convention member state. If the work is published (for example, a blog posting) then the place of publication is its country of origin, which is most probably the location of the server from which it was first made available to others, if known.[31] If it is unpublished, as is likely for documents produced for internal purposes, the country of origin is that of which the author is a national and thus the place of recording is immaterial for the question whether copyright subsists.[32]

Problems of location will thus only arise in respect of non-Berne countries, or in a Berne jurisdiction which imposes formalities requirements for reasons other than qualifying for copyright protection. This issue was discussed by the US courts in *Moben v 335 LLC*,[33] where the defendant was sued for copyright infringement of a graphic work uploaded to a server in Germany from which it immediately became accessible worldwide. There was no dispute that the defendant had made copies of the work in the US, without licence, but the defendant argued that this immediate accessibility amounted to first publication in the US. If this were so, the action could not be brought until the plaintiff had registered copyright in the work in the US. The court rejected this argument, holding that first publication had occurred on the server to which the work was uploaded, that is, in Germany.

The EU *sui generis* database right is more problematic where databases are hosted on cloud infrastructure. Database right subsists if the database's 'makers or right holders are nationals of a Member State or … have their habitual residence in the territory of the Community'.[34] This wording has some unexpected consequences – for example, a UK

---

[31]   This point has not definitively been decided anywhere. If publication is via a cloud platform the precise server may be unknown, unpredictable and quite possibly merely fortuitous. A pragmatic approach, such as that of the Court of Justice of the European Union in Case C-173/11 *Football Dataco Ltd and Ors v Sportradar GmbH and Anor (Legal protection of databases)* [2012] OJ C 379, 7, is likely to be the only solution, and the place of establishment or habitual residence of the publisher would be an attractive choice.

[32]   *Berne Convention*, art. 5(4)(c).

[33]   Unreported, D Delaware, 6 October 2009.

[34]   Directive 96/9 on the legal protection of databases [1996] OJ L77, 20, art. 11(1).

national who had been resident in Hong Kong for several years and created a database there would still benefit from database right if unauthorized extraction or reutilization occurred in an EU country – but anomalies of this kind are to be expected from legislation which substantially pre-dates the arrival of the cloud. More challenging is the question of infringement where either the hosting of the database itself, or the person extracting or reutilizing its contents, is located outside the EU's geographical territory.

The most likely scenario involves the US, as the major cloud service providers are all US corporations and much of their cloud infrastructure is located there. US law provides no *sui generis* protection for databases which consist of factual information, and only limited copyright protection for any elements of creativity in a database's structure.[35] Thus if a database protected by EU database right is hosted on a US-located cloud server, the right will only be infringed if the acts of extraction or reutilization take place in the EU, rather than at the server. A similar though reverse problem arises if a database is hosted on an EU-located cloud server but acts of extraction or reutilization are undertaken by a person located in the US.

In *Football Dataco Ltd & Ors v Sportradar GmbH & Anor (Legal protection of databases)*[36] the Court of Justice of the European Union declined to decide where cross-border acts of extraction took place. It did, though, consider the question of reutilization by means of making the database contents available to the public. Observing that:

> Categories based on concepts, such as time and space, the meaning of which becomes highly ambiguous in the world of virtual reality, are rendered ineffective by the networked configuration of a global communication medium, the content of which is constantly being renewed and which even today remains highly resistant to the discipline of a legislative framework that can be effective and efficient only if it is set up with the support of the international community of States as a whole[37]

the Court decided to adopt a pragmatic approach to the question. In that case the Austrian defendant Sportradar hosted extracts from the claimant's database in its home country, from which it made them available to persons in the UK. The court held that the process of making available consisted of a number of connected acts, some of which occurred in

---

[35] *Feist Publications Inc v Rural Telephone Service Company Inc* 499 US 340 (1990).
[36] C-173/11 (n 31).
[37] Ibid para. 55.

Austria and others where the targeted recipients were located, the UK. Thus reutilization occurred in both countries.

It is unclear whether this reasoning should be applied to acts of extraction, but a plausible case can be made. Copying parts of a database in country A has a higher potential impact on the database owner's economic interests[38] if those parts are recorded to permanent storage for subsequent reutilization. Thus a recording in country B is a continuing part of the extraction process, so that extraction should be considered to have occurred in both A and B.

But none of these difficulties about infringement affect the basic conclusion that IP rights subsist in information generated within the cloud, and their ownership is no different than if the information had been generated outside.

What *is* potentially different, or perhaps more accurately an entirely new issue, is the question of ownership of the metadata and derived information which cloud service providers generate using the information owned by their customers. For the purposes of this chapter, 'metadata' is data about the customer's data, that is, information about the relationships between the customer, the customer's data and applications and any provider or third party applications or data, such as logs of data accesses or application usage by the customer or their individual employees or end users. 'Derived information' is new data generated by the provider through analysis of customer data or its metadata. The dividing line is, of course, blurred.

Cloud service providers will, as a matter of course, generate and store metadata whilst providing their services.[39] The purpose of producing this information is both to enable and enhance the customer's use of the service, and also for the provider's own management purposes, such as for charging or billing customers. Additionally, the fact that service

---

[38] Infringement only occurs if the extraction or reutilization appropriates a substantial part of the economic value of the database – C-203/02 *British Horseracing Board Ltd and Others v William Hill Organization Ltd* [2004] paras 78–80.

[39] Metadata presents known privacy risks, and thus in many countries telecoms service providers are limited in the metadata they can collect – Directive 2002/58/EC of the European Parliament and of the Council of 12 July 2002 concerning the processing of personal data and the protection of privacy in the electronic communications sector [2002] OJ L201/37, arts 6 and 9. It is not suggested here that ownership rights require regulation of this kind, but as section II demonstrates, there are real risks to confidentiality that might not be adequately addressable through contract, particularly in the case of consumers. This point will form an element of future work on this topic.

providers have possession of and technological control over the customer's information allows them to use data mining[40] tools to trawl through customer information, either individually or on a collective basis, and thereby generate new and potentially valuable information. As a hypothetical example, a service provider with a number of motor insurers as customers could mine their data to extract information on the accident rates and types for different makes and models of vehicle. As a real example, Facebook and Google collect metadata and mine customer information to generate new information about their customers' interests, activities and preferences. This new information can be exploited commercially, often for marketing purposes, and is part of the 'price' which customers (to an extent unknowingly) pay for their use of these ostensibly 'free' services.

None of these activities present any threat to a customer's ownership of IP rights in information, but they do have a potential impact on its confidentiality. That impact is small if the provider is only using this derived information for its internal activities of running the service, and in any event the provider will have an express or implied licence to do so. The danger of breach of confidentiality is increased, however, once the provider discloses the derived information to third parties.

There is, unsurprisingly, no known instance of a cloud service provider deliberately exploiting derived information which identifiably links to its customers without first obtaining the customer's consent (as do Google and Facebook, for example). This would be commercial suicide once the fact became known. Instead, providers aggregate customer information, analyse that data and exploit the results. In theory the data are anonymized, so there is no risk of a breach of confidence.

Unfortunately anonymization of data is not a complete safeguard against confidentiality breaches. In a recent article Paul Ohm has alerted lawyers to advances in reidentification science, which uses the recombination of separate databases to build connections between items of data and thereby identify the person to whom they relate.[41] A service provider's obligation is probably only to take reasonable care to preserve confidentiality[42] and not absolute, and so the provider will have fulfilled this obligation if the derived information cannot, in the light of the state of technology at the time, foreseeably identify the customer via the use of

---

[40] Jiawei Han and Micheline Kamber, *Data Mining: Concepts and Techniques* (3rd ed., Burlington Massachusetts, Morgan Kaufmann 2011).

[41] Paul Ohm, 'Broken Promises of Privacy: Responding to the Surprising Failure of Anonymization' (2010) *UCLA LR* 1701.

[42] *Weld-Blundell v Stephens* [1919] 1 KB 520.

reidentification technology. However, a wise provider will need to keep alert to new developments in reidentification, as a failure to adapt to new technologies can also amount to a failure to take reasonable care.[43]

II. CONTROL

If cloud use presents few threats to the ownership of information, what are the real problems? To answer this we must switch our attention from ownership to questions of use.

One important side effect of owning something is that the owner can control its use by others. Information presents a particular difficulty here because it is by its nature a *non-rivalrous* good. Its possession, use or enjoyment by one person does not prevent any other person from also possessing, using or enjoying it. Thus in order to restrict the use of information by others, something needs to be done to make the work *excludable*, or in other words to ensure that it cannot be used unless the owner agrees. One way in which a cloud user might do this is via technical restrictions, such as encrypting the information so that no one else can use it. But encryption has drawbacks as well as advantages, and so users often rely on the laws of intellectual property or confidence, each of which grants rights which enable the owner of information to control some or all uses of that work.

But in order for a cloud service to work, the service provider must necessarily make some uses of the customer's information. The terms of service will grant permission for this, in the form of a licence. So far as the customer is concerned, ownership of the information now becomes irrelevant as a means of controlling its use. Instead, the customer needs to be certain that the licence does not permit uses which the customer would wish to constrain.

This is where the real problem lies, and there are several reasons why it is an intractable problem.

First, the actual uses of information which the service provider makes are largely invisible to the customer. This is because of information's non-rivalrousness: no matter what the provider is doing with the information, the customer can continue to use it unhindered. This is very different from physical property – for example, if I lend my car to another I cannot use it myself, and can to some extent monitor the borrower's use, perhaps by checking the distance driven and inspecting

---

[43]   *The TJ Hooper* (1932) 60 F 2d 737 (ship-to-shore radio).

the car for damage. All that most cloud customers can do to discover the likely uses of their information is to read the disclosures made by the provider, either in the terms of service or the service description. As we shall see, these are unlikely to be very informative.

Secondly, the service provider is likely to have little knowledge of any limitations the customer would wish to place on use of information. Indeed, each customer is likely to desire different restrictions, or at least would do so if the matter had been considered. Further, the provider is likely to be very unsure about its future plans and how they will require use of customer information: cloud business models are evolving rapidly and are very different from what they were even two years ago. All this leads to very open drafting of licence terms, under which the provider is granted a wide range of permissions to use customer information.

Finally, even if customers were to stop relying on information ownership to control use, there is little or no scope to negotiate terms of service. The vast majority of cloud services are sold as commodities, which customers can either take or leave. Even in major commercial cloud transactions, the scope for negotiating limitations on information use is very limited.[44]

If we return to the cloud service provider terms mentioned in section I.A we will see that these licence terms define the provider's use rights very broadly. Dropbox takes the least expansive licence, but even so is entitled to do anything with the customer's information which is necessary to provide the service.[45] Google goes substantially further, also taking rights to do whatever is needed to develop new services:

> The rights you grant in this license are for the limited purpose of operating, promoting, and improving our Services, and to develop new ones.[46]

It is worth noting that neither Dropbox nor Google give any detail about what uses they might make of customer information, so that these licence terms are really no more than promises about the motives and purposes behind whatever uses they decide to make.

---

[44] W. Kuan Hon, Christopher Millard and Ian Walden, 'Negotiated Contracts for Cloud Services' in Millard (ed.) (n 17) ch. 4.

[45] 'Dropbox Terms of Service' (n 18): 'We may need your permission to do things you ask us to do with your stuff, for example, hosting your files, or sharing them at your direction ... You give us the permissions we need to do those things solely to provide the Services'.

[46] 'Google Terms of Service' (n 19).

Facebook takes by far the most extensive use rights over its customers' information:

> you grant us a non-exclusive, transferable, sub-licensable, royalty-free, world-wide license to use any IP content that you post on or in connection with Facebook (IP License). This IP License ends when you delete your IP content or your account unless your content has been shared with others, and they have not deleted it.[47]

This term allows Facebook to make any use of the information, for whatever purpose it desires, without limitation of any kind except after the information or the customer's account has been deleted.

The more detailed examination of cloud terms of service in Chapter 12 indicates some of the other ways in which terms are drafted in favour of service providers and permit a wide range of uses of customer information.

This position is clearly unsatisfactory from the customer's perspective, and ought to be seen as unsatisfactory by service providers as well. To persuade customers to adopt the undoubted benefits of migrating to the cloud, providers need to overcome their customers' fears and doubts. And given the high value placed on information ownership, as we saw at the beginning of this chapter, vague and open licence terms are highly unlikely to be persuasive.

But moving from the current situation where terms are necessarily drafted by service providers and not open to negotiation is clearly difficult. How it might be achieved is the subject of the next sections of this chapter.

III. ACCOUNTABILITY

Many authors have suggested that the concept of accountability could, when applied to cloud computing, help mitigate the risks of information misuse, particularly in respect of privacy, confidentiality and IP rights.[48] There are numerous definitions of accountability, but all have two elements in common: transparency about how information is intended to

---

[47] 'Facebook Statement of Rights and Responsibilities' (n 20).

[48] Daniel J. Weitzner, Harold Abelson, Tim Berners-Lee, Joan Feigenbaum, James Hendler and Gerald Jay Sussman, 'Information Accountability' (2008) 51(6) *Communications of the ACM* 82; Siani Pearson, 'Towards Accountability in the Cloud' (2011) *IEE Internet Computing* July/August 64.

be stored and processed; and verification of what has actually happened to that information. Some add a third element, remediation.[49]

To achieve greater control over information uses a cloud customer needs first to know, or to be able to discover, what uses are actually being made of each relevant piece of information. Because cloud services are often layered, with different elements of the service being provided by different providers, the customer will want to know *who* is storing and processing the information. There may be a need to know *where* it is being stored and processed, for example, for data protection compliance purposes. Customers will certainly want to discover any disclosures or other uses of the information which go beyond what is necessary for the provision of the service. They will want to know the likelihood of these things in advance so that they can decide whether to enter into that particular cloud relationship – this requires transparency. They will also want to know whether what was supposed to happen did actually happen, and if anything which was not supposed to happen occurred – this can be achieved through verification.

Remediation can either be built into the accountability system itself, or effected through external organizations such as courts and regulators.

Much of the academic literature on accountability relates to the governance of transnational institutions. In this context accountability requires a decision-maker to explain how it arrived at its decision, which in turn permits those affected by the decision to question the justifications or challenge the outcome. All are agreed that a fundamental prerequisite for accountability is transparency.[50] According to Hale, transparency:

---

[49] Andreas Schedler, 'Conceptualizing Accountability' in Andreas Schedler, Larry Diamond and Marc F. Plattner (eds), *Self-Restraining State: Power and Accountability in New Democracies* (Boulder Colorado: Lynne Rienner Publishers 1999) chs 2, 13, 17: 'A is accountable to B when A is obliged to inform B about A's (past or future) actions and decisions, or justify them and to be punished in the case of misconduct'; see also Weitzner et al. (n 48) 86: 'Information accountability means that information usage should be transparent so it is possible to determine whether a use is appropriate under a given set of rules'.

[50] Josep Ibáñez, 'Who Governs the Internet? The Emerging Regime of e-Commerce' in Jean-Christophe Graz and Andreas Nölke (eds), *Transnational Private Governance and Its Limits* (London: Routledge 2008) 142, 153.

has become the international community's standard response to accountability concerns at international institutions, appearing in the pronouncements of government and international officials, corporate executives, and activists alike.[51]

Transparency requires an organization to disclose all the information which is necessary for outsiders to determine if it is acting properly. It confers on them, at least in theory, 'the ability to know what an actor is doing and the ability to make that actor do something else'.[52]

Hale argues that transparency, on its own, goes a substantial distance towards holding a transnational actor to account. The three mechanisms of market pressure, public criticism and internal norms act as powerful enforcement mechanisms in many cases. Market pressure works through the decisions of suppliers and customers; in the cloud context, customers will be more likely to choose a service provider whose proposed and actual uses of their information are acceptable. Providers will tend to modify their information uses in order to attract customers. Public criticism acts intangibly, but there is evidence that it, too, works to change behaviour.[53]

In the cloud context, Facebook provides a useful case study of how transparency can lead to changes in information use. In 2007 Facebook launched Beacon, an advertisement system which, when a Facebook user transacted with a partner company, immediately posted details of the transaction to that user's Facebook newsfeed. As a consequence, these details were sent to other Facebook users who subscribed to that newsfeed.[54] User opposition grew rapidly, and within a month Beacon was changed to an opt-in system, rather than opt-out.[55] All this was a

---

[51]   Thomas N. Hale, 'Transparency, Accountability, and Global Governance' (2008) 14 *Global Governance* 73.

[52]   Ibid 75.

[53]   Hale cites the World Bank Inspection Panel, pointing out that the mere release of information was sufficient to change behaviour in over half of the cases examined, and to produce substantial change in a quarter of them – ibid 83–5; see also the series of reversals of privacy policy by software as a service (SaaS) provider Facebook, following widespread public criticism – Chris Reed, *Making Laws for Cyberspace* (Oxford: Oxford University Press 2012) 213–14.

[54]   For example, it is reported that one user purchased a diamond as a present for his wife, and was naturally upset when she immediately learned about it via Facebook, 'Facebook's Beacon Settlement Approved by Judge' (*Inside Facebook*), www.insidefacebook.com/2010/03/18/facebooks-beacon-settlement-approved-by-judge/, accessed 1 February 2014.

[55]   Mark Zuckerberg, 'Thoughts on Beacon' (*Facebook*, 5 December 2007), http://blog.facebook.com/blog.php?post=7584397130, accessed 1 February 2014.

consequence of transparency. Subsequent remediation, as a result of the settlement in a class action brought by Facebook users, led to Beacon's final discontinuance in 2009 and the establishment of a Privacy Foundation for Facebook.[56]

A mere 18 months later in February 2009, Facebook generated more controversy when it unilaterally deleted a section from its terms which read:

> You may remove your User Content from the Site at any time. If you choose to remove your User Content, the licence granted above shall automatically expire, however you acknowledge that the Company may retain archived copies of your User Content.

The effect of deleting this term was that Facebook would have unlimited rights to use content indefinitely, under the licence granted when users signed up. As we have seen, this licence permits use by Facebook for any purposes whatsoever. Once a journalist discovered the change and alerted users, over 38,000 of them joined a Facebook group to protest at the change[57] and there was substantial adverse publicity in the media. Within a few days, Facebook was forced to announce that it was reinstating the term,[58] again as a consequence of transparency.

Since then Facebook has made further attempts to share the data of its users as widely as possible,[59] but in large part these changes have been opposed successfully by users as being contrary to the social norms which they expect to govern their use of the service. Remediation via law has, of course, played a part, through the criticisms made by the EU's Article 29 Working Party[60] and a decision of the Canadian Privacy

---

[56]   Order of Judge Seeborg, C 08-3845 RS, 17 March 2010; 'Case Comment: *Lane v Facebook Inc*: United States – Privacy – Internet' (2010) 16(1) *CTLR N5*.

[57]   Nick Graham and Helen Anderson, 'Are Individuals Waking Up to the Privacy Implications of Social Networking Sites?' (2010) 32 *EIPR* 99, 101.

[58]   'Facebook "Withdraws" Data Changes' (*BBC News*, 18 February 2009), http://news.bbc.co.uk/1/hi/technology/7896309.stm, accessed 1 February 2014.

[59]   'Facebook Faces Criticism on Privacy Change' (*BBC News*, 10 December 2009), http://news.bbc.co.uk/1/hi/technology/8405334.stm, accessed 1 February 2014; 'Facebook U-Turns on Phone and Address Data Sharing' (*BBC News*, 18 January 2011), www.bbc.co.uk/news/technology-12214628, accessed 1 February 2014; 'Germans Question Facebook Tagging Privacy' (*BBC News*, 3 August 2011), www.bbc.co.uk/news/technology-14391788, accessed 1 February 2014.

[60]   EU Article 29 Working Party, *Opinion 5/2009 on Online Social Networking* (01189/09/EN WP 163, 12 June 2009).

Commissioner,[61] but customer opposition has proved equally effective, and far faster, in countering changes to information use which customers find objectionable.

Transparency is inevitable for Facebook. It provides a uniform set of services to all its customers, and because it has such a high profile any changes to the ways it uses customer information are likely to be detected very quickly. But how is transparency and verification to be achieved for those cloud relationships which are more diverse, and subject to far less external scrutiny?

The answer proposed by the EU-funded A4 Cloud project[62] is the development of technical tools which enable customers to interrogate and obtain automated reports from providers about the uses made of customer information. These tools are still under development, but as currently proposed they will aim to assist in meeting three objectives:[63]

Objective 1
Develop tools that enable cloud service providers to give their users appropriate control and transparency over how their data is used, confidence that their data is handled according to their expectations and is protected in the cloud, delivering increased levels of accountability to their customers.

Objective 2
Create tools that enable cloud end users to make choices about how cloud service providers may use and will protect data in the cloud, and be better informed about the risks, consequences and implementation of those choices.

---

[61]   *CIPPIC v Facebook,* Case 2009-008, www.priv.gc.ca/cf-dc/2009/2009_008_0716_e.cfm, accessed 1 February 2014.
[62]   'Overview' (*Cloud Accountability Project,* 2014), www.a4cloud.eu/, accessed 1 February 2014.
[63]   Siani Pearson, Vasilis Tountopoulos, Daniele Catteddu, Mario Sudholt, Refik Molva, Christoph Reich, Simone Fischer-Hubner, Christopher Millard, Volkmar Lotz, Martin Gilje Jaatun, Ronald Leenes, Chunming Rong and Javier Lopez, 'Accountability for Cloud and Other Future Internet Services' in *Proceedings of the 2012 IEEE 4th International Conference on Cloud Computing Technology and Science (CloudCom)* (Taipei, Taiwan, 3–6 December 2012) 629, doi: 10.1109/CloudCom.2012.6427512, accessed 1 February 2014.

Objective 3

Develop tools to monitor and check compliance with users' expectations, business policies and regulations.

The scope of A4 Cloud is limited to data protection and confidential information, but it is clear that the tools could be extended to cover potentially all uses of customer information.

The most important functions which the tools will perform include:[64]

- Enabling customers to specify technical policies about use of their information, which will apply across the supply chain of layered service providers, and access logs which demonstrate policy compliance;
- Collecting evidence about information use for the purposes of audit and attribution of responsibility for each use;
- Automatically monitoring policy compliance across the supply chain.

If these tools are successful, and are adopted by cloud service providers, they will facilitate a high level of transparency and verification for customers.

An important point to note is these tools will be individually configurable by customers, so that each customer is able to set its own limitations on use and monitoring requirements. This level of individualization is not really achievable through legal drafting, even in those high value contracts where negotiation of terms is possible, because of the complex matrix of information and its potential uses and the difficulties of coping with frequent changes to contract terms. Tools of this kind are what Lessig described as computing code having the effects of law.[65] Potentially, they even supersede law in some cases. If such tools were available to deal with information ownership issues, all that the contract would need to state is that the provider undertakes to comply with the information policies set by the customer using the tools. The tools would provide transparency and verification, whilst the role of the contract clause would be limited to remediation.

Of course, accountability cannot solve all the problems of information use on its own. But it assists customers to make a more fully informed choice when signing up to a cloud service. And if information *is* used or disclosed in an inappropriate way, accountability provides the evidence

---

[64]   Ibid 631–2.
[65]   Lawrence Lessig, *Code and Other Laws of Cyberspace* (New York: Basic Books 1999).

which the customer needs to seek a legal remedy or, more likely, negotiate a solution with the service provider.

IV. CLOUD COMMUNITY NORMS

The discussion of accountability in section III explains how it might be used to enable the customer to control use of information placed or generated in the cloud. Accountability requires the provider to agree to inform the customer about these uses, and the principle is uncontroversial (though putting it into effect is a technical challenge) because all the cloud players agree that the customer owns that information.

Dealing with uses of derived information, generated by the provider from its own metadata and via data mining, is more difficult. The service provider will be the owner of that information, and so will wish to use it for whatever purposes it thinks fit. But because it is derived from information which customers own, those customers will feel proprietorial about it and will want some element of control over its use. Accountability is not a solution on its own, because in most cases derived information will aggregate customer information and metadata, so that it will not be possible to identify which individual elements of the derived information engage a particular customer's interests. Even if it were possible to make this link, transparency about uses of the derived information would disclose the provider's business partners and working methods, both of which are commercially confidential.

Thus we need to develop a set of external rules and guidelines which regulate the uses of derived information by cloud service providers. But where are these to come from?

I have argued elsewhere[66] that national laws are incapable of producing appropriate regulation for cyberspace activities. The lawmaking process is too slow and cumbersome for fast-moving technologies, particularly in coping with the rapid change which is inevitable. And because cloud technologies operate with little or no reference to physical geography, they can only be properly regulated by a globally uniform set of rules. National law does not produce uniformity.

---

[66]   Chris Reed, *Making Laws for Cyberspace* (Oxford: Oxford University Press 2012); Chris Reed, 'Cloud Governance: The Way Forward' in Christopher Millard (ed.), *Cloud Computing Law* (Oxford: Oxford University Press 2012) ch. 14.

As Murray has shown, the process of achieving a regulatory settlement is necessarily a dialectic one.[67] There is a continuous process of communication between law makers and individuals (and also with the other modalities of regulation, norms, markets and code in Lessig's terminology[68]) through which each modifies the other's position to produce changes in the regulatory settlement. This dialogue identifies the collective, and competing, norms of the community, which have to be reflected and balanced in the regulatory settlement if that settlement is to be accepted by members of the community.[69]

Achieving an effective dialogue is difficult, as we have already seen in the example of Facebook. That regulatory settlement was reached through adversarial confrontation, with Facebook pushing for the changes it wanted and its customers pushing back hard. It is clear that a stable settlement has not yet been reached.

In my view, an effective consensus on the cloud community's norms for information use is unlikely to be achieved without establishing formal structures for dialogue. Those structures will need to be properly representative of all elements of the cloud community, which extends beyond customers and providers to include those individuals whose information is processed in the cloud and national governments and other regulators who have a duty to protect citizens and ensure the proper functioning of commerce and society.[70] Building a global representative structure is one of the major challenges for the cloud in the coming years.

---

[67] Andrew Murray, *The Regulation of Cyberspace* (Abingdon: Routledge-Cavendish 2007) 25.

[68] Lessig (n 65) 85–99.

[69] Reed (n 66) ch. 7.

[70] Ibid 370–71.

8. Cloud computing and copyright

George Yijun Tian[*]

I. INTRODUCTION

Cloud computing (CC) has significantly changed the way in which information is collected, stored, handled and distributed by individuals, businesses and government agencies. In a recent study, Gartner identifies the top ten strategic technology trends for 2014, and three of them are directly related to CC technology.[1] Like many other technology developments, CC brings us both opportunities and risks. One recent study by International Data Corporation (IDC) predicted that CC will generate as much as $1.1 trillion in annual revenue by 2015.[2] On the other hand, CC poses significant questions about how the collection, handling and distribution of content and personal information are appropriately undertaken in this new environment. It brings new challenges for the existing content regulation (such as copyright law) and traditional models of commercializing and protecting copyright work.

This chapter examines the recent development of national CC policies and strategies and examines whether existing content regulation provides sufficient legal certainty for the development of the content industry in

* The author is grateful to Professor Jill McKeough, Acting Senior Deputy Vice-Chancellor (SDVC) of the University of Technology Sydney (UTS) and Commissioner for the Australian Law Reform Commission (ALRC) Inquiry into Copyright Law, for her intellectual guidance and valuable comments throughout the writing of this chapter. The author is also grateful to Professors Anne Cheung and Rolf Weber for their kind support and valuable comments during that time. He would also like to thank Dr Clement Chen and other editors for their kind support and help with proofreading and formatting.

1 'Gartner Identifies the Top 10 Strategic Technology Trends for 2014' (*Gartner*, 8 October 2013), www.gartner.com/newsroom/id/2603623, accessed 13 April 2014.
2 Willis Wee, 'Cloud Computing's Role in Job Creation in Asia' (*Tech in Asia,* 9 March 2012), www.techinasia.com/cloud-computing-job-asia, accessed 14 April 2014.

the new cloud environment. Section II provides an overview of the recent development of CC and its benefits. Section III examines and compares the recent development of CC-related national Information and communications technology (ICT) policies and strategies in major jurisdictions, such as the US, the UK, the EU, Japan, China, and Australia. Sections IV and V explore issues relating to copyright liability of CC users and providers respectively. It examines whether the existing content regulations, particularly Internet service provider (ISP) safe harbour law, are sufficient to address these challenges. Some recent development of CC-related copyright infringement cases in Australia and the US are examined.[3] Section VI, by drawing on the lessons from the recent development of case law and studies in the US, argues that it is necessary to introduce a US-style fair use exception to provide more legal certainty for CC users and providers, and that ISP safe harbour provisions and fair use exception need to work collaboratively in promoting the development of the content industry in the new cloud environment.

II. BENEFITS OF CLOUD COMPUTING

Unlike traditional modes of IT consumption, CC delivers several overlapping benefits and flexibilities. Firstly, computational resources are elastic and can be shared by many simultaneous remote users and can be scaled up or down with demand. This may arguably significantly reduce the operational costs of service providers. Secondly, CC services can be sold in economically efficient, pay-as-you-go models, much like a utility service. This may arguably reduce the cost for service users. Thirdly, operational expertise, including IT management and maintenance, can be outsourced to the cloud service providers.[4] This may arguably create many new working opportunities. For example, cloud specialists will be required, ranging from cloud product managers and consultants, to network managers and engineers, in order to help businesses shift to, and

---

[3] *National Rugby League Investments Pty Ltd v Singtel Optus* [2012] 201 FCR 147.

[4] David R. O'Brien and Urs Gasser, 'Cloud Computing and the Roles of Governments' in Urs Gasser and Jonathan Zittrain (eds), *Internet Monitor 2013: Reflections on the Digital World* (2013) 26, http://blogs.law.harvard.edu/internet monitor/files/2013/12/IM2013_ReflectionsontheDigitalWorld.pdf, accessed 13 April 2014; Peter Mell and Timothy Grance, 'The NIST Definition of Cloud Computing' SP 800-145 (*National Institute of Standards and Technology Information Technology Laboratory*, September 2011) 2, http://csrc.nist.gov/publications/nistpubs/800-145/SP800-145.pdf, accessed 13 April 2014.

maintain, the new cloud environments. One recent study by IDC found that public and private IT cloud services will produce nearly 14 million jobs worldwide by 2015, and more than half of those jobs will come from small and medium-sized enterprises (SMEs).[5]

Another study, conducted by KPMG International and *Forbes Insight*, on the status and impact of cloud adoption around the world, finds CC technology has been accepted by an increasing number of enterprises.[6] The study showed that an increasing number of enterprises expect to: '(1) move more business processes to the cloud in the next 18 months, (2) gain more budget for cloud implementation and (3) spend less time building and defending the cloud business case to their leadership'.[7] It is clear that 'the business is becoming more comfortable with the benefits and associated risks that cloud brings'.[8]

As one commentator observed, 'the benefits of cloud computing, including ease of use and cost savings, are just too great to ignore', and 'cloud computing has become a mainstream technology choice for many organizations as corporate hesitation to move applications to the cloud has given way to increasing acceptance of the cloud, especially among business users'.[9]

---

[5]   Wee (n 2).

[6]   KPMG and *Forbes Insight* conducted a web-based survey of 674 senior executives in organizations using the cloud across 16 countries to assess global cloud adoption. 'The Cloud Takes Shape: Global Cloud Survey – The Implementation Challenge' (*KPMG International*, February 2013) 26, www.kp mg.com/FR/fr/IssuesAndInsights/ArticlesPublications/Documents/the-cloud-takes-shape.pdf, accessed 15 April 2014. The survey further stated:

> Of the respondents, 11 percent were from organisations with revenues in excess of 20 billion US dollars (USD), 26 per cent with revenues of between USD1 billion and USD20 billion, 29 percent with revenues of between USD500 million and USD999 million and 34 percent with revenues of between USD100 million and USD499 million.

[7]   Ibid 25. The survey finds that: 'the majority of organisations around the world have already begun to adopt some form of cloud (or "as-a-service") technology within their enterprise'.

[8]   Ibid.

[9]   Jackie Gilbert, 'Rapid Adoption of Cloud Apps Exposes Risk' (*Austin Business Journal*, 18 January 2013), www.bizjournals.com/austin/print-edition/2013/01/18/rapid-adoption-of-cloud-apps-exposes.html?page=all, accessed 15 April 2014.

III. CLOUD COMPUTING POLICY AND STRATEGY IN MAJOR COUNTRIES

The potential benefits of CC technology have also been well-recognized by an increasing number of governments around the world. Major economies in the world have all developed their own national ICT policies or strategies (and even detailed regulations) in order to cultivate and guide the development of the emerging cloud computing industry and to balance the benefits of different stakeholders in the new cloud environment.[10] Some examples are noted below.

The US government's Federal Cloud Computing Strategy provides a 'comprehensive strategy that involves multiple levels of government'.[11] A critical component of the strategy is the 'cloud first' policy. It sets up a 'top-down requirement' for all executive branch agencies to transition legacy IT assets to cloud computing within an 18-month period.[12]

Japan's Smart Cloud Strategy sets forth a high-level plan to 'maximize the use of cloud services', 'promote the widespread use of ICT', and 'amass and share a wealth of information and knowledge beyond the boundaries of companies and industries across the entire social system'.[13] In doing so, they aim to create 'new economic growth' and bolster 'Japan's international competitiveness'.[14]

---

[10]   O'Brien and Gasser (n 4) 25; The Department of Finance and Deregulation, 'Opportunities and Applicability for Use by the Australian Government' (Cloud Computing Strategic Direction Paper, Version 1.0 April 2011), www.finance.gov.au//files/2012/04/final_cloud_computing_strategy_version_1.pdf, accessed 15 April 2014. International governments, such as those of the United States, the United Kingdom, Canada, New Zealand and Australia all 'see cloud services as an opportunity to improve business outcomes through eliminating redundancy, increasing agility and providing information and communication technology (ICT) services at a potentially cheaper cost', ibid 7.

[11]   Urs Gasser and David R. O'Brien, 'Governments and Cloud Computing: Roles, Approaches, and Policy Considerations' (No. 2013/23, August 2013) 3, www.wti.org/fileadmin/user_upload/nccr-trade.ch/wp3/WP_Government_and_Cloud_Computing_083013.pdf, accessed 15 April 2014.

[12]   Ibid 5.

[13]   Ibid 3.

[14]   Ibid; Yasuo Sakamoto, 'Smart Cloud Strategy' (May 2010) (NIST Cloud Computing Forum and Workshop, Washington DC, 5–7 June 2012) 1, http://collaborate.nist.gov/twiki-cloudcomputing/pub/CloudComputing/ForumVAgenda/2_Smart_Cloud_Strategy_of_Japan_Yasuo_Sakamoto.pdf, accessed 15 April 2014.

In China, the central government's 12th Five-Year Plan has designated CC as a Strategic and Emerging Industry ('SEI', under the category of Next-Generation IT).[15] As with many of China's top technology initiatives, China's central government authorities aim to adopt a coordinated and top-down approach to guide the development of cloud computing policy and standards in order to promote local companies and technology.[16]

Much like the US government, the UK government introduced the Government Cloud Strategy, which introduced a high-level vision, objectives, and implementation strategy for the UK's 'G-Cloud'. By implementing a large-scale reform effort, the UK government aims to solve IT problems such as wasteful duplication of resources and systems, over-capacity, insufficient integration, and central control.[17]

The European Commission (EC) also announced its commitment to cloud computing and a long-term plan for establishing 'a common set of rules to develop a cohesive market structure among the EU member states for cloud service providers'.[18] More specifically, it states the EU policies will focus on 'enabling and facilitating faster adoption of cloud computing throughout all sectors of the economy which can cut ICT costs, and when combined with new digital business practices, can boost productivity, growth and jobs'.[19]

Recently, the Australian government issued its National Strategy for Cloud Computing, which sets out 'new rules for government agencies to

---

[15]   The US-China Business Council (USCBC), 'China's Strategic Emerging Industries: Policy, Implementation, Challenges, and Recommendations' (March 2013) 13, http://uschina.org/sites/default/files/sei-report.pdf, accessed 16 April 2014.

[16]   Robert O'Brien, 'Cloud Computing in China: An Insider's Perspective on the Chinese Attempt to Catch-Up to Amazon' (*Context China*, 1 May 2013), http://contextchina.com/2013/05/cloud-computing-in-china-an-insiders-perspective-on-the-chinese-attempt-to-catch-up-to-amazon/, accessed 16 April 2014. He further stated: 'Mushero believes the government is more likely to make a difference as an early adopter of cloud services than by attempting to innovate through top-down, heavily funded R&D programs'.

[17]   UK Government, Cabinet Office, 'Government ICT Strategy' (30 March 2011) 4, www.cabinetoffice.gov.uk/sites/default/files/resources/uk-government-government-ict-strategy_0.pdf, accessed 16 April 2014.

[18]   Gasser and O'Brien (n 11) 5.

[19]   Ibid; European Commission, 'Unleashing the Potential of the Cloud in Europe' (COM, 2012) 529, http://media.cloudscapeseries.eu/Repository/document/Presentations/KenDucatel_Unleasing%20the%20Potential%20of%20cloud%20Computing%20in%20Europe.pdf accessed 16 April 2014.

consider cloud first in procurement and to begin moving websites into the public cloud'.[20] The strategy aims to maximize the value of CC in government, support the cloud sector, as well as promote cloud services to small business, not-for-profits, and consumers.[21]

Although a number of major economies have developed their own national strategies or policies to promote wide implementation of new CC technology models and rapid growth of CC industries, a significant question remains as to whether these new technical choices are actually lawful under the copyright law in various countries.[22] And, it seems that most governments have not yet set up detailed policies/regulatory guidelines for protecting copyright content in the new cloud environment.

IV. COPYRIGHT LIABILITY OF CLOUD USERS

Potential copyright challenges that both CC service providers and users have to consider include in particular: (1) the potential risks to CC service providers for copyright infringement activities conducted by their subscribers; and (2) whether the existing ISP safe harbour legislation is sufficient to strike a sound balance between different stakeholders.

As some commentators pointed out, 'copyright laws are a major consideration for businesses considering cloud computing, as there are serious copyright and confidentiality concerns once you start putting your data in a cloud computing environment'.[23] Indeed, a large amount of data or content stored in the cloud is subject to copyright protection, including films, texts, photographs, computer games, computer programs, and software.

---

[20] Josh Taylor, 'Australian Government Unveils National Cloud Strategy' (*ZD Net*, 29 May 2913), www.zdnet.com/au/australian-government-unveils-national-cloud-strategy-7000016001/, accessed 16 April 2014.

[21] Ibid; 'The National Cloud Computing Strategy' (*Australian Government Department of Communications*, 2013), www.communications.gov.au/digital_economy/cloud_computing, accessed 16 April 2014.

[22] James North, Ravi de Fonseka and Kieran Donovan, 'Australia: Fair Use Exception to Copyright Infringement – The Cloud Is the Limit' (*Mondaq*, 20 February 2014), www.mondaq.com/australia/x/293866/Copyright/Fair+use+exception+to+copyright+infringement+The+cloud+is+the+limit, accessed 16 April 2014.

[23] Federated Press, 'Addressing Data Ownership, Privacy, Security and Compliance Concerns' (Sixth Cloud Computing Law Workshop, Toronto, Canada, 5 March 2013), www.federatedpress.com/pdf/CU/6CCL1303-E.pdf, accessed 16 April 2014.

Generally speaking, under copyright law in most countries, a person who creates a work is automatically the copyright holder. Copyright registration is unnecessary. A copyright owner has exclusive rights in using and exploring their work, including storing or distribution through the cloud. For any other users, reproduction or exploitation of such a work is generally prohibited, even in the cloud. In other words, if a user exercises the exclusive rights of the copyright holder, infringement is likely to occur.

A.   Copyright Liability and Terms of Use

As discussed earlier in Chapter 1, based on the nature of services, CC services can be divided into three categories: SaaS, PaaS and IaaS. It seems SaaS and IaaS present more copyright problems than PaaS does.[24] PaaS may be less of a problem because a developer (a user of PaaS) is the creator of a work and therefore automatically the copyright owner. There is no copyright issue here since the created work is not used by an end-user but by the developer.

When using SaaS, the cloud software is temporarily stored in the user's computer's random access memory. If the terms of use for a SaaS application contains a licence that authorizes its users to make copies of the software, its users will not be at risk of copyright infringement. However, sometimes, a cloud provider may fail to mention reproduction rights in its terms of use. For example, the terms of use for IBM SmartCloud for Social Business does not explicitly mention anything on whether its users can make temporary copies of the cloud software.[25] This will then raise questions, such as: (1) whether a SaaS user commits a copyright infringement; and (2) whether this may give SaaS providers 'a right to demand cessation of use and compensation'.[26] (Appropriate reform of copyright law to overcome these problems will be discussed below.)

---

[24]   Christian Solmecke, 'The Legal Aspects of Cloud Computing under Copyright Law' (*Wilde Beuger Solmecke*, 13 September 2013), www.wbs-law.de/eng/the-legal-aspects-of-cloud-computing-under-copyright-law-45886/, accessed 13 April 2014.

[25]   'IBM Terms of Use: SaaS Specific Offering Terms' (*IBM*), https://apps.na.collabserv.com/manage/catalog/trial/termsOfUse/showTerms, accessed 16 April 2014; 'IBM SaaS General Terms of Use' (*IBM*), www-03.ibm.com/software/sla/sladb.nsf/sla/tou-gen-terms/, accessed 16 April 2014.

[26]   Solmecke (n 24); see also 'Oracle Software as a Service Agreement' (*Oracle*, 2012), www.oracle.com/us/products/applications/crmondemand/soft

The terms of use of an IaaS service provider will be a starting point to identify potential copyright infringement also. The terms of use will normally contain specific clauses on whether users can download software or contents to their computers or devices and whether such contents can be shared with others. For example, with respect to download and use of IaaS software, Dropbox Terms of Service explicitly states:[27]

> Some of our Services allow you to download client software ('Software') which may update automatically. So long as you comply with these Terms, we give you a limited, nonexclusive, nontransferable, revocable license to use the Software, solely to access the Services ...

As to content sharing and copyright infringement, the Dropbox Terms of Service provides:[28]

> You're responsible for your conduct, Your Stuff and you must comply with our Acceptable Use Policy. Content in the Services may be protected by others' intellectual property rights. Please don't copy, upload, download or share content unless you have the right to do so.
>
> ...
>
> We respect the intellectual property of others and ask that you do too. We respond to notices of alleged copyright infringement if they comply with the law, and such notices should be reported using our DMCA [Digital Millennium Copyright Act] Process. We reserve the right to delete or disable content alleged to be infringing and terminate accounts of repeat infringers.

If a user breaches these rules, they may receive a warning letter or even face court action for copyright infringement.[29] As such, before storing copyright content to the cloud or accessing contents provided by a cloud provider, it is important to carefully read the terms of use of cloud service providers.

---

ware-service-us-439842.pdf, accessed 16 April 2014. It seems that the agreement has explicitly excluded users' rights to make copies, and it stated: 'except as expressly provided herein, no part of the services may be copied, reproduced, distributed, republished, downloaded, displayed, posted or transmitted in any form or by any means, including but not limited to electronic, mechanical, photocopying, recording, or other means ...'.

[27]   'Dropbox Terms of Service' (*Dropbox*, 20 February 2014), www.dropbox.com/terms2014, accessed 16 April 2014.

[28]   Ibid.

[29]   Solmecke (n 24).

B.   Statutory Exemption for Private Copies under Traditional Copyright Law

While protecting the rights of copyright owners and creators, copyright laws in most countries provide for exceptions. This means that, in certain circumstances, an individual may download and upload copyright works or contents to the cloud without consent from the copyright holder.[30] For example, under German copyright law, an individual can reproduce a copyright work provided 'it is only for private purposes' and 'in limited numbers', such as sharing a copyright-protected MP3 music file with close friends and relatives.[31] This is also referred to as the 'personal use' doctrine. The US copyright law contains a similar 'fair use' doctrine, which has broader coverage. These doctrines may arguably apply to the use and distribution of copyright contents in the cloud environment. (More detail on the application of the copyright exemptions, such as the US fair use doctrine, in the cloud environment will be discussed later.)

C.   Exceptions under Digital Copyright Law

Most countries have amended their copyright law in response to the rapid development of digital technology, particularly the Internet. For example, the US enacted the Digital Millennium Copyright Act (DMCA) in 1998. Certain new amended provisions in copyright laws, such as Internet service provider (ISP) safe harbour provisions and the provisions on anti-circumvention of technical measures, may have direct an impact on the effects of implementing the existing copyright exemptions. For example, under copyright law in most countries, the right to make a private copy is excluded if a work is protected with technical measures, such as digital rights management (DRM) technologies, to prevent it from being copied.[32] Therefore, if a cloud provider applied any anti-circumvention technology to prevent the copyrighted work from being transferred to other users (including close friends), any conduct circumventing such measures would then be treated as illegal.

Moreover, many cloud providers may use technical measures to restrict user access to purchased content within a particular time frame. For example, users can only watch a video for a certain number of days and

---

[30]   Ibid.

[31]   Ibid.

[32]   DRM technologies attempt to control what a user can and cannot do with the media and hardware they have purchased. 'DRM' (*Electronic Frontier Foundation*), www.eff.org/issues/drm, accessed 16 April 2014.

then access is denied. If any users circumvent such a technical measure and view the video after their licence expires, they will breach the copyright law also.

V. COPYRIGHT LIABILITY OF CLOUD SERVICE PROVIDERS

For cloud providers, potential liability for copyright infringement might include two aspects: direct liability and indirect liability. With respect to direct liability, if cloud providers use their own facilities to participate in the copyright infringement, such as uploading and distributing copyrighted content, they are clearly breaching copyright law.[33] In considering indirect liability (contributory/vicarious liability), a core question is whether or not, or in what circumstance, a cloud provider should be liable for the copyright infringement activities of their subscribers.[34] For example, a question may arise on whether a cloud provider breaches copyright through offering copyright-protected files for downloading (rather than uploading), or through merely providing a platform to facilitate the exchange of the copyrighted content.

Clearly, indirect liability is the major concern of most cloud providers. As mentioned above, ISP safe harbour provisions in new digital copyright laws are mainly designed to address the ISP's indirect liability issue.

A. What Is Safe Harbour Legislation?

The history of the Internet service provider safe harbour can be traced back to the World Intellectual Property Organization (WIPO) Internet Treaties, adopted in December 1996. The treaty explicitly required member countries to provide 'immunity' ('safe harbour') to limit ISP liability for their subscribers' online infringement acts, and suggested that copyright liability should not apply to a person or entity serving as a conduit, who 'provi[des] ... physical facilities for enabling or making a communication'.[35]

---

[33] Yijun Tian, *Re-Thinking Intellectual Property: The Political Economy of Copyright Protection in the Digital Era* (London and New York: Routledge 2009), ch. 5, 196.

[34] Ibid, 197.

[35] 'Concerning Article 8' in *Agreed Statements Concerning the WIPO Copyright Treaty*, WIPO doc. no. CRNR/DC/96 (20 December 1996), at

As such, safe harbour provision is particularly important for online service providers, such as Google (as one of the largest companies providing information location tools) and Facebook, to avoid any potential legal liability for the copyright infringement conduct of their subscribers. For example, their subscribers may upload unauthorized copyright content through their website/network without notifying them.

B.   FTA and US-Style ISP Harbour Laws

Following the WIPO Internet Treaties, many countries have amended their copyright laws and included their own ISP safe harbour provisions. For example, Australia introduced its own ISP safe harbour legislation in 2000. The Copyright Amendment (Digital Agenda) Act 2000 ('DAA') included an ISP safe harbour provision for both defining and limiting the liability of ISPs in relation to both 'direct' (liability of their own infringement) and 'authorization' liability (vicarious or contributory liability for their subscribers' infringement) for copyright infringement on the Internet.

The landscape has changed as a result of the conclusion of the Australia–United States Free Trade Agreement (FTA) in 2004.[36] The FTA explicitly requires Australia to 'provide rules for the liability of ISPs for copyright infringement, reflecting the balance struck in the U.S. Digital Millennium Copyright Act (DMCA) between legitimate ISP activity and the infringement of copyrights'.[37]

This not only requires Australia to introduce a regime requiring ISP compliance with right holders' requests if an ISP wants to obtain immunity for the infringing actions of its subscribers (the US Notice and Takedown Regime),[38] but also requires Australia to provide 'avenues for content owners to subpoena ISPs for information about ISP users who

---

www.wipo.int/treaties/en/text.jsp?file_id=295166, accessed 13 February 2015; L.H. Holmes, 'Note and Comment: Making Waves in Statutory Safe Harbours – Re-Evaluating Internet Service Providers' Liability for Third-Party Content and Copyright Infringement' (2001) 7 *Roger Williams University Law Review* 215, 233.

[36]   Trade Minister Mark Vaile concluded an agreed text for the Australia–United States FTA (AUSFTA) with his US counterpart, United States Trade Representative (USTR) Bob Zoellick on 8 February 2004.

[37]   USTR, 'Trade Facts: Free Trade "Down Under" – Summary of the AUSFTA' (*iPRSonline*, 8 February 2004), www.iprsonline.org/resources/docs/2004-02-08-ustr-australia.pdf, accessed 12 March 2014.

[38]   Ibid; AUSFTA, ch. 17; AUSFTA, full text, www.dfat.gov.au/trade/negotiations/us_fta/final-text/index.html, accessed 12 March 2014.

are suspected of using the services to store unauthorized material' (the US Subpoena Procedures).[39]

After the ratification of the FTA, Australia amended the Copyright Act 1968 (Cth) and included a limitation on remedies available against carriage service providers in 2005. Many commentators believe that the US-style safe harbour scheme 'would obviously be more favourable to copyright holders and place more obligations on ISPs'.[40]

In fact, Australia is not the only country affected by the FTA. In almost all FTAs after 2000, in which the US was a party, a specific provision exists requiring FTA parties to introduce the US DMCA-style ISP safe harbour legislation. For example, the US and Chile signed the US–Chile Free Trade Agreement (USCFTA) in June 2003.[41] By including a special intellectual property rights (IPR) chapter (Chapter 17),[42] the USCFTA attempted to force Chile into compliance with its obligations under the Agreement on Trade-Related Aspects of Intellectual Property Rights (TRIPS Agreement),[43] and to comply with the requirements under the WIPO Internet Treaties, such as prohibiting 'consumers from tampering with anti-pirating codes placed on audio-visual and software products', and setting up safe harbour for ISP liabilities for online infringement acts conducted by their subscribers.[44] In the Asian and Pacific areas, Singapore became the first nation to ratify a free trade agreement with the

---

[39]   Tian (n 33) ch. 5.

[40]   Arthur Robinson, 'Australia–United States Free Trade Agreement: Impacts on IP, Communications and Technology' (*Allens*, February 2004), www.aar.com.au/pubs/ip/foftafeb04.htm or www.aar.com.au/pubs/pdf/ip/foftafeb 04.pdf, both accessed 16 April 2014.

[41]   USTR, 'United States and Chile Sign Historic Free Trade Agreement' (Press Release, 6 June 2003), www.ustr.gov/about-us/press-office/press-releases/ archives/2003/june/united-states-and-chile-sign-historic-freetr, accessed 16 April 2014.

[42]   USTR, 'Chapter 17: IPR' in The US–Chile Free Trade Agreement (*USTR*, 2003), www.ustr.gov/trade-agreements/free-trade-agreements/chile-fta/final-text http://www.ustr.gov/about-us/press-office/press-releases/archives/2003/june/united-states-and-chile-sign-historic-freetr, accessed 16 April 2014.

[43]   Chile has been a WTO member since 1 January 1995 and a member of GATT since 16 March 1949. See also WTO, 'Chile and the WTO', at www.wto.org/english/thewto_e/countries_e/chile_e.htm, accessed 13 February 2015. As a member of the WTO, Chile needs to comply with all agreements under the WTO, including the TRIPS Agreement.

[44]   Craig R. Woods, 'Comment and Case Notes: The United States–Chile Free Trade Agreement – Will it Stop Intellectual Property Piracy or Will American Producers be Forced to Walk the Plank?' (2004) 10 *Law and Business Review of the Americas* 425, 431–2 (introducing the IP provisions in the US–CFTA);

US.[45] The two countries concluded the United States–Singapore Free Trade Agreement (USSFTA) in May 2003. Like its counterpart, the USCFTA, the USSFTA also contained a special IPR chapter (Chapter 16), which requested Singapore to harmonize its IP laws with those of the US, and to import the US DMCA model to 'strengthen and modernize' its copyright protection in the digital age, including ISP safe harbour legislation.[46]

Since many countries introduced the US-style safe harbour legislation, the juridical experiences of the US courts in implementing safe harbour law to cloud service providers are arguably very influential for other countries in dealing with similar matters. Some key questions that courts have to answer may include whether the ISP safe harbour provisions can adapt to new cloud environments, whether the existing immunity is broad enough to cover all cloud services, as well as understanding the relationship between ISP safe harbour immunity and traditional copyright exceptions (such as fair use exceptions).

C.   Recent US case law on safe harbour

Recent court cases in the US have painted a fairly sunny picture for online intermediaries, including cloud service providers, so long as they 'operate responsibly, within the DMCA's safe harbours, and avoid actively inducing infringement, their roles as intermediaries should not subject them to liability for copyright infringement'.[47] In case after case, US courts have extended safe harbour immunities to online service providers.

'Summary of the US–Chile Free Trade Agreement' (*Office of the United States Trade Representative*, December 2001), www.ustr.gov/about-us/press-office/factsheets/archives/2001/december/free-trade-chile-summary-us-chile-free-trad, accessed 16 April 2014.

[45]   Kenneth Chiu, 'Harmonizing Intellectual Property Law between the United States and Singapore: The United States–Singapore Free Trade Agreement's Impact on Singapore's Intellectual Property Law' (2005) 18 *Transnational Lawyer* 489, 489 (noting that this agreement 'was the first of its kind between the United States and any Asian Pacific country').

[46]   Ibid 503.

[47]   Marc Aaron Melzer, 'Copyright Enforcement in the Cloud' (Winter 2011) 21 *Fordham Intellectual Property, Media and Entertainment Law Journal* 403, 439. He further stated:

Courts have applied this approach when reviewing the conduct of SaaS providers, such as Veoh, so the rule should apply all the more to PaaS and IaaS providers, who arguably have less direct interaction with and control

For example, in *Io Group, Inc. v Veoh Networks, Inc.*,[48] Io Group initiated litigation against Veoh for copyrighted videos that Veoh users had uploaded to the website. After a step-by-step review of the requirements of section 512 of the DMCA (Digital Millennium Copyright Act), the court concluded that Veoh qualified for safe harbour protection. In *UMG Recordings, Inc. v Veoh Networks*,[49] UMG Recordings sought a copyright infringement judgment against Veoh based on UMG-produced music videos that third-party users had uploaded to the Veoh service. After examining the technical processes by which the videos were manipulated, stored and accessed using Veoh's system, the court, again, made a decision in Veoh's favour. In *Viacom Int'l Inc. v YouTube, Inc.*,[50] content creator Viacom sued YouTube for copyright infringement based on the presence of user-uploaded copyright videos on the YouTube website. The court granted summary judgment to YouTube on all of Viacom's claims for direct and secondary infringement, and found that they qualify for safe harbour provision (17 U.S.C. s. 512(c)).[51]

Since Australia and many other countries imported the US safe harbour law model, their safe harbour legislation should, arguably, be broad enough to protect online intermediaries and for the development of new business/service models, such as CC services. If this interpretation is followed, it seems that there is no immediate need to strengthen the protection of intermediaries by expanding the existing safe harbour provision.

D.   'Copyright Gap'

Nevertheless, many cases and studies showed that the legal certainty for US CC providers cannot simply be credited to its safe harbour law. It seems that the US safe harbour law and the US fair use doctrine (broad copyright exceptions) have worked together in order to strike a sound

---

over the content that their customers place on their systems, unless the provider induces infringement by its customers.

[48]   *Io Group Inc. v Veoh Networks Inc.*, 586 F Supp 2d 1132, 1155 (ND Cal 2008).

[49]   *UMG Recordings Inc. v Veoh Networks Inc.*, 665 F Supp 2d 1099, 1118 (CD Cal 2009).

[50]   *Viacom Int'l Inc. v YouTube Inc.*, 718 F Supp 2d 514, 529 (SDNY 2010); *Viacom International Inc. et al. v YouTube Inc. et al.*, 1:07-cv-02103, No. 452 (SDNY 18 April 2013).

[51]   Melzer (n 47) 428–9; *Viacom International Inc. et al. v YouTube Inc. et al.*, 1:07-cv-02103, No. 452 (SDNY 18 April 2013).

balance of different stakeholders in the new cloud environment. However, when importing the US-style safe harbour law, many countries have not imported the US style of broad fair use exceptions. This may place CC providers in these countries in a position of legal uncertainty for copyright infringement.

VI. GAPS OF COPYRIGHT LAW AND FAIR USE AS A SOLUTION

A. Industry Concerns and Gaps in Australian Copyright Law

One example of a jurisdiction with significant legal uncertainty for CC providers is Australia. Many online intermediaries and cloud service providers are keen to have an expanded safe harbour immunity for ISPs. For example, search giant Google recently made a submission to the Australian federal communications minister Malcolm Turnbull's media regulation reforms,[52] identifying two important areas for reform.[53] First, the company requested the extension of copyright safe harbours to online intermediaries – like search engines and forums – in order to provide more legal certainty for the operation of online intermediaries. Second, it expressed strong support for a recommendation made by the Australian Law Reform Commission (ALRC) to repeal complex and technology-specific copyright exceptions and replace them with a US-style fair use provision. Google stated that the introduction of fair use would ensure that Australian copyright laws could keep pace with the digital world in a manner that continues to incentivize creation and protect Australian copyright owners.[54]

Like many other countries, due to the lack of a US-style broad fair use exception, the existing copyright law does have many potential problems. As Google observed, the current Australian Copyright Act contains 'multiple, detailed provisions which are not suitable for a digital age'.[55] For example, a basic Internet function like caching is dealt with in three

---

[52] 'Deregulation' (*Australian Government Department of Communication*, 2014), www.communications.gov.au/deregulation, accessed 16 April 2014.

[53] Google Australia, 'Deregulation: Initiatives in the Communications Sector' (Submission to The Hon. Malcolm Turnbull, MP, Minister for Communications, 17 December 2013), www.communications.gov.au/__data/assets/pdf_file/0009/214983/Google.pdf, accessed 16 April 2014.

[54] Ibid.

[55] Ibid; Australian Copyright Act 1968 (Cth), ss 43A, 116AB and 200AAA.

separate places in the Act, with three different legal treatments. More-over, basic Internet functions such as search indexing and crawling have not been explicitly covered by a specific exception in Australian copyright law. This arguably creates great legal uncertainties for a CC service provider to operate a cache or provide search indexing services in Australia.

The provision of a CC service (for example, Dropbox, online back-up of data) often involves caching, indexing, data transfer and other technical functions that require moving or copying data. As such, both cloud users and cloud service providers may be under the risk of infringing copyright in the course of using or providing such services. For example, a cloud user that stores personal files in the cloud may not benefit from the format-shifting exception because the file is stored on remote servers, which the user does not actually own. Similarly, a cloud service provider, which shifts a user's stored files around from server to server, making copies each time, may be under the risk of infringing copyright also.

The recent *Optus TV Now* case[56] in Australia highlights the issue. In that case, the Full Federal Court found that 'Optus infringed copyright in sports broadcasts by providing a cloud-based DVR [digital video recorder] service'.[57] Through the service, users/subscribers are able to indicate the free-to-air broadcasts they would like to record, and Optus would record the chosen programmes on its servers so that the subscriber could watch them later. Although the copies were made at the customer's request, the Court held 'Optus' role in making the infringing copy was so overt that the copy was not made by the subscriber alone'.[58]

Some commentators were critical of the decision:

---

[56]   *National Rugby League Investments Pty Limited v Singtel Optus Pty Ltd* [2012] FCAFC 59.

[57]   North, Fonseka and Donovan (n 22); John Fairbairn and Charles Alexander, 'Alert: Full Federal Court Finds Optus TV Now Service Infringes Copyright' (*Minter Ellison*, 30 April 2012), www.minterellison.com/pub/na/20120430_optustvnow/, accessed 16 April 2014.

[58]   North, Fonseka and Donovan (n 22); see also, Maurice Gonsalves, James Lawrence and Philippa Macaskill, 'Full Federal Court Finds in Favour of NRL, AFL and Telstra in Optus TV Now Appeal' (*King and Wood Mallesons*, 27 April 2012), www.mallesons.com/publications/marketAlerts/2012/Pages/Full-Federal-Court-finds-in-favour-of-NRL-AFL-and-Telstra-in-Optus-TV-Now-appeal.aspx, accessed 16 April 2014. They stated: 'The decision will be welcomed by owners and exclusive licensees of broadcast and film copyright because it confirms their ability to control copying of their works, particularly when this occurs in a commercial context'.

The logical question that follows an outcome like that in *Optus TV Now* is whether the exceptions in the Copyright Act are so inflexible that they fail to account for emerging technologies. The judiciary has historically been reluctant to afford language in the Copyright Act a technologically neutral meaning, leaving it to the Parliament to update the legislation in piece-meal fashion.[59]

These issues were recently examined by the ALRC. The ALRC recommended the repeal of technology-specific copyright exceptions and replacing them with a US-style fair use provision which would ensure that Australian copyright laws could keep pace with the digital world in a manner that continues to incentivize creation and protect Australian copyright owners.[60] The chapter will next examine what fair use exception is and why it may serve as a solution.

B.   Fair Use as a Solution

1.   What fair use is

A 'fair use' is referred to as any copying/reproduction of copyrighted work done for a limited and 'transformative' purpose, such as to comment upon, criticize, or parody a copyrighted work.[61] For example, section 107 of the US Copyright Law[62] contains a list of the various purposes for which the reproduction of a particular work may be considered 'fair', such as criticism, comment, news reporting, teaching, scholarship, and research.[63] Such uses can be done without permission from the copyright owner. In other words, fair use is a defence against a claim of copyright infringement. Once a use qualifies as a fair use, it would then not be considered as an illegal infringement.

---

[59]   North, Fonseka and Donovan (n 22).

[60]   Google Australia (n 53) 4.

[61]   US Copyright Office, 'Copyright: Fair Use' (FL-102, June 2012), www.copyright.gov/fls/fl102.html, accessed 16 April 2014.

[62]   Title 17 U.S. Code para. 107 – Limitations on exclusive rights: Fair use.

[63]   Ibid s. 107 also sets out four factors to be considered in determining whether or not a particular use is fair:

1)   The purpose and character of the use, including whether such use is of commercial nature or is for nonprofit educational purposes;
2)   The nature of the copyrighted work;
3)   The amount and substantiality of the portion used in relation to the copyrighted work as a whole; and
4)   The effect of the use upon the potential market for, or value of, the copyrighted work.

As such, fair use may arguably serve a powerful defence for online service providers and their subscribers. If, for instance, copyright holders cannot establish a copyright infringement by online service subscribers (for example, the users of services like Facebook) in the first place, then it is unlikely they would be able to initiate litigation against online service providers themselves for contributory liability.[64]

2. Why fair use?

As many commentators observe, 'fair use can encourage innovation and can be flexibly applied to changing technologies (like cloud servers that store and move customer data regularly)'.[65] When the US courts decide on the liabilities of online service providers, in addition to safe harbour legislation, they often refer to the fair use provision also (for example, *YouTube* case mentioned above). In other words, it seems that the ISP safe harbour legislation and fair use exception work together to provide legal certainty for online intermediaries and public users in the USA.[66]

Over the past decades, the fair use regime in the US copyright law has demonstrated a sound flexibility for catching up with changing technologies (like the Internet and cloud services) and encouraging innovation.[67] As the ALRC noted, 'if fair use existed in Australia, the Copyright Act would not need to be updated simply because consumers now want to store purchased copies of copyright material in the cloud rather than on a hard drive'.[68]

---

[64] George Yijun Tian, 'Don't Sue Us for Search: Google's Unnecessary Safe Harbour Appeal' (*The Conversation,* 2014), http://theconversation.com/dont-sue-us-for-search-googles-unnecessary-safe-harbour-appeal-24405, accessed 16 April 2014.

[65] For example, US courts' willingness to accept that innovative cloud services can be captured by the fair use doctrine, long before the legislature gets around to considering such technology, is testament to its flexibility. In *Cartoon Network et al. v Cablevision*, the US Second Circuit Court of Appeals accepted that 'a cloud-based DVR service fell within fair use'; North, Fonseka and Donovan (n 22).

[66] Melzer (n 47).

[67] North, Fonseka and Donovan (n 22). Indeed, as many commentators observed, 'fair use can encourage innovation and can be flexibly applied to changing technologies [like cloud servers that store and move customer data regularly]' and 'Broadly worded and technology-neutral, it aims to take into account the context in which copyright material is used – making it better positioned to be able to cope with new uses of works', ibid.

[68] Ibid.

Moreover, a recent study showed that 'the courts' willingness to accept that innovative cloud services can be captured by the fair use doctrine' would have a deep impact on the rapid growth of CC industries. For example, in *Cartoon Network et al. v Cablevision,* the US Second Circuit Court of Appeals accepted that 'a cloud-based DVR service fell within fair use'.[69] A 2013 study commissioned by Harvard Business School found that the *Cartoon Network et al. v Cablevision* decision led to 'additional incremental investment in U.S. cloud computing firms that ranged from US$728 million to approximately US$1.3 billion over the two-and-a-half years after the decision'.[70] By contrast, the study revealed that more restrictive rulings on cloud services in France and Germany during the same period resulted in a total decrease in French and German venture capital (VC) investment of US$87 million or a loss of 'almost US$270 million in traditional R&D investment in these two countries during the same period'.[71]

This provides further evidence that the introduction of a flexible copyright regime (such as through the introduction of a US-style fair use doctrine) may create huge economic benefits for Australia and other countries. As such, it seems that ALRC's recommendation on the repeal of existing technology-specific exceptions with copyright restrictions with broader rules (such as a US-style fair use exception) would serve as the best resolution in the long run.

---

[69]   *The Cartoon Network LP LLLP v CSC Holdings Inc.* 536 F.3d 121 (2nd Cir 2008), www.ca2.uscourts.gov/decisions/isysquery/339edb6b-4e83-47b5-8caa-4864e5504e8f/1/doc/07-1480-cv_opn.pdf, accessed 16 April 2014; see also Optus, *Copyright and the Digital Economy* (Submission in response to ALRC Discussion Paper, Public Version, August 2013), www.alrc.gov.au/sites/default/files/subs/725._org_optus_alrc_dp_public.pdf,accessed 16 April 2014. Optus stated in the submission (para. 2.16):

Optus notes the developing body of United States cases that have concluded that fair use includes third party recording on behalf of end-users. For example, the *Aereo* and *Cablevision* cases and more recently the *Dish Networks* case. These cases deal with cloud-based DVR services, allowing end-users to remotely record broadcasts on servers owned and located by the third party service provider.

[70]   Chris Borek, Laurits R. Christensen, Peter Hess, Josh Lerner and Greg Rafert, *Lost in the Clouds: The Impact of Copyright Scope on Investment in Cloud Computing Ventures* (International Think-tank on Innovation and Competition (INTERTIC)), www.intertic.org/Conference/Lerner.pdf, accessed 16 April 2014, 2.

[71]   Ibid; North, Fonseka and Donovan (n 22).

VII. CONCLUSION

As discussed above, a brief review of the history of safe harbour legislation and recent ISP-related case law in the US makes it clear that there is no immediate need to strengthen the protection of online intermediaries and CC providers by expanding the existing safe harbour provision. For jurisdiction outside the US, the introduction of the fair use exception alone, as recommended by the ALRC, may serve as the most feasible approach for providing legal certainty for CC users and providers.

Like Australia, many countries only introduced the US safe harbour law rather than the US fair use doctrine. Thus, the resolution for Australia is arguably applicable for other countries also. It is imperative to make ISP safe harbour law and fair use exceptions work together in order to promote innovative CC business models, to enhance the development of the content industry, and to strike a sound balance of different stakeholders in the cloud environment.

9. Towards the seamless global distribution of cloud content

Peter K. Yu[*]

> [A]s time goes on ... the world will realize that at least for intellectual property the days of the nation-state are over.
>
> Sir Robin Jacob, former Lord Justice of Appeal[1]

I. INTRODUCTION

In the age of cloud computing, consumers expect content to be accessible anywhere, anytime. Although we rarely carry suitcases of books, CDs, DVDs or other cultural products across national borders, many of us now store a large volume of self-created or lawfully obtained content in the cloud. Using SaaS (software as a service), such as Facebook, Gmail, Instagram, Tumblr or Twitter, Internet users communicate with others via the cloud regardless of their present location.

Since their arrival, cloud platforms and related services have posed considerable challenges to copyright holders. Thus far, many of the cloud-related discussions have focused on unauthorized content distribution through cloud lockers – the most notorious being Megaupload and Rapidshare. Such discussions resemble the earlier discussions on peer-to-peer file-sharing technology and Internet intermediary liability. Some commentators have also raised questions concerning the ownership of intellectual property in works stored in the cloud as well as privacy-related matters discussed in other chapters in this volume.

[*] This chapter draws on research from the author's earlier article in the *Cardozo Arts and Entertainment Law Journal*. The author is grateful to Marketa Trimble for her valuable comments and suggestions, and Linzey Erickson, Jeffrey Kappelman, Nicholas Krob and Erica Liabo for excellent research and editorial assistance.

[1] Hon. Mr Justice [Robin] Jacob, 'International Intellectual Property Litigation in the Next Millennium' (2000) 32 Case Western Reserve J Intl L 507, 516.

Notwithstanding the myriad challenges cloud computing has posed to copyright holders, one cannot overlook the boundless opportunities this new technology has provided to rights holders for distributing copyright content across the world. To a large extent, the global distribution of cloud content has brought back the age-old discussion concerning the proper response to disruptive technology and the copyright industries' repeated and arguably short-sighted efforts to protect outdated business models.[2]

To complicate matters further, cloud platforms and related services have raised new questions that have not been widely discussed in the digital technology debate. Because these platforms facilitate simultaneous multijurisdictional access to copyright content, they unsurprisingly are on a collision course with the territoriality principle in intellectual property law. Specifically, cloud computing has raised challenging questions concerning what laws to apply and whether those laws allow the protected content to be distributed.

This chapter begins by discussing the concept of territoriality in copyright law. It highlights two sets of territoriality questions implicated by cloud computing. The chapter then explores the justifications for and drawbacks of introducing geographical restrictions in cloud platforms. In view of the many drawbacks of these restrictions and the immense yet unfulfilled potential of cloud computing, this chapter concludes by identifying five areas in which adjustments can be introduced to promote the global distribution of cloud content. These adjustments also seek to address the territoriality challenges posed by existing nation-based copyright laws.

II. CLOUD COMPUTING AND TERRITORIAL RIGHTS

Commentators have widely discussed the copyright challenges posed by cloud computing. In a discussion paper for a recently concluded copyright law consultation, the Australian Law Reform Commission (ALRC) devoted an entire section to the challenges posed by this new technology. As the consultation document declared:

> The exceptions [in the copyright system] that allow users to make copies of certain content for private and domestic use may not always apply if the copies are stored on remote computer servers that the user does not own. A

---

[2] Peter K. Yu, 'Digital Copyright and Confuzzling Rhetoric' (2011) 13 Vanderbilt J Entertainment & Technology L 881, 887–91.

technology-neutral approach to copyright policy might suggest that whatever users may do using technology in their own home, they should be able to do using technology stored remotely. However, such a technology-neutral policy applied to private copying may prevent rights holders from obtaining remuneration for certain uses of their copyright material.

Companies that offer cloud computing services may also risk infringing copyright, for example by reproducing or communicating copyright material originally uploaded to their servers by their customers. In performing necessary technical functions, cloud computing service providers may risk infringing copyright, just as internet service providers may risk infringing copyright when they index and cache internet content. It is unclear whether these technical functions would be captured by the existing exceptions in the Copyright Act for the making of temporary reproductions 'as part of the technical process of making or receiving a communication' or 'incidentally made as a necessary part of a technical process of using a copy of the material.[3]

In Europe, the Court of Justice of the European Union (CJEU) recently issued the opinion of *ITV Broadcasting Ltd v TVCatchup Ltd*, considering questions referred for a preliminary ruling by the High Court of Justice (England and Wales).[4] In this case, British television broadcasters ITV, Channel 4 and Channel 5 challenged the legality of a service enabling paying subscribers to view live streams of unlicensed content provided through free-to-air television broadcasts. Although the case involved many complicated factors concerning the changing technological environment, the CJEU eventually held:

> [The right of communication to the public] covers a retransmission of the works included in a terrestrial television broadcast
>
> – where the retransmission is made by an organisation other than the original broadcaster,
> – by means of an internet stream made available to the subscribers of that other organisation who may receive that retransmission by logging on to its server,
> – even though those subscribers are within the area of reception of that terrestrial television broadcast and may lawfully receive the broadcast on a television receiver.

Across the Atlantic, the US Supreme Court also handed down the decision of *American Broadcasting Companies v Aereo, Inc.*, which

---

[3] Australian Law Reform Commission, *Copyright and Digital Economy: Issues Paper* (IP 42, 2012) 27.
[4] Case C-607/11 *ITV Broadcasting Ltd v TV Catch Up Ltd* (7 March 2013).

raised similar questions concerning the right of public performance.[5] In this case, major US television broadcasters challenged the legality of a service allowing paying subscribers to receive online streams of un-licensed content provided through over-the-air television broadcasts. During the oral argument, a number of justices expressed concern that a broad decision against Aereo could stifle the future development of cloud computing and other yet-to-develop communications technologies. In the end, Justice Stephen Breyer wrote a narrow majority decision, holding that Aereo made public performances within the meaning of the 1976 Copyright Act. As he declared: 'an entity that transmits a performance to individuals in their capacities as owners or possessors does not perform to "the public," whereas an entity like Aereo that transmits to large numbers of paying subscribers who lack any prior relationship to the works does so perform.'[6]

To be certain, the issues the ALRC, the CJEU and the US Supreme Court recently explored are highly important to copyright law reform at the domestic level, including reform related to cloud computing. Never-theless, this new technology has raised additional challenges when content is distributed via remote servers located outside the user's physical location. For instance, these challenges will occur when copy-right content is uploaded to a foreign server (think about Amazon Cloud Drive, Dropbox, iCloud or even Megaupload). They will also arise when a larger transnational conglomerate work compiles many smaller com-ponent 'works' authored by individuals located in different parts of the world (think about Wikipedia).[7] In either situation, cloud platforms are likely to create what Jane Ginsburg referred to as '[t]he disjunction between territorial treatment of copyright claims and the ubiquity of cyberspace'.[8] This disjunction has raised two sets of territoriality ques-tions, which will be discussed below.

---

[5]   134 S Ct 2498 (2014).

[6]   Ibid 2510.

[7]   'Virtual Reality, Appropriation, and Property Rights in Art: A Roundtable Discussion' (1994) 13 Cardozo Arts & Entertainment LJ 91, 94–7. On copyright issues relating to Wikipedia, see Jeremy Phillips, 'Authorship, Ownership, Wikiship: Copyright in the Twenty-First Century' in Estelle Derclaye (ed.), *Research Handbook on the Future of EU Copyright* (Cheltenham, UK and Northampton, MA, USA: Edward Elgar Publishing 2008).

[8]   Jane C. Ginsburg, 'Copyright without Borders? Choice of Forum and Choice of Law for Copyright Infringement in Cyberspace' (1997) 15 Cardozo Arts & Entertainment LJ 153, 155.

A. Independence of Right

The first set of questions covers what we generally describe as the independence of right doctrine.[9] Under this doctrine, rights holders do not have unitary protection throughout the world. Instead, they obtain nation-based rights in countries such as Australia, Brazil or China. What type of rights they obtain, how strong these rights will be and whether these rights are to be effectively enforced depend largely on the intellectual property system each country has put in place. While the territoriality principle has been used to justify national discretion, such discretion is also strongly supported by the principle of national sovereignty and concerns about international comity.

Thus far, the continued national divergences in laws, policies and institutions have created a 'territorial mess' that greatly hinders the global distribution of copyright content.[10] The challenges are further exacerbated by additional differences in market capacities and consumer expectations. To address this territorial mess, countries have worked hard to harmonize their laws in the past two centuries.

Since the 1880s, countries, especially those in continental Europe, have begun working together to address cross-border challenges by establishing international intellectual property agreements. These agreements ranged from the Berne Convention for the Protection of Literary and Artistic Works (Berne Convention) to the Agreement on Trade-Related Aspects of Intellectual Property Rights (TRIPS Agreement) of the World Trade Organization (WTO) to the 1996 Internet Treaties of the World Intellectual Property Organization (WIPO).

A case in point is the Berne Convention, the predominant international copyright treaty. Article 5(2) of the Convention expressly states:

> The enjoyment and the exercise of these rights ... shall be independent of the existence of protection in the country of origin of the work. Consequently, apart from the provisions of this Convention, the extent of protection, as well as the means of redress afforded to the author to protect his rights, shall be governed exclusively by the laws of the country where protection is claimed.

---

[9] On the difference between the territoriality and independence of intellectual property rights, see Frederick M. Abbott, 'Seizure of Generic Pharmaceuticals in Transit Based on Allegations of Patent Infringement: A Threat to International Trade, Development and Public Welfare' (2009) 1 WIPO J 43, 44.

[10] Peter K. Yu, 'Region Codes and the Territorial Mess' (2012) 30 Cardozo Arts & Entertainment LJ 187, 187.

Although commentators suggested that the lack of registration, substantive examination or other administrative procedure may make the independence of right doctrine less relevant to copyright law than to trademark or patent law,[11] there is no denying that global exploitation rights do not yet exist under the current nation-based copyright laws. Instead, countries introduced the national treatment concept and international minimum standards to foster certainty, predictability and harmony. While national treatment prohibits discrimination against foreign authors, international minimum standards seek to offer authors an adequate level of protection.

B.   Jurisdiction and Scope of Protection

The second set of territoriality questions concerns the territorial reach of prescriptive jurisdiction and the scope of the relevant copyright law.[12] Both issues are usually resolved at the discretion of nation-based institutions, such as the legislature or the judiciary. Under US case law, for example, federal statutes are not to be construed to apply to conduct abroad absent clear Congressional intent to that effect.[13] Thus, courts are generally reluctant to apply copyright laws to infringing activities outside the United States unless there is direct infringement within the country.

The seminal case in the area is the 1994 case of *Subafilms, Ltd v MGM-Pathe Communications Co.*[14] In this case, Subafilms and Hearst Corporation sued MGM/UA for unauthorized foreign distribution of The Beatles's *Yellow Submarine*. Interpreting the US Copyright Act as conferring rights no further than the national border, the US Court of Appeals for the Ninth Circuit held that authorizing within the United States acts that occur entirely abroad did not violate domestic copyright law.

After *Subafilms*, however, several courts have declined to follow the Ninth Circuit's decision, maintaining that the court had ignored changing economic reality, technological conditions and consumer expectations. Instead, they sought to justify the application of US law by identifying

---

[11]   William Patry, 'Choice of Law and International Copyright' (2000) 48 American J Comparative L 383, 394–5.

[12]   On the distinction between these two issues, see Marketa Trimble, 'Advancing National Intellectual Property Policies in a Transnational Context' (2015) 74 Maryland L Rev 203.

[13]   *Equal Employment Opportunity Commission v Arabian American Oil Co.* 499 US 244 (1991).

[14]   24 F3d 1088 (9th Cir 1994).

some connection between the infringing act and the US territory. In doing so, they not only strengthen the protection of US copyright works abroad, but also remove the territoriality-based loophole from US copyright law.

C. Summary

The distribution of copyright content via cloud platforms has raised many difficult yet important questions. If the platform is located entirely within the country, these questions will concern whether existing copyright law meets the challenges posed by this new and disruptive technology. For instance, will the right of public performance cover the cloud-based dissemination of copyright content? Will the 'replicat[ion] within the cloud for reasons of performance, availability, backup, ... redundancy' and parallel processing infringe on the right of reproduction?[15] Should the answer to either question be positive, will the potential infringement be exempted by a relevant limitation or exception – for example, an exception for 'temporary reproduction' in regard to cloud-based or cloud-driven replication?

If the cloud platform involves remote servers located outside the country, such distribution will raise two additional sets of territoriality questions: (1) What is the applicable law? (2) Will such law be applied extraterritorially? As an illustration, consider the unauthorized distribution of US copyright content via remote cloud servers in Hong Kong. Such distribution will implicate both US and Hong Kong copyright laws. It may also implicate the laws of other jurisdictions, especially if it has substantial adverse effects in third countries.

The first set of questions focuses on what law(s) should apply: US law, Hong Kong law, the laws of other jurisdictions, or all or none of the above? Because cloud platforms often involve storing multiple copies of the protected work on servers in different countries, the multijurisdictional nature of acts involving these platforms makes it very likely that the laws of more than one jurisdiction will apply. The second set of questions concerns whether infringement has taken place under the applicable law if the infringing act occurred outside the national border. For instance, if the court finds US law applicable, it will still have to explore whether an act committed in Hong Kong will constitute infringement under that specific law.

---

[15] Ian Walden, 'Law Enforcement Access to Data in Clouds' in Christopher Millard (ed.), *Cloud Computing Law* (Oxford: OUP 2013) 287.

III. JUSTIFICATIONS FOR INTRODUCING GEOGRAPHICAL RESTRICTIONS

Although one could tackle these territoriality questions head-on, content providers, thus far, have avoided these difficult questions by introducing geographical restrictions. By controlling the location in which their copyright content is being accessed or used, these providers transform the borderless digital environment back into territorially based distribution platforms. If past distribution strategies used by the music, movie and television industries provide any guide, similar restrictions will be increasingly placed on authorized cloud-based distribution platforms.

To understand why content providers have resorted to geographical restrictions, this section discusses four sets of justifications that copyright holders, industry groups and commentators have advanced thus far. Although cloud computing may not yet provide sufficient concrete examples to fully illustrate these justifications, this chapter draws on research the author conducted earlier on another form of geographical restrictions: DVD region codes.[16] Used commonly to protect movies, television programmes, computer software and online games, these technological restrictions were introduced in the late 1990s to limit content access to only the authorized geographic region – for example, Region 1 for the United States, Region 2 for the United Kingdom or Region 3 for Hong Kong.

While DVD region codes provide a textbook illustration for the use of geographical restrictions to protect copyright content, these restrictions can be found on many other consumer products – including those developed before the digital age (such as power plugs and sockets). Today, region codes have been widely used to protect not only movies and television shows, but also music, computer software, online games and, surprisingly, even printer toner cartridges.[17] When keyed to local wireless providers, lockout codes have also been successfully deployed in

---

[16] To provide an example, a US tourist who purchased a DVD at the Hong Kong International Airport may not be able to view the DVD at home in the United States despite the lawful purchase in Hong Kong. The purchased DVD from Hong Kong will have a Region 3 flag while the DVD player may only be able to play Region 1 or Region ALL DVDs. On DVD region codes, see Yu (n 10).

[17] Ibid 257.

cell phones to provide geographical restrictions, even though these codes technically do not have the same design and functionality as DVD region codes.[18]

More recently, a growing number of YouTube accounts have imposed geographical restrictions to prevent viewers from having access to all content, thereby taking away YouTube's earlier strength as a region-free platform for disseminating and viewing content. Apple's iTunes Store 'has [also] established different pricing structures for different countries; their [digital rights management] protects against consumer arbitrage, and their servers ensure that anyone trying to log onto, say, the U.S. iTunes website from a U.K. computer will be automatically redirected to the British site'.[19] In addition, to meet user needs and to ensure data retention in a contracted-for location, cloud providers have begun introducing the so-called regional cloud, or cloud services within a 'regional zone'.[20] In short, geographical restrictions are now ubiquitous; they can be found in not only consumer goods but also cloud services.

A. Sequential Release

Out of the four most widely cited justifications for introducing geographical restrictions to protect copyright content, the first concerns the need for products to arrive at different markets at different times. The need to segment the global market is indeed the most widely cited justification for DVD region codes. As the DVD Copy Control Association declared on its website:

> Movies are often released at different times in different parts of the world. For example, a film that opens in December in the U.S. might not premier[e] in Tokyo until several months later. By the time that Tokyo premier[e] occurs, the film may be ready for DVD distribution in the U.S. Regional DVD coding allows viewers to enjoy films on DVD at home shortly after their region's theatrical run is complete by enabling regions to operate on their own schedules. A film can be released on DVD in one region even though it is still

---

[18]   Ryan L. Vinelli, 'Bringing Down the Walls: How Technology Is Being Used to Thwart Parallel Importers amid the International Confusion concerning Exhaustion of Rights' (2009) 17 Cardozo J Intl & Comparative L 135, 139.

[19]   Tarleton Gillespie, *Wired Shut: Copyright and the Shape of Digital Culture* (Cambridge, MA: MIT Press 2007) 267.

[20]   Simon Bradshaw, Christopher Millard and Ian Walden, 'Standard Contracts for Cloud Services' in Millard (n 15) 55; W. Kuan Hon and Christopher Millard, 'How Do Restrictions on International Transfers of Personal Data Work in Clouds?' in Millard (n 15) 274–5.

being played in theaters in another region because regional coding ensures it will not interfere with the theatrical run in another region. Without regional coding, all home viewers would have to wait until a film completes its entire global theatrical run before a DVD could be released anywhere.[21]

The studios' need for sequential distribution is understandable. There are practical reasons for releasing movies in different parts of the world at different times. For instance, foreign release may be delayed due to 'the complications and differing costs of local/video duplication, dubbing and/or sub-titling, promotion, or dealing with censors'.[22] Directors, actors, writers and producers may also need to travel from one region to another to promote a movie.[23] It is not new that movies with significant marketing campaigns perform better at the box office.[24]

Apart from these practical needs, timing can affect a movie's box office performance. For example, a summer movie shown in the United States during the Fourth of July weekend may have weak ticket sales in Australia and New Zealand if shown at the same time; the Southern hemisphere is still in the middle of winter at that time. Likewise, a blockbuster movie opening in the United States during Thanksgiving may perform much better if shown a month or two later in Hong Kong, during either Christmas or the Chinese New Year. Because of the need for different release dates, DVD region codes were introduced to provide the technological fix needed to prevent foreign DVDs from not only under-cutting the box office for the theatrical release, but also disrupting the whole distribution cycle in foreign markets.[25]

---

[21]   'Frequently Asked Questions and Answers' (*DVD Copy Control Association*), www.dvdcca.org/faq.aspx, accessed 28 April 2014.
[22]   Claude E. Barfield and Mark A. Groombridge, 'The Economic Case for Copyright Owner Control over Parallel Imports' (1998) 1 J World Intellectual Property 903, 930.
[23]   Ibid 929; Brian Hu, 'Closed Borders and Open Secrets: Regional Lockout, the Film Industry, and Code-Free DVD Players' (Spring 2006) *Mediascape* 4, 4; Peter K. Yu, 'Anticircumvention and Anti-Anticircumvention' (2006) 84 Denver U L Rev 13, 75.
[24]   Mark S. Nadel, 'How Current Copyright Law Discourages Creative Output: The Overlooked Impact of Marketing' (2004) 19 Berkeley Tech LJ 785, 797; Harold L. Vogel, *Entertainment Industry Economics: A Guide for Financial Analysis* (8th edn, Cambridge: CUP 2011) 127–8.
[25]   Susan P. Crawford, 'The Biology of the Broadcast Flag' (2003) 25 Hastings Communications & Entertainment LJ 603, 607; Gillespie (n 19) 264; Nadel (n 24) 827; Vogel (n 24) 126.

B. Price Discrimination

The second widely cited justification concerns price discrimination.[26] Such discrimination provides a profit-maximizing mechanism through which content providers 'charge[ ] a high price to high valuation users and a low price to low valuation users'.[27] Such a mechanism not only allows these providers to recoup costs in the home market before exporting the product abroad,[28] but also enables them to price the product according to the cost of living in foreign countries. For instance, region codes allow Mexican consumers to buy DVDs of Hollywood movies at local retail prices, not the higher US retail prices.

Price discrimination is important because it can benefit both consumers and producers. Consumers living in countries with much lower costs of living will have access to products they otherwise cannot afford.[29] Without geographical restrictions, content providers understandably would be reluctant to sell products at discount prices, fearing that those discounted products would eventually enter their primary markets as parallel imports – unauthorized goods legally imported from abroad, usually at discount prices.[30] By enlarging the global market to cover customers who otherwise could not afford the product, content providers will also be able to increase the customer base and thereby maximize profit.[31] The providers' increased ability to take advantage of economies of scale and scope will, in turn, make the venture more profitable.[32] If profits are ploughed back into production, or if the profit potential could encourage content providers to make larger upfront investments, price

---

[26]   Rostam J. Neuwirth, 'The Fragmentation of the Global Market: The Case of Digital Versatile Discs (DVDs)' (2009) 27 Cardozo Arts & Entertainment LJ 409, 422–3; Vogel (n 24) 126; Yu (n 10) 206–9.

[27]   Michael J. Meurer, 'Price Discrimination, Personal Use and Piracy: Copyright Protection of Digital Works' (1997) 45 Buffalo L Rev 845, 850.

[28]   Neuwirth (n 26) 423.

[29]   Frederick M. Abbott, *Parallel Importation: Economic and Social Welfare Dimensions* (Winnipeg: International Institute for Sustainable Development 2007) 6; Barfield and Groombridge (n 22) 931; William W. Fisher III, 'Property and Contract on the Internet' (1998) 73 Chicago-Kent L Rev 1203, 1239; Keith E. Maskus, 'The Curious Economics of Parallel Imports' (2010) 2 WIPO J 123, 127.

[30]   Peter K. Yu, 'The Copyright Divide' (2003) 25 Cardozo L Rev 331, 436.

[31]   Glynn S. Lunney, Jr, 'Copyright's Price Discrimination Panacea' (2008) 21 Harvard J L & Technology 387, 388.

[32]   Vinelli (n 18) 143.

discrimination will create a virtuous cycle that benefits consumers in the form of newer and better products.[33]

C. Distribution and Licensing Arrangements

The third justification concerns distribution and licensing arrangements.[34] Although content providers could directly distribute products throughout the world, they often establish distribution and licensing agreements instead.[35] Such arrangements make sense for both practical and business reasons. By making the licensed product more attractive to local consumers, regional distributors and exclusive licensees could add value to the original work.

Consider the movie industry again for an illustration. Movie producers 'often customize the products to meet local market demands, including dubbing/sub-titling, duplication of the customized product, special packaging and advertising'.[36] In transition economies, such as China and Russia, or in Latin America or Africa, these distributors and licensees can help studios navigate through the complex local business environment.[37] In addition, 'newer and smaller motion picture companies ... [may] need to raise capital for production, usually in large amounts, ... by selling or licensing rights to particular territories and media or both before a picture is produced'.[38] The same is also true for blockbuster projects that are very costly for even established studios to produce. Thus, by conferring exclusive control over a geographical region, studios provide local distributors or licensees with the much-needed incentive to invest in regional distribution and marketing efforts.[39]

Because distribution and licensing agreements are based on countries or geographical regions, the distributor in one country or region may not have rights to release the DVD in another. Even if the distributor is a subsidiary of a large conglomerate targeting the worldwide market, the distributors in different regions may be formed as separate legal entities

---

[33]   Abbott (n 29) 8; Maskus (n 29) 123; Vinelli (n 18) 142.
[34]   Jim Taylor, Mark R. Johnson and Charles G. Crawford, *DVD Demystified* (3rd edn, New York: McGraw-Hill 2006) 5–19; Yu (n 10) 209–13.
[35]   Vogel (n 24) 127.
[36]   Barfield and Groombridge (n 22) 930.
[37]   Peter K. Yu, 'From Pirates to Partners: Protecting Intellectual Property in China in the Twenty-First Century' (2000) 50 American U L Rev 131, 209–10.
[38]   Barfield and Groombridge (n 22) 930.
[39]   Emily Dunt, Joshua S. Gans and Stephen P. King, 'The Economic Consequences of DVD Regional Restrictions' (2002) 21(1) *Economic Papers* 32, 39; Maskus (n 29) 128.

based on different regulatory standards, corporate governance structures and tax arrangements. These distributors may also have different strategies for marketing, distribution, post-sale remedies and intellectual property enforcement.

D.   Censorship Ratings and Regulatory Standards

The final justification concerns the practical needs created by the considerable divergences in regulatory standards across the world.[40] As far as movies are concerned, film ratings vary largely from country to country. In the United States, for example, the film ratings were formulated by the Motion Picture Association of America. Even more problematic, the ratings and regulations for movies can be quite different from those for television programs.[41] The theatrical version of a movie can also be quite different from the DVD version in the same market.[42]

Out of the six regions used in DVD codes, Region 6 provides the most obvious example of how movie studios need to adjust their distribution strategies in response to local regulations. Unlike all other regions, this region includes only one country: China. The need for such a distinction is understandable, considering China's aggressive censorship of media content.[43] By having a different region code from the ones used in other countries, studios can easily adjust the content based on what is allowed under Chinese content regulations. After all, what is shown in the United States, Europe or Japan may not be shown in China.

In addition to movie censorship, region codes can be used to address piracy and counterfeiting problems. For instance, China and Southeast Asia, both hotbeds of movie piracy, belong to two separate regions: Region 6 for China and Region 3 for Southeast Asia.[44] Having separate

---

[40]   Caitlin Fitzsimmons, 'Restricting DVDs "Illegal" Warns ACCC', *Australian IT* (27 March 2001) 33; Neuwirth (n 26) 426.

[41]   On content filtering on television, see Monroe E. Price (ed.), *The V-Chip Debate: Content Filtering from Television to the Internet* (Mahwah, NJ: Erlbaum 1998).

[42]   Rebecca Caldwell, 'DVDs without the XYZ', *Globe and Mail* (23 February 2001) R5.

[43]   On censorship in Chinese cinema and the importation quota for foreign movies in China, see Mary Lynne Calkins, 'Censorship in Chinese Cinema' (1999) 21 Hastings Communications & Entertainment LJ 239; Carl Erik Heiberg, 'American Films in China: An Analysis of China's Intellectual Property Record and Reconsideration of Cultural Trade Exceptions amidst Rampant Piracy' (2006) 15 Minnesota J Intl L 219.

[44]   Fitzsimmons (n 40).

region codes allows movie studios to respond to piracy problems – perhaps by deploying additional technological protection measures or introducing holograms or other hard-to-copy packaging features. Even if no additional measures or features are introduced, the use of separate region codes (Regions 3 and 6) will ensure that the geographically restricted DVDs, if pirated, will not compete with DVDs sold in the primary markets in North America, Europe and Japan (Regions 1 and 2).

E. Summary

In sum, one can identify at least four justifications for introducing geographical restrictions to protect copyright content. Although the examples in this section were drawn primarily from DVD region codes and the movie industry, the discussion here will apply well to other industries that now embrace geographical restrictions, such as providers of television programs, music, computer software and online games. In addition, because the nature and goals of DVD region codes are similar to the geographical restrictions now deployed on cloud platforms, and because these platforms have already begun to serve as distribution channels for copyright content, this discussion will provide insights into the justifications behind restrictions on cloud platforms and related services.

IV. DRAWBACKS OF INTRODUCING GEOGRAPHICAL RESTRICTIONS

The previous section explained why movie studios and other content providers consider it important to introduce geographical restrictions to protect copyright content. Although some of these justifications are understandable, especially from the content providers' standpoint, one can question whether geographical restrictions are now obsolete or would actually achieve their intended goals. For example, region codes seem somewhat outdated in an environment where a growing number of movies are released on the same day. Such release is especially common for blockbuster movies, due in part to the concerns about digital piracy and in part to the fear that spoilers will become available on the Internet.

In addition, region codes as presently deployed by the movie industry do not provide an effective price discrimination tool. If such a tool is to be effective, economies that are not similarly situated should not be grouped together. The case that makes the least economic or geographical sense is Region 5, which includes not only India and Russia – two of the

BRICs (Brazil, Russia, India, China and South Africa) – but also some members of the European Union as well as all countries in Africa except Egypt and South Africa. To put it bluntly, Region 5 seems to be the region about which Hollywood does not care much; this region has very little to do with price discrimination.

While this section can continue to criticize DVD region codes based on the four justifications mentioned above – as I did in a recent article[45] – these codes provide only one example of the geographic restrictions used to protect copyright content. Whether the deployed restrictions will be expedient and effective will depend on the industry, product and market involved. Just because one set of geographical restrictions has raised problems does not mean that another set cannot be satisfactory. Cloud platforms, for instance, may rely on restrictions that are of a much finer grain than DVD region codes, such as Internet protocol addresses. As a result, these platforms may pose fewer problems.

Nevertheless, regardless of whether geographical restrictions can be more tailored and suitable, the use of these restrictions to protect copyright content has many shortcomings. This section will identify four specific areas in which geographical restrictions will create, or have created, unintended consequences that harm both content providers and consumers.

A. Consumption

The first set of unintended consequences concerns consumption. With increased globalization and frequent consumer travel, a model that conditions the enjoyment of digital content on the place of purchase or first usage is seriously outdated. As consumer lifestyles, habits and preferences continue to change, geographical restrictions could eventually backfire on content providers by reducing consumption.

Consider, for example, the inconvenience that geographical restrictions have caused to people travelling abroad for a temporary period of time. Unless they plan to stay abroad for a more extended period, most of them are unlikely to subscribe to new services that are geographically confined. In fact, consumers are unlikely to join a new service unless they know for sure that the service will still be accessible after they return home.

For frequent travellers, the purchase decision will become even more complicated. Instead of thinking about whether they want the service in

---

[45]   Yu (n 10) 200–16.

the first place, they also need to think in advance about whether they would use the service in the place of purchase. In the end, if they cannot decide on the spot where the service will be used, they likely will turn down the service. If they unfortunately are unaware of the issues involved, or if they fail to consider these issues when signing up for the service, they will become deeply disappointed when they find out that the service they purchased is inaccessible outside the place of purchase.

Even worse, the inconvenience that geographical restrictions have caused may force consumers to turn to websites or services that distribute content without the content providers' authorization. Although quite a number of expatriates are eager to pay a subscription fee to enjoy movies and television shows from their native countries, geographical restrictions deployed in the broadcasters' or service providers' official websites (think about BBC iPlayer) have prevented them from obtaining access even with the subscription fee. While some of these frustrated potential subscribers choose alternative entertainment content, usually from competitors outside their native countries, others opt to watch those shows by paying a subscription fee to third-party services that may not share revenue with the original distributor, such as My Expat Network.[46] Some potential subscribers may even turn to unauthorized streaming sites on the Internet, even though all three groups of viewers were initially willing to pay a monthly subscription fee.

B.   Competition

The second set of unintended consequences pertains to the anti-competitive effects of geographical restrictions. To some extent, one can view these restrictions as post-sale mechanisms that content providers deploy to control the way consumers use their work after making a lawful purchase. By exercising such control, and thereby reducing competition, content providers can artificially inflate the selling price, often to the detriment of local consumers.[47]

---

[46]   Other third-party services include those 'retransmitting television programs themselves (e.g., ivi in the United States, TV CatchUP in the United Kingdom, shiftTV in Germany, and ManekiTV in Japan) ... [and those] enabling users to share retransmission of television programs (e.g., Justin.tv and WorldTV)'. Marketa Trimble, 'The Future of Cybertravel: Legal Implications of the Evasion of Geolocation' (2012) 22 Fordham Intellectual Property, Media & Entertainment LJ 567, 573–4.

[47]   Jonathan Band and Masanobu Katoh, *Interfaces on Trial 2.0* (Cambridge, MA: MIT Press 2011) 1.

Such control has also resulted in fewer choices for consumers. A case in point is a geographically confined platform that provides only the US version of the television show *The Office*, but not the original UK version. While this platform will satisfy viewers who are content to watch only Steve Carell's American remake of the show, it is unlikely to meet the needs of those who prefer Ricky Gervais' original version or want to watch both versions.

Even if the content is the same, the version offered in the country of origin may be superior to the one offered outside. When US movies or television series are released in multiple regions, it is not unusual for Region 1 DVDs to have better quality content than those released outside the United States.[48] Many of these DVDs also carry fewer special features, such as commentaries, interviews, bloopers and behind-the-scene footage.[49]

As if these shortcomings were not problematic enough, competition is particularly important to small markets that do not generate sufficient economies of scale and scope. For instance, it is not unusual for retailers in Hong Kong or Singapore to import goods from both the United Kingdom and the United States. Not only can the prices in these two countries be quite different, the available goods can vary as well. For example, *Harry Potter and the Philosopher's Stone* (the UK version) has British spellings, while *Harry Potter and the Sorcerer's Stone* (the US version) has American spellings. Even if the content is the same and the price is more or less the same at source, the two prices can fluctuate dramatically when currency exchange rates, transportation costs, package discounts, and other short-term and long-term factors are taken into consideration.[50]

---

[48]   Paul Zach, 'DVDs Made for SE Asia out in the Market', *Straits Times* (27 September 1997) 6.

[49]   Sherwin Loh, 'Listen to Your Customers', *Straits Times* (19 August 2009) 50; Sun Qixiang, 'The DMCA Anti-Circumvention Provisions and the Region Coding System: Are Multi-Zone DVD Players Illegal after the *Chamberlain* and *Lexmark* Cases?' (2005) U Illinois J L Technology & Policy 317, 332–3.

[50]   Barfield and Groombridge (n 22) 923, 935; Margreth Barrett, 'The United States' Doctrine of Exhaustion: Parallel Imports of Patented Goods' (2000) 27 Northern Kentucky L Rev 911, 959; Seth E. Lipner, *The Legal and Economic Aspects of Gray Market Goods* (New York: Quorum Books 1990) 3; Vinelli (n 18) 143.

C. Cultural Rights

The third set of unintended consequences focuses on the protection of cultural rights. It goes without saying that the enjoyment and exercise of these rights depend largely on the existence of cultural materials. Because geographical restrictions reduce access to these important materials, they threaten to intrude on the consumers' enjoyment and exercise of their cultural rights.

For foreign students, expatriate workers and immigrant families, having access to cultural materials is of paramount importance. This is particularly true when parents want to teach children their native language or culture.[51] Content distributed on global cloud platforms therefore can come in handy – whether as movies in the native language or foreign movies with subtitles in that particular language.

Geographical restrictions can also hamper the ability of domestic students to learn foreign languages.[52] Indeed, globally distributed cloud content can play a very important role in language and cultural education, especially given the wide availability of computers with Internet access in the classroom, at home and now even via smart devices on the street.[53] As Rostam Neuwirth rightly reminded us, 'the population of countries where films broadcast on television are not dubbed usually show stronger foreign language skills than in those countries where films are dubbed'.[54]

D. Censorship

The final set of unintended consequences relates to censorship. As noted earlier, DVD region codes or other geographical restrictions allow content providers to adjust content based on either the requirements of censorship regulations or through self-censorship. While such adjustments no doubt help content providers accelerate market entry and maximize profit, they also help facilitate censorship in countries having strong information control environments.[55]

In previous works, I noted how US intellectual property policies – including the support of widespread deployment of DVD region codes

---

[51] Hu (n 23) 2; James C. Luh, 'Breaking Down DVD Borders', *Washington Post* (1 June 2001) E1.

[52] Peter Ecke, 'Coping with the DVD Dilemma: Region Codes and Copy Protection' (2005) 38 *Die Unterrichtspraxis / Teaching German* 89; Hu (n 23) 2.

[53] Taylor, Johnson and Crawford (n 34) 3.

[54] Neuwirth (n 26) 452.

[55] Hu (n 23) 4; Neuwirth (n 26) 426.

and other geographical restrictions – have threatened to undermine the country's longstanding interests in promoting free speech, free press and other civil liberties abroad.[56] Without these restrictions, individuals in repressive countries who successfully obtain copyright content from the outside may still be able to obtain information censored by the authorities or self-censored by content providers. With these restrictions, however, it is much harder and much more costly for these individuals to obtain the uncensored version, even if they are willing to take risks. After all, they now need to acquire not only the content, but also the technology or equipment needed to view such content.

Moreover, censorship is not limited to countries having strong information control environments: it can also be found in the United States or other Western democracies. In the United States, for instance, there is a long history of movie censorship, which spans from the Hays Office and the Motion Picture Production Code to the film ratings system currently used by the Motion Picture Association of America (MPAA).[57] Even today, one can still find different products on the two sides of the Atlantic. A case in point is Stanley Kubrick's *Eyes Wide Shut*. While its Region 2 version (for Europe and Japan) includes the original material, the orgy scene on Region 1 DVDs has been digitally altered to meet the MPAA censorship ratings.[58] Thus, without the ability to circumvent geographical restrictions, Canadian and US film students will have a very difficult time studying the late director's original conception of his final film.

E. Summary

In sum, the strength of the justifications for introducing geographical restrictions to protect copyright content varies according to the type of product or service, the nature of the industry involved and the geographically based proxy used to facilitate content control and restrictions.

---

[56]   William P. Alford, 'Making the World Safe for What? Intellectual Property Rights, Human Rights and Foreign Economic Policy in the Post-European Cold War World' (1997) 29 New York U J Intl L & Politics 135, 144–5; Rebecca MacKinnon, *Consent of the Networked: The Worldwide Struggle for Internet Freedom* (New York: Basic Books 2012) 105; Robert S. Rogoyski and Kenneth Basin, 'The Bloody Case that Started from a Parody: American Intellectual Property Policy and the Pursuit of Democratic Ideals in Modern China' (2009) 16 UCLA Entertainment L Rev 237, 239; Yu (n 37) 174.

[57]   On movie censorship in the United States, see Edward de Grazia and Roger K. Newman, *Banned Films: Movies, Censors and the First Amendment* (New York: Bowker 1982).

[58]   Hu (n 23) 2; Neuwirth (n 26) 426–7.

Regardless of how important these justifications are, geographical restrictions come with serious unintended consequences that harm both content providers and consumers.

V. FIVE AREAS FOR POSSIBLE ADJUSTMENTS

The previous two sections have examined both the justifications for and drawbacks of introducing geographical restrictions to protect copyright content. One drawback that has not yet been discussed is how these restrictions, if deployed in the cloud, will greatly undermine the immense potential provided by cloud computing technology and cloud-based distribution platforms. This drawback is particularly harmful considering that this new technology can help facilitate the global distribution of copyright content, making such distribution faster, less costly and more user-friendly. When conglomerate works such as Wikipedia are involved, the need to develop a distribution strategy that matches the global user base becomes even more important and urgent.

To help realize the full potential of cloud platforms and to facilitate the global distribution of copyright content, this section identifies five areas where adjustments can be introduced to address the challenges posed by the territoriality principle in intellectual property law and the continued national divergences in laws, policies and institutions in the copyright field. While some of the identified adjustments may be easier to introduce than the others, the harder-to-introduce adjustments can also be more effective. Moreover, many adjustments can be introduced at the same time or *ad seriatim*. Thus, it is more important to identify the potential adjustments than assessing their strengths and weaknesses and their ease of introduction and implementation.

A. Treaty

The first set of adjustments concerns international treaties. This set of adjustments is arguably the hardest to introduce, but is likely to be the most effective in the long run. Although international treaties tend to lag behind technological developments, leading to a cat-and-mouse chase between the two,[59] introducing treaty-based adjustments to the existing

---

[59] Peter K. Yu, 'Trade Agreement Cats and the Digital Technology Mouse' in Bryan Mercurio and Ni Kuei-Jung (eds), *Science and Technology in International Economic Law: Balancing Competing Interests* (Abingdon, UK: Routledge 2014).

international intellectual property regime is important if nation-based rights are to collapse into a single global unitary right.

Although no such right presently exists in the international intellectual property regime, a close parallel can be found in the community trade mark (CTM) and community design systems in the European Union. As a region-wide, unitary trademark, CTM came into existence following the adoption of the Council Regulation on the Community Trade Mark in December 1993 and the establishment of the Office for Harmonization in the Internal Market. Instead of having national trademarks in the then 12, and now 28, members of the European Union, rights holders can enjoy the protection of a single unitary CTM throughout the European Union.

As of this writing, plans are underway to implement the EU-based unitary patent system, which can be traced back to the negotiations surrounding the establishment of the Convention for the European Patent for the Common Market in Luxembourg in December 1975. This recently adopted system gives nationally granted patents unitary effect within the 25 participating members of the European Union.[60] Thus far, six EU members – Austria, Belgium, Denmark, France, Malta and Sweden – have ratified the Agreement on the Unified Patent Court; the entry into force of this agreement will be needed if the unitary patent system is to begin operation.

Within the copyright field, the European Commission has also explored the need for region-wide unitary copyright titles. From December 2013 to March 2014, the Commission held a consultation on the modernization of the EU copyright regime. A key focus of this consultation is 'to increase the cross-border availability of content services in the Single Market, while ensuring an adequate level of protection for right holders'.[61] This consultation also built on the practical industry-based solutions explored in the recently concluded 'Licences for Europe' Stakeholder Dialogue, which the Commission launched in February 2013.[62]

---

[60] The three non-participating countries are Italy, Spain and the most recent EU member, Croatia.

[61] Commission of the European Communities, *Public Consultation on the Review of the EU Copyright Rules* (2013) 8. On this consultation, see Giuseppe Mazziotti, 'Managing Online Music Rights in the European Digital Single Market: Current Scenarios and Future Prospects' in Jan Rosén (ed.), *Intellectual Property at the Crossroads of Trade* (Cheltenham, UK and Northampton, MA, USA: Edward Elgar Publishing 2012).

[62] 'Licences for Europe: Ten Pledges to Bring More Content Online' (*Commission of the European Communities*, 13 November 2013), ec.europa.eu/

To be certain, countries, including members of the European Union, are still very unlikely to agree to an international agreement that facilitates the development of a global, unitary copyright. The reasons are twofold. First, copyright subsists in the original work upon creation – or, in some jurisdictions, fixation (that is, when the work is expressed in a tangible medium). Because no registration or examination is required, it is sometimes hard to know when copyright protection is secured. Even more complicated, Article 5(2) of the Berne Convention expressly states that '[t]he enjoyment and the exercise of these rights shall not be subject to any formality'. Registration and other formalities affecting the enjoyment and exercise of copyright are therefore prohibited.

Second, and more importantly, it took the European Union quite a few decades to establish both the CTM and the unitary patent system. Given the considerable diversity within the international community, it is very unlikely that a world copyright system will emerge any time soon. If it took the 12 earlier EU members decades to create just the CTM, one can imagine how many more decades it will take the more than 180 WIPO members in Africa, Asia, Australasia, Europe, and North and South America to establish a global, unitary copyright.

Thus, it is very unlikely that countries will agree to develop a world copyright system anytime soon. Nevertheless, the unlikelihood of developing such a system does not mean that countries could not agree on the establishment of a unitary right in special situations, such as those involving the Internet and cloud platforms. As commentators have widely discussed in the past two decades, territorially based intellectual property rights do not sit well with the Internet, even though copyright holders, industry groups and policymakers continue to retrofit national boundaries back into the digital environment. Even if one is reluctant to introduce a unitary right – such as an Internet- or cloud-based global exploitation right – treaties can be used to facilitate international exhaustion of rights in situations involving both the Internet and the cloud. Such exhaustion prevents rights holders from retaining any right of distribution or commercial exploitation after the copyright work has been marketed with their consent in any part of the world.

Thus far, negotiations on exhaustion of rights – and, by extension, parallel importation – have been highly contentious in the WTO. As Vincent Chiappetta recounted, during the negotiation of the TRIPS Agreement, countries had to 'agree to disagree' over the exhaustion

---

internal_market/copyright/docs/licences-for-europe/131113_ten_pledges_en.pdf, accessed 16 May 2014.

issue.[63] While the United States and the European Communities favoured national or regional exhaustion, Australia, Hong Kong, New Zealand and Singapore preferred international exhaustion.[64] Although Article 6 neither mandates nor forbids international exhaustion, it states that the mandatory WTO dispute settlement process will not be 'used to address the issue of the exhaustion of intellectual property rights'.

Notwithstanding the compromise struck in Article 6 by developed and developing countries during the TRIPS negotiations, the exhaustion debate has been slowly changing, especially in light of digital technology, the increasingly globalized marketplace and the multijurisdictional nature of acts involving the Internet – and, in this case, the cloud. While the European Union has now embraced regional exhaustion, the recent US Supreme Court decision of *Kirtsaeng v John Wiley & Sons, Inc.* confirmed that the first sale doctrine in US copyright law applies to copies of copyright works lawfully made within the United States and abroad.[65]

Indeed, after *Kirtsaeng* and an earlier, but similar case, *Quality King Distributors, Inc. v L'Anza Research International, Inc.*,[66] a growing number of commentators have suggested that the United States has, in effect, a global exhaustion regime in the copyright field. Many commentators have also considered the national exhaustion approach outdated. As William Patry wrote:

> There should be worldwide exhaustion of digital rights once a work has been licensed in one country. National or regional exhaustion is a relic of the analog world. Societies should be required to maintain free, publicly accessible online databases of which works they claim the right to administer, as well as contact information for the rights holders sufficient to permit users to contact the rights holders directly. There should be legally required fixed time periods to distribute monies, specially for foreign rights holders. If foreign money is not distributed within the requisite time period, the foreign rights holder or the home society of the rights holder may bring suit and are entitled to attorney's fees or penalties.[67]

---

[63]   Vincent Chiappetta, 'The Desirability of Agreeing to Disagree: The WTO, TRIPs, International IPR Exhaustion and a Few Other Things' (2000) 21 Michigan J Intl L 333.

[64]   Jayashree Watal, 'From Punta del Este to Doha and Beyond: Lessons from the TRIPS Negotiating Processes' (2011) 3 WIPO J 24, 26.

[65]   133 S Ct 1351 (2013).

[66]   523 US 135 (1998). This case concerned the application of the first sale doctrine in US copyright law to copies of copyright works lawfully made within the United States but exported abroad.

[67]   William F. Patry, *How to Fix Copyright* (Oxford: OUP 2011) 182.

To be certain, treaty-based adjustments are difficult to introduce. Nevertheless, the past two decades have not seen a higher momentum to push for treaty-based reforms at WIPO. Since the adoption of the WIPO Copyright Treaty and the WIPO Performances and Phonograms Treaty in December 1996, no new substantive international intellectual property agreement has been established at WIPO. In June 2012, however, close to 50 WIPO members signed the Beijing Treaty on Audiovisual Performances, which offers protection to audiovisual performers under the existing international copyright system. A little more than a year later, WIPO also adopted the Marrakesh Treaty to Facilitate Access to Published Works for Persons Who Are Blind, Visually Impaired, or Otherwise Print Disabled (Marrakesh Treaty). Upon ratification, this landmark instrument will provide easy or ready access to copyright publications to hundreds of millions of individuals with print disabilities.

The Marrakesh Treaty is interesting, because it includes a provision that explicitly covers the 'cross-border exchange of accessible format copies'. Article 5(1) specifically states: 'Contracting Parties shall provide that if an accessible format copy is made under a limitation or exception or pursuant to operation of law, that accessible format copy may be distributed or made available by an authorized entity to a beneficiary person or an authorized entity in another Contracting Party.' Thus, even though Article 5(5) states that '[n]othing in this Treaty shall be used to address the issue of exhaustion of rights', the Marrakesh Treaty allows an accessible format copy made under the permitted conditions in one country to be distributed or made available under similar conditions in another.

Moreover, since the 2013 General Assembly, WIPO Director General Francis Gurry has noted the importance of creating 'a seamless global digital marketplace'.[68] As he recently explained in an interview with the *Intellectual Property Watch*:

> For as long as it is easier to get content illegally than it is to get it legally, there is an encouragement to piracy. We have to make the conditions to get it legally better than illegally and that is the global digital marketplace.
> Let me give you [an] example: if one of the HBO series comes out in a new season in, for example, the US but is not available in the new season in certain other countries. What do people do? Do they wait patiently for three months? No, because they are addicted! So this is where I think our objective

---

[68] Francis Gurry, 'Address by the Director General' (*World Intellectual Property Organization*, 23 September 2013), www.wipo.int/about-wipo/en/dgo/speeches/a_51_dg_speech.html, accessed 7 June 2014.

ought [to] be a seamless global legal digital marketplace and I think everyone has agreed on this.[69]

Although Gurry did not believe the creation of this new marketplace should be 'a legislative exercise', he noted the need to establish 'a multi-stakeholder dialogue' to facilitate such creation. It remains to be seen whether such a dialogue would help kick start discussions that lead to the development of a new international instrument or a soft law recommendation at WIPO.

B. Law

The second set of adjustments, which is less difficult than the first to introduce, pertains to the development of choice-of-law principles that are particularly useful for cloud platforms and related services. Because the Berne Convention focuses on national treatment, it arguably does not provide any choice-of-law principles for determining copyright owner- ship and infringement. Instead, courts have developed their own prin- ciples to address these issues.

For instance, in the 1998 case of *Itar-Tass Russian News Agency v Russian Kurier, Inc.*,[70] a seminal US case in the area, several Russian journalists sued a New York-based Russian newspaper for allegedly infringing upon the copyright in their newspaper and magazine articles which were originally published in Russia. After examining the two different interpretations of national treatment, the US Court of Appeals for the Second Circuit held that national treatment is not a choice-of-law provision. Instead, the appellate court developed federal common law to fill in the gaps left by the US Copyright Act.

As far as copyright ownership is concerned, the Second Circuit found that the applicable law was the law of the state that had the most significant relationship to the copyright work and the parties involved – in this case, Russian law. With respect to the infringement issue, however, the court applied the oft-used conflict-of-laws principle of *lex loci delicti* (law of the place of the wrong). Under this tort principle, the court applied the law of the country in which the infringement occurred – in this case, the United States.

In the 1990s and early 2000s, the Hague Conference on Private International Law sought to draft a new Convention on Jurisdiction and

---

[69]   Catherine Saez, 'WIPO Director Gurry Speaks on Naming New Cabinet, Future of WIPO', *Intellectual Property Watch* (8 May 2014).

[70]   153 F3d 82 (2nd Cir 1998).

Foreign Judgments in Civil and Commercial Matters. Although the drafting exercise was ultimately unsuccessful, due in no small part to the emerging challenges posed by the Internet,[71] the draft Convention paved the way for the development of two related projects: the American Law Institute Project on Principles on Jurisdiction and Recognition of Judgments in Intellectual Property Matters and the Max Planck Group on Conflict of Laws in Intellectual Property (CLIP) Principles.[72]

Like the draft Hague Convention, both projects started with a focus on jurisdiction and enforcement of judgments. Unlike the Convention, however, both projects go beyond the original focus to cover choice-of-law issues. Although it is too early to tell how influential these two projects will eventually become, or whether later efforts to redraft the Hague Convention will be fruitful, it is not difficult to note the importance of developing coherent choice-of-law principles in light of the territoriality challenges posed by the Internet and cloud computing technology.

In addition to these two projects, as well as other similar projects in Japan and South Korea and under the auspices of the International Law Association,[73] commentators have suggested new choice-of-law approaches that may be useful in the context of cloud platforms and related services. For example, Graeme Dinwoodie called for courts to 'decide international copyright cases not by choosing an applicable law, but by devising an applicable solution'.[74] As he reasoned:

> International copyright disputes implicate interests beyond those at stake in purely domestic copyright cases. National courts should thus be free to decide

---

[71] Avril D. Haines, 'The Impact of the Internet on the Judgments Project: Thoughts for the Future' (*Hague Conference on Private International Law*, February 2002), www.hcch.net/upload/wop/gen_pd17e.pdf, accessed 24 May 2014.

[72] On the draft Hague Convention and the proposal advanced by Rochelle Dreyfuss and Jane Ginsburg that eventually became the draft American Law Institute Principles, see American Law Institute, *Intellectual Property: Principles Governing Jurisdiction, Choice of Law, and Judgments in Transnational Disputes* (Philadelphia: American Law Institute 2008); 'Symposium on Constructing International Intellectual Property Law: The Role of National Courts' (2002) 77 Chicago-Kent L Rev 991. On the CLIP Principles, see European Max Planck Group on Conflict of Laws in Intellectual Property, *Conflict of Laws in Intellectual Property: The CLIP Principles and Commentary* (Oxford: OUP 2013).

[73] Trimble (n 12).

[74] Graeme B. Dinwoodie, 'A New Copyright Order: Why National Courts Should Create Global Norms' (2000) 149 U Pennsylvania L Rev 469, 476.

an issue in an international case using different substantive copyright rules that reflect not only a single national law, but rather the values of all interested systems (national and international) that may have a prescriptive claim on the outcome. This approach to choice of law may unleash the generative power of common law adjudication as a means of developing international copyright norms. And it would accommodate the concerns of dynamic flexibility without compromising the values of national diversity or pluralistic perspective in a way that public law-based copyright lawmaking does not.[75]

Paul Berman also advocated '[a] cosmopolitan approach to international adjudication [that] allows courts to engage in a dialogue with each other concerning the appropriate definition of community affiliation and the appropriate scope of prescriptive jurisdiction'.[76]

C. Business

The third set of adjustments involves private ordering. Of all the five areas discussed in this section, contract-based adjustments are the easiest to adopt. They are also the most practical. Nevertheless, these adjustments vary considerably according to the parties involved and the power disparity between them. In light of the drastic changes to technological, environment and consumer expectations brought about by the Internet and cloud computing technology, it is high time content providers rethink their geographically based distribution strategies.

In the past decade, content providers have spent a considerable amount of time, energy, effort and resources on developing responses to copyright challenges posed by the Internet and new communication technologies. As difficult as these challenges may be, these providers, sadly, have not spent enough time rethinking their global distribution strategies. For instance, they could have thought about how to set up a distribution system based on a global platform, as opposed to a few platforms designed around arbitrarily selected regions. They could also have explored ways to allow rights holders in different regions to share in revenues generated through a single global distribution platform – with the assistance of collecting societies, perhaps.[77]

---

[75] Ibid.
[76] Paul Schiff Berman, 'Towards a Cosmopolitan Vision of Conflict of Laws: Redefining Governmental Interests in a Global Era' (2005) 153 U Pennsylvania L Rev 1819, 1865.
[77] Patry (n 67) 182.

To be certain, distributors may be reluctant to make their programming available online even though widespread demand exists. A case in point is the British Broadcasting Corporation (BBC), whose iPlayers include region-based restrictions.[78] These restrictions are understandable considering that the British public broadcaster has already licensed its programming out to other foreign distributors. While *Downton Abbey* has been shown on PBS in the United States, many other BBC shows, including the famous *Doctor Who* series, are being shown on BBC America.

In addition, the BBC may be conscious of the fact that a show needs to generate enough publicity in the United Kingdom or other Commonwealth markets before it could become successful in the United States or receive worldwide distribution. The BBC may also not have acquired all the rights in the underlying materials for the show to be broadcast in the United States or other parts of the world. In fact, until content providers start thinking more seriously about adopting a global distribution strategy, they may remain reluctant to obtain global rights for use in their works, as those rights tend to be more costly, more difficult and more time-consuming to secure.

Nevertheless, content providers need to be conscious of changing consumer lifestyles, habits and preferences as well as the increasing demand for borderless enjoyment of entertainment content. It does not make much business sense when customers cannot obtain desired programming despite their willingness to pay reasonable prices.[79] More importantly, the inability for these potential customers to view the content has eventually fuelled the demand for its unauthorized distribution.

To some extent, content providers are shooting themselves in the foot when they choose not to meet consumer demand. As Pink Floyd's first manager reminded us, 'The flagrant spread of "Internet piracy" in developed countries is a reflection of the failure of the industry as a whole to develop an appropriate copyright response to the distribution and remuneration options made possible by the new technologies.'[80] Likewise, William Patry observed, 'successful Internet business models are based on satisfying consumer preferences, honed and targeted through information provided by consumers. Such business models offer

---

[78]   Marie Boran, 'Stream of Online TV Shows and Movies Starts Flowing', *Irish Times* (2 December 2011) 6.
[79]   Patry (n 67) 183.
[80]   Greg Kot, *Ripped: How the Wired Generation Revolutionized Music* (New York: Scribner 2009) 2.

more choices, more consumer satisfaction (since they are based on consumers' own preferences), and therefore ultimately lead to greater revenue.'[81]

Indeed, the arrival and growing popularity of cloud platforms and related services have made it particularly urgent for content providers to reconsider their use of geographical restrictions to ensure that willing consumers can pay for products they want. As Patry continued, 'the best way to prevent the sale of unauthorized goods is to flood the market with authorized goods'.[82] The highly influential *Hargreaves Review of Intellectual Property and Growth* also declared: 'Where enforcement and education alone have so far struggled to make an impact on levels of copyright infringement, there has been more evidence of success where creative businesses have responded to illegal services by making available lower priced legal products in a form consumers want.'[83]

D. Government

The fourth set of adjustments is similar to the third, except that it concerns content generated by governments or other public entities – for example, works created by government employees or funded by taxpayers (such as content created by or for public broadcasters). While the type of territoriality challenges confronting this type of content is similar to those confronting content owned by private content providers, the resistance towards global content distribution may be lower when compared with the private sector.

To be certain, governments may be wary about the global distribution of content generated by their employees or funded by taxpayers. They may also believe that their focus and priority should be on promoting the interests of their own nationals. Indeed, it is not uncommon to find extant laws on Crown, parliamentary or government copyright in Commonwealth jurisdictions. Nevertheless, many jurisdictions now have laws removing copyright protection from government works. For instance, section 105 of the US Copyright Act stipulates that 'copyright protection … is not available for any work of the United States Government'. Works created by employees of the US federal government are therefore ineligible for copyright protection. Even for jurisdictions with Crown,

---

[81]   William Patry, *Moral Panics and the Copyright Wars* (New York: OUP 2009) 11.

[82]   Patry (n 67) 256.

[83]   Ian Hargreaves, *Digital Opportunity: A Review of Intellectual Property and Growth* (Newport, UK: Intellectual Property Office 2011) 79.

parliamentary or government copyright, a growing number of them have introduced easy-to-use licensing mechanisms to facilitate greater access to and use of the protected content. In June 2010, the Australian Parliament announced its plan to port its central website across to a Creative Commons licence.[84] Such a licensing arrangement has opened up the parliamentary website, which contains bills, committee and parliamentary reports, and other key public documents.

Moreover, the global distribution of government-generated content could induce other governments to do the same. Reciprocity and international comity are key factors for determining whether copyright law should be extraterritorially applied. By facilitating the promotion of the country or the governed territory to foreign tourists, investors and workers, greater global distribution can also provide indirect benefits to taxpayers.

As if such benefits were not enough, the global distribution of government-generated content can create 'soft power', widely discussed by Joseph Nye, Robert Keohane and other commentators.[85] Because the Internet has provided individuals with an unprecedented opportunity to obtain information about the way of life in other countries,[86] such distribution can benefit the international community by enabling nationals in other countries to make informed judgments about possibilities of life. Such enablement is especially valuable to residents in countries having strong information control environments (where proxy servers are used to hide the user's identity and physical location).[87]

Finally, the action that governments take in this area could induce greater voluntary action on the part of the private sector. As Deborah Hurley, the former director of the Harvard Information Infrastructure Project, reminded us, 'governments, by placing their large thumbs firmly on the side of the scale tipped toward more access to information, would

---

[84] Jessica Coates, 'The Australian Parliament Goes CC: With v3.0' (*Creative Commons Australia*, 7 June 2010), creativecommons.org.au/weblog/entry/301, accessed 24 May 2014.

[85] Robert Keohane and Joseph Nye defined 'soft power' as 'the ability to get desired outcomes because others want what you want'. Robert O. Keohane and Joseph S. Nye, *Power and Interdependence* (3rd edn, New York: Addison-Wesley Longman 2001) 220. On soft power, see Joseph S. Nye, Jr, *Soft Power: The Means to Success in World Politics* (New York: PublicAffairs 2004).

[86] Peter K. Yu, 'Bridging the Digital Divide: Equality in the Information Age' (2002) 20 Cardozo Arts & Entertainment LJ 1, 23.

[87] Peter K. Yu, 'Moral Rights 2.0' (2014) 1 Texas A&M L Rev 873, 888–94.

reframe the debate and send a strong signal to other content providers'.[88] Thus, by distributing content globally via cloud platforms, governments would help jumpstart adjustments that private businesses can introduce.

E. Technology

The final set of adjustments focuses on the technology needed to protect against the intrusion on cultural rights and to ensure equitable global access to lawfully obtained copyright content. Thus far, Internet users have deployed geolocation tools (including proxy servers) to view or use online content that they otherwise would not be able to by virtue of their geographical location. If such tools are banned, technological adjustments will have to be introduced, with additional support from the relevant limitations or exceptions in copyright law.

One such technological adjustment is Marketa Trimble's proposed 'digital passport'. As she explained:

> [L]egal cybertravel [that is, the evasion of geolocation that prevents the user from viewing certain Internet content from the user's physical location] might be conditioned upon the use of a digital passport that would identify not only the user's location or domicile but also the user's identity or account; such a condition would permit cybertravel but require that the user maintain accurate information about his or her identity. This solution would allow cybertravel but defeat anonymization; users would be able to obscure their current location if, for instance, the digital passport required information about the user's domicile or residence but not the user's current location.[89]

By ensuring that consumers can enjoy their lawfully purchased services when they are travelling or working abroad, Professor Trimble's 'digital passport' and other similar technological adjustments will make the implicated services more attractive. The adjustments therefore will benefit not only consumers but also content providers. To be certain, content providers may have priced the service based on content availability in only the user's home country – for example, the user will have to pay a higher premium price for global access. In reality, however, many of these providers may simply have a tough time negotiating the licences needed to ensure user access outside the place of purchase.

---

[88]   Deborah Hurley, *Pole Star: Human Rights in the Information Society* (Montreal: International Centre for Human Rights and Democratic Development 2003) 36–7.
[89]   Trimble (n 46) 639.

Indeed, there has been a growing demand for 'cross-border portability of subscription services', which was a priority issue for the European Commission's recently concluded 'Licences for Europe' Stakeholder Dialogue. As the Commission observed in a document announcing the pledges made by major content providers, 'Today, subscribers to audio-visual services online, e.g. consumers watching movies via an Internet service provider or web-store, are often denied access to services legally bought in their own EU country when they cross national borders.'[90] While this stakeholder dialogue and the associated pledges focused on access to content and services within the European Union, the lack of cross-border portability affects users throughout the world.

The need for such portability is highly understandable. As the European Commission declared in an earlier document entitled *A Digital Agenda for Europe*:

> Consumers expect, rightly, that they can access content online at least as effectively as in the offline world. Europe lacks a unified market in the content sector. For instance, to set-up a pan-European service an online music store would have to negotiate with numerous rights management societies based in 27 [now 28] countries. Consumers can buy CDs in every shop but are often unable to buy music from online platforms across the EU because rights are licensed on a national basis. This contrasts with the relatively simple business environment and distribution channels in other regions, notably the US, and reflects other fragmented markets such as those in Asia ... .[91]

The lack of cross-border portability of content and services can also backfire on content providers. As William Patry observed:

> Many tens of millions of dollars are left on the table in Europe alone because of the inability to get pan-European licenses. Instead, licensees have to negotiate on a country-by-country basis with national collecting societies, music publishers, and record labels (to name only the top three groups), to say nothing of countries where there are no collecting societies. Authors lose because deals aren't done; the public loses because there is a dearth of authorized, complete services; copyright law as system loses for both these reasons.[92]

---

[90]   'Licences for Europe: Ten Pledges to Bring More Content Online' (n 62).
[91]   'A Digital Agenda for Europe' (COM (2010) 245 final/2, 2010) 7.
[92]   Patry (n 67) 186.

To some extent, the need for cross-border portability reminds us of some earlier proposals concerning a right to hack or a right to circumvent. For example, Congressman Richard Boucher introduced, in January 2003, the Digital Media Consumers' Rights Act, seeking to restore the historical balance struck by fair use in copyright law.[93] Julie Cohen argued that 'licensees ... should be accorded rights of electronic self-help when necessary to preserve the balance that the Copyright Act is intended to establish'.[94] Andrew Shapiro underscored the need for allowing people to engage in what he described as 'fair hacking' or a 'fair breach', in analogy to fair use.[95] As part of the Canadian copyright law reform, Michael Geist further proposed to 'include a positive user right to circumvent a technological measure for lawful purposes'.[96]

Although these decade-old proposals sought to protect fair use or first sale rights, or to restore the traditional balance in the copyright system, they were similar to the technological adjustments identified in this section. Like the identified adjustments, these earlier proposals sought to ensure that consumer expectations are met. Moreover, if technological adjustments are indeed needed to protect against the intrusion on cultural rights, it would not be too far-fetched to argue that these adjustments are required by the pre-existing obligations in international human rights treaties that relate to the protection of cultural rights.[97]

VI. CONCLUSION

Cloud computing technology has provided one of the most logical platforms for the global distribution of copyright content. While it is understandable why content providers are eager to bring their current geographically based business models into the cloud, this chapter has shown that this approach is ill-advised on two counts. First, although justifications exist to introduce geographical restrictions, these restrictions come with serious unintended consequences that harm both content

---

[93]   [2003] HR 107, 108th Cong.
[94]   Julie E. Cohen, 'Copyright and the Jurisprudence of Self-Help' (1998) 13 Berkeley Technology LJ 1089, 1092.
[95]   Andrew L. Shapiro, *The Control Revolution: How Internet Is Putting Individuals in Charge and Changing the World We Know* (New York: PublicAffairs 1999) 179.
[96]   Michael Geist, 'Anti-Circumvention Legislation and Competition Policy: Defining a Canadian Way?' in Michael Geist (ed.), *In the Public Interest: The Future of Canadian Copyright Law* (Toronto: Irwin Law 2005) 248–9.
[97]   Yu (n 10) 246.

providers and consumers. Second, and more importantly, geographical restrictions will likely hamper the future development of cloud computing. To ensure that cloud computing technology can be fruitfully developed, this chapter identifies five sets of adjustments that can be introduced to facilitate the authorized global distribution of cloud-based copyright content. It is my hope that the seamless global distribution of this content will help fully realize the potential of cloud computing – to the benefit of content providers, technology developers and, most importantly, consumers.

10. Lost in translation: transforming healthcare information for the digital and cloud domains

Terry Sheung-Hung Kaan[*]

I. INTRODUCTION

Between paper records and the cloud, two distinct steps are involved in the translation of healthcare and medical data from the analogue to the digital domain. The first step involves the conversion from data held on paper to electronic database systems. Generally held within a single institution or a group of related institutions in a client-server model within institutional boundaries, this translation of such biomedical data from the analogue to the digital is the first but fundamental step towards its use in the cloud. But to make the leap to the cloud, a further step must be taken to free the data from the confines and limitations of local infrastructure and design. This chapter examines both steps, and surveys the progress made at both bars as well as the obstacles associated with each. The argument is made that the fundamental nature of the initial transition from the analogue to the digital domain needs to be recognized accordingly, and appropriate care and attention be given to the design and process of this transition.

In the realm of biomedical information and records, there seemed to have been reasonable grounds for optimism and hope at the dawn of the era of mass adoption of modern information technology. In his 1968 address entitled 'Hospital Records in the Computer Age',[1] Sir Richard

* The author wishes to thank the Warden and Fellows of Merton College, Oxford University for a Visiting Research Fellowship for Trinity Term 2013. A portion of the research for this chapter was undertaken during the term of the Research Fellowship.

1 Richard Doll, 'Hospital Records in the Computer Age' (1968) 61(7) *Proc R Soc Med* 709.

Doll (who subsequently became Regius Professor of Medicine at Oxford) wrote that he was 'convinced that computers have a great deal to offer medicine and that they will eventually transform its practice'. Even more boldly, he predicted that 'the progressive transfer of decision-making to data-processing machines will become a characteristic feature of hospital medicine during the next fifty years'.[2] A little short of that predicted half-century later, ambition has collapsed in hubris in the wake of the National Programme for IT debacle in England.

The National Programme for IT was launched in 2000 by the then Prime Minister Tony Blair with the declared intent of making the English National Health System (NHS) 'the healthcare system the world most envies'.[3] The plan was simple enough: to convert the unruly quagmire of paper and electronic records held by individual healthcare institutions to a modern, fully integrated, national-level electronic records' system that would be accessible to healthcare givers across the country. Patient records would be liberated from the confines of individual healthcare institutions and specific providers, consequently freeing patients to access healthcare across the entire national system, and providing healthcare providers with vitally complete and integrated information about their patients.

But even this simple (if broad) ambition was not to be. By May 2011, the £11.4 billion National Programme for IT ('the National Programme') had suffered the indignity of being the subject of a critical report by the Comptroller and Auditor General. The report concluded that, of the £6.4 billion already spent on the National Programme by the end of March 2011, 'the £2.7 billion spent on care records systems so far does not represent value for money, and we do not find grounds for confidence that the remaining planned spend of £4.3 billion will be different'.[4]

By September of the same year, the Government had announced that 'it would dismantle the National Programme but keep the component parts in place with separate management and accountability structures'.[5,6]

---

[2] Ibid 709.

[3] Linda Beecham, 'Tony Blair Launches Radical NHS Plan for England' (2000) 321 *BMJ* 317.

[4] The National Audit Office, *The National Programme for IT in the NHS: An Update on the Delivery of Detailed Care Records System* (HC 2010–12, 888, 2011) 4 and 13 (The NAO Report).

[5] Committee of Public Accounts, *The Dismantled National Programme for IT in the NHS* (HC 2013–14, 294) 5 (The HC CPA Report).

[6] Denis Campbell, 'NHS Told to Abandon Delayed IT Project' (*The Guardian*, 22 September 2011).

As the Government is still bound by continuing contractual obligations under the original plan, the total cost of the National Programme to taxpayers is uncertain, with the Department of Health putting the forecast at £9.8 billion.[7] Billed as 'what would have been the world's largest civilian computer system',[8] it has come in for severe criticism even from some of the professional stakeholders it was intended to serve.[9]

Amidst the politically charged recriminations, however, are perhaps some themes worth investigating in attempting to understand why such a national-level project (no doubt closely watched by other countries with similar ambitions) could have ended in such a manner, with a view to avoiding the same pitfalls in the planning and implementation of similar national programmes in other countries.

The sheer scale of the ambition appears to have been a significant factor, as well as the rapidly evolving state of technology. A health secretary of the succeeding government, Andrew Lansley, laid the blame on the imposition of 'a top-down IT system on the local NHS, which didn't fit their needs'.[10] Yet others have criticized the 'lack of clinical engagement, with the focus upon technology and not service change. There was no comprehensive sell programme to clinicians or NHS Executives to ensure they understood the concept and had bought into it'.[11] Other commentators within the healthcare professions have been more critical, characterizing the National Programme as being 'politically driven' from the outset by a newly elected New Labour government eager to make its mark without a true appreciation of the risks that the scale of the ambitions would inevitably involve.[12]

---

[7]   The HC CPA Report (n 5) 5.

[8]   Rajeev Syal, 'Abandoned NHS IT System Has Cost £10bn So Far' (*The Guardian*, 18 September 2013).

[9]   'Editorial' (2011) 378 *The Lancet* 542.

[10]   Campbell (n 6).

[11]   Rhys Hefford, 'Why the NHS National Programme for IT Didn't Work' (*CIO UK*, 2 December 2011), www.cio.co.uk/insight/strategy/why-nhs-national-programme-for-it-didnt-work/, accessed 24 April 2014.

[12]   Ann Robertson, David Bates and Aziz Sheikh, 'The Rise and Fall of England's National Programme for IT' (2011) 104 J R Soc Med 434, 434–5.

II. FROM ANALOGUE TO DIGITAL: THE CHALLENGES OF CONVERSION

A. Lost in Translation

The first step towards any notion of involvement of the cloud in the realm of medical practice or the healthcare professions is the conversion of existing patient records from paper-based systems to digital systems. Although simple enough as an idea in itself, the reality of even the most basic and modest of conversion schemes at the most restricted level of the local institution or even single clinic is much more complicated than that, unless the intent is simply to reduce paper records to the form of digitized images, which arguably is really not digital conversion at all. In the classic patient record card, the physician is essentially free to enter information at will in free-form with no concern about compulsory data fields, or standardized ways of entering data or even describing conditions.

In this chapter, the argument is advanced that a major cause of difficulties in the conversion of healthcare records from the analogue to the digital domain lies in the failure of IT system designers, clinicians and healthcare institutional managers alike to realize that transition to the digital domain inevitably entails fundamental changes to the very nature of the data, and that these changes in turn have profound consequences for the uses and users of the data. The full dimensions and implications of these changes have yet to be fully understood and appreciated in the body of law and ethics, with the result that national legislatures are but taking the first hesitant steps towards a comprehensive regime for the regulation of the accession and use of such data in the healthcare and biomedical research sector, let alone any move towards any international consensus on how such data are to be treated. From the IT system designers' point of view, the changed nature of the data gives rise to new legal and ethical obligations (many of which are currently uncertain in scope and reach). Moreover, new classes of uses and potential stake-holders will have to be anticipated and considered, and management responses carefully considered.

Even something as seemingly simple as notes of a clinical consultation poses problems in translation. As Sir Richard Doll observed, such clinical notes can 'vary in complexity from the terse comment ... that the patient "has budgerigar" – an important reminder of a topic of conversation rather than a possible source of infection – to the detailed psychiatric history and neurological examination of 2,000 or more words and symbols'.[13] So the point is that the clinical record in its traditional paper format was written by an expert, with the intention that it should serve to jog the memory of the same expert at the next consultation of the patient, or for the elucidation of a fellow professional trained in the same arcane art of the physician's notes, which may to the trained insider speak as much from what is not mentioned as from what is. The IT design must accommodate the learning and argot of a highly trained and skilled profession, and especially bear in mind that clinical notes written on paper records were very unlikely to have been written with a view to future reduction to a digital state with its compulsory record fields of a modern database.

Electronic databases do not lend themselves to free-form entry, particularly if other uses and applications for the electronic medical records are contemplated (which uses and applications will be explored later in this chapter). In particular, electronic databases are constructed using standardized fields (for example, 'Name', 'Date of Birth', 'Home Address', 'Allergies') to record information. So healthcare providers who have to deal with electronic medical records are not free to enter information as they like, but must enter it in a standardized format. This, of course, leads to the question as to what fields should be included in the system. The temptation is always to include more, but the greater the number of fields, the greater the likelihood more of them will be irrelevant to the consultation at hand, and the greater administrative burden on physicians already sorely pressed for time. There is also the argument that the inclusion of some kinds of data may cause harm.[14] Clearly, inaccurate or inaccurately entered data will have that effect, but so too will the inclusion of unreliable data. For example, would the methodology for a test result from a decade ago satisfy current criteria of reliability? Another example would be medical data such as test results from research trials which do not measure up to clinical diagnostic standards for the exclusion of false positives and negatives.

An artificially constrained choice of fields also introduces the potential danger of relevant information not being entered because the physician was not prompted for it by the system. Information *desired by the system* is not the same as information desired by the *physician* (think billing vs clinical purposes). An abundance of caution in the inclusion of fields may

---

[13]   Doll (n 1) 711–12.
[14]   Kimberley Shoenbill, Norman Fost, Umberto Tachinardi and Eneida Mendonca, 'Genetic and Electronic Health Records: A Discussion of Ethical, Logistical and Technological Considerations' (2014) 21 *J Am Med Inform Assoc* 171, 172–3.

mean that the electronic record will end up being composed largely of an unmanageable clutter of empty fields through which the physician must trawl to find the desired pearls. Instead of aiding as intended, the imprecision of fields and the 'noise' induced by such a system may actually make the physician's diagnosis more difficult. The physician's art of putting forward a complex diagnosis and postulate may be forcibly reduced to fixed options dictated by the design of the fields.[15]

And then there is the question of what to include. The physician's notes on paper or cards do not constitute all of the records of the patient. Among other equally important parts of the patient's clinical record to consider are diagnostic images (a challenge from their sheer size), laboratory test results and pathology reports. Some kinds of clinical records cannot be converted at all. For example, if biopsies have been taken and tissue preserved and retained, these physical samples obviously cannot be 'digitized' and must remain in their corporeal form, and so a physical (and therefore 'analogue') archive must still be retained. So then, how is the new electronic database to be linked to these unconvertible analogue and physical archives?

Local legal rules (and institutional confidence in the new electronic database systems) may dictate that the analogue records' system be maintained alongside the digital system for a period – not an inconsiderable imposition on the clinician hard-pressed for time. The forced double-entry may also open the door to errors if vital information is recorded in one system and not the other, and the defective record subsequently relied upon for the follow-up treatment of the unfortunate patient.

B. Purposes

Before considering what purposes the translated data may be put to, it may be useful to consider the arguments for moving data from the analogue into the digital domain. In the NHS, as in many other countries, computerization in the healthcare institution setting found its first footing not in clinical care applications, but in the more mundane role of the automation of administrative functions (particularly accounting, billing and finance). So, at least initially, conversion was not necessarily aimed solely or largely at furthering better and safer clinical diagnosis and

---

[15] Sir Richard Doll gives a good illustration of this in his discussion of the difficulties of taxonomic classification of seemingly simple 'symptomatological datum' such as headaches and coughs, in Doll (n 1) 19.

treatment. For the NHS's National Programme, the 'anticipated qualitative benefits' included 'increased patient safety through reducing duplicated information that is more likely to contain omissions, and efficiency improvements by, for example, automating back office administration'.[16]

In a review of the NHS's computing policy in the 1970s, it was observed that when computers were first introduced in the medical field in the 1960s, their initial impact was 'predominantly through financial and payroll applications, and then they were used increasingly by research workers, particularly for computational and data analysis'.[17] Not without concern, the author noted that despite the 'burst of enthusiasm' then for harnessing computers in the healthcare sector from the 1960s, little was shown in the way of 'effective contribution to service medicine' despite the resources thrown towards that end.

So, in addition to the simplistic model in which paper-based healthcare records are converted into the digital domain for the same kind of clinical use as before the conversion, at least some other potential new uses and demands begin to be identifiable. Clearly, demand will increase for access to the electronic patient records for administrative and back-office use, particularly billing and financial applications. These uses arguably have nothing to do with the clinical care of the patient, and may (and some might argue, should) be separated out from any clinical system. Then there may be some administrative uses for the electronic medical record which *does* relate to the administrative aspects of the clinical care of the patient (but not to the clinical care itself), such as the scheduling of consultations and appointments.

C. Consolidation and Conflation

So one of the first fundamental changes occurring in the initial stages of 'computerization' in the institutional healthcare setting is *consolidation* and *conflation* of various formerly disparate and discrete sources and systems of information – each originally created to serve quite different objectives and purposes. Some sources may fit quite well with each other (at least in principle) such as medical records from different clinics or surgeries within the same system. But others may sit uncomfortably with each other, and the resulting consolidated database may well give rise to troubling issues of harmonization and integration. A simple example of this might be the consolidation of patient billing databases (in other

---

[16]   The NAO Report (n 4) 21.
[17]   Michael Alderson, 'A Review of the National Health Service's Computing Policy in the 1970s' (1976) 30 *Brit J Soc Med* 11, 11.

words, billing records) with pharmaceutical dispensing records and patient clinical consultation records (clinical records). If the patient's employer is the bill payer, the consolidation of billing records with clinical records may give rise to issues of whether employers may assert the right to know what kind of medications the employee has been prescribed, and why.

The failure by IT systems' designers to appreciate this fundamental change consequent on the simple consolidation and conflation of disparate databases created originally for different purposes may give rise to unforeseen challenges down the road if IT system designers are only given briefs on what each database was created for, and on their present uses. The obvious danger is, of course, this effectively freezes the system design in a patchwork of historical perspectives that take no account of the inevitable interaction of various components of the merged databases, let alone the consequences and implications of potential future uses.

D. New Uses and New Implications

The implications of the conversion of data from the analogue to the digital domain is well understood by graphic artists, photographers, movie-makers and those dealing with images. In the conversion, the very nature of the data is fundamentally altered and acquires dimensions and attributes not present in the original. As digital photographers understand, the conversion of an image from the analogue into the digital domain means more than just the means by which the image is stored. The conversion to the digital domain opens up a whole new dimension and world of possibilities of new uses and manipulations not possible in the analogue domain. The digital image can be much more readily manipulated with software than for analogue images.

The difference is like the printed page of a physical book which can only be read (and then only by one person at a time) for the purpose for which the book was written, whether for entertainment, aesthetic fulfillment or reference. But the same information presented on the physical pages of a book, if translated into the digital domain, can be manipulated in an infinite variety of ways. This may range from interface manipulations, such as being presented in a variety of font types and sizes to suit individual readers reading the text on-screen on a computer or on e-book readers. But more powerful uses may include effortless indexing of the text and making it available to sophisticated searches such as with the use of Boolean operators. To put it simply, one of the most important and indispensable tools of contemporary life – the modern Internet search engine service – would not have been possible without the existence of a large body of publications in the digital domain. If a single work can be manipulated and worked on in this way, consider the possibilities if hundreds of thousands of works were combined and subject to manipulation, access and review in the same way. It is a completely new dimension – the ability not only of being able to sift and search for relevant information within a single database (for example, a book), but also to search *across* and therefore *compare* information across many databases. One implication of this property of the digital domain is, therefore, the ability to search for patterns across large sets of consolidated databases that may not be discernable or revealed from the examination of individual databases.

This has important implications and consequences directly relevant in the context of healthcare and clinical databases in the digital domain. When individual consultation records (all records of an individual patient's consultations or clinical interactions with the various clinics or surgeries, doctors and hospitals in a given healthcare system) are gathered together in the digital domain, a *longitudinal electronic medical record* (longitudinal EMR) is created for that particular patient. This was what was sought by the Detailed Care Record proposal in the original NHS National Programme. The advantages of such a longitudinal EMR in digital form are various. But one particularly relevant to the present discussion is that, if designed appropriately to be accessible from anywhere, then a much more complete clinical record of the individual patient's medical history and treatment regimes is presented to the treating physician than if the patient's records remained in the discrete silos of paper records held by the individual clinics or hospitals that the patient may have visited.

Obviously, in an emergency, when the patient cannot rely on being treated by a physician familiar with his or her past history, such access to a longitudinal EMR is especially vital and useful. So, from many single or incomplete records scattered across many institutions and healthcare access points, a more complete picture and *reliable* profile of a given patient can be built up. The comparison is analogous to a single snapshot in time versus a movie of an individual's life.

Just like in the digitization of books and publications, the next dimension that arises from conversion into the digital domain is the ability to search for, discover or predict patterns when many separate databases are merged or linked into large-scale consolidated ones. In the context of clinical records, the longitudinal EMRs of individual patients can likewise be merged or consolidated into large-scale *longitudinal EMR databases*. When a hospital group combines all the longitudinal EMRs of its patients into a single clinical database, some powerful new tools and possibilities become available. From the perspective of hospital administrators, these databases offer new insights for patterns of diseases in the local population that they serve. These insights can then be harnessed towards more targeted and efficient allocation of resources for treatment. They can also be put to the improvement of clinical audit processes through the investigation of patterns of diseases and treatment outcomes (including the incidence of unexpected adverse outcomes and possible iatrogenic injuries) which would not be possible with paper-based analogue records. For clinicians, information on patterns reveals the efficacy of different treatment options and infection control programmes, as well as alerting them to the presence of nosocomial diseases and (especially relevant in the age of SARS and MERS) emergent zoonotic diseases.

These advantages and uses are already well known to public health authorities interested in the epidemiology of diseases in their local populations. Most advanced medical jurisdictions operate some kind of disease registries at the local, regional and national levels which provide public health authorities with timely warnings of emergent diseases and conditions requiring a public health response. Yet the recent experience of disease registries in the UK has exposed new fault lines created by the power of digital databases.

Sometimes the existing law may be inadequate to support technological progress, or may even hinder it. Before 2000, it was the practice of healthcare institutions and physicians in the UK to contribute relevant clinical information about their patients to various national registries, notably cancer registries. In most cases, the transfer of information was done as a matter of accepted practice, without explicit consent being taken from the patients to which the information related. In September 2000, the General Medical Council (GMC) issued guidance drawing attention to the need for the consent of the patient as a precondition for the transfer of information to such registries.[18] Predictably, the research community was appalled with the very real prospect of the streams of information to the disease registries drying up as a result of the guidance if it was enforced. Evidence was given before the House of Lords Select Committee on Science and Technology by eminent experts warning that 'the whole cancer registry system would collapse if the requirement for informed consent and/or anonymisation prior to

---

[18] The General Medical Council, 'Confidentiality: Providing and Protecting Information' (September 2000), accessible at http://www.gmc-uk.org/confidentiality_sep_2000.pdf_25416426.pdf (last accessed 17 February 2015).

registration were to be enforced', and that 'cancer registries were absolutely vital to research and medical care in providing basic information on the health of the nation'.[19]

The GMC did not budge from its view that explicit consent was required by the common law for the transmission of personal medical information to the databases. In the end, however, it accepted a government undertaking to implement legislation allowing for the transmission of such information on a statutory basis in the public interest without the need for explicit patient consent. The GMC accordingly allowed a one-year moratorium on the implementation of its guidance, and the necessary legislation was eventually passed.[20]

From the perspective of public health planners and biomedical researchers alike, even longitudinal EMR databases on the largest of scales (for example, at the national level which was the ambition of the NHS National Programme) suffer from several particularly grave flaws. By its very nature, a longitudinal EMR database is a retrospective record, and not a prospective one. It is a record of the medical state of people not when they are healthy (which is most of the time) but only when they were ill (and therefore, in a physiological condition not representative of their normal state). It tends towards over-representation by the elderly suffering from multiple co-morbidities in the last few years of their lives. So although it speaks much of what has happened to a small and unrepresentative population at a difficult time in their lives, it is silent on the state of health of the majority for most of the time. For researchers and clinicians alike, this skewed nature of longitudinal EMR databases makes it difficult to gather an accurate picture of the progress of diseases and conditions in the *general* population (as opposed to the ill population) over the course of a lifetime.

It is to achieve a more representative longitudinal EMR database that the concept of a *biobank* has been mooted. Instead of a database comprising mainly records of interventions for the ill, why not have a database of volunteers of a demographic profile representative of the local population, recruited at a time when they are still young and healthy, and then track their individual longitudinal health profile over a

---

[19] Science and Technology Committee, *Fourth Report* (HL 2000–01) para. 7.29 (ch. 7 'Ethics, Privacy and Consent').

[20] Health and Social Care Act 2001, s. 60, currently National Health Service Act 2006, s. 251. An account of this is given by Calvin Ho, 'Privacy in Medical Research: Re-Thinking the Role of Law and its Relationship with Ethics' in Terry Kaan and Edison Liu (eds), *Life Sciences: Law & Ethics – Recent Developments in Singapore* (Singapore: Academy Publishing 2006) 176–80.

lifetime, until exit by death? Because the biobank starts out with a demographically representative profile of the young and healthy, disease and morbidity patterns in the general population can be better studied and traced, particularly if physical material such as blood, urine, saliva, tissue or genetic samples can be added to the otherwise purely informational longitudinal EMR records. The concept has its roots in influential research programmes such as the Framingham Heart Study. The first study of its kind, an initial batch of 5,209 volunteers were recruited from 1948 with the aim of studying 'the expression of coronary artery disease in a "normal" or unselected population and to determine the factors pre-disposing to the development of the disease through clinical and laboratory exam and long term follow-up'.[21]

The modern expression of the biobank ambition is probably best represented by the UK Biobank Project.[22] The largest project of its kind in the world, it has already achieved its initial target of recruiting 500,000 volunteers between the ages of 40 to 69 between 2006 and 2010, all of whom have 'undergone measures, provided blood, urine and saliva samples for future analysis, detailed information about themselves and agreed to have their health followed. Over many years this will build into a powerful resource to help scientists discover why some people develop particular diseases and others do not'.[23]

But even the vast scale of the UK Biobank does not make it a truly *national* project. The apotheosis and dream of biomedical researchers, clinicians and public health planners and policy-makers alike would be a national-level biobank integrated with a national longitudinal EMR database capturing the majority of the citizens in the country. Only a few countries (mostly small ones) have attempted to build such a system. The

---

[21] Syed S. Mahmood, Daniel Levy, Ramachandran S. Vasan and Thomas J. Wang, 'The Framingham Heart Study and the Epidemiology of Cardiovascular Disease: A Historical Perspective' (2014) 383 *The Lancet* 999, 1000. This review article gives a good account and historical perspective of the Framingham Heart Study. More information can be found at the project's website at www.framing-hamheartstudy.org.

[22] The UK Biobank Coordinating Centre, 'UK Biobank: Protocol for a Large-Scale Prospective Epidemiological Resource' (*Biobank*, 21 March 2007), www.ukbiobank.ac.uk/wp-content/uploads/2011/11/UK-Biobank-Protocol.pdf?ph pMyAdmin=trmKQlYdjjnQIgJ%2CfAzikMhEnx6, accessed 1 May 2014.

[23] The UK Biobank, 'About UK Biobank', www.ukbiobank.ac.uk/about-bio bank-uk/, accessed 1 May 2014.

poster child of these attempts is that of Iceland's.[24] The history of this project may prove to be an object lesson for the healthcare professions, national health planners, legal professionals and IT systems designers alike on the kinds of pitfalls likely to be encountered in building such a comprehensive system. Brought into being by legislation in the form of the Act on a Health Sector Database and the Biobanks Act,[25] the Icelandic government sought to harness the unique genetic characteristics of its tiny but genetically homogenous population by combining various existing sources of personal, genealogical and medical information into a national health sector database.[26]

Deep disquiet was expressed, however, by some concerned that such a national database programme, even if equipped with opt-out provisions, would erode fundamental privacy rights.[27] The original version of the Act on a Health Sector Database was successfully challenged before the Icelandic Supreme Court in 2003 in the case of *Ragnhildur Guðmunds-dóttir v The State of Iceland.*[28] In that case, the applicant successfully challenged the law on the grounds that its provision for the transfer of the health data of her deceased father to the national health sector database

---

[24] For a survey on national biobanks, see Helen Swede, Carol L. Stone and Alyssa R. Norwood, 'National Population-Based Biobanks for Genetic Research' (2007) 9 *Genet Med* 141–9.

[25] Act on a Health Sector Database, No. 139/1998 as amended by Act No. 77/2000, No. 55/2009, No. 162/2010, No. 126/2011 and No. 34/2012, and the Biobanks Act, No. 110/2000, as amended by Act No. 27/2008 and Act No. 48/2009. English translations of these and other Icelandic legislation are available from the website of the Icelandic Ministry of Welfare at http://eng.velferdarraduneyti.is/legislation/acts_of_parliament/, accessed 3 May 2014.

[26] For a general account of the beginnings of the project and the Act on a Health Sector Database, see Hilary Rose, 'The Commodification of Bioinformation: The Icelandic Health Sector Database' (*The Wellcome Trust*, 2001), www.wellcome.ac.uk/stellent/groups/corporatesite/@msh_grants/documents/web_document/WTD003281.pdf, accessed 20 May 2014.

[27] Geneviève Cardinal and Mylene Deschenes, 'Surveying the Population Biobankers' in Bartha Maria Knoppers (ed.), *Populations and Genetics: Legal and Socio-Ethical Perspectives* (Boston: Martinus Nijhoff 2001) 37–94, at 69–70.

[28] *Ragnhildur Guðmundsdóttir v The State of Iceland* (Icelandic Supreme Court No.151/2003, delivered 27 November 2013). An English translation of this decision was available on http://epic.org/privacy/genetic/iceland_decision.pdf, accessed 1 May 2014. An insightful commentary on this decision and its consequences may be found in Renate Gertz, 'An Analysis of the Icelandic Supreme Court Judgment on the Health Sector Database Act' (2004) 1 *SCRIPTed* 241–58.

violated her constitutional rights to privacy because 'information could be inferred from such data relating to the hereditary characteristics of her father which might also apply to herself'.[29] The decision forced the subsequent amendments to the Act.

III. RELATIONAL INFORMATION, CONSENT AND THE CHALLENGES OF PRIVACY

In the context of this chapter, the main interest raised by the GMC guidance controversy and the *Ragnhildur Guðmundsdóttir* case is the recognition that the kind of data mining and manipulations of information translated and consolidated into the digital domain raises new and vexing questions about the protection of the privacy of the individual. Individual privacy would not have been an issue had the information remained in the analogue domain. Rothstein ably captures the problem thus:

> In today's mostly paper-based health records system, privacy is protected largely by fragmentation, inefficiency, illegibility, and general chaos. It would be virtually impossible for any adult to collect all of his or her health information maintained by numerous health care providers in different locations over years or decades. If a patient is unable to locate all of his or her health records, then third parties are also unable to do so. There is no question that fragmentation promotes health privacy, but it does so at a very high cost in terms of undermining coordination of care, efficiency, and health care quality.[30]

A. Assumptions as to Privacy, Uses and Users

The point which Rothstein makes is often an overlooked one in the rush to convert the analogue to the digital. When information is stored in the analogue domain, a certain set of assumptions are made in relation to the information both by those taking the information, and by those that the information pertains to. The simplest case is that of information given by a patient to a doctor, say in the 1960s or even the 1970s. No thought would have been given to the digitization of the information or to its possible eventual consolidation and conflation with other scattered records pertaining to that particular patient, or to consolidation and

---

[29] Ibid.
[30] Mark Rothstein, 'Health Privacy in the Electronic Age' (2007) 28 *J Leg Med* 487, 489.

conflation with the records of many thousands or even millions of other persons. The assumption made by both the giver and the taker of the information is that the information would be stored in a particular form (the paper record), for the use of that particular user of the information (the physician taking the information) or other colleagues as may have been authorized by the physician or the patient himself, for the purpose only of the clinical treatment and follow-up of the patient. And possibly, the same paper record might also be used for ancillary administrative purposes such as billing, although this would generally only occur in a small clinical setting, as larger institutions would have a separate set of records (whether in paper or digital format) for billing and accounting purposes – these would not form part of the clinical record of the patient.

From the legal and ethical perspectives, consent is taken from the patient for the taking of the information for the use of a *specific user* or implied group of specific users (the patient's general physician, and the physician's colleagues in the same practice). Likewise, the consent is for a *specific use*: the clinical treatment and benefit of the patient. Unless specifically asked for, there is no consent for any other *uses* (such as for research) or for access by other *users* (such direct access by insurers, health maintenance organizations, or even national health programme administrators and planners). So the information contained in the traditional paper record is constrained in both intended uses and users. Rothstein's point is that the very nature of traditional paper records serves to protect the implicit privacy boundaries and implicit agreement as to permissible uses and users.

Conversion to the digital domain, however, fundamentally undermines these assumptions of privacy assured by the nature of the paper record. Once in the digital domain, the information becomes accessible to many more kinds of potential uses, and many more kinds of potential users. Not all of these uses or users will have interests aligned to that of the patient. Indeed, arguably *most non-clinical* potential new stakeholders claiming the right to access the *clinical* information (as opposed to administrative and billing information relating to the patient) are *unlikely* to have interests entirely in agreement with that of the patient. So Rothstein argues that although the primary rationale for the taking of clinical information is the furtherance of the health of the patient, the reality is that:

> any entity with an interest in an individual's current or future health status might have an interest in having access to the individual's health records.

With few exceptions, such entities may lawfully require that the individual execute an authorization for the disclosure of all his or her health records.[31]

The most familiar example is, of course, the authorization for access to health information that insurance companies generally require of prospective clients as a precondition of insurance, and similar pre-conditions imposed by employers on prospective employees for pre-employment health examinations and screenings. With easy access to consolidated longitudinal data pertaining to the health of their employees, employers, too, may be tempted to assert an interest in data-mining the health records of their employees. For example, is the company present-ing payment for any prescription for drugs that may be associated with the treatment or rehabilitation of substance abuse, or a sexually transmit-ted disease or any other kind of condition about which some may be minded to make a moral judgment?

In the UK, the bluntest expression of this precarious balance between the privacy rights of individuals and the assertion of rights by third-party stakeholders may be found in the uneasy truce between the insurance industry and persons carrying the genes for heritable diseases that may have a significant impact on their life expectancies. The insurance industry, understandably, asserts the right to require prospective cus-tomers to disclose the results of any genetic tests that may be positive for such heritable diseases. In a fully digitized national health database system, it would be straightforward for insurance companies to demand access to such information. In such a situation, a direct conflict of interests is created by the very existence of a system purportedly established for the exclusive clinical benefit of the patient. The fear is, of course, that if patients felt that they would be at risk of raised insurance premiums if they went for genetic testing of suspected heritable diseases, then they would avoid such testing. Or patients would simply have themselves tested abroad. Neither option is in the clinical interest of the patients, as their physicians would be denied an accurate picture of the health of their patients. In the UK, the current arrangement is that insurance companies have agreed with the government to voluntarily limit the scope of such demands for disclosure of genetic test results until 1 November 2017. The reality of this arrangement is simply that the real decisions in law and ethics have been postponed for another day, with nothing having been conceded by the insurance industry.[32]

---

[31]   Ibid 496.

[32]   HM Government and the Association of British Insurers, 'Concordat and Moratorium on Genetics and Insurance' (*UK Department of Health*, 2011),

But as is clear from the discussion above of the establishment of large-scale longitudinal EMR databases and purpose-built research biobanks, the most pressing new use asserting itself in the digital domain is that of research. Information in the digital domain lends itself to the kind of digital mining, analysis and manipulation which would be impossible in the analogue world, even assuming that the analogue records were themselves not fragmented. With digitization on a large scale, the health information of an individual is no longer the only information that is important. Consolidation and conflation of the health records of many thousands of individuals give rise to new classes of informational assets not captured in any single individual's longitudinal health records. For public health authorities and planners, such new classes of informational assets will include invaluable epidemiological information on the patterns of diseases in the local population.

B.   Relational Information in the Digital Domain

For biomedical researchers and interested third parties (including insurance companies) operating on a smaller perspective, yet another class of information can be extracted from digital databases: that of *relational information*. In the digital domain, it may be possible to construct a probabilistic health profile of a target person without access to the health records of the actual target person: all that is required is sufficient information about persons closely related to the target person. For this reason, the normal privacy controls in the analogue world do not work as well in the digital world, if at all. A person can secure his or her privacy by refusing consent to access to paper health records, but such refusal may count for nothing if an interested third party has access to sufficient relational information in the digital domain. As made plain by the *Ragnhildur Guðmundsdóttir* case, consolidation and conflation of analogue records to the digital domain brings into existence new threats to the privacy of individuals which could not be contemplated in the analogue world.

To sum up, the conversion of paper records into the digital domain, therefore, raises many new and fundamental implications for privacy not only for the individuals to which the records relate, but also for the family members of these individuals. And these implications endure beyond the death of the individuals concerned. Clinical records collected

www.gov.uk/government/publications/agreement-extended-on-predictive-genetic-tests-and-insurance, accessed 3 May 2014.

for the purposes of the treatment of the living survive their original intent and function to continue to be useful to biomedical researchers – and to third parties such as insurers.

The English common law has yet to really engage these new implications for privacy. For the most part, decisions in both law and ethics have merely been postponed for demands by the insurance industry for access to information about predictive genetic test results. In reaching so far beyond the original intent of the parties (traditionally the patient and his or her physician), the question is then whether the terms of the original consent (whether expressed or implied) to the taking and keeping of the information can accommodate such a whole new slew of uses and users. The argument is that it does not, and that from the perspectives of both the law and the body of ethics that conversion from the analogue to the digital may well require the retaking of a broader consent from patients.

A simple illustration will suffice: if a patient's paper records are digitized and consolidated with a larger database, there will be the question of whether research access should be permitted at any point in the future, especially given that the stored information is likely to survive the patient. Appropriate access controls may be devised to satisfy ethical requirements (and institutional review boards and medical journals), but these controls relate only to the ethical acceptability of the research objectives and protocol. They will not, and cannot, address the basic question of whether legally and ethically acceptable consent had been obtained in the first place for the patient's information to be included in a database potentially open to research use.

So the first relates to the research *use* of information, whereas the second relates to the legality (in legal and ethical terms) of the *accession* of the data to the research database. And what if the patient is no longer alive? Can consent by proxy be ever obtained, and if so, from whom, or is it the case that data relating to the deceased must be purged from databases if no consent was ever taken for research use? In designing databases, therefore, IT system designers may well need to keep in mind the necessity for accommodating an effective distinction between information for which the patients have given their consent for research use, and that for which they have not. Without the ability to distinguish and segregate these two kinds of data for a specific class of user (researchers in this case), the entire database may be legally and ethically compromised from the research access point of view.

C. Control

Another fundamental issue yet to be addressed by both the common law and by the body of ethics is the question of control. In the traditional paper-based records setting, this was not a serious issue as both the scope of use and users were limited by the physical nature of the manner of storage of the information, as well as the very limited range of uses for the information.

Given the potential new uses, users and longevity of the transformed information, what kind of rights should patients retain over the use of their information, and how is control to be shared between patients, physicians and administrators? As Rothstein asks, should patients have the right to delete, block or otherwise redact sensitive information to render them inaccessible to specific uses or users?[33] One complication is that different people are sensitive about different things. An activist lobbying for changes in public attitudes towards discrimination against people living with AIDS may not be concerned about releasing information about his or her own HIV-positive status, but many other people will be. So arguably, the complication is that sensitivity of information can only be determined subjectively by the patient to whom the information relates, and not by reference to any allegedly objective criteria.

IV. FUTURE PERFECT: THE LURE OF THE CLOUD AND THE CHALLENGES AHEAD

A. The Impact of Privacy Concerns

That privacy is a significant social concern in the transfer of health records from the analogue to the digital domain is not in doubt. In the United Kingdom, considerable variation exists in the attitudes of various demographic segments of the population to the establishment and use of EMRs. In the first large-scale study of its kind in the UK,[34] while it was reported that an overwhelming majority (89.71 per cent of 2,857 respondents) supported the use of EMRs 'for personal health care provision', there was much less agreement on how much of their

---

[33]   Rothstein (n 30) 492.

[34]   Serena A. Luchenski, Julie Reed, Cicely Marston, Chrysanthi Papoutsi, Azeem Majeed and Derek Bell, 'Patient and Public Views on Electronic Health Records and Their Uses in the United Kingdom: Cross-Sectional Survey' (2013) 15 J Med Internet Res e160.

personal records should be used in this way, with just 66.75 per cent favouring the inclusion of 'their complete, rather than limited, medical history'. Significant differences occurred between different age groups, with older people and some minorities a surprising level of support for research access use (81.38 per cent) was reported, but the majority added the caveat that the information should be anonymized. The take-home lesson may be that public attitudes and concerns are rather less monolithic than public policy planners and IT designers may wish to assume, and are capable of making quite informed distinctions between the kind of 'intended use, the type of information being shared, and whether health information is anonymized or not'.[35]

In the wake of the collapse of the original National Programme, fresh controversy has arisen over the UK government's proposals for a NHS medical database. The government has agreed to delay the launch of the sharing of healthcare data by six months after 'acknowledging that there was insufficient public support in the scheme'.[36] Also, the Royal College of General Practitioners is 'calling for a new national advertisement campaign and a personally addressed letter sent to every person in the country' to inform them of the proposed scheme and its implications for privacy.[37] Perhaps too, privacy concerns may make for tempting political and media targets. The danger is that public perception and appreciation of privacy issues may be distorted by either sensational or uneven coverage with disproportionate attention being given to the occasional slip-ups rather than the overall benefits and gains achieved by a given system.

In the United States, social concerns over privacy issues have found legislative expression in legislative provisions such as the 1996 Health Insurance Portability and Accountability Act (HIPAA) and its accompanying Security Rule and Privacy Rule.[38] These rules have considerable teeth. With fines of up to US$1.5 million per calendar year and ten years

---

[35] Ibid Introduction.

[36] Peter Walker, James Meikle and Ramdeep Ramesh, 'NHS in England Delays Sharing of Medical Records' (*The Guardian*, 18 February 2014).

[37] Laura Donnelly, 'Patients Should Be Warned before NHS Shares Medical Records, Doctors Say' (*The Telegraph*, 18 February 2014).

[38] The US Department of Health and Human Services gives the following background to the two Rules on its website, see 'Summary of the HIPAA Privacy Rule', www.hhs.gov/ocr/privacy/hipaa/understanding/summary/index.html, accessed 3 May 2014.

in prison for violations of the Privacy Rule,[39] the clear legislative intent is to have EMR 'owners take privacy and security seriously'.[40]

But that is not the only effect that the HIPAA regulations are likely to have. Despite some optimistic projections for the future of EMRs in the cloud domain,[41] one of the most daunting challenges to the migration of healthcare information systems to the cloud, particularly in the more ambitious paradigms of PaaS (Platform as a Service) and IaaS (Infrastructure as a Service) as defined by the National Institute of Standards and Technology (NIST),[42] is the administrative burden, cost and risks of compliance with the extraordinarily complicated rules mandated by the HIPAA. In any of the three modes of engagement in cloud services as defined by NIST, data inevitably will potentially pass into or through the hands of cloud software, platform or infrastructure administrators or providers, making compliance with the HIPAA rules a potential minefield that attracts not just civil but penal sanctions.

One approach to the management of exposure to such liability is the 'Business Associate Contracts' mandated by the HIPAA rules, under which the obligations of confidentiality of third parties (the 'business associates') who have to handle or who have access to the data are made clear and made part of the terms of the cloud services contract.[43] The Health Information Technology for Economic and Clinical Health (HITECH) Act of 2009 was enacted in an attempt to clarify the burden of liability of business associates, but the net effect may have been to add

---

[39]   See the US Department of Health and Human Services summary of the penalties for violations and non-compliance with the Privacy Rule, 'Summary of the HIPAA Privacy Rule', ibid.

[40]   Eugene J. Schweitzer, 'Reconciliation of the Cloud Computing Model with US Federal Electronic Health Records Regulations' (2012) 19 *J Am Med Inform Assoc* 161, 162.

[41]   See Scott Good, 'Why Healthcare Must Embrace Cloud Computing' (*Forbes*, 2 May 2013), www.forbes.com/sites/centurylink/2013/05/02/why-healthcare-must-embrace-cloud-computing/, accessed 3 May 2014. The article cites a 'recent study by the firm MarketsandMarkets [which] indicates that the healthcare cloud computing market, which is only currently about 4% of the industry, is expected to grow to nearly $5.4 billion by 2017'.

[42]   Peter Mell and Timothy Grance, 'The NIST Definition of Cloud Computing' SP 800-145 (*National Institute of Standards and Technology Information Technology Laboratory*, September 2011), http://csrc.nist.gov/publications/nist pubs/800-145/SP800-145.pdf, accessed 3 May 2014.

[43]   For an account of business associate contracts, see Schweitzer (n 40) 164; and 'Business Associate Contracts' (*US Department of Health and Human Services*, 25 January 2013), www.hhs.gov/ocr/privacy/hipaa/understanding/cover edentities/contractprov.html, accessed 3 May 2014.

even more fine print to the mix. Yet clearly such contracts cannot entirely limit civil and penal liability even where the law (such as the HITECH Act does) attempts to ease the move to the cloud.

If compliance within a single jurisdiction is problematic, then the lack of international agreement and harmonization of national rules relating to privacy standards in the handling of information in the cloud may well prove to be the biggest obstacle to the true adoption of cross-border cloud platforms: one system that satisfies the requirements of US national and state laws may well run foul of European ones.

B. Fragmentation and Inertia

But even when there is political will and a clear legal framework, and assuming that privacy concerns can be assuaged, many barriers stand in the way of the construction of health databases at the national level. In the United States, little progress has been made on the proposal for a national population health record database (PopHR) mooted by the American Medical Informatics Association in 2007. Despite general agreement on its utility, the PopHR proposal was for anonymized patient data to be made available in electronic form as a source of population health data and statistics – an idea similar to that of disease registries. Even when data is already held in electronic form, fragmentation of the source data is one of the most serious problems – not only is data held by different entities with different access rules and protocols, they may also be held in incompatible formats. Finance is a common bone of contention, and simple 'policy and politics'.[44] Simple and vital population health statistics are surprisingly difficult to come by.

V. CONCLUSION

The aim of this chapter has not been to discourage the transition from the analogue domain to the digital one, and then finally to the cloud. It is simply to point out that care should be taken to study and understand the implications and consequences of the very real and fundamental changes in the nature of the information that accompanies this transition, and of the potential new uses and users that are likely to arise. As with the transition of data from the analogue to the digital domain, the transition

---

[44] Daniel J. Friedman and R. Gibson Parrish II, 'The Population Health Record: Concepts, Definition, Design, and Implementation' (2010) 17 *J Am Med Assoc* 359, 360.

from local to cloud storage is inevitable. Given the current range of cloud platforms, hosting and infrastructural services offered, the existence of mature and appropriate cloud technologies and platforms is no longer the real barrier to the adoption of cloud technologies and platforms. The real obstacles lie in more prosaic practical, social, ethical and legal concerns relating to the digitization of information in the first place. Only when these issues (which relate largely to the first fundamental step of moving information from the analogue to the digital domain) have been satisfactorily settled, can there be an effective large-scale move to the cloud paradigm for healthcare and medical databases and information systems.

In this respect, it is probably better to study and learn from the experience of others, rather than suffer the reinvention of the wheel. Social concerns such as privacy need to be taken into account, but so too, there must also be a corresponding understanding by legislators and policy-makers that knee-jerk reactions to such concerns may result in hardwiring rules and regulations that hobble and stifle innovation. Forty years down the road, we may perhaps agree that Sir Richard Doll was presciently spot-on in his future-gazing: that computers have much to offer medicine, and that they would eventually transform its practice. They already have. But they have also opened a whole Pandora's Box of ethical, legal and social issues that we are just only beginning to understand and come to grips with.

11. International genomic cloud computing: 'mining' the terms of service

Edward S. Dove, Yann Joly and Bartha M. Knoppers

I. INTRODUCTION

The genomic research community is facing a big data challenge.[1] The cost of genetic sequencing is falling faster than that of storage and bandwidth, and thanks to advanced technologies for genetic sequencing and analysis, more data have been generated than ever before. Consider that the average human whole-genome sequence contains approximately three billion data points (known as 'base pairs') and generates roughly 100 gigabytes of data, and that the whole genome of a tumour and a matching normal tissue sample consumes one terabyte of uncompressed data.[2] A project utilizing thousands of genomes (not to mention phenotypic data and the linking of local data with online public data) for disease research would quite quickly generate petabytes of data.[3]

Yet, genetic sequencing machines currently are incapable of generating a single string containing billions of properly organized nucleotides.

---

[1]   Genomics can be defined as the study of the complete DNA sequence (in other words, the entire set of genes) found in humans, both anatomically (sequences and organization) and physiologically (expression and regulation). The genome is the complete set of genes needed by a human being for its development and functioning.

[2]   Aisling O'Driscoll, Jurate Daugelaite and Roy D. Sleator, '"Big Data", Hadoop and Cloud Computing in Genomics' (2013) 46 J Biomed Inform 774. The authors note that since 2008, genomic data is outpacing Moore's Law (the observation that, over the history of computing hardware, the number of transistors in a dense integrated circuit doubles approximately every two years) by a factor of 4.

[3]   One petabyte equates to 10^{15} bytes of digital information.

Instead, they produce shorter, fragmented and unordered sections, each only a few hundred or thousand nucleotides long. Researchers must rely on technicians and computers to properly organize them. At the same time, the current reality is that the amount of genomic data and associated clinical data needed to procure the statistical power required to advance biomedical research and clinical practice exceeds the technical capacity of any single site or server. This is especially the case in rare disease research or cohort studies that look at genetic factors responding to specialized treatments. If a genomic researcher has one million samples, each with hundreds of thousands of attributes and thousands of basic elements, yet only 100 have the characteristics being searched for, quite clearly the data set becomes overwhelmingly huge.

For instance, the International Cancer Genome Consortium (ICGC)[4] and its member project, The Cancer Genome Atlas (TCGA),[5] have analysed and released the data from over 10,000 donors, generating more than 1.5 petabytes of raw and interpreted data. It is estimated that when the ICGC project is complete in 2018, it will comprise more than 50,000 individual genomes with an estimated 10 to 15 petabytes of data.[6] While the interpreted results are available for browsing, mining and download-ing at a site-specific data portal (in Toronto) and the raw sequencing data are archived at two sites (the European Genome-Phenome Archive (EGA) in the UK, and at cgHub in the University of California, Santa Cruz in the United States), there are many compelling scientific reasons for researchers to have remote access to the raw sequencing data. Foremost, pan-cancer analyses can be performed to identify commonalities and differences among the various cancer types.

Certain projects have been successfully designed to handle specific privacy issues surrounding identifiability for large-scale community pro-jects. For example, Bio-PIN allows a biospecimen donor to be registered without any identity data, and a distinguishing biological PIN code (called Bio-PIN) is produced based on that individual's unique biological characteristics (for example, nucleotides that are not part of any geno-type) in a way that the resulting PIN code cannot be linked back to the individual.[7] This not only ensures anonymity, but also enables a secure, two-way, individual-controlled, web-based communication with the

---

    [4] International Cancer Genome Consortium, www.icgc.org, accessed 25 July 2014.
    [5] The Cancer Genome Atlas, cancergenome.nih.gov/, accessed 19 July 2014.
    [6] ICGC (n 4).
    [7] J.J. Nietfeld, Jeremy Sugarman and Jan-Eric Litton, 'The Bio-PIN: A Concept to Improve Biobanking' (2011) 11 *Nat Rev Cancer* 303.

research platform, such as a biobank.[8] Similarly, DataSHIELD enables analysis of pooled (but not shared) data based on parallel local processing, distributed computing, and advanced asymmetric encryption algorithmic methods.[9]

Yet, the biggest challenge in 21st century data-intensive science is more fundamental: comprehensive analyses of genomic data sets to advance biomedical research and clinical practice cannot be done without greater collaboration, a vast computer infrastructure and advanced software tools. Simply buying more servers for a local research site is no longer an optimal or even feasible solution to handle the data deluge. Rosenthal and others observe:

> As biomedical research transitions to a data-centric paradigm, scientists need to work more collaboratively, crossing geographic, domain, and social barriers. Interdisciplinary collaboration over the Internet is in demand, making it necessary for individual laboratories to equip themselves with the technical infrastructure needed for information management and data sharing. For example, a research group may need to include data from clinical records, genome studies, animal studies, and toxicology analyses. The era of spreadsheet-based research data storage is approaching its limits.[10]

As a result, researchers are increasingly turning to cloud computing, both as a solution to integrate data from genomics, systems biology and biomedical data mining, and as an approach to mine and analyse data to solve biomedical problems.[11]

---

[8]   A biobank is an organized collection of human biological material and associated information stored for one or more research purposes.

[9]   Madeleine J. Murtagh, Ipek Demir, K. Neil Jenkings, Susan E. Wallace, Barnaby Murtagh, Mathieu Boniol, Maria Bota, Philippe LaFlamme, Paolo Boffetta, Vincent Ferretti and Paul R. Burton, 'Securing the Data Economy: Translating Privacy and Enacting Security in the Development of DataSHIELD' (2012) 15 *Public Health Genomics* 243; Susan E. Wallace, Amadou Gaye, Osama Shoush and Paul R. Burton, 'Protecting Personal Data in Epidemiological Research: DataSHIELD and UK Law' (2014) 17 *Public Health Genomics* 149.

[10]   Arnon Rosenthal, Peter Mork, Maya Hao Li, Jean Stanford, David Koester and Patti Reynolds, 'Cloud Computing: A New Business Paradigm for Biomedical Information Sharing' (2010) 43 *J Biomed Inform* 342, 343.

[11]   Stephen H. Friend and Thea C. Norman, 'Metcalfe's Law and the Biology Information Commons' (2013) 31 Nat Biotechnol 297; Vivien Marx, 'Genomics in the Clouds' (2013) 10 Nat Methods 941. For example, as part of its Ten Thousand Genomes Program (AUT10K), the advocacy group Autism Speaks is using Google Cloud Platform to create an enormous database of sequenced genomes from people with autism and their family members. The goal is to facilitate new discoveries about autism by making the data openly accessible. See

II. GENOMIC CLOUD COMPUTING

Though an evolving paradigm, genomic cloud computing can be defined as a scalable service where genetic sequence information is stored and processed virtually (in other words, in the 'cloud') usually via networked, large-scale data centres accessible remotely through various clients and platforms over the Internet.[12] Rather than buying more servers for the local research site, as was done in the past, genomic cloud computing allows researchers to use technologies such as application programming interfaces (APIs) to launch servers. Various cloud computing platforms have emerged for genomic researchers, including Galaxy,[13] Bionimbus[14] and DNAnexus,[15] which allow researchers to perform genomic analyses using only a web browser. These platforms in turn may run on specific clouds provided by cloud service providers (CSPs).

Different deployment models of cloud computing have emerged in recent years (for example, commercial/public, community, hybrid and private), and each carry different technical, legal and ethical considerations for researchers (please see discussion in Chapter 1).[16] In this chapter, we focus on commercial CSPs that typically process data transnationally, have built-in security mechanisms, and can handle the

---

Lily Hay Newman, 'Autism Speaks Is Using Google Cloud Platform to Amass and Analyze a Trove of Autism-Related Genomes', (*Slate*, 13 June 2014), www.slate.com/blogs/future_tense/2014/06/13/using_google_cloud_platform_autism_speaks_is_doing_research_on_a_database.html, accessed 21 July 2014.

[12]   Lincoln D. Stein, 'The Case for Cloud Computing in Genome Informatics' (2010) 11 *Genome Biol* 207.

[13]   Enis Afgan, Dannon Baker, Nate Coraor, Hiroki Goto, Ian M. Paul, Kateryna D. Makova, Anton Nekrutenko and James Taylor, 'Harnessing Cloud Computing with Galaxy Cloud' (2011) 29 *Nat Biotechnol* 972.

[14]   Allison P. Heath, Matthew Greenway, Raymond Powell, Jonathan Spring, Rafael Suarez, David Hanley, Chai Bandlamudi, Megan E. McNerney, Kevin P. White and Robert L. Grossman, 'Bionimbus: A Cloud for Managing, Analyzing and Sharing Large Genomics Datasets' (2014) 21 *J Am Med Inform Assoc* 969.

[15]   Jeffrey G. Reid, Andrew Carroll, Narayanan Veeraraghavan, Mahmoud Dahdouli, Andreas Sundquist, Adam English, Matthew Bainbridge, Simon White, William Salerno, Christian Buhay, Fuli Yu, Donna Muzny, Richard Daly, Geoff Duyk, Richard A. Gibbs and Eric Boerwinkle, 'Launching Genomics into the Cloud: Deployment of Mercury, a Next Generation Sequence Analysis Pipeline' (2014) 15 *BMC Bioinformatics* 30.

[16]   Jonathan J.M. Seddon and Wendy L. Currie, 'Cloud Computing and Trans-Border Health Data: Unpacking U.S. and EU Healthcare Regulation and Compliance' (2013) 2 *Health Policy and Technology* 229.

large volume of data generated by international genomic research projects. They allow customers to build, manage and scale an infrastructure based on their needs. Large commercial CSPs have the advantage of often already having public genomic data sets on their cloud infrastructure, which save researchers time and effort in organizing and paying for the transfer of common data such as reference genomes.[17]

In this chapter, we also focus on Infrastructure as a Service (IaaS) cloud computing, which provides raw computing resources, including processing power (known as 'compute') and storage to the user. Often this service allows users to install their own operating systems and applications on the provider's infrastructure. In other words, IaaS provides an ability to 'rent' the compute space and mount bespoke research tools for genomic analysis on the cloud.[18]

Cloud contracts can be either non-negotiable 'standard-form' contracts or negotiated contracts tailored to fit the specific requirements of the cloud service customer. Typically for scalability reasons, however, commercial CSPs provide non-negotiable, standard-form contracts that apply to all types of data. Both types of contracts are generally called 'terms of service' and cover terms and conditions, service level agreements, acceptable use policies, and general security and privacy policies – the latter of which can often be quite lengthy and complex. Sometimes these documents, or key parts of them, may be folded into the terms of service; other times they are incorporated by reference.

Genomic cloud computing provides several benefits. First, it is, relatively speaking, low-cost in terms of allowing access to resources due to its 'elasticity' – an on-demand service wherein one pays for what one needs. This shifts the need from purchasing many information technology resources in-house (in other words, capital expenditure) to 'renting' such resources from third parties when needed (in other words, operating expenditure). For genomic researchers, this tends to mean paying for computing time and transfer. Moreover, large CSPs are able to buy data transit in bulk so as to increase network connectivity and the bandwidth necessary for international data transfer; this reduces internal bandwidth costs and passes on the savings to their customers. Second, cloud

---

[17]   Marx (n 11) 941. Amazon Web Services' cloud contains public data sets including, for example, the US National Institute of Health's sequence database, GenBank.

[18]   See, for example, the Genome Analysis Toolkit (GATK), a toolkit for commercial applications developed by Appistry and the Broad Institute, available for download and installation on a cloud. www.broadinstitute.org/gatk/, accessed 27 July 2014.

computing may afford greater data security, as large-scale cloud-based infrastructure typically has the capacity to invest in and implement state-of-the-art encryption, firewalls and auditing capabilities. Third, genomic cloud computing also offers increased data storage capacity, efficient processing and 'scaled up' genomic analysis through increased computing power, which can accelerate discovery and innovation and avoid the 'researchers' bottleneck' where researchers are forced to size their work to the infrastructure their organization built. Finally, with efficiency and economies of scale, cloud computing services are becoming not only a cheaper solution but also a more environmentally friendly way to build and deploy IT services.[19]

However, as recognized by governments and scholars alike, these benefits do not come without some concerns.[20] In addition to data security concerns,[21] reliability can plague even the biggest names in cloud computing. In 2008, 2011 and 2012, for example, Amazon's data centres suffered multiple outages, including one due to heavy thunderstorms, bringing down a number of popular websites and services and

---

[19]   Cloud computing is seen to deliver energy savings through external data storage and data bundling on powerful mainframe computers. See Ingrid Gottschalk and Stefan Kirn, 'Cloud Computing as a Tool for Enhancing Ecological Goals?' (2013) 5 *Business & Information Systems Engineering* 299. At the same time, however, the growing demand of cloud infrastructure has drastically increased the energy consumption of data centres. See Jayant Baliga, Robert W.A. Ayre, Kerry J. Hinton and Rodney S. Tucker, 'Green Cloud Computing: Balancing Energy in Processing, Storage, and Transport' (2011) 99 *Proceedings of the IEEE* 149.

[20]   Paul M. Schwartz, 'Information Privacy in the Cloud' (2013) 161 Univ PA Law Rev 1623; Konstantinos K. Stylianou, 'An Evolutionary Study of Cloud Computing Services Privacy Terms' (2010) 27 J Comput Inf Law 593; Article 29 Data Protection Working Party, 'Opinion 05/2012 on Cloud Computing' (WP 196, 1 July 2012); European Commission, 'Unleashing the Potential of Cloud Computing' COM (2012) 529 final; European Parliament, 'Resolution of 10 December 2013 on Unleashing the Potential of Cloud Computing in Europe' (2013/2063(INI)), www.europarl.europa.eu/sides/getDoc.do?type=TA&language=EN&reference=P7-TA-2013-0535, accessed 24 July 2014.

[21]   Ponemon Institute LLC, *Data Breach: The Cloud Multiplier Effect* (Traverse City, MI: Ponemon Institute 2014), citing responses from more than 600 US-based IT and IT security practitioners who are familiar with their company's usage of cloud services. Many of those surveyed do not believe their organizations are properly vetting cloud services for security: 72 per cent believed their CSP would not alert them to a data breach that involved theft of confidential data.

preventing users from logging in to access their data.[22] One outage led a technology commentator to remark: 'The duration of the outage has surprised many, since Amazon has a lot of backup computing infrastructure. If Amazon can't safeguard the cloud, how can we rely on it?'[23] In addition, closure of CSPs can cause concern about data control and migration. In 2013, for example, Nirvanix, a well-funded and established CSP, suddenly ended its cloud service and gave its customers only two weeks to save and migrate their data.[24] Similarly, in January 2012, to the surprise of many, Google discontinued Google Health and gave users a year within which to make alternative arrangements for their data.[25]

As genomic researchers rely on data donated by patients and participants and are bound to abide by laws and research ethics policies, it is critical to respect the privacy and autonomy of patients and participants by proactively assessing the full range of legal issues surrounding genomic cloud computing. This risk assessment is all the more important given that the terms of service of CSPs are generic documents that have not been developed with sensitive health or genomic data specifically in mind.

In this chapter, we discuss several key legal issues, namely data control; data security, confidentiality and transfer; and accountability. Without question, one of the most pressing issues in genomic cloud

---

[22] Mike Gunderloy, 'S3 Outage: The Aftermath' (*GigaOM*, 21 July 2008), http://gigaom.com/2008/07/21/s3-outage-aftermath, accessed 21 July 2014; Derrick Harris, 'Cloud Platforms Heroku, DotCloud & Engine Yard Hit Hard by Amazon Outage' (*GigaOM*, 21 April 2011), http://gigaom.com/2011/04/21/more-than-100-sites-went-down-with-ec2-including-your-paas-provider, accessed 21 July 2014; Nick Bilton, 'Amazon Web Services Knocked Offline by Storms' (*New York Times.com*, 30 June 2012), http://bits.blogs.nytimes.com/2012/06/30/amazon-web-services-knocked-offline-by-storms, accessed 21 July 2014; Nicole Perlroth, 'Amazon Cloud Service Goes Down and Takes Popular Sites With It' (*New York Times.com*, 22 October 2012), http://bits.blogs.nytimes.com/2012/10/22/amazon-cloud-service-goes-down-and-takes-some-popular-web-sites-with-it, accessed 21 July 2014.

[23] Dean Takahashi, 'Amazon's Outage in Third Day: Debate over Cloud Computing's Future Begins' (*VB News*, 23 April 2011), http://venturebeat.com/2011/04/23/amazons-outage-in-third-day-debate-over-cloud-computings-future-begins, accessed 21 July 2014.

[24] Tom Coughlin, 'Nirvanix Provides Cautionary Tale for Cloud Storage' (*Forbes*, 30 September 2013), www.forbes.com/sites/tomcoughlin/2013/09/30/nirvanix-provides-cautionary-tail-for-cloud-storage/, accessed 21 July 2014.

[25] Aaron Brown and Bill Weihl, 'An Update on Google Health and Google PowerMeter' (*Google Blog*, 24 June 2011), http://googleblog.blogspot.ca/2011/06/update-on-google-health-and-google.html, accessed 30 July 2014.

computing – and indeed cloud computing generally – is privacy. While CSPs and researchers alike push for greater harmonization of the global data protection regulatory framework, many data protection authorities and other regulators question whether cloud computing can truly be compliant with the current frameworks as they exist, and if not, whether alternative solutions to protect privacy are needed. As the issue remains unsettled, the room for privacy concerns widens.

The issues identified in this chapter should be borne in mind by genomic research organizations when negotiating legal arrangements to store genomic data on large commercial CSPs' servers. Depending on the nature of the data and research environment, researchers must determine whether specialized secure private or hybrid clouds (which large CSPs may offer) are required to ensure that sensitive data (for example, clinical data) remains within an organization and follows appropriate regulations, or whether commercial clouds may be used to analyse and distribute publicly available data,[26] perhaps subject to approval by a data access committee that authorizes scientific researchers and other end users.[27] The points raised in this chapter are based on a review of several publicly available CSP terms of service. Critical reviews of privacy legislation in various jurisdictions and academic literature on cloud privacy were also

---

[26]   R.L. Grossman and K.P. White, 'A Vision for a Biomedical Cloud' (2012) 271 J Intern Med 122; Y. Tony Yang and Kari Borg, 'Regulatory Privacy Protection for Biomedical Cloud Computing' (2012) 3 Beijing Law Rev 145. Depending on the jurisdiction, regulations may require that cloud-based genomic analyses be performed only on de-identified sequence data to interpret genomic variants.

[27]   For example, cloud computing services are now permitted by the US National Institutes of Health for 'controlled access' genomic and associated phenotypic data obtained from NIH-designated data repositories under the auspices of the NIH Genomic Data Sharing Policy. Investigators who wish to use cloud computing for storage and analysis will need to indicate in their Data Access Request, which is reviewed by a data access committee, that they are requesting permission to use cloud computing and must identify the cloud service provider or providers that will be employed. They also will need to describe how the cloud computing service will be used to carry out their proposed research. See National Institutes of Health, 'NIH Position Statement on Use of Cloud Computing Services for Storage and Analysis of Controlled-Access Data Subject to the NIH Genomic Data Sharing Policy' (2015), http://gds.nih.gov/pdf/NIH_Position_Statement_on_Cloud_Computing.pdf, accessed 3 April 2015. See also National Center for Biotechnology Information, 'NIH Security Best Practices for Controlled-Access Data Subject to the NIH Genomic Data Sharing (GDS) Policy' (2015), http://www.ncbi.nlm.nih.gov/projects/gap/pdf/dbgap_2b_security_procedures.pdf, accessed 3 April 2015.

undertaken. As there are other types of CSPs, and this is a quickly evolving area, other issues can arise in the course of genomic cloud computing. Genomic researchers are therefore encouraged to seek legal advice before concluding agreements with cloud providers.

III. LEGAL ISSUES

A. Data Control

Cloud computing with commercial CSPs entails the outsourcing (or off-shoring) of data and services to third party providers. Any genomic or health-related data that used to be stored locally may thereafter be stored in the cloud, including in a 'cloud stack' format whereby multiple layers of services are provided by separate CSPs. Attributable to a multi-tenant environment (in other words, where a single instance of software runs on a server and serves multiple client-organizations), and possibly geographically dispersed data centres, genomic researchers place their computation and data on machines they cannot directly control. To a large extent, control over computation and data is thereby relinquished, the latter of which arguably challenges established international privacy law principles of openness and transparency.[28] Among the risks associated with cloud computing are unauthorized access (or reuses for which consent has not been obtained from researchers, patients or participants), data corruption, infrastructure failure, or unavailability. In case something goes wrong, it can be difficult to discern the source of the problem, and, in the absence of solid evidence, it is nearly impossible for the parties involved to hold each other responsible for the problem if a dispute arises.

Data control issues are manifest in several areas of a CSP's terms of service:

1. Amendments to terms of service
First, control issues arise in the ability for many commercial CSPs to amend the terms of service, frequently without explicit notification to customers. Often included in CSPs' imposed standard-form contracts is the possibility for the CSP to vary terms via unilateral notice (see Box

---

[28] See, for example, OECD, 'Recommendation of the Council concerning Guidelines Governing the Protection of Privacy and Transborder Flows of Personal Data' C(80)58/FINAL (2013), as amended on 11 July 2013 by C(2013)79.

11A.1 in the Appendix for an example). This privilege, which is commonly seen in IT and online contracts, obliges customers to check the CSP website for changes to the terms of service, even if the CSP does not mark the changes or indicate the date of last change or review. Some may provide notice only of 'material' changes to the terms of service. Further, CSPs will consider the continued use of their cloud service as deemed acceptance of the new terms of service in the absence of any explicit objection to the amended terms or cessation of use.

Consequently, researchers should ensure proper notification of amendments to terms of service with a reasonable period of time for response and acceptance.

2. Data preservation and deletion

Second, control issues are encountered in terms of service sections regarding data preservation (what happens to data when the contractual relationship with the CSP ends) and deletion (the removal of data from the cloud). Even though control is potentially problematic, researchers should to the greatest extent possible put themselves in a position to control what data are moved to the cloud, as well as to control what data remain in the cloud. They should also ensure that they can retrieve genomic data when needed and that a CSP cannot retain it or use it after the contract ends, subject to legal or regulatory requirements and/or authorization of the researchers.

Regarding preservation, some CSPs will preserve data for a grace period following the end of the agreement (for example, 30 days). Other CSPs may stipulate that they will delete the data immediately upon the end of the agreement, no matter the circumstances. Others simply may not discuss at all what will happen, providing neither a grace period nor an undertaking to delete the data. Consequently, researchers should ask for clarification of the CSP's data preservation policy regarding how long the grace period lasts (if applicable), commitments to comprehensively delete the data, and any costs that may be involved. Additionally, researchers should ensure that data exit and migration strategies are well planned before importing genomic data into a cloud. Indeed, the Nirvanix experience demonstrates that it is much easier to import data than to recover it or move it to another CSP; a cloud exit strategy is as valuable as a cloud deployment strategy.[29]

Regarding deletion, researchers should consider what happens to their genomic data after the relationship with a CSP comes to an end: what is

---

[29]   Supra, p. 243.

their exit strategy and end-of-contract transition? Researchers should also consider whether they can retrieve their data with relative ease to move it elsewhere. Upon termination of the cloud computing services, does the CSP ensure that the genomic data will be deleted comprehensively, including duplicates or backups, from its servers (and any sub-processors' servers) upon the researchers' retrieval of it? Is there evidence provided of permanent deletion? If this cannot be ensured, a CSP may be seen to assume responsibility, under data protection laws of certain jurisdictions such as those in Europe, for the security of any non-deleted personal data. It should be noted that under the proposed European General Data Protection Regulation, a new right to transmit personal data in the same format could require CSPs to allow customers to move their data to competitors offering similar products or services.[30]

3. Data monitoring

Third, control issues arise in terms of service sections pertaining to data monitoring. Can the CSP monitor hosted genomic data, and if so, what form should the monitoring take and what conditions should apply? Even though most commercial CSPs encrypt data while in transit and at rest, researchers should still verify that the data are encrypted (and find out how they are encrypted). Additionally, if it is researchers that encrypt the data, they should query whether they want the CSP to have access to decryption keys.[31] While monitoring of traffic data or bandwidth con-sumption may be acceptable, researchers could be concerned with a CSP monitoring personal data or aggregate genomic data uploaded to the cloud, even if such monitoring is to ensure compliance with an accepted use policy. Researchers may want the CSP to agree, if possible, to treat any genomic or health-related data obtained from monitoring or support

---

[30] Gerhan Gunasekara, 'Paddling in Unison or Just Paddling? International Trends in Reforming Information Privacy Law' (2014) 22 *International Journal of Law and Information Technology* 141, 159. The proposed Regulation creates a 'right to data portability', which includes 'the right to transmit … personal data and any other information provided by the data subject and retained by an automated processing system, into another one, in an electronic format which is commonly used, without hindrance from the controller from whom the personal data are withdrawn'. See European Commission, 'Proposal for a Regulation of the European Parliament and of the Council on the protection of individuals with regard to the processing of personal data and on the free movement of such data (General Data Protection Regulation)', COM(2012) 11 final 2012/0011 (COD), art. 18(2).

[31] This said, strong data encryption can make it more difficult to index the data, multiplying access costs. See Rosenthal and others (n 10) 350.

or maintenance activities as subject to confidentiality provisions, or to restrict the purposes for which CSPs can monitor such data. Additionally, researchers should ensure that their own organization has data encryption capabilities and good management infrastructure for control over data stored on a cloud. At the same time, researchers should be aware of their own policies for giving authorization and access privileges to staff to provide login details to CSP employees for certain situations (for example, support).

B. Data Security, Confidentiality and Transfer

On a structural level, there is a contrast between the nature of cloud computing, built on the idea of 'locationlessness' (or at least disparate localization), and data privacy laws, which are still based on geographic borders and location-specific data processing systems. Cloud computing is largely built on the idea of seamless, borderless sharing and storage of data. This can run into tension with different national jurisdictions governing citizens' rights over privacy and protection of personal data. Indeed, as cloud computing enables personal (health) data to be transferred across borders, where little consensus exists about which authorities have jurisdiction over the data, cloud customers and providers will each need to understand and comply with the different rules in place – to the extent such rules exist. In an environment where data exchange by researchers is no longer a point-to-point transaction within one country, but instead is characterized by transnational, dynamic and decentralized flow, the legal distinction between national and international data use may become less meaningful than in the past.

At the same time, the global nature of genomic cloud computing means that it is difficult to know which laws apply, let alone how to ensure compliance with the applicable laws. For example, while national regulatory frameworks such as the Clinical Laboratory Improvement Amendments (CLIA)[32] or the Health Insurance Portability and Accountability Act of 1996 (HIPAA)[33] establish guidelines for clinical data storage and sharing in the US, there remains no international law on the use and storage of clinical data. In addition, the nascent stage of cloud

---

[32]   Clinical Laboratory Improvement Amendments of 1988 (CLIA), 42 U.S.C. para. 263a.

[33]   Health Insurance Portability and Accountability Act of 1996 (HIPAA), Pub. L. No. 104–191, 110 Stat. 1936 (1996). See also Centers for Medicare & Medicaid Services, 'The Health Insurance Portability and Accountability Act of 1996', www.cms.hhs.gov/hipaa/default.asp, accessed 14 July 2014.

computing, particularly in the genomics context, leads to uncertainty about how existing laws, especially privacy and data protection laws, will be applied. Though it is now well established that data sets such as genome sequences may uniquely identify an individual,[34] there has not yet been an attempt to reach community consensus on safeguarding privacy in genomic cloud computing, particularly regarding well-defined cloud computing-attuned standards, guidelines or model contractual agreements.[35] This said, researchers probably will be more interested in the applicable law for the CSP who is providing the services, rather than where data are stored, as CSPs must comply with and be subject to the laws of their headquartered jurisdiction.[36]

1. Data security and confidentiality

One of the greatest concerns about storing genomic data in the cloud is whether the data are secure. Researchers may fear that storing data in the cloud will lead to potential unauthorized access to participant or patient data, and liability and reputation damage that could result from a mandatory breach notification, such as that stipulated in HIPAA.[37] Misappropriation or disclosure of private health information through a genomic data breach can result in serious privacy consequences such as genetic discrimination in healthcare, employment and private insurance. Studies have shown that it is technically feasible for a data intruder to access a researcher's genomic database, combine the sensitive data with publicly available information, and determine that a specific person is linked with a disease.[38] However, it should be noted that documented

---

[34] Yaniv Erlich and Arvind Narayanan, 'Routes for Breaching and Protecting Genetic Privacy' (2014) 15 *Nat Rev Genet* 409–21.

[35] However, on a general level, regulators have begun to develop model terms for cloud computing service level agreements, paying particular attention to security and personal data protection in the cloud. See, for example, European Commission's Cloud Select Industry Group – Subgroup on Service Level Agreements (C-SIG-SLA), *Cloud Service Level Agreement Standardisation Guidelines* (24 June 2014), https://ec.europa.eu/digital-agenda/en/news/cloud-service-level-agreement-standardisation-guidelines, accessed 28 July 2014.

[36] This is distinct from any governing law and forum selection clauses (in other words, choice of forum for settling disputes) in the terms of service. CSPs may assert that the terms of service are covered by the laws of a specific jurisdiction, which may not be the jurisdiction in which the CSP has its principal place of business.

[37] Health Insurance Portability and Accountability Act (HIPAA) Administrative Simplification Rules, 45 C.F.R. paras 164.400–14.

[38] Erlich and Narayanan (n 34).

instances of genetic discrimination remain very rare outside the context of a few monogenic dominant genetic disorders.[39]

Even though genomic data stripped of identifiers (including names, addresses, birthdates and the like) may not constitute 'personal health information' for HIPAA or other similar health information privacy law purposes, recent literature suggests this could well change.[40] Consequently, researchers have reason to seriously consider the security issues of genomic cloud computing and the role of privacy laws.

Such issues arise in terms of service sections addressing data security and confidentiality, along with CSP privacy policies, and data location and transfer. Depending on the sensitivity of the data, research organizations may want to establish data access committees which oversee the terms of access to cloud-stored data. Similarly, US-based researchers might want (or even require) CSPs to hold 'trusted partner' status before storing genomic or clinical data in the cloud, or have them sign a HIPAA 'business associate agreement' (BAA).[41] Many commercial CSPs are now able to provide a BAA, which describes what a CSP can and cannot do with 'protected health information' under HIPAA guidelines, including a prohibition on further disclosing the data to another entity other than those permitted or required by the contract or by law. However, applying such extensive national requirements would not be conducive to the type of global data exchange needed for the development of a healthy, productive genomic research sector. The desire of participants and patients to encourage beneficial research that could eventually lead to the development of a cure for serious afflictions should not be neglected in order to achieve an 'ideal' level of privacy protection. Considering these issues together, researchers should verify the data elements to be stored in the cloud, including whether the data constitute sensitive personal data or personal health information. Genomic data should be secured in a way that protects the privacy of everyone whose data are analysed. Researchers should also consider restricting access to cloud-stored genomic data

---

[39]   Yann Joly, Ida Ngueng Feze and Jacques Simard, 'Genetic Discrimination and Life Insurance: A Systematic Review of the Evidence' (2013) 11 *BMC Medicine* 25.

[40]   Laura L. Rodriguez, Lisa D. Brooks, Judith H. Greenberg and Eric D. Green, 'The Complexities of Genomic Identifiability' (2013) 339 *Science* 275.

[41]   HIPAA restricts covered entities from disclosing 'personal health information' to non-affiliated third parties unless specific contractual arrangements have been put in place. See HIPAA Administrative Simplification Rules (n 37), 45 C.F.R. paras 164.502(e), 164.504(e), 164.532(d) and (e).

(individual-level) to bona fide researchers approved by data access committees.

Often, genomic data security and confidentiality questions may be answered by consulting privacy or data protection laws, as well as internal organizational policies and research funding requirements. Data protection laws may provide only broad principles-based guidance, such as requiring the adoption of safeguards that are commensurate with the sensitivity of the data – and data protection laws across the globe frequently treat genomic data as sensitive, thereby requiring strict safe-guards.

Many CSPs offer to make 'best efforts' or to take 'reasonable and appropriate measures' to secure data against accidental/unlawful loss, access or disclosure, but this is distinct from a legal representation that the service will be uninterrupted or error free, or that data will be fully secure or not otherwise lost or damaged. Indeed, few commercial CSPs will make this latter type of comprehensive representation. At the same time, CSPs themselves must be cognizant of strict privacy and data protection laws in jurisdictions where data may be processed, especially in Europe. For example, section 9 of Germany's Federal Data Protection Act (BDSG) mandates the need for 'necessary technical and organizational measures' to be put in place for a cloud service, and section 9(a) grants audit rights to cloud customers to examine a CSP's 'data protection strategy and their technical facilities'.[42] Commercial CSPs should be in a position to implement security and compliance features that enable compliance with relevant regulations and international guidelines, be it HIPAA,[43] Good Clinical Practice (GCP) guidelines,[44] European data protection laws or dbGaP Security Best Practices Requirements.[45]

Researchers should carefully examine a CSP's approach to securing and protecting data, with an understanding that CSPs may not want to fully disclose their security practices, lest doing so compromise their cloud's security itself. Many commercial CSPs offer security 'white

---

[42] Federal Data Protection Act (BDSG) (Germany), Federal Law Gazette I, 66 (2003), www.bfdi.bund.de/EN/DataProtectionActs/Artikel/BDSG_idFv01092 009.pdf?__blob=publicationFile, accessed 13 July 2014.

[43] HIPAA Administrative Simplification Rules (n 37).

[44] International Conference on Harmonisation of Technical Requirements for Registration of Pharmaceuticals for Human Use (ICH), 'Guideline for Good Clinical Practice E6' (10 June 1996), www.ich.org/fileadmin/Public_Web_Site/ ICH_Products/Guidelines/Efficacy/E6_R1/Step4/E6_R1__Guideline.pdf, accessed 15 July 2014.

[45] 'dbGaP Security Best Practices Requirements' (n 27).

papers' that researchers can consult to review the security controls. Important questions to consider include: does data security appear to be a priority? What are the physical, administrative and digital security measures? Is the CSP willing to show specific documentation (for example, ISO 27001, ISO 27002 or ISO 27018 policies and procedures)?[46] How well are web-based applications protected? Are there API access restrictions? Are there multi-factor authentication, automatic session timeouts, and logging functions for auditability? Will the CSP provide prompt notification of service interruptions or a potential data compromise? Are cloud customers indemnified for unscheduled downtime? Does the CSP make data backups or are researchers solely responsible for doing so? Do the CSP's security measures accord with the researchers' own security policies or practices regarding the secure storage of genomic data? Given the sensitivity of genomic data, researchers should consider whether a CSP agrees to report any data losses or security breach incidents within a short period of time (for example, less than 24 hours).

There are several aspects researchers should consider with respect to data security and confidentiality. First, they should ensure that CSPs have been independently audited against comprehensive and internationally recognized and respected information security standards, such as those promulgated by the International Organization for Standardization (ISO) and Statement on Standards for Attestation Engagements (SSAE). Second, they should ensure that the third party audit certifications are current and maintained throughout the duration of the cloud service. Third, researchers should consider how cloud computing can impact data protection and confidentiality, both within the laws of jurisdictions and also within the ethical and legal requirements of the research organization and/or funders. If a CSP is unwilling to commit to a general obligation to comply with all applicable data protection and confidentiality laws relating to genomic data, researchers should alternatively attempt to secure a confidentiality or non-disclosure agreement, or a commitment by

---

[46] ISO 27001 is a well-known international standard for initiating, implementing, maintaining and improving an information security management system. ISO 27002 establishes detailed guidelines and general principles for information security management within an organization. ISO 27018 was released in August 2014 and is intended to be used in conjunction with the information security objectives and controls in ISO 27002 to create a common set of security categories and controls that can be implemented by a public cloud computing service provider that processes Personally Identifiable Information (PII).

the CSP to be contractually bound to the ethical and legal requirements applicable to the researchers' institution.

Yet, general commitments to laws may be the best that researchers can hope for at this time, along with strong adherence to security measures such as data encryption, both when at rest and during transfer. At their end, CSPs should institute good privacy and security principles such as data minimization (only retaining the data needed for business purposes and disposing of it after its useful life has expired); user access control (only granting access to those who need certain data); vulnerability management (constant scanning of systems to ensure data protection); segregation and segmentation of services (walling off sensitive services from less sensitive ones to apply rigorous security controls effectively); data monitoring (mechanisms that allow for quick detection of attacks and countermeasures); and training and awareness (proper training to ensure employees know about security protocols, the limitations of encryption and dangers of phishing attacks).

2. Data location and transfer

Data location and transfer is a critical issue for researchers, given its intersections with data protection laws, ethical guidelines, and consent forms that may (or may not) address data storage and sharing. In addition to cloud-to-cloud data transfer, which raises questions of data, application and service interoperability, researchers should be aware that most commercial CSPs process, store or temporarily move data to any country where the CSP or its agents maintain facilities (see Box 11A. 2 in the Appendix for an example). This is done for service-related reasons, namely for security, backups, support and cost efficiency. Intra-cloud data transfer (that is, transfer within the same CSP) is permissible under most data protection laws, provided there is compliance with the relevant data export provisions, such as consent from 'data subjects', model contractual clauses, or Binding Corporate Rules.[47]

However, many commercial CSPs may not always tell their customers where the data are going at any given moment. This can cause problems in regions such as Europe, where data protection laws prohibit the transfer of data to third countries without 'adequate protection' for the

---

[47] Binding Corporate Rules (BCRs) are provisions in European data protection law that allow a multinational company to transfer personal data to its affiliates and subsidiaries in foreign (non-European) jurisdictions without 'adequacy' status, provided it submits its global privacy policies and practices to a 'lead' jurisdiction's data protection authority (typically in the country of the company's European headquarters) for review and prior approval.

data. Some CSPs may store data in locations unknown to researchers (and 'data subjects', in other words, research participants), and some American CSPs may not have signed on to the US-EU Safe Harbor Agreement (nor may they be able to, as some commentators assert IaaS clouds by definition cannot fulfil any of the Safe Harbor Agreement Principles[48]). As a result, Europeans' genomic and health-related data may be denied lawful entry into the cloud, absent express consent. Indeed, in 2011, Germany's data protection authorities adopted a cloud computing orientation guide which suggested that German users of cloud computing services are forbidden from transferring sensitive data (which includes genomic and health data) to a US CSP without the express consent of the individual.[49]

This said, 'sensitive' genomic and health-related data may still be transferred – legally and ethically – if researchers apply sound strategies to managing the data, including obtaining consent from participants or patients, protecting the identity of data through de-identification or other privacy enhancing mechanisms, and applying certain restrictions on data access. If there are transfers of personal data from one jurisdiction to another, researchers should verify that a CSP is in compliance with data export laws and regulations (for example, US-EU Safe Harbor Agreement Principles if feasible, EU-standard contractual clauses based on EU Data Protection Directive 95/46/EC) and that the CSP has adequate oversight mechanisms to monitor ongoing compliance with these laws and regulations.

At the same time, large commercial CSPs increasingly assure customers with sensitive data that their data will remain in particular countries or regional zones of choice, even for remote access. Researchers concerned about the location of genomic and health-related data storage should be mindful of the specific locations where data are stored on CSP servers, and it may be that researchers want their data stored only in locations providing an equivalent or greater level of protection for genomic and health-related data to that applicable where the data originated. Even when the data are kept in a specifically determined country, special attention should be paid to provisions allowing temporary or emergency transfer of data to additional undisclosed locations.

---

[48]   Seddon and Currie (n 16) 236.
[49]   Working Groups on Technology and Media of the Conference of Federal and State Data Protection Commissioners, 'Cloud Computing: An Orientation Guide' (2011), www.bfdi.bund.de/EN/Topics/technologicalDataProtection/Artikel/OHCloudComputing.pdf?__blob=publicationFile, accessed 22 July 2014.

Likewise, researchers should be mindful of the long-arm reach of certain laws, such as the US Patriot Act,[50] which allows the US government to access any data within US territory or within a US-based company (even when there is a subsidiary or operations outside the US) without giving notice and without informing the person concerned of the accessed information.[51] A recent US court case found that US Internet service providers (for example, Microsoft or Google and other companies offering cloud services via the Internet) with EU subsidiaries are required to comply with warrants and subpoenas from US law enforcement agencies relating to data held in the EU.[52] Researchers should be mindful, therefore, of CSPs in jurisdictions that permit wide surveillance and law enforcement access to data; they should look to structure services, to the extent possible, which can protect data of patients or participants from access requests by law enforcement agencies. Some jurisdictions, such as Europe, have responded to concerns of US governmental reach by promoting CSPs that claim to never share personal data with other companies or governments and keep all data in non-US data centres where privacy laws may be stronger.[53] It should be noted, however, that many other jurisdictions, including throughout Europe, have national security legislation that gives police and intelligence agencies far-reaching access to data in the cloud in cases justified by national security, frequently without court authorization.[54] Depending on legal/regulatory requirements and the sensitivity of the data, to assuage

---

[50] The Uniting and Strengthening America by Providing Appropriate Tools Required to Intercept and Obstruct Terrorism Act of 2001 (USA PATRIOT Act), Pub. L. No. 107–56, 115 Stat 272 (2001). The Act permits the Federal Bureau of Investigation to obtain an order (called 'Section 215 Orders') from the Foreign Intelligence Surveillance Court demanding any data it deems relevant to an investigation into international terrorism or espionage.

[51] Ibid., para. 215.

[52] *In re Matter of a Warrant* (2014) US District Court – Southern District of New York, 13 Mag 2814, www.nysd.uscourts.gov/cases/show.php?db= special&id=398, accessed 12 July 2014. Microsoft filed objections with the district court, where, on 31 July 2014, the chief judge adopted and affirmed the magistrate judge's order in a bench ruling. Microsoft filed a notice of appeal to the United States Court of Appeals for the Second Circuit. At the time of writing, the case remains undecided.

[53] Mark Scott, 'European Firms Turn Privacy Into Sales Pitch' (*New York Times.com*, 11 June 2014), http://bits.blogs.nytimes.com/2014/06/11/european-firms-turn-privacy-into-sales-pitch/, accessed 12 July 2014.

[54] Winston Maxwell and Christopher Wolf, 'A Sober Look at National Security Access to Data in the Cloud: Analyzing the Extravagant Claims About U.S. Access that Ignore Access by Foreign Jurisdictions' (2014) Hogan Lovells

national security law concerns, researchers should consider requesting CSPs to store data and applications only in designated regions.

While not always made public, researchers should attempt to determine in which jurisdictions the CSP maintains servers and which agents (in other words, sub-contractors) can access their data. They should investigate as much as possible the trail of data storage and transfer, and the ability to have tools that can verify the locations of data storage or transfer. It is important that a CSP will transfer genomic and health-related data only in an encrypted manner over secure networks and that the CSP will continue to be responsible for managing its agents' compliance with data security and confidentiality.

C. Accountability and Liability

Finally, researchers should be mindful of what may happen in the event that something goes wrong. In short, what happens when the cloud fails? With more services being built on top of cloud computing infrastructures, a power outage, closure, bankruptcy or breakage/failure can create a domino effect, effectively taking down large amounts of Internet services and Internet-based applications. In cases of failure, what forms of arbitration exist for stakeholders, and what is the responsibility of CSPs? Traditional privacy and data protection laws may not provide much clarity regarding responsibility and accountability, given that cloud computing introduces a new element into the data provider-data collector/data processor-data controller dynamic.

Accountability issues appear in the standard clauses in contracts addressing liability. Researchers should be mindful of the breadth of a CSP's waiver of liability (see Box 11A.3 in the Appendix for an example). CSPs who have terms of service governed by laws of US states rather than European countries may waive all liability for any unauthorized access or use, corruption, deletion, destruction or loss of any data maintained or transmitted though its servers, regardless of who is at fault. Thus, any damage caused to researchers' data, such as losses arising from security breaches, data breach or loss, denial of service, performance failures, inaccuracy of the service, and so on, even if attributed to the CSP or its agents, may be excluded from any liability. In light of these issues, researchers should determine the chain of responsibility for

White Paper, www.hoganlovells.com/custom/documents/hogan-lovells-a-sober-look-at-national-security-access-in-the-cloud-(2014-update).pdf, accessed 30 July 2014.

preserving the confidentiality and integrity of genomic data. They should also request full indemnity for liability related to privacy and security.

Given the potential concerns about misuse or damage to genomic data, researchers should be aware that direct liability is typically excluded by CSPs.[55] Researchers should also be aware of the importance of negotiating for a clause that imposes liability on the CSP for, at a minimum, wilful or gross negligence with respect to defined types of breach or loss, such as breach of confidentiality, privacy or data protection laws, data loss/corruption or breach of regulatory or security requirements that could give rise to regulatory sanctions.

IV. CONCLUSION

Genomic cloud computing is an emerging technology platform for the biomedical research community. Many cloud computing issues remain unsettled. The legal challenges canvassed in this chapter can provide a useful starting point for researchers to consider when negotiating legal arrangements to store genomic data in the cloud. Just as financial institutions and insurers increasingly use the cloud to manage their data and services (and hold our personal information in an encrypted state), migrating genomic and other health-related data to the cloud is part of the evolution of existing technologies and large-scale genome science. But it comes with its own challenges. All stakeholders should come to the table and work together towards common solutions that enable trust. Collaboration between large biobanks and genomic research consortia on these legal issues to present a common position to commercial CSPs will be a major determinant of success.

In any environment, cloud computing or otherwise, there is no such thing as zero risk. Dedicating more resources to secure genomic and health-related data will be critical for researchers harnessing the cloud. But so too will it be critical to have an open discussion with CSPs of the risks *and* benefits of cloud computing – the latter of which is equally important. Transparent practices will be critical to build trust among participants (government, organizations and individuals) for genomic cloud computing. Transparency prevents abuse by organizations and encourages participants to share their data. The broad access, computing power and speed of cloud computing impels organizations responsible for

---

[55] Direct liability tends to mean liability for losses to the cloud customer relating to data loss or compromise in the cloud.

sensitive data to institute and maintain clearly defined policies on transparency.

In fact, this push for greater transparency is one of the stated aims of the newly launched Global Alliance for Genomics and Health,[56] a broad and diverse coalition of leading health and research organizations united with a global mission to accelerate progress in science and medicine. Seeking to develop and promulgate harmonized approaches (both technical and regulatory) for the effective and responsible sharing of genomic and clinical data across jurisdictions, the Global Alliance is uniquely situated to bring together various stakeholders for open dialogue about genomic cloud computing best practices, and for the design of a flexible and risk-based framework to improve the potential of cloud technologies in the genomics space.

We emphasize the need for multi-stakeholder involvement because introducing genomics into clinical practice through cloud computing 'is not only a linear function of computing capacity but it [also] requires the input from diverse disciplines'.[57] CSPs should consider the specific challenges of genomic and health-related data. Researchers should consider scrutiny of cloud contracts as only one part of the risk assessment process of data migration to the cloud. They should also assess which functions should be migrated to the cloud and how, as well as which internal controls to develop, data will be encrypted and backed up internally, and, after contractual agreement with a CSP, how monitoring will be conducted. Ultimately, diligent genomic cloud computing means leveraging security standards and evaluation processes as a means to protect data, whether local or remote. More importantly, diligent genomic cloud computing entails many of the same good practices that researchers should always consider in securing their local infrastructure. In itself, there is nothing magical about an outsourced relationship with a CSP.

At the same time, broader and non-technical questions remain. Scholars of ethical, legal and social issues (ELSI) in genomics may need to consider whether consent practices should be refined to specifically address the possibility that genomic and health-related data will be processed in the cloud, and any ensuing ethical and legal implications.

---

[56]   Global Alliance for Genomics and Health, www.genomicsandhealth.org, accessed 28 July 2014.

[57]   Barbara Prainsack, Silke Schicktanz and Gabriele Werner-Felmayer, 'Geneticising Life: A Collective Endeavor and its Challenges' in Barbara Prainsack, Silke Schicktanz and Gabriele Werner-Felmayer (eds), *Genetics as Social Practice: Transdisciplinary Views of Science and Culture* (Farnham, UK: Ashgate 2014).

Further research will be needed to uncover the legal and ethical issues associated with other types of cloud computing. Such research would be best informed if it is evidence-based and seeks the views of various stakeholders. This will be critical to better develop cloud computing policy and 'best practices' for the genomics community. That CSPs and genomic and ELSI researchers consider these issues together is not only evidence of due diligence, but a sign of ethical conduct and respect for patients and participants whose data are being used to advance bio-medical science across the globe.

ACKNOWLEDGEMENTS

The authors wish to acknowledge the funding support from the Discovery Frontiers: Advancing Big Data Science in Genomics Research program (grant no. RGPGR/448167-2013, 'The Cancer Genome Collaboratory'), which is jointly funded by the Natural Sciences and Engineering Research Council (NSERC) of Canada, the Canadian Institutes of Health Research (CIHR), Genome Canada, and the Canada Foundation for Innovation (CFI), and with in-kind support from the University of Chicago and the Ontario Research Fund of the Ministry of Research and Innovation.

APPENDIX: EXAMPLES OF CLAUSES FROM CURRENT CSP TERMS OF SERVICE

BOX 11A.1   EXAMPLE OF AMENDMENT CLAUSE

Modifications to the Agreement

We may modify this Agreement (including any Policies) at any time by posting a revised version on the ... Site or by otherwise notifying you in accordance with Section ... The modified terms will become effective upon posting or, if we notify you by email, as stated in the email message. By continuing to use the Service Offerings after the effective date of any modifications to this Agreement, you agree to be bound by the modified terms.

BOX 11A.2   EXAMPLE OF DATA TRANSFER AND STORAGE CLAUSE

Facilities and Data Transfer

[CSP] may process and store ... Customer Data in the United States or any other country in which [CSP] or its agents maintain facilities. By using the Services, Customer consents to this processing and storage of ... Customer Data. The parties agree that [CSP] is merely a data processor.

Transient Storage

[CSP] Customer Data may be stored transiently or cached in any country in which [CSP] or its agents maintain facilities.

BOX 11A.3   EXAMPLE OF LIMITATIONS OF LIABILITY CLAUSE

Limitations of Liability

We and our affiliates or licensors will not be liable to you for any direct, indirect, incidental, special, consequential or exemplary damages ... neither we nor any of our affiliates or licensors will be responsible for any compensation, reimbursement, or damages arising in connection with: ... Any unauthorized access to, alteration of, or the deletion, destruction, damage, loss or failure to store any of your content or other data ...

---

12. Practical aspects of licensing in the cloud

Alan Chiu and Geofrey Master

I. INTRODUCTION: ALL ABOUT LICENSING IN THE CLOUD ENVIRONMENT

In this digital age, people use the World Wide Web to access information; to stay in touch with friends worldwide; and to access and share files and information anywhere at anytime. Enterprises use the Internet to access and utilize an increasing array of sophisticated business applications and technology infrastructure. All of these services are incredibly easy to initiate and use, often requiring minimal data entry (including the occasional input of credit card information). A series of clicks and the service is there and fully operational. It is not surprising that, in this easily accessible cloud environment with such a powerful array of capabilities,[1] there is significant confusion about the legal implications, rights and responsibilities attached to these activities. What seems like a free, easy and open environment actually carries significant consequences

---

[1] As broadly summarized by David Linthicum in his report, the major categories or patterns of cloud computing technology are the following:

- storage-as-a-service;
- database-as-a-service;
- information-as-a-service;
- process-as-a-service;
- application-as-a-service;
- platform-as-a-service;
- integration-as-a-service;
- security-as-a-service;
- management-/government-as-a-service; and
- infrastructure-as-a-service.

David Linthicum, *Selecting the Right Cloud* (InfoWorld Special Report, September 2009) 6.

for users: consequences which may come as significant surprises with unexpected impacts on both individual and business users.

One example where confusion about the cloud is rife is the seemingly common perception that everything on the Internet is owned by the public and can be freely used without any limitation. This perception is fundamentally wrong. In fact, intellectual property rights (mainly copyright in this context) continue to subsist in most, if not all, information posted on, shared over or transmitted via the Internet. Equally immediate, when a user uploads data onto the Internet, that upload is invariably subject to terms that define the access and use rights of other cloud users, as well as the ownership retained (or relinquished) by the uploading user in such data. These rights constitute an actual or constructive contract (license) granted to the service or platform provider and potentially other Internet users as well. Although sometimes they are difficult to discern, which will be discussed below, the terms of this contract define rights of use to the data for certain purposes or within certain limitations.

Regardless of the cloud services involved, there are license rights that define the various parties' rights in, and to, data in the cloud environment as well as other key rights and obligations, whether the cloud service customer is a licensor or a licensee or, as is frequently the case, both.

The following are representative scenarios reflecting licensing in cloud services:

(i) *Customer owned data* – Where the customer uploads and stores data using cloud storage (whether that data is a photo, a word document, a sound track, logo or software) he or she does so under a grant of rights, whether express or implied, to the storage service provider. This grant extends, at a minimum, to the right to make such copies as may be required to enable the provider to perform the storage, processing, backup and retrieval functions through the servers making up the storage facility. Often these servers are situated in different locations (or even different jurisdictions), which may also vary at times based upon aggregate demand and the provider's platform and arrangements for data balancing. The grant of these rights is called content licensing. Further, when a customer engages a service provider to provide Infrastructure-as-a-Service (IaaS) or Platform-as-a-Service (PaaS), the customer may upload their own proprietary (or licensed) software for integration into such cloud services. For this, the customer similarly licensed (or sub-licensed in the case of third party software uploaded by the customer) such software to the service provider for system integration.

As discussed below, the exact contractual terms of these license grants may be clearly expressed and agreed to by the parties, but often they are at least partly implied through the actions and conduct of the parties. In the case of express licenses, as may be contained in the terms of service agreed to by the customer at service initiation, the scope of the licenses may be broad. In fact, such terms may extend well beyond the immediate requirements of the services being provided. For example, a relatively common right included under these licenses grants the provider the right to use the customer data for the benefit of the provider itself, including for further development of the services for all customers of that provider.

(ii) *Service provider owned/licensed software* – Whenever a customer engages a cloud service, the service provider must also grant a license to the customer for at least the necessary rights to use the provider's software interface and functionality or other components essential to the delivery and use of the relevant services.

Cloud customers, especially in public clouds, may be unaware that they are granting content licenses to the service providers at all, much less the actual nature, scope and duration of such licenses. Even though the customers may retain ultimate ownership of their own data, there is a very real risk that they may have lost control over it.[2] Often equally important other rights or obligations are contained (or not contained) in the contract terms governing use of a cloud service, and these may also be unappreciated by the customer.

In this chapter, we provide an overview of the complexities of the cloud services contracting process and discuss in detail some of the key issues and challenges to cloud licensing in practice.

II. ESSENTIAL TERMS IN A CLOUD LICENSE

A. The Frequent Challenge of Determining Terms

Ideally, the terms and conditions under which any cloud solution is provided should be expressly and comprehensively stated in a written, static, readily accessible and understandable agreement. Again ideally,

---

[2] This echoes the view expressed by Professor Chris Reed in Chapter 7.

these terms and conditions should be known and understood by both the customer and the provider. This is often not the case.

The growth of the cloud services' delivery model has been rapid, and has challenged consumers' ability (and perhaps willingness) to effectively assess and manage the legal implications and risks presented in contracting for, and utilizing, cloud solutions. In fact, the sheer ease of initiation and use of cloud services belie the legal significance of the undertaking. From the initial set-up (including the contracting), to the operational use of the services and through to termination arrangements, cloud services present new but familiar variations on the risk and opportunity trade-offs presented in traditional technology service arrangements. Specifically, virtually all of the major issues long recognized as involved in IT outsourcing present themselves in cloud services.[3]

Cloud solutions, by their very nature, are more susceptible (when compared to prior bespoke technology solutions) to the customer proceeding with adoption and use without a clear understanding of the full contractual dimensions of the arrangement being undertaken. This may be the result of commando-click-through practices, where the customer clicks acceptance to online terms without even making an effort to review them. In other cases, even when making that dutiful effort to review and understand cloud solution terms of service, the customer may still not fully understand the contract being entered. Of course, there have always been those customers who do not read contracts, but with the proliferation of click-through contracts over the Internet, the practical ease of elective ignorance has never been greater and this has often contributed to reduced vigilance around contracting.[4] In fact, one of the greatest strengths of the cloud, its sheer ease of use and access, has no doubt contributed to this, sometimes reducing the contracting process to seemingly nothing more than navigating the Internet.

The terms of service for cloud solutions are often prepared by the provider and frequently cover only limited issues. Determining actual contract terms applicable to the services is more difficult where issues are missing. In such cases, those missing terms may be implied where

---

[3]   Fredrik Motzfeldt (ed.), 'The Cloud Risk Framework: In Forming Decisions about Moving to the Cloud' (*Marsh Risk Consultants*, May 2012, 3–4), http://f.datasrvr.com/fr1/812/29871/3424_MA12-11623_Cloud_Computing_Frmwk_UK_04-2012_final_nocrps.pdf, Accessed 14 July 2014.

[4]   Simon Bradshaw, Christopher Millard and Ian Walden, 'The Terms They Are A-Changin' ... Watching Cloud Contracts Take Shape' (2011) 7 *Issues in Technology Innovation*, 1–12, and at www.brookings.edu/research/papers/022/04/cloud-computing contracts, accessed 14 July 2014.

required for the contract to make commercial sense. Terms may be implied by law, such as the rights of the provider (or a third party) under copyright or patent law; or may be implied in fact where necessary to give efficacy to the cloud arrangement. Terms may also be drawn from what is viewed as the reasonable expectations of the parties, including as reflected in their actions or conduct. The result is that, frequently with cloud solutions, especially public cloud solutions, any comprehensive understanding of terms only starts with those expressly required by the provider in the accept-before-entering gateway, and so must be supplemented through implied terms. Once established, implied terms can be enforced, but the burden of establishing implied terms can be difficult and raises risks for either or both of the parties.

The frequent lack of certainty over precise terms may be acceptable (and even appropriate) for a cloud solution subject to purely casual use. Think of a purely personal email service used for non-critical communications. However, to the extent a cloud service begins to involve critical functions or sensitive data, it becomes increasingly important for the customer to have a clear understanding of the terms and rights, so that suitability for its use can be evaluated. Again, however, one of the core strengths of the cloud, the practical ease of initiation of use, has led to the situation where adoption of cloud services has frequently outpaced prudent evaluation and management of risk.

The need for the customer to evaluate the suitability of available contract terms relative to their requirements is very stark in the case of cloud solutions, especially the public cloud, where there may be little or no opportunity for the customer to actually have input on the terms available. Often the choice facing the customer is acceptance of the provider's standard terms or foregoing the adoption of the cloud solution entirely. Such a stark set of alternatives is complicated further by both the speed and the ease of acceptance and adoption. The result is that customers may unwittingly make bad trade-offs between cost savings and flexibility versus risk.

A further consideration in cloud contracting is that the party seeking to affirmatively enforce a right or obligation inevitably has some greater threshold burden than the counter-party, especially if the right or obligation to be enforced is not expressly part of their agreement, so must be established as an implied term. Again, cloud solutions present a dilemma: their ease of contracting, while a core strength, also presents significant oversight challenges. Opportunities promising a quick fix, cost savings and flexibility may drive quick decisions that have significant business and risk consequences. Wanting or needing a particular right of assurance in a contract is far from establishing it.

The take-it-or-leave-it reality of many public cloud solution contracts is another important consideration. Providers are often resistant to any modification to their contract terms. Some of this resistance may be the traditional resistance of any party in any transaction to changes in its established (and desired) terms, but many cloud solutions involve technical practices or arrangements that place very practical limits on the ability of the provider to accommodate certain customer desired arrangements, much less give contractual assurance of doing so. Further, one of the core characteristics of the cloud is ease of provisioning – including contracting, where providers are often not set up to expend effort and resources on contracting or accommodating variations in terms or services for individual customers. Even where a provider may be able and willing to accommodate a customer's particular requirement, the accommodation may drive the provider's costs: ones which must be passed on to the customer and so adversely impact the financial benefits of the solution. For the customer, achieving full value from a cloud solution inevitably demands a careful and responsible balancing of the cost savings and functionality benefits, with risk and strategy.

B.   Essential Contract Terms: What Terms a Good Cloud Contract Should Contain

Moving beyond the pitfalls and challenges often faced in contracting for cloud services, we now consider the substantive terms a good cloud services contract should contain. In doing this, significant leverage can be drawn from prior experience of technology delivery, namely traditional outsourcing. Outsourcing has been through a critical evolution in contracting over the past two decades. The cloud represents merely the latest means of delivery of technology solutions, following on from initial modern outsourcing and offshoring.[5] Each of these delivery models involved stabilization and growth phases heavily driven by contracting models, and in each the contracting pressures were the same – developing a model to support practice that gave sufficient assurances to customers to permit adoption of the service. Thus, we can evaluate the issues present in contracting for cloud solutions through contrasting cloud license and contract issues and terms with classic outsourcing contract issues and terms. Such an exercise provides a means to critically

---

    [5]   Jonathan Crane, 'The Death of Outsourcing, and other IT Management Trends' (*Forbes*, 28 December 2012), www.forbes.com/sites/ciocentral/2012/12/28/the-death-of-outsourcing-and-other-it-management-trends/, accessed 14 July 2014.

analyse important customer protection provisions many of which were developed through outsourcing contracts. The practical challenge is how to combine this contracting experience and learning from outsourcing with the flexibility and standardization essential to cloud computing solutions.

The business environment in which the cloud operates presents many challenges, as business users face new and changing legislation and regulations (such as data protection) impacting the provision and use of cloud computing services. Further, capability and competition within the cloud and outsourcing market is growing as cloud service contract arrangements and terms are evolving.

In our discussion, we will focus on the following essential contractual issues:

1. License grant
2. Service commitments
3. Service quality protections
4. Customer control rights
5. Compliance obligations
6. Data and security protections
7. Intellectual property protections
8. Service continuity protections
9. End of term assistance

Our discussion will deal with each of these issues respectively. Much of this discussion will compare and contrast representative approaches to the issues taken in the traditional outsourcing model as a primary point of reference. This traditional approach to services will be contrasted with the approach frequently found in the pure public or utility cloud model, which generally represents the spectrum extreme in cloud services contracting – more the pure cloud approach. Then, reflecting a middle-ground approach, we will discuss these issues in the context of private or hybrid cloud model solutions, where the provider may be in a better position to be responsive to specific (individual) customer needs.[6]

The following discussion will largely use the terms 'contract' and 'license' interchangeably. While acknowledging that all licenses are indeed contracts but not all contracts are licenses, this interchangeable use of the terms is a device for ease of discussion and to illustrate the

---

[6] For the purpose of this discussion and as a point of reference, a representative private or hybrid cloud solution could be cloud provision of an enterprise application, as seen in business-focused SaaS offerings.

various considerations raised in connection with the placement and use of data in the cloud. Nonetheless, because of the important role that licensing concepts play in many cloud solutions, the natural tendency is often to refer to the cloud service contract as a license, hence the reference in our title to practical aspects of licensing in the cloud.

1. Scope of license grant: threshold issue

The first, and in many respects pivotal, set of contract issues associated with any cloud solution contract is the literal license grant. This set of issues encompasses the subject, the permissible users and the use of the license. Most cloud service arrangements involve at least two sets of license grants: a grant by the provider to the customer and a grant by the customer to the provider. This discussion will focus primarily on the provider-to-customer grant, which is the grant establishing the scope and nature of the cloud services. In most cases, the customer-to-provider grant is largely ancillary to the services and focused on addressing the use to which the customer's data (including software) must be put by the provider in performing the cloud services.[7]

(a) Subject of license   The first consideration in any right of use or license grant is the subject matter of the grant. In cloud computing, this subject matter (the service) may be software (in the case of Software-as-a-Service (SaaS)) or it may be a technical platform (in the case of Platform-as-a-Service (PaaS)) or it may be infrastructure, which is a combination of software and technical platform (in the case of Infrastructure-as-a-Service (IaaS)). In identifying the subject, it is important to consider how that subject is itself scoped – for example, whether use of software includes use of its source code, which may be important if the customer needs to make modification or enhancement, including for the purposes of interfacing or integrating with other software or processes. Similarly, it is important whether the software provided includes updates and new versions and whether the customer has the discretion to move to such updates or new versions. This is an area where the nature of cloud computing often drives limits in the customer's discretion regarding implementation of software updates or new versions. Often the SaaS model is built as a 'one-size-fits-all' solution where software updates are uniformly rolled out for all users of the service, or

---

[7]   The customer-to-provider grant is entirely important and is rife with critical issues such as potential loss of data or control and regulatory compliance. This grant will be discussed further below in the topic of intellectual property.

with limited flexibility for customers to select different release or version levels for their use. While this uniformity can stand as one of the core strengths of cloud computing for software services – enabling customers to keep current with versions and releases without undertaking the upgrade implementation themselves, it can also be a limitation of the cloud solution, as customers are taken to upgrades, ready or not.

(b) Permissible users The next issue to be addressed in analysing a cloud solution is determining who has the right to use the solution. Customer requirements here are often driven by the customer's identity (for example, whether they are an individual or a business enterprise) and the purpose or purposes for which the solution is being implemented (for example, is it for casual personal use or business use). Other important matters include the number of users permitted (dependent on the number of staff of the business requiring access) and whether the customer may allow third parties (such as their customers or contractors) to access the services.

(c) Permissible use License grants frequently also address the permissible uses for which the solution may be put by the user(s). User rights can be expressed as general or specific, and specific grants may clearly provide that only expressly permitted uses are allowed. Such an exclusivity provision makes the grant defining scope of permissible use critical. Use limitations may be based on aspects of the solution, such as access, use, execution, reproduction, display, performance, distribution, modification and creation of derivative works of the software/platform; or based on the activities of the customer, such as use in operations of a defined business or geography. It is critical that the customer has a clear understanding of the scope of use for which they require the cloud solution, and ensure that the user rights provided under the contract terms are sufficient to meet those requirements.

The pricing arrangements of a cloud solution may be closely parallel to, or effectively define, the license grant terms. For example, charges may be based on specific use of the solution – such as, access to and use of different software modules, or numbers of users (named or concurrent) or size of cloud storage. Through such arrangements, the customer uses the service on a pay-as-you-go basis.[8] Where no specific level or volume

---

[8] W. Kuan Hon, Christopher Millard and Ian Walden, 'Negotiating Cloud Contracts' (2012) 16(1) *Stanford Technology Law Review* 127.

of service is granted, however, the customer may increase and decrease usage of the service as needed (and available).

(d)   Terms and termination   Contract provisions relating to the contract period and circumstances of termination vary dramatically among cloud solutions and drive very important considerations for the customer. These provisions largely define the extent to which the provider is making a threshold commitment to deliver or provision the solution and, correspondingly, the level of assurance the customer may have that the solution will continue to be available for their use. The core issues are how long the solution is committed as available and, if there is a committed period of provision, under what circumstances provision may nonetheless be terminated by the provider. A closely related issue is the right to partial termination, including suspension of the services for a limited time.

If there is no, or a limited committed, term of provision of a cloud solution – there is a correspondingly limited reason for termination rights. In many cloud computing solutions, the committed contract period is short with little or no advance notice for termination (by either party) required. However, if the customer has a specific business need, longer committed period contracts and termination periods may be necessary to enable the customer to prudently incorporate the solution into their operations. When providers seek to offer cloud solutions targeting serious business operations, it becomes increasingly important to offer specific committed contract periods. With a move to fixed service provision commitment periods, the issues around early termination become significant.

The first issue with any committed term in a cloud solution is the length of the committed period, including any renewal rights and whether such renewal rights are automatic or subject to an election to not renew by either (or both) of the parties. In service arrangements, committed periods may range from short notice periods (of, say, 30 days) to multi-year terms. In evaluating the certainty of continued availability of a cloud solution, it is important for the customer to consider the minimum term that may in fact be applicable under the contractual arrangement.

Where a cloud contract contains a committed period, the conditions or circumstances under which either party may terminate the agreement prior to the expiration of its term become relevant. Typically, service contracts provide that termination rights are available to a party in circumstances of material breach by the other party – recognizing that what constitutes a material breach may vary between the parties. Although some termination rights are parallel for customer and provider, traditional service arrangements often provide broader termination rights to the customer for breaches by providers than to the provider for breaches by the customer, reflecting the broader scope of (performance) responsibilities of providers (and thus a wider range of potential material breaches). In traditional outsourcing arrangements, it is common that the scope of potential material default by the customer giving rise to a termination right by the provider is limited to non-payment. Another traditional default circumstance giving rise to termination rights (typically also a termination right for the customer) is multiple non-material breaches that constitute material default due to frequency – 'a terminating party should have regard to the overall circumstances and its position would be strengthened if it could permit to a breakdown in relations and the prospect of continuing a substandard performance'.[9] Additionally, rights of termination for convenience and circumstances of *force majeure* are frequently included in licenses with fixed terms.

2. Service commitments

(a) Commitment to contract terms This issue concerns the extent to which the provider retains the ability to unilaterally make changes in the services.

In the traditional outsourcing contracting model, terms of the service can only be modified by mutual agreement. Provisions such as *force majeure* may provide relief from performance obligations in certain circumstances,[10] but the provider generally has no unilateral rights to alter or modify their performance obligations during the term of the agreement.

This commitment to contract terms is not always present in the pure public cloud contract. Rather, providers of pure public or utility cloud solutions, such as Facebook (cloud-based online social media) and Dropbox (cloud-based online file storage), have terms of service that often reserve for the provider the ability to change those terms at any time and at their own discretion. Sometimes this right is expressly stated as a unilateral right to make changes, and other times the right is more

---

[9] Sarah Walker and Carolyn Greene, 'What Constitutes a "Material Breach" Is Becoming a Central Problem for Those Wishing to Terminate Long-Running IT Contracts' (*The Lawyer*, 8 January 2007), www.thelawyer.com/get-out-flaws/123688.article, accessed 14 July 2014.

[10] In the cloud computing context, *force majeure* typically covers power cuts, strikes, failure of telecom services, third party failures, natural disasters and any other event beyond the control of the service provider.

indirectly preserved through incorporation of external documents (often linked) such as policies and procedures that can be varied by the provider from time to time. In some cases, the provider commits to provide some level of notice of changes, but in most cases customers have to monitor the provider's website for changes to the contract terms. Enforceability of such changes may be limited to a degree of reasonableness under applicable law, but the existence of such a unilateral provider right in any cloud solution is a significant and defining consideration for the customer, inevitably sowing uncertainty for them. Cloud solutions marketed for business adoption, such as an SaaS model for enterprise applications utilizing a private or hybrid deployment model, tend to address this issue in a manner closer to traditional outsourcing, providing the customer with assurance that contract terms can be changed only by mutual agreement between the provider and the customer.

(b) Commitment to services   This issue involves the extent to which the cloud service contract commits the provider to deliver specified and expressly defined services, or gives the provider latitude in the services that may be delivered.

The traditional outsourcing contract is premised on a detailed, customized service definition often contained in extensive, descriptive statements of work. These service descriptions may contain common elements between a provider's customers, but they are frequently tailored to the customer's specific operational and practice requirements and so the outsourcing contract and delivery models are fully oriented towards this.

The pure public cloud solution, on the other hand, typically provides high-level, general definitions of standard services that are common to all customers and that are often provided on an 'as is' basis, under which no express commitment is made by the provider that the services will in fact conform to the high-level, general services definition. The middle-ground approach, seen frequently in SaaS private or hybrid cloud solutions, involves contracts that may contain relatively detailed service definitions in descriptive statements of functionality or work, but not customized service definitions tailored to a customer's specific operational or practice requirements. This cloud model takes a one-size-fits-all approach to common services for representative customers, in order to preserve that efficiency which marks cloud solutions.

(c) Minimum term commitment   This issue involves the extent to which the cloud service contract commits the provider and the customer to

maintain the contract for a specific period of time, subject to defined termination rights, such as in the case of uncured default by one of the parties.

On this issue, the outsourcing model has traditionally been based on a commitment period of years applicable for the service provider. Although the typical term in outsourcing agreements has been shortened over the past ten years, outsourcing contracts routinely provide for an initial term of three to seven years, with optional extension terms of one to two years exercisable by the customer. Outsourcing contracts typically also provide a right to the customer to terminate early (for convenience) with a notice period and the payment of pre-established termination charges.

The pure utility cloud contract, on the other hand, typically provides little or no minimum term, reflecting, as will be discussed below, the frequent absence of performance commitments generally by the provider. In such circumstances the provider is not obligated to make the services available.

The middle-ground private or hybrid cloud contract often carries a relatively short minimum term, but in some cases may require a notice period prior to termination by either party.

3. Service quality protections

(a) Testing and acceptance   This issue involves the extent to which the cloud service contract makes provision for the customer to test and accept the services (or other deliverables) as part of the initial performance or delivery.

The traditional outsourcing contract model often builds a level of user testing and acceptance into the initial implementation of the services. In addition, testing and acceptance are commonly built into the project methodology around all deliverables following the initial implementation, including transformations of service delivery. These procedures are designed to provide assurance to the customer that the services meet the customer's pre-defined operational and practice requirements and, to some degree, assurance to the provider that the customer will accept (often a prerequisite to payment) if the requirements are in fact met.

The pure utility cloud solution contract typically does not provide for testing and acceptance, either at service initiation or subsequent delivery level (such as software upgrades). In some cases, a trial period may be allowed to permit the customer to make a determination of whether they want to proceed with actual adoption and production use, but often this is effectively accommodated by allowing the customer to terminate the services whenever they decide the solution does not meet their operational or practice requirements.

The middle-ground private or hybrid model contract often allows for testing of key transition milestones during initial implementation and subsequent deliverables during the term, although these tend to be generic and aimed at permitting the customer to make a go-no-go decision rather than confirming a delivery commitment on part of the provider.

(b) Commitment to service levels   Service levels and their related provisions constitute one of the main contractual devices in establishing, measuring and reporting service performance. This issue involves the extent to which the provider gives contract commitments that the services will conform to certain pre-defined performance requirements.

Service levels typically play a very important role in the traditional outsourcing contracting model. Outsourcing agreements often provide detailed and customer specific service levels which serve as both a contractual commitment of service performance (for example, establishing service availability, response time, transaction rate, processing speed, accuracy and the like) and the basis of credits (penalties) for failed performance. Typically, these are provided through a comprehensive service level methodology providing the ability of the customer to modify service levels and credits to address both problem areas and evolving areas of the customer's concern, together with detailed reporting of the provider's performance against the service level requirements. In many cases, certain pre-defined levels of service level failures may be the basis of termination rights, exercisable by the customer.[11] Recognizing that in no event can service levels effectively address the full range of performance, outsourcing contracts typically also provide more general performance requirements, such as the commitment to perform the services with reasonable skill, care and diligence.

Pure utility cloud solution contracts typically do not include significant provider commitments to service levels and, where service levels may be included, they are often a component of the general service description which either does not provide for service level credits or establishes

---

[11]   Such provisions based on service levels entitling the consumer to terminate the service contract may include such a right when: (i) the service performance level drops below a defined point in any measurement period; or (ii) a certain value of service credit becomes payable within a prescribed period (for example, in a year); or (iii) a service level is not met for a certain number of consecutive measurement periods.

unrealistic hurdles to obtaining credits. Understandably, for standardized and low-cost solutions, the pure utility cloud providers are reluctant to guarantee (with penalty for non-compliance) the quality and reliability of the service. However, as providers seek to broaden the acceptability of public cloud solutions in business environments, many are reconsidering offering some service level commitments as a way to accommodate their customers' needs and attract new business. Even in such cases, however, often the service level provisions function in a defensive manner by being structured so as to restrict the provider's responsibility to limited credits which function as exclusive remedies, or their equivalent, for failure to attain the defined service level.

The middle-ground private or hybrid solution contracts more commonly contain service level provisions, although these service levels tend to be focused more on supplier technology rather than reflecting the specific customer's needs associated with the solution. Nonetheless, these service levels may carry meaningful service credits for failure to attain the provider-defined service levels. In general, only those customers with high subscription and upfront payment of significant fees have the power to negotiate for service level commitment.[12] In larger cloud service projects, providers and customers may agree on a significant list of key performance metrics to express the level of performance with which both parties are comfortable, while cloud service projects on a smaller scale, typically, will cover far fewer performance metrics.[13] It is therefore important to decide which performance metrics are most crucial in achieving the customer's business needs and objectives and to select

---

[12] City of Los Angeles, 'Professional Services Contract between the City of Los Angeles and Computer Science Corp. for the SaaS E-Mail and Collaboration Solution (SECS)' (10 November 2009), https://sites.google.com/a/lageecs. lacity.org/la-geecs-blog/home/faqs-1/C-116359_c_11-20-09.pdf?attredirects=0&d =1, accessed 14 July 2014.

[13] Some key service quality metrics are proposed by Joe McKendrick: (i) availability rate metric; (ii) outage duration metric; (iii) mean-time between failures metric; (iv) reliability rate metric; (v) network capacity metric; (vi) storage device capacity metric; (vii) server capacity metric; (viii) web application capacity metric; (ix) instance starting time metric; (x) response time metric; (xi) completion time metric; (xii) storage scalability (horizontal) metric; (xiii) server scalability (horizontal) metric; (xiv) server scalability (vertical) metric; (xv) mean-time to switchover metric; and (xvi) mean-time system recovery metric; see Joe McKendrick, '16 Key Service Quality Metrics to Boost Cloud Engagements' (*ZDNet*, 22 July 2013), www.zdnet.com/16-key-service-quality-metrics-to-boost-cloud-engagements-7000018353/, accessed 14 July 2014.

metrics that are measurable and auditable, with the metric standards, measurement mechanisms and reporting requirements documented clearly and concisely.

4. Customer control rights

(a) Rights to determine architecture   This issue involves the extent to which the services contract gives the customer rights with respect to the technical architecture that the provider utilizes in performance and delivery of the services.

The traditional outsourcing model contract typically gives the customer the right to approve the architecture utilized by the provider. This approval may be part of the initial contractual arrangement, with assurance provided to the customer that changes will not be made in the technical architecture via change control protections. Also, the customer typically has the right to dictate changed technical architecture, although implementation may involve additional services and carry new charges.

The pure utility cloud solution contract invariably gives the customer no right to approve technical architecture. Similarly, the middle-ground private or hybrid cloud model also gives the customer no right to approve technical architecture. In fact, it is one of the core distinctions of the cloud (over traditional bespoke outsourcing) that it essentially offers customers one-size-fits-all solutions.

(b) Change control rights   This issue involves the extent to which the services contract provides customer protection from changes made by the provider in the services: changes which impact those services or the customer's use of them.

The traditional outsourcing contract model requires that any change in the services which has a direct or indirect impact on the services or the customer's use of the services must be consented to by the customer. This customer protection provides assurance that the services will not be changed in a way that results in additional costs to the customer or diminishes required functionality.

The pure utility cloud contracting model, with solutions that are driven by a common, one-size-fits-all service typically allows the provider to make changes in the services without notice to or consent by the customer. The middle-ground private or hybrid cloud contract frequently requires that the provider gives notice to the customer of changes and allows the customer to terminate the contract if the changes have an adverse effect on the services or the customer, but the provider has no obligation to obtain the customer's consent to the changes.

5. Compliance obligations

(a) Assistance in complying with laws   This issue involves the extent to which the services contract obligates the provider to assist or accommodate the customer in meeting the customer's legal compliance requirements, particularly with respect to the activities and operations of the customer involving use of the services.

Compliance with laws is an important element in the traditional outsourcing model contract. Typical provisions obligate the provider to comply with all laws applicable to the services and their delivery and performance, and that they assist with the customer's compliance related to the services. These provisions are premised on the recognition that a customer cannot transfer their compliance responsibilities to a third party, so necessarily needs to build in assurances promoting compliance.

The pure public cloud solution's standardized offering affords limited flexibility to adjust the services to a specific customer's legal requirements. Some of this inflexibility arises from the frequent heavy reliance on subcontractors in public clouds.[14] In reality, it may be almost impossible for the provider to assist the customer in complying with local laws given the cross-border nature of the cloud offering. Although providers may endeavor to perform the services in compliance with applicable laws, the contract invariably will not include commitments respecting specific compliance. Combined with the provider's reserved ability to make unilateral changes in the services (often without notice), the result is that a customer facing legal compliance considerations must continually monitor the services and their use to ensure due compliance. In some cases, the customer's ability to accurately monitor the services is not feasible with a cloud solution, rendering some solutions inappropriate for certain uses.

The middle-ground private or hybrid cloud model often provides a certain level of flexibility to configure the service to meet varying customer compliance requirements. These more tailored solutions are also frequently designed and operated in a manner allowing the customer more assurances on legal compliance.

(b) Audit rights   This issue involves the rights granted to the customer to audit the provider and their provision of the services.

---

[14]   Gavin Clarke, 'Apple's iCloud Runs on Microsoft and Amazon Services: Who Says Azure Isn't Cool and Trendy Now' (*The Register*, 2 September 2011), www.theregister.co.uk/2011/09/02/icloud_runs_on_microsoft_azure_and_amazon, accessed 14 July 2014.

In the traditional outsourcing model contract, customers are typically provided with well-defined rights to undertake operational and financial audits of the provider and the services (including subcontractors).

The pure utility cloud solution contract typically provides no audit rights for the customer, especially with respect to subcontractors. In fact, the provider in pure utility cloud solutions frequently does not even disclose whether subcontractors have been used.

In this area, the middle-ground private or hybrid cloud solution often provides some audit rights. Typically, however, these rights do not include any right of physical access to the provider's facilities for audit or review purposes.

(c) Liability   Contractually, one of the core compliance assurance mechanisms is the potential exposure of liability for failure to perform according to the terms.[15] Thus, one of the threshold issues in any services contract is the extent to which the provider may be exposed to liability for non-performance of contractual obligations.

Industry practice for the traditional outsourcing model is for liability to be limited to direct damages and further limited to a pre-defined (or calculable) limit on liability, subject to certain exclusions for breaches or defaults under the contract.[16] Typically indirect and punitive damages are expressly disclaimed, except in cases of significant misconduct, such as gross negligence, fraud or willful abandonment.

The pure public cloud solution provides extremely limited liability for breaches or failures of any type. It is common practice that the providers' standard service contracts will exclude liability as much as possible. In some cases, the provider will undertake that the services will be performed (if at all) in accordance with reasonable skill and care,[17] but

---

[15]   Blaha Ralf, Marko Roland, Zellhofer Andreas, and Liebel Helmut, *Rechtsfragen des Cloud Computing*, (Medien und Recht-Wien 2011) 44.

[16]   Charles Goetz and Robert Scott, 'Liquidated Damages, Penalties and the Just Compensation Principle: Some Notes on an Enforcement Model and a Theory of Efficient Breach' (1977) 77(4) *Columbia Law Review* 554–94.

[17]   For example, in the Apple's iCloud Terms and Conditions, Apple stipulates that:

> Apple shall use reasonable skill and due care in providing the Service, but ... Apple does not guarantee or warrant that any Content you may store or access through the Service will not be subject to inadvertent damage, corruption [or] loss ...

Apple Inc., 'iCloud Terms and Conditions', section s (page 2), www.apple.com/legal/internet-services/icloud/en/terms.html, accessed 14 July 2014.

will generally not provide monetary compensation in the event the provider fails to comply with the given undertaking. In such circumstances, the public cloud contract may state that the provider will use commercial endeavors to rectify problems of non-performance. Often, this undertaking is the consumer's 'sole and exclusive' remedy for non-performance.

The middle-ground private or hybrid cloud model often has a narrowly defined scope of potential damages: direct damages only, subject to a limited maximum usually defined either by reference to the contract price or charges or to a fixed sum, and subject to certain exclusions from such limitations. All losses that are special, indirect or consequential are most frequently excluded entirely under the contract. Additionally, in order to limit their potential liability exposure, the provider will normally seek to disclaim liabilities for certain events or incidents, including service outages and data loss, delays, delivery failures, or other damage resulting from the transfer of data over communication networks and facilities. It is important for the customer to fully understand the protection offered under the service contract and to evaluate in advance whether the risks are acceptable in the context of their intended use of the services before entering into the contract.

6. Data and security protections

(a) Location of data This issue concerns provisions restricting or identifying where the customer's data used in conjunction with the cloud service may be stored or processed. Location of the customer's data can have significant implications for both security and legal compliance.

In traditional outsourcing contracts, permissible locations for the provider's storage and processing of the customer's data are defined and approved. Changes to these locations (at least involving material changes, including any transfer to a different country) require approval of the customer or, at a minimum, compliance with the change control processes (which itself likely requires the customer's approval).

In pure public cloud contracts, there are typically no restrictions on where the customer's data may be processed or stored. In fact, in many cases, the technical infrastructure used by providers may itself limit even the provider's ability to control, or even know, the location of data processing and storage: for example, where networks of third parties are utilized to provide storage and processing.

Private or hybrid cloud solutions are more likely to provide assurances about the location of data, frequently fixing data location by country. Nonetheless, even with such assurances, broader consideration must be given to the locations from which the provider may access the customer's data, resulting in the potential for deemed exports or transfers as a result of access from a foreign jurisdiction.

(b) Information security   Information security is a major consideration in any service contract. This issue focuses on the extent of assurance that the customer's data provided to (or created by) the provider in connection with the services will be protected from access, use or alteration by unauthorized third parties.

Outsourcing contracts typically contain detailed information security provisions, focused on security to meet the customer's specific requirements. Additionally, the customer under an outsourcing contract usually has the right to require changes in the provider's security practices, subject to the possibility of the additional work constituting new services for which there may be additional charges.

In the case of pure public cloud solutions, information security provisions are typically included in the contract. These solutions, however, tend to be standardized offerings and based on use of the provider's standard controls, with little or no ability to make modifications for any specific requirements of the customer.

Middle-ground private and hybrid cloud solutions tend to treat security as a service, and may provide optional arrangements from a pre-established suite of security offerings.

(c) Return, disposal or destruction of customer data   This issue involves the extent to which the service contract gives assurances that the provider will return or destroy the customer's data, and the timing of that return or destruction.

With traditional outsourcing, the contract gives the customer clear and direct commitments from the provider that customer data will be returned or destroyed at the customer's option, not only at the termination of the agreement, but also when the data is no longer needed for the performance of the services. Similarly, outsourcing contracts typically commit the provider to returning the customer's data at any time upon the customer's request.

Pure public cloud contracts typically contain little or no assurance that all of the customer's data will be found and erased, or returned. As with limitations on some provider's control of the location of their customers' data, the technical structure of many pure public cloud solutions places limitations on the providers' ability to give assurances about return or destruction.

Middle-ground private and hybrid cloud solutions typically provide that data will be returned or destroyed, although the alternative selected is sometimes at the determination of the provider.

7. Intellectual property protections

(a) IP rights of customers' data   The data in the cloud can be any data, in any form, each and any of which enjoys some level of intellectual property protection (most frequently copyright in this context). It is well established that copyright subsists in original works (including electronic data) unless: (i) it is *de minimus* and hence does not meet the minimum threshold for copyright protection; (ii) it is copied from others; or (iii) the copyright has already lapsed. In some cases, data, for example a drug formula, may also be protected as a trade secret or a potentially patentable subject matter. This issue involves the intellectual property (IP) ownership of the data which customers may provide or produce through utilization of the services, and the extent to which the provider is allowed to use such data.[18]

The traditional outsourcing model stringently protects the customer's ownership of their data and specifies clearly the provider's right to access, store, process, make necessary copies and use the customer's data (and its associated IP rights) for the purpose of providing the service. Similarly, the outsourcing contract will detail ownership of any intellectual property developed by the provider (including jointly with customer), and will allocate these rights through ownership and license rights. Essentially, it is a content license granted by the customer to the provider and it is common to see that such license covers use by the service provider and their subcontractors and strictly limits use to such purposes.

The pure utility cloud model generally provides that the customer retains ownership of the data it provides and grants a use license to the provider. The big players in the market, such as Google[19] and Apple

---

[18]   W. Kuan Hon, Christopher Millard and Ian Walden, 'Negotiating Cloud Contracts' (2012) 16(1) *Stanford Technology Law Review*, 126.

[19]   Google's Terms of Service provide:

You retain ownership of any intellectual property rights that you hold in that content. In short, what belongs to you stays yours. When you upload, submit, store, send or receive content to or through our Services, you give Google (and those we work with) a worldwide license to use, host, store, reproduce, modify, create derivative works (such as those resulting from translations, adaptations or other changes we make so that your content works better with (iCloud[20]), make it clear in their terms of service that, by utilizing their services, the customer grants a worldwide, perpetual and royalty-free license to the provider to use the customer's data. Some providers specify that the license grant is for use of the data for the purpose of providing, promoting or improving the services but some are silent on the scope of such content license. More likely than not, the license is a perpetual one which does not end upon termination or expiration of the service. Such broad licenses raise risks for IP owners putting data on a public cloud. These risks include the risk that trade secrets may lose the necessary element of confidence. As for patent rights, risks arise as the novelty required for patent registration may be compromised by placing patentable subject matters on a public cloud under such a broad license. The maintenance of novelty may be lost when the data is accessible to a large number of people within an enterprise without proper access controls. It remains to be seen how courts will approach such a situation, leaving this a considerable business risk. Another issue is the risk of data loss: loss of control of the customer's IP, which may result in the absence of a clear commitment by the provider to safeguard access to the data and to permanent and complete erasure or prompt return of the data when it is no longer used with, or needed for, the services (as discussed further below in connection with end of term assistance).

The middle-ground private or hybrid model typically provides that the customer retains ownership of data (and its associated IP) provided or processed through the cloud services and grants a content license to the

---

our Services), communicate, publish, publicly perform, publicly display and distribute such content. The rights you grant in this license are for the limited purpose of operating, promoting, and improving our Services, and to develop new ones. This license continues even if you stop using our Services (for example, for a business listing you have added to Google Maps) ...

Google Inc., 'Google Terms of Service' (page 2), www.google.com/policies/terms/, accessed 14 July 2014.

[20] Apple's iCloud Terms and Conditions provide:

by submitting or posting such Content on areas of the Service that are accessible by the public or other users with whom you consent to share such Content, you grant Apple a worldwide, royalty-free, non-exclusive license to use, distribute, reproduce, modify, adapt, publish, translate, publicly perform and publicly display such Content on the Service solely for the purpose for which such Content was submitted or made available, without any compensation or obligation to you.

Apple Inc., 'iCloud Terms and Conditions', section s (page 6), www.apple.com/legal/internet-services/icloud/en/terms.html, accessed 14 July 2014.

provider. It is particularly important for business customers with high-value IP,[21] business data and trade secrets to have an express provision in the contract covering IP ownership, scope of the content license, termination right of the content license and return and removal of data upon termination. Unlike the pure public cloud model, such rights may be protected in middle-ground private and hybrid model contracts.

IP considerations also drive a number of other issues previously seen in cloud computing arrangements. For example, preservation of confidentiality and novelty critical to IP protection highlights the importance of the contract clearly defining access rights. Use of end-to-end encryption to prevent unauthorized access and preserve confidentiality and/or novelty of the data can also be utilized to mitigate risk. Further, because IP protection is largely territorial (local law driven), location of cloud data storage or processing has a significant impact on the IP rights. If the provider's servers storing customer data are located in a country where the customer's data is not protected under local IP laws or where IP rights are difficult to enforce, risks would increase if the customer's IP is locally stolen or misappropriated. Hence, location of data storage by the service provider is a major risk factor for IP-rich customers, making countries with strong IP regimes preferred, and assurances that the customer's data will remain there important.

(b) Ownership of developed materials   This issue involves the extent to which the service contract provides that the customer retains ownership of the intellectual property rights of the data (including metadata) and materials that may be developed through provision of the services.

The traditional outsourcing model clearly defines and allocates the customer's and the provider's respective rights in the IP developed through performance of the services. Once ownership is established and defined in developed materials, either special license provisions may be provided for such IP or the contract's usual provisions respecting licenses to the parties' IP may apply.

Pure public cloud solutions typically allow customers to retain ownership of their own data, but frequently do not define ownership of data created (even derivative) or IP developed in the course of the provision of the services. Such arrangements raise risks of unauthorized use and potential loss of ownership and control.

---

[21]   Herbert Zech, Lizenzen für die Benutzung von Musik, Film und E-Books in der Cloud (*Zeitschrift für Urheber- und Medienrecht (ZUM)* 2014) 6.

Typically the middle-ground private or hybrid cloud contract provides that the customer retains ownership of any data provided or processed or created through the cloud services. These provisions frequently also provide limited rights to ownership of customizations of the services (such as customized software interface), with license-back (to the provider) rights.

(c) Non-infringement warranty and indemnity   This issue involves the extent to which the cloud contract requires the provider to warrant that the cloud services do not infringe the intellectual property rights of the third party and to indemnify the customer against costs and damages associated with third party claims of such infringement. This issue also encompasses the potential warranty and indemnity by the customer to the provider against claims by a third party that the data or other material provided by the customer, or the use to which the customer puts the cloud services, infringes the third party's intellectual property rights.

The traditional outsourcing contract contains a provider's warranty of non-infringement and indemnities against third party claims that the cloud services (at least when used as contemplated under the contract) infringe the third party's IP rights. Less frequently, the contract may provide for a warranty and indemnities from the customer that data they provide (and make available for use by the provider), or uses to which they put the services, infringe third party IP rights. A number of ancillary significant issues associated with any indemnity arise from outsourcing, such as the extent to which the indemnity is subject to, or excluded from, some or all of the limitations of liability contained in the contract and the scope of remedies available to the indemnitee in the event of an actual or alleged infringement, as discussed further below. Indemnities are frequently the subject of significant negotiation in any outsourcing transaction.

The public cloud solution frequently omits warranties and indemnities by the provider entirely and broadly sweeps such issues within the general 'as is' condition under which the services are provided.[22] It is

---

[22] For example, Dropbox provides the following in their Terms of Service:

> To the fullest extent permitted by law, Dropbox and its Affiliates, Suppliers and Distributors, make no warranties, either express or implied, about the services. The services are provided 'as is'. We also disclaim any warranties and merchantability fitness for a particular purpose and non-infringement.

Dropbox, Inc., 'Dropbox Terms of Service' (page 2), www.dropbox.com/privacy #terms, accessed 14 July 2014.

more common, however, that pure public cloud solutions include indemnities and even warranties from the customer, particularly in respect of data or materials provided or used by the customer in connection with the cloud services. This is in addition to their applicable infringement notice and take-down procedures imposed in compliance with the safe harbor provisions under the US Digital Millennium Copyright Act 1998, Electronic Commerce Directive 2000 or other similar legislation.

The middle-ground private or hybrid cloud contract often includes some level of provider infringement indemnification, but less frequently include warranties of non-infringement. Typically, this indemnification is limited to infringement associated with deployment of the cloud services, but it is often narrowly scoped and subject to extensive exceptions. As with pure public cloud solutions, middle-ground private or hybrid cloud solutions frequently impose a greater level of customer non-infringement warranties and indemnities, including agreement to the provider's notice and take-down policy.

(d) Infringement remedies   This issue involves the scope and nature of the remedies provided should there be a claim of infringement against the customer (or provider in the case of a non-infringement warranty or indemnity by the customer) arising from the provision or use of the cloud services. The remedies provided under an indemnity are a critical component of the indemnity itself, as they define the scope of potential liability and responsibility of the indemnitor.

The traditional outsourcing contract typically provides express indemnity remedies in the event that the services infringe third party rights. These remedies typically consist of the obligation to indemnify for costs of defense and any judgment or settlement, and to either obtain any necessary rights in order to continue the provision and use of the services, or to replace or modify the services so that they do not infringe a party's rights, without material decrease in functionality. Frequently, the actual choice of these remedies is at the election of the provider. With its primary focus on services, the outsourcing model typically does not allow the provider the right to cease performance (withdraw the service), leaving the provider obligated to either obtain necessary rights or modify or replace the infringing portion of the services, at the risk of breaching the contract for its failure to do one or the other. A related issue of significance is whether such defined remedies are the exclusive remedies of the indemnitee for any infringement or if others are available, such as the ability to terminate the agreement or make claim for other damages. A warranty of non-infringement may itself serve as the basis of the exercise of rights under the contract in the event it is breached, including a claim of material default that may give rise to a termination right.

The pure utility cloud terms of service typically offer little or no committed remedy in case of infringement, which is consistent with the provider's frequent right to unilaterally terminate provision of the services.

The middle-ground private or hybrid cloud contract more likely than not includes some remedies in the case of an infringement. These remedies typically include the modification or replacement alternatives found in the traditional outsourcing arrangement, but frequently there is also a right for the provider to terminate the services if they determine neither of these options to be commercially viable, usually with a refund to the customer of amounts paid, sometimes reduced based upon use up to the time of termination.

8.   Service continuity protections

(a)   Personnel continuity   This issue involves the extent to which the service contract gives the customer assurances that the provider will seek to maintain key personnel to provide support for the services. Such continuity can be an important element in assuring the customer that the services will be appropriately performed.

The traditional outsourcing model provides for the identification of a group of provider personnel or positions that the provider is obligated to seek to maintain for the provision of services to the customer over a defined period of time and often offers protection with respect to a provider's general personnel turnover.

The pure public cloud solution never gives provider commitments regarding personnel continuity.

The middle-ground private or hybrid model may provide some commitment to continuity for a limited number of key personnel for particularly crucial functions or activities.

(b)   Non-suspension/interruption   This issue involves the extent to which the contract expressly prohibits the provider from interrupting or suspending the services.

The traditional outsourcing contract prohibits any suspension of services (subject to defined termination rights by the provider) and requires detailed business continuity planning. Outsourcing contracts typically also state that under no circumstances can the provider withhold the customer's data, including specifically for the purpose of gaining an advantage in the event of a dispute.

Consistent with the lack of general commitment respecting the provision of the service, pure public cloud terms of service frequently expressly acknowledge potential interruptions of services and make no commitment regarding business continuity.

The middle-ground private or hybrid cloud contract frequently provides certain rights to limit users to protect the integrity of the services and may contain provisions regarding business continuity procedures and practices.

9. End of term assistance

(a) Termination assistance Exit or termination arrangements represent a critical set of considerations associated with any adoption of services, especially in business operations. It is important that, as part of a customer's adoption of a cloud solution, they carefully evaluate and provide for a viable exit strategy, taking into account the support they can expect from the provider and the demands they expect to face at that time. The provisions in service contracts concerning the parties' respective obligations when the service or contract is terminated are critical. These obligations must be evaluated by the customer in light of their anticipated options at the time the services end. It is particularly important in the cloud context where the customer may have transferred, shared or stored data in the cloud or developed a degree of reliance on the cloud services as part of their business operations. This issue involves the extent to which the contract commits the provider to assist the customer at the termination of the services in connection with the customer's transition of the services to internal or successor provision.

The traditional outsourcing contract contains detailed provisions addressing the obligations of the provider to support the customer in transitioning to successor provision at the termination of all or part of the services (including extension of services to the extent that additional time is required for the successor arrangements). These provisions are aimed at assuring the customer has access to appropriate support to avoid disruption of its operations. Such comprehensive provisions address most of the elements of service provision from return of the customers' data, to the infrastructure (equipment, software and personnel) used in the service delivery.

The pure public cloud terms of service typically provide a right for the customer to access its data in cases of termination, except in some cases where the termination is by the provider for the customer's default. Consistent with the overall absence of service assurances in the pure public cloud model, contracts do not provide for further assistance to avoid disruption of the customer's operations.

The middle-ground private or hybrid cloud model may provide the customer with some ability to extend services and some reasonable assistance in transition to a successor arrangement.

(b) Data transmission format for data return   One of the most critical components of an end of service transition is the provider's return, retention and deletion of customer's data. It is important that customer's data is returned in a format that is reasonably accessible and compatible with the systems which they will be using or at least have access to for conversion purposes during the cloud services termination phase.

(c) Data security for data return   Data security must be considered at all stages of engaging cloud services, including the termination phase. At termination, customers should understand the level of data security applied in the transmission of data and be prepared for appropriate remedial action in the event of data leakage. Addressing these issues at the time of termination, however, may well be too late for effective arrangements. It is critical that the customer evaluates the full life-cycle risks associated with any cloud solution from the time of initial adoption.

(d) Data retention (by providers)   Even where providers have committed to permanently delete customer data upon termination, in reality this process may involve an extended period, often up to one to three months before data is in fact deleted. Additionally, providers may retain backup copies, logs and other information which may have been shared with other users (such as a photo on Facebook) for a longer period. However, it is worth noting that data privacy laws in many jurisdictions prohibit retention of personal data for too long.[23]

---

[23]   For example, under Data Protection Principle 2(3) of the Hong Kong Personal Data (Privacy) Ordinance (Cap.486), when a data user (for example, a business entity) engages a data processor (for example, a cloud service provider), whether within or outside Hong Kong, to process personal data (for example, data of club members, end customers and patients) on the data user's behalf, the data user must adopt contractual or other means to prevent any personal data transferred to the data processor from being kept longer than is necessary for the processing of that personal data. Hence, for compliance purposes, the Hong Kong customers should consider imposing a shorter retention period for personal data stored or processed on the cloud. In any event, customers are encouraged to negotiate for notification of some sort from the provider before deletion of data.

(e) Deletion of data   Deletion of data in the cloud is a much more complicated process than a mere click of a mouse. The existing standard terms offered by cloud providers (particularly public clouds) generally do not specify in any detail the arrangements for data deletion upon termination of the service contract. Even where the provider has offered to delete the customer's data at the customer's request, it is extremely difficult to achieve complete and permanent erasure.[24] Complete erasure of data is even more difficult in a cloud environment where multiple locations for data storage and data processing are involved.[25] The challenges associated with securely deleting data in the cloud stand as yet another specific consideration that customers must carefully evaluate as part of their decision to adopt cloud services.

(f) Other termination support   Bearing in mind that cloud providers will offer limited termination support, under the existing market practice, enterprise solution customers should develop and maintain through the life of the cloud services a termination plan that, based upon the assistance available from the provider, gives them adequate assurance that they will be able to successfully transition the services back to in-house or a successor provider.

III. CONCLUSION

It is important to recognize that characterization of a particular cloud offering as public versus private or hybrid is undoubtedly a significant

---

[24] For electronic data, the common file deletion command only removes file pointers to the data, leaving the data on disk sectors of a hard disk which remains recoverable by the use of common forensic tools. Data deletion from a computer system requires repeat overwriting of the data and metadata for a certain number of times until they are no longer retrievable.

[25] So, it is unlikely to be a true statement if the service provider claims that your data will be removed permanently from its cloud system. Dropbox gives what would seem a realistic description of their data erasure practice:

> We'll retain information you store on our Services for as long as we need it to provide you the Services. If you delete your account, we'll also delete this information. But please note: (1) there might be some latency in deleting this information from our servers and back-up storage; and (2) we may retain this information if necessary to comply with our legal obligations, resolve disputes, or enforce our agreements.

Dropbox, Inc., 'Privacy Policy' (posted 20 February 2014 and effective 24 March 2014), www.dropbox.com/privacy2014, accessed 14 July 2014.

over-simplification that does not tell the whole story when it comes to license or other contract rights. There is a great variability among cloud offerings within each category. The result is that the customer's due diligence is essential. It is vital that the customer reads the service descriptions for such important aspects of the service as processing locations, data backups, redundancy, encryption, security, transition process and options for customer control. Even beyond literal contractual assurances, the provider's form of contract often provides significant insight into the way the service is structured, and in cloud solutions this structure often defines the ability of the provider to meet customers' requirements.

Any service arrangement carries certain risks for the parties that may be influenced or driven by practical realities in the technical structure of the solution and the operations of the parties. These risks can be significantly exacerbated for the customer by lack of certainty (or understanding) of the contract or license terms, leading to poor decision-making in connection with the adoption of cloud solutions. One of the greatest risks associated with the adoption of any cloud solution by a customer is failure to understand the full range of their rights, responsibilities and requirements associated with the solution and its operations. In this sense, cloud computing does not present fundamentally different considerations from other service and licensing arrangements through which the customer obtains rights to services and software usage. Rather, cloud computing presents certain nuanced differences from traditional services and licensing which are driven by the technical structure and operation of cloud computing. Past experience, based on prior service and licensing arrangements offers valuable signposts for charting responsible approaches to the adoption of any cloud computing solution.

Index

accountability
  cloud data ownership, and 153–8
  cloud service reliability, and 256–7
  definition 152–3
  EU governance policy objectives
    156–8
  purpose 157–8
  remediation, and 153, 155–6
  transparency, and 152–6
Amazon 14, 57, 111, 242–3
America Online (AOL) 84
*American Broadcasting Companies v
  Aereo* 182–3
anonymized data 71, 75–8
  anonymization 98–9
  browser-generated information 81–2
  data combination, and 84–5
  data erasure, and 77–8
  data fingerprints 82–3
  data quality and size 91–2
  de-identification, and 79–80, 90–91
  definition 78–80, 86–7
  EU policy on 77–80
  identifiers, and 80–83
  judicial rulings 85–8
  law reform proposals 90–91
  pseudonymous data, and 79–80
  re-identification, and 77–80, 83–8,
    90–91, 93–4
  reuse of data, risk assessments
    92–3
  technological challenges 75–6
  US policy on 91
  vs. anonymous data 78–80
anonymous data 71
  Big Data technology, and 97–8
  Bio-PIN codes 238–9
  vs. anonymized data 78–80
Apple 68, 188

Asia-Pacific Economic Cooperation
  Cross-Border Privacy Rules (CBPR)
    37–8
Australia
  cloud policy developments 164–5,
    181–2
  cloud policy limitations 174–6
  Copyright Amendment (Digital
    Agenda) Act 2000 170
  copyright law
    Creative Commons licensing 209
    fair use doctrine 174–7
    government works protection 209
    protection gaps 174–6
    safe harbor provisions 170
  cross-border data flow controls 35
  data protection 35
  National Strategy for Cloud
    Computing 164–5
  personal data, definition 74

BBC iPlayer 207
big data 71, 95, 97–8
binding corporate rules (BCR) 37, 111,
  113
Bio-PIN 238
biomedical information *see* medical
  records
biomedical research *see also* genomic
  research
  EU data protection regime 99–100
  Icelandic biobank policy 226–7
  medical records, use in 230–33
  national biobank proposals 225–6
Boucher, R. 212
broadcasting
  cloud streaming copyright challenges
    182–3
  geographical restrictions 212–13

EU regime, in 129–30
  generally 35–6, 43–4, 65
Cross-Border Privacy Rules
  (CBPR)(APEC) 37–8
cybertravel 210

data, definition 7
data fingerprints 82–3
data loss, risks of 17, 67
data mining 84–5, 149, 158
data ownership
  accountability, and 152–8
  applicable law 141–2
  cloud challenges 139
  community norms, role of 158–9
  confidentiality 144–5, 149–50
  contract law influences 145
  copyright 141–2, 145
  country of origin 146
  customer relationships 142–3
  data mining 149
  database rights 142, 146–8
  derived information 148–9, 158–9,
    283–4
  encryption 150
  endowment effect 139–40
  information generated in cloud
    145–50, 158–9
  information placed in cloud 140–45
  metadata 148–9
  ownership concept 139–40
  privacy rights, and 140
  terms of service 150–51
  transparency 152–6
  TRIPS Agreement protection 143–4
  uploaded data, misconceptions about
    262
  use controls 150–52
data processing
  activities, context of 108
  automated data certificates 112
  consent 35, 87–8, 93–4, 105, 137
    right to withdraw 114
  controller representative
    requirements 106–7
  controller *vs.* processor distinction
    101–3

data transfers to sub-processors
    112–13
  definition 100–101
  disclosure to third parties 113–16
  establishment, classification of 108–9
  EU regime applicability 103–7
  information policies 113–15
  justifications for 104–5
  private international law jurisdiction,
    and 128
  Safe Harbor Agreements 110–13,
    116–17, 254
  safeguard exceptions 110–11
  surveillance, and 115–16
data protection *see also* cross-border
    data flows; medical records;
    outsourcing
  accountability 32, 34
  best efforts policies 251
  cloud challenges 29, 33–41, 99–100
  collection restrictions 30–31, 34
  compensation controls 38
  consent 137
  controller representative requirement
    106–7
  controller *vs.* processor distinction
    101–3
  data breach management 34
  data collection restrictions 30–31
  data erasure/exit policies 31, 33,
    77–8, 246–7
  data quality 31
  data storage 36, 246–7
  data transfer restrictions 32
  data use restrictions 34
  data users, and 29, 41–2
  definitions
    EU regime 69–70, 72–7, 88–90,
      97–100
    personal data 73–4
    processing 100–101
    US regime 74–5, 86–7, 89
  formal contractual relationships, and
    39
  identity management/authentication
    33
  individual participation 32, 34